UNDERSTANDING URBAN POLITICS

Institutions, Representation, and Policies

TIMOTHY B. KREBS
UNIVERSITY OF NEW MEXICO

ARNOLD FLEISCHMANN
EASTERN MICHIGAN UNIVERSITY

ROWMAN & LITTLEFIELD
Lanham • Boulder • New York • London

Executive Editor: Traci Crowell
Assistant Editor: Deni Remsberg
Higher Education Channel Manager: Jonathan Raeder

Credits and acknowledgments for material borrowed from other sources, and reproduced with permission, appear on the appropriate page within the text.

Published by Rowman & Littlefield
An imprint of The Rowman & Littlefield Publishing Group, Inc.
4501 Forbes Boulevard, Suite 200, Lanham, Maryland 20706
www.rowman.com

6 Tinworth Street, London SE11 5AL, United Kingdom

British Library Cataloguing in Publication Information Available

Library of Congress Cataloging-in-Publication Data
Names: Krebs, Timothy B., 1966– author. | Fleischmann, Arnold, author.
Title: Understanding Urban Politics : Institutions, Representation, and Policies / Timothy B. Krebs, University of New Mexico, Arnold Fleischmann, Eastern Michigan University.
Description: First edition. | Lanham : Rowman & Littlefield, [2020] |
Identifiers: LCCN 2019049132 (print) | LCCN 2019049133 (ebook) | ISBN 9781538105214 (cloth) | ISBN 9781538105221 (paperback) | ISBN 9781538105238 (epub)
Subjects: LCSH: Municipal government—United States. | Political participation—United States. | Public policy (Law)—United States. | United States—Politics and government.
Classification: LCC JS331 .K75 2020 (print) | LCC JS331 (ebook) | DDC 320.8/50973—dc23
LC record available at https://lccn.loc.gov/2019049132
LC ebook record available at https://lccn.loc.gov/2019049133

~~ief Contents

Contents

UNDERSTANDING URBAN POLITICS

Institutions, Representation, and Policies

TIMOTHY B. KREBS
UNIVERSITY OF NEW MEXICO

ARNOLD FLEISCHMANN
EASTERN MICHIGAN UNIVERSITY

ROWMAN & LITTLEFIELD
Lanham • Boulder • New York • London

Executive Editor: Traci Crowell
Assistant Editor: Deni Remsberg
Higher Education Channel Manager: Jonathan Raeder

Credits and acknowledgments for material borrowed from other sources, and reproduced with permission, appear on the appropriate page within the text.

Published by Rowman & Littlefield
An imprint of The Rowman & Littlefield Publishing Group, Inc.
4501 Forbes Boulevard, Suite 200, Lanham, Maryland 20706
www.rowman.com

6 Tinworth Street, London SE11 5AL, United Kingdom

British Library Cataloguing in Publication Information Available

Library of Congress Cataloging-in-Publication Data
Names: Krebs, Timothy B., 1966– author. | Fleischmann, Arnold, author.
Title: Understanding Urban Politics : Institutions, Representation, and Policies / Timothy B. Krebs, University of New Mexico, Arnold Fleischmann, Eastern Michigan University.
Description: First edition. | Lanham : Rowman & Littlefield, [2020] |
Identifiers: LCCN 2019049132 (print) | LCCN 2019049133 (ebook) | ISBN 9781538105214 (cloth) | ISBN 9781538105221 (paperback) | ISBN 9781538105238 (epub)
Subjects: LCSH: Municipal government—United States. | Political participation—United States. | Public policy (Law)—United States. | United States—Politics and government.
Classification: LCC JS331 .K75 2020 (print) | LCC JS331 (ebook) | DDC 320.8/50973—dc23
LC record available at https://lccn.loc.gov/2019049132
LC ebook record available at https://lccn.loc.gov/2019049133

♾️™ The paper used in this publication meets the minimum requirements of American National Standard for Information Sciences—Permanence of Paper for Printed Library Materials, ANSI/NISO Z39.48-1992.

List of Figures, Tables, Boxes, and Maps

FIGURES

TABLES

BOXES

MAPS

Preface

URBAN POLITICS TEXTBOOKS frequently employ a limited perspective on the governance of America's cities. This text seeks to address that concern. Cities are remarkable places where people, commerce, entertainment, culture, danger, and design merge to generate massive amounts of economic activity, cultural variety, threats, and new ways of living and responding to the challenges of modern society. The decisions that shape cities are not guided solely by things beyond the control of local elected and appointed officials. Indeed, they are influenced by the same kinds of political tugs of war that characterize higher levels of government.

Cities do many things that are critical to the functioning and performance of particular places but also to the national and international economies. While broader economic, social, demographic, and cultural forces shape the context of cities, we agree with Paul Peterson that there are limits to what cities can do. However, this overlooks—as numerous scholars have demonstrated over the years—the essential political character of urban governance.

For too long, scholars of urban politics have overlooked or under-appreciated this kind of approach in favor of an "apolitical" urban politics devoted to study-ing the impact that economic forces have on shaping decisions and constraining actors in city politics. Others have taken a historical approach, which, we argue, ignores much of what political science, especially recent scholarship, has to say about the politics and governance of cities. Globalization and place-centered approaches represent another angle by which to analyze cities. While forces of globalization and the peculiar circumstances of any one city are often beyond the control of city leaders and institutions, according to our method of analysis, they are merely conditions that local leaders and institutions must confront if they are to navigate the future successfully. Lastly, although regime theory rightfully places individuals and groups—and, yes, politics—at the center of theorizing about cities, its case-study orientation and inability to yield meaningful expecta-tions and predictions about urban politics leave it wanting as well.

Our Approach to Examining Urban Politics

Our political framework focuses on four main features: the role of institutions in establishing the political "rules of the game," the representativeness of city gov-ernment, the influence of citizen participation in local democracy, and how each of these features influences the adoption and implementation of public policies. We place individuals, organizations, and groups at the center of urban politics. In so doing, we embrace the idea that human agency is central to what happens in urban politics. Our approach is grounded in the notion that politics is politics whether it occurs at the national, state, or local level. What students of political science need in a text is a treatment of urban politics that ties in with other approaches in political science that seek to produce reasonable explanations and useful generalizations, albeit with consideration of the factors that make the local level different in several ways.

Cities may not decide war and peace, but they affect the quality of our daily lives in more profound ways than either the national or state governments, and they are the venues of profound political conflict of the most basic and personal kind. Our approach takes this notion seriously and seeks to present what we know about cities in an accessible but comprehensive way.

How will we carry this approach throughout this book? It means that we will take an empirical approach to the study of urban politics in America. This does not mean that we will base our understanding solely on quantitative research. Rather, we seek to incorporate work that places individuals, groups, organizations, and institutions at the center of our understanding. In urban research, this tends to include much of what is broadly categorized as American political development, an approach that seeks to identify and explain patterns, trends, and changes over time. That requires looking carefully at the kinds of incentives faced by participants in local politics, including current opportunities and barriers, as well as the effects of previous actions, many of which occurred decades earlier.

We have discovered with a collective 40-plus years of teaching urban politics that undergraduates often enter our classes ill-equipped to understand politics and governance at the level of government closest to them, namely, their city. This is in part a reflection of the invisibility of urban politics in our nation's media coverage except when something truly extraordinary happens. Students have few visuals of urban politics like they have of national politics, with its seemingly endless cable and network news coverage. Moreover, many students have no real background in local government and do not know even the basic sorts of things that students in other American politics courses might know about their subject matter. What we seek to do, therefore, is to give students the kinds of visuals and information that they can readily integrate with what they are learning or have learned in their other courses.

Key Features of the Book

We have attempted to produce a text built on cutting-edge research that asks critical questions aimed at engaging students to explore local politics on their own. This includes several elements:

- A set of guiding questions at the start of each chapter will generate critical thinking as you delve into chapter details.
- In order to enhance your understanding of the basics of urban politics in America, each chapter has key terms in bold text, followed by their definitions and useful examples. Key terms are repeated at the end of each chapter, as well as being listed with their definitions in a glossary at the end of the book.
- To encourage further exploration, each chapter contains a set of discussion questions after the conclusion.
- Each chapter also includes a set of research exercises that we hope will engage students to become scholars of the city on their own. These assignments can

complement or replace a traditional research paper, and they ask you to rely on local media, government sources, and other information.

- The book's website has flash cards to help you master key terms, practice questions to help you prepare for tests, a resource guide for staying current with urban politics and doing solid research, and other useful tools.

A great thing about studying urban politics is that it is right outside your door and in your community every day. It does not take place in a far-away place like Washington, DC, or a state capital, and what cities do and what they accomplish (or not, as the case might be) can have lasting impacts on your life opportunities. We hope that this text will serve as a catalyst for you to understand more fully the politics of cities, which are, after all, where the vast majority of the world's residents call home.

Organization of the Book

This book is divided into four parts. Part I includes three chapters that lay the groundwork for the rest of the book. Chapter 1 explores the many meanings (and confusion) regarding what "urban" is, traces the major population changes in American urban development, and briefly analyzes what local governments do and what is different about politics at the local level. Chapters 2 and 3 provide a history of American urban development, especially major population movements, economic shifts, changes in local politics, and national policies affecting cities.

The three chapters in Part II examine political institutions, namely, the organizations and procedures that are central to urban politics and policy making. Chapter 4 covers intergovernmental relations—the many ways that local governments interact both with each other and with the state and national governments. Chapter 5 examines local legislatures, and chapter 6 considers the local executive branch, including mayors, city managers, local bureaucracies, and constitutional officers required by states.

Part III looks closely at participation and representation in urban politics. Its three chapters examine elections and voting, local campaigns, and nonvoting forms of civic engagement, especially interest groups, political parties, contacting, and protest.

Part IV dives into local policy making. Chapter 10 covers the policy process and the delivery of local services. Chapter 11 explains the complex world of local government finances and budgets. The last two chapters examine specific policies. Chapter 12, "Building the City," analyzes economic development, land use, housing, and infrastructure. Finally, chapter 13 looks at the quality of life, namely, local policies on public safety, the environment, "morality" issues, and urban amenities.

A Few Words of Thanks

We would like to thank several people for helping to bring this project to fruition. First, hats off to Michael Leo Owens of Emory University for telling Arnold Fleischmann to write his own textbook instead of thinking about editing a reader to make up for problems with the existing texts. Fleischmann would also like to thank his graduate school mentors, Dave Perry and Al Watkins, for pushing him to use the past to explore the politics of Sunbelt cities. He's come a long way from his small-town Wisconsin upbringing. Lastly, thanks to Eastern Michigan University for teaching releases to work on this project.

Timothy Krebs wants to thank Dr. John Pelissero, his mentor and friend, who inspired him to study urban politics at Loyola University Chicago. His guidance, teaching, and confidence have left an indelible mark on his life and career. He also wants to thank the College of Arts and Sciences at the University of New Mexico for its support of this project. Finally, he wants to thank his family, especially his children, Ethan and Nora, who have endured many nights and hours where Dad was busy working and distracted. He loves them dearly and greatly appreciates their patience and support. This book is for them.

We would also like to thank Traci Crowell for sticking with this project over a few years and for her steady encouragement and useful feedback, the production team at Rowman & Littlefield, Karen Trost for her great editorial help in organizing and presenting each and every chapter, and the external reviewers of the proposal and draft chapters, who were immensely helpful: Vladimir Kogan (Ohio State University), Brian Adams (San Diego State University), Carlos Vargas-Ramos (Columbia University), Thomas J. Vicino (Northeastern University), Geoffrey Willbanks (University of Texas at Tyler), Bruce Ransom (Clemson University), Anirudh V. S. Ruhil (Ohio University), Chris Warshaw (Massachusetts Institute of Technology), Joshua Chanin (San Diego State University), José E. Cruz (University of Albany—SUNY), Sarah Reckow (Michigan State University), and Lisa Schweitzer (University of Southern California). Many undergraduate students at both Eastern Michigan University and the University of New Mexico helped shape this book by providing valuable feedback to draft chapters and exercises. We thank them. Last, but not least, thank you to John Wagner, an advanced Ph.D. student in the political science department at the University of New Mexico, who produced all of the ancillary materials that accompany this text.

About the Authors

Timothy B. Krebs is professor of political science at the University of New Mexico, where he joined the faculty in 2002 after 4 years at the University of North Carolina at Greensboro. His teaching includes undergraduate and graduate courses in American politics, urban politics, urban management, state and urban policy, and campaigns and elections. Krebs received his BA from Loyola Marymount University in Los Angeles and earned his PhD from Loyola University Chicago in 1997, where he wrote an award-winning dissertation. His publications have appeared in the *American Journal of Political Science*, *American Politics Research*, *Political Research Quarterly*, *Social Science Quarterly*, *Urban Affairs Review*, and other outlets.

Arnold Fleischmann has been a professor at Eastern Michigan University since 2009, where he served as Political Science department head until 2016. Previously, he taught for more than 20 years at the University of Georgia. His teaching has included basic undergraduate and graduate classes in American politics, as well as specialized courses in urban politics, urban policy, state politics, and politics and sexual minorities. Fleischmann received his BA from the University of St. Thomas (Minnesota) and his PhD from the University of Texas. He has been coauthor of three editions of *Politics in Georgia* (University of Georgia Press), has published seven other book chapters, and has had articles in the *Journal of Politics*, *Political Research Quarterly*, *Social Science Quarterly*, *Public Administration Review*, *Urban Affairs Review*, *Journal of Urban Affairs*, and other scholarly journals.

PART I

LAYING THE GROUNDWORK

1

STUDYING URBAN POLITICS

GUIDING QUESTIONS

1. In what ways are "urban" areas identified in the United States, and how do we measure changes in them?
2. How does local politics compare to politics at the state and national levels?
3. How are local governments organized in the United States? What roles does each type of government perform?
4. How do local governments interact with one another and with higher-level governments? How are institutions and representation related to politics at the local level?

FROM THE FIRST CENSUS in 1790 until the one in 1880, the US Census Bureau defined a line on a national map as the start of the "frontier," an area consisting of locations with fewer than two people per square mile (it is worth noting that the measure did not count Native Americans). The frontier in 1790 essentially extended west from the Appalachians. By 1890, the bureau concluded that with so many settled areas in the West, there was no longer a frontier line.[1] Thomas Jefferson saw westward expansion as an equalizer, but perhaps not one that could undermine slavery.[2] Frederick Jackson Turner's classic 1893 essay also captured the mental link between frontier and opportunity.[3]

The end of a frontier line did not eliminate the American mentality of striking out to conquer the frontier. Indeed, historian Kenneth Jackson describes this view in the rise of US suburbs—what he called the "crabgrass frontier."[4] Over the years, the bureau has also struggled to identify urban areas. This chapter helps lay the foundation for the rest of the book by explaining the many meanings of the term *urban*, tracing early US urbanization, and analyzing what is different about local politics and government compared to the state and national levels.

FIRST THINGS FIRST: WHAT IS "URBAN," ANYWAY?

Given the title of this text, a good starting point is to define *urban*. At first glance, this might seem like an easy task. However, even the US Census Bureau has used a number of different definitions over the years.[5]

Census Definitions

With significant population movements after the Civil War, the Census Bureau began differentiating urban and rural areas in the late 1800s. The national census occurs every year ending in zero. With the 1910 census, the bureau defined an **urban area** as an incorporated place (think of a city or village with its own local government) with at least 2,500 residents. Even with such a low population threshold, the US remained primarily a rural nation. Only 46.3 percent of the population lived in urban areas in 1910, but the definition covered quite a range—from three cities with over one million residents to nearly 1,200 places with just 2,500 to 5,000 inhabitants.[6] The 1950 census recognized densely populated areas outside large cities as urban, and what is now the federal Office of Management and Budget (OMB) adopted uniform national standards for identifying different types of urban areas.

For many years, the Census Bureau has gathered data for areas as small as individual city blocks. The focus on larger concentrations starts with the **Core Based Statistical Area (CBSA)**, which consists of the counties or equivalent entities associated with at least one core urbanized cluster with a population of at least 10,000, plus any adjacent counties with a high degree of social and economic integration with the core as measured through commuting ties with counties associated with the core.[7] This definition is the foundation for a key distinction in thinking about urban areas. **Metropolitan Statistical Areas (MSAs)** are CBSAs with a core urbanized area of at least 50,000 people. **Micropolitan Statistical Areas**, first identified for the 2000 census, are CBSAs with a core urban cluster of between 10,000 and 50,000 people. Think of these as smaller urban centers that would have a mix of wholesale and retail, medical services, financial and legal services, government installations, transportation, and maybe even educational institutions not found elsewhere in the region.

Applying these definitions is a very dynamic process that is easier to understand with examples. The OMB reconsiders criteria and data regularly in defining specific CBSAs, and the Census Bureau does population estimates between censuses. Mainly because of population growth, this means that more counties can be added to an existing MSA, new MSAs can be identified, and the MSA name can be changed as large suburbs grow around a central city. For example, Metropolitan Atlanta was defined as five counties in the 1970 census. Just 40 years later, the MSA was renamed Atlanta-Sandy Springs-Roswell for 2010, when it covered twenty-nine counties. CBSAs are "artificial" economic and social—not political—designations, so the Columbus, Georgia, MSA in 2010 included four counties in Georgia and two in a different time zone in Alabama. Also in 2010, the OMB identified a new micropolitan area in Georgia (Vidalia) about a three-hour drive southeast of Atlanta.

Even the above definitions do not capture the full range of urbanization in the United States. The OMB and the Census Bureau have a category acknowledging that metropolitan or micropolitan areas can grow together into a pretty seamless pattern called **Combined Statistical Areas (CSAs)**. CSAs consist of two or more adjacent metropolitan or micropolitan statistical areas that have substantial employment interchange. As anyone flying into the New York City area recognizes, the New York-Newark CSA seems to go on forever. Indeed, this CSA includes thirty-five counties in New York (five are the boroughs that make up New York City), New Jersey, Connecticut, and Pennsylvania. The Chicago-Naperville CSA includes thirteen counties in Illinois but extends to six in northwest Indiana and Kenosha County, Wisconsin. The Los Angeles-Long Beach CSA extends east all the way from the Pacific Ocean to California's border with Arizona and Nevada.[8]

Growth of Urban Areas

Chapters 2 and 3 explore in more detail the population movements, economic changes, and political developments associated with American urbanization. As background for that analysis, we provide a brief description of historical population changes. Figure 1.1 shows the distribution of the US population from the first census in 1790 through the 2010 census.

Perhaps the most apparent pattern in figure 1.1 is the convergence of the lines for urban and rural percentages; an urban majority first emerged with the 1920 census. This trajectory reflects the transformation of the economy from agriculture to manufacturing and services, vast internal population movements and large-scale immigration, and significant improvements in technology. All of these shifts boosted growth in the nation's cities. Cities were not insignificant earlier, however. Many of the key events during the Revolution occurred in economically important coastal cities like Boston, New York, and Philadelphia. The country expanded aggressively to the west after gaining independence, including the Louisiana Purchase in 1803, the annexation of Texas in 1845, and statehood for California in 1850. These areas were largely rural, but westward growth was also powered by the development of economic centers like New Orleans, Pittsburgh, St. Louis, Chicago, and San Francisco.

Two of the lines in figure 1.1 are shorter: The metropolitan statistical area (MSA) population was not calculated consistently until 1960, and micropolitan areas were not included in the census before 2000. The conclusion is clear: Of the 309 million people in the US in 2010, 84 percent lived in MSAs. However, the figure does not capture the growth of suburbs and decline of many cities after World War II and the resurgence of central cities this century (see chapter 3).

Along with multiple definitions of what is considered urban are assorted notions of urbanization. Common dictionary definitions are only a starting point. They often treat urbanization as "the quality or state of being urbanized or the process of becoming urbanized," which seems redundant, although

Figure 1.1 Percentage of the US Population Living in Rural, Urban, Metropolitan, and Micropolitan Areas, 1790–2010 Censuses

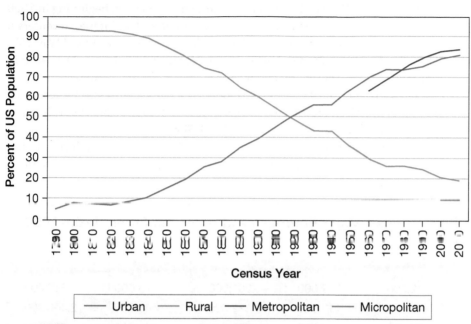

Source: US Census Bureau, *Census of 1990, Selected Historical Decennial Census Population and Housing Counts: Urban and Rural Population*, table 4; *Statistical Abstract of the United States: 1993*, Part 2, table 38; 2000 and 2010 calculations from the bureau's *American Fact Finder* tool.

Merriam-Webster does add that the first use of the term was in 1888.[9] Such definitions get a bit more specific with the meaning of *urban*: "relating to, characteristic of, or constituting a city"[10] or "of, relating to, or designating a city or town."[11] Other definitions are more specific, treating urbanization as a process in which "large numbers of people become permanently concentrated in relatively small areas, forming cities."[12] Such descriptions seem to assume that urban settlements are not only more densely populated than rural areas, but also include a range of businesses and occupations, as well as a mix of nonagricultural land uses and perhaps collective means of dealing with public safety, health, commerce, and necessities such as transportation, water, and sanitation.[13]

Keep in mind that urbanization was not something that first occurred in the United States. Many early cities were the political and economic centers of empires in Asia and Europe. Rome is thought to have had at least one million residents for several centuries after the rise of Christianity. Constantinople's population fluctuated between 300,000 and 700,000 between the years 800 and 1700, and rose to nearly a million with the rise of the Ottoman Empire. In Russia, the positions of Moscow and St. Petersburg shifted seemingly with the whims of the czars. Warfare and disease also had significant impacts on urbanization in Europe.[14]

As the Spanish empire expanded in the Americas, explorers conquered major Aztec and Inca cities. The Spanish built colonial cities to administer their holdings in North America, as did the French, English, and Dutch.[15] As empires grew in North America and elsewhere, European capitals became major urban centers, as did other commercial hubs. Table 1.1 displays the population of major European cities from 1700 to 1900 and compares large US cities, beginning in 1800. The data demonstrate the rise of the major commercial and imperial centers in Europe before the major boundary changes that occurred after World War I. The table also shows the rapid rise after independence of American industrial, shipping, and financial centers that grew to rival their European predecessors.

As the old mercantile system of shipping raw materials to Europe declined in the face of American industrialization, Charleston dropped from the fifth-largest city in 1800 to #15 in 1850 and #68 in 1900. Similarly, New Orleans was among the five largest US cities from the 1810 to the 1850 censuses. As industrialization and westward expansion ramped up, especially after the Civil War, New Orleans

TABLE 1.1 Population of Major European and American Cities, 1700–1900					
City	1700	1750	1800	1850	1900
Europe					
Amsterdam	172,000	219,000	201,000	225,000	510,000
Berlin		113,000	172,000	446,000	2,400,000
Constantinople	700,000	660,000	570,000	785,000	900,000
Lisbon	188,000	213,000	237,000	257,000	363,000
London	550,000	676,000	861,000	2,320,000	6,600,000
Madrid		123,000	169,000	263,000	600,000
Moscow	130,000	161,000	238,000	373,000	1,100,000
Naples	207,000	324,000	430,000	416,000	600,000
Paris	530,000	560,000	547,000	1,314,000	3,300,000
St. Petersburg		138,000	220,000	502,000	1,439,000
Vienna	105,000	169,000	231,000	426,000	1,662,000
United States					
Baltimore			26,514	169,014	508,957
Boston			24,937	136,881	560,892
Brooklyn[a]				96,838	
Chicago				29,963	1,698,575
New Orleans				116,375	287,104
New York			60,515	515,547	3,437,202
Philadelphia			41,220	121,376	1,293,697
St. Louis				77,860	575,238

[a] Brooklyn was an independent city until its 1898 merger with Manhattan, the Bronx, Queens, and Staten Island to form the five boroughs of modern-day New York City. It is included in the New York total for 1900.

Source: For European cities, Tertius Chandler and Gerald Fox, *3000 Years of Urban Growth* (New York: Academic Press, 1974), 17–20, 321–335; for American cities, US Census Bureau, "Population of the 100 Largest Cities and Other Urban Places in the United States: 1790 to 1990," https://www.census.gov/population/www/documentation/twps0027/twps0027.html.

dropped to twelfth-largest in 1900 as it was eclipsed by places like Buffalo, Cleveland, Cincinnati, and Pittsburgh.

Just as urban centers grew in Europe during the 1600s and 1700s, the later emergence of American cities was associated with the growth of government. Unlike the dominance of national governments in much of Europe, the decentralization of the American federal system early on produced a proliferation of local governments, with each state setting up its own system. This raises another key issue: What is the scope of local government in the United States?

WHAT'S DIFFERENT ABOUT LOCAL GOVERNMENT AND POLITICS?

Health care? Trade? Immigration? Terrorism? Abortion? These issues never seem to go away in national politics and pit Americans against one another in increasingly polarized debates. Many of these conflicts are common at the state level as well. Things seem different at the local level, however.

Many Americans take for granted the work of cities, counties, townships, and special districts. These governments administer roads and transit systems, water and sewers, courts and jails, a wide range of inspections and licenses, elementary and secondary schools, airports, and much, much more. J. Eric Oliver characterizes the work of local government as "managerial." Within this context, Oliver argues that national elections are often about ideology, policy preferences, ethnic or religious identification, or similar perspectives. At the local level, the focus is on services and taxes, with elections usually focusing on the performance of incumbents.[16] This view is reinforced in part by surveys indicating that Americans have far more trust and confidence in their local governments than they do in those governing them in their state capitals or Washington, DC (see figure 1.2).

The data in figure 1.2 are from Gallup polls generally conducted in the fall of the year indicated. Respondents were asked if they had a great deal, a fair amount, not very much, none at all, or no opinion in response to a question of "how much trust and confidence" they had regarding "the state where you live when it comes to handling state problems" or "local governments in the area where you live when it comes to handling local problems." Because the role of the federal government was divided into separate international and domestic questions, the figure also covers responses to the question, "How much trust and confidence do you have in our federal government in Washington when it comes to handling domestic problems?" The lines in figure 1.2 are the percentage of respondents in the national survey answering "a great deal" or "a fair amount" of the time. Note that there are some gaps in the data for years when surveys did not ask about state or local government.[17]

The trends are interesting in several respects. All three levels saw a decline in trust beginning in the late 1990s. After that, however, the trust level for local governments remained fairly steady at around 70 percent, even with the Great Recession that began in 2007. In contrast, trust in state governments fluctuated widely, with major drops between 2001 and 2003, and again during the Great Recession, only to rise as the economy improved and hover somewhat above

Figure 1.2 Percent Reporting a Great Deal or a Fair Amount of Trust and Confidence in the Federal Government, Their State Government, or Local Governments in Their Area

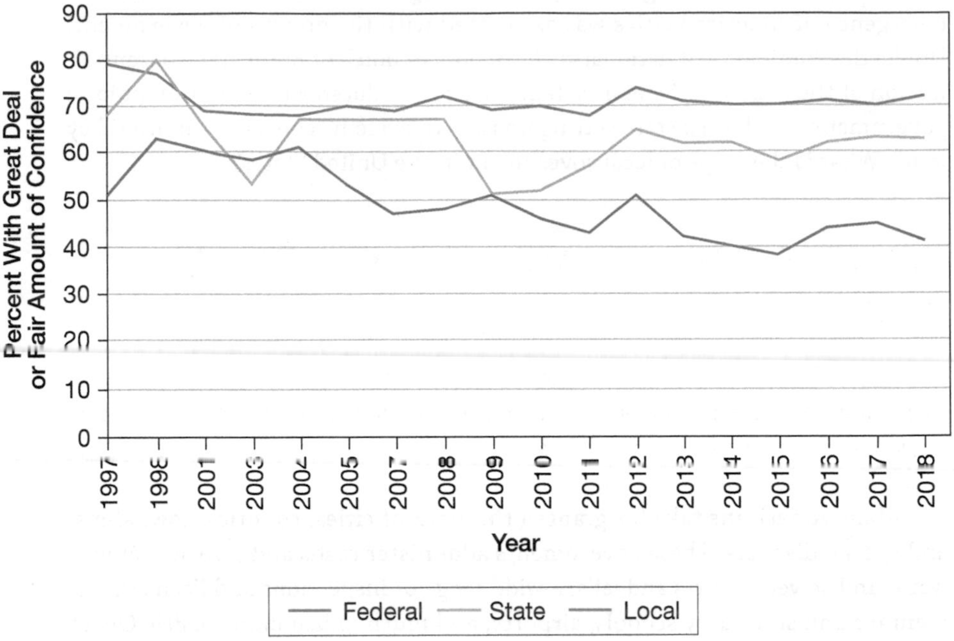

Source: Gallup, "Trust in Government: Gallup Historical Trends," http://news.gallup.com/poll/5392/trust-government.aspx.

60 percent. Trust of the federal government shows a long-term slide, although it would be higher had international problems been examined. Those levels of trust decline, however, the longer the United States is involved in Afghanistan and Iraq.

Overall, figure 1.2 suggests that local government employees and elected officials work in a political environment that is relatively supportive of their work. That does not mean an absence of political conflict, however. One temptation in examining politics at the local level is to assume that it is the same as national or state politics but on a smaller scale. Nothing could be further from the truth. In most ways, national and state policies generally do not depend on a person's location within their boundaries. For instance, a monthly Social Security check is the same no matter where the person lives. The federal income tax rate for individuals and businesses and federal laws covering criminal activity do not vary from state to state, and your "Forever" stamp is good everywhere. Similarly, residents of a state face the same requirements for getting a license to drive, practice law, teach in public schools, or get married. Speed limits on freeways in rural areas are the same. State universities usually charge state residents the same tuition rate if they are in the same program and taking the same course load. Charging more—sometimes much more—to students from other states and countries is a common practice, however.

In contrast, at the local level, *where* a person lives, works, or does business *is everything*. As most households recognize, public schools vary from one district to another and even among different neighborhoods in the same school district. Crime differs from one section of a city to another, as can policing practices, including the presence of local "speed traps." There are also differences in the quality and availability of parks, libraries, streets, public transportation, and other services, as well as conditions like entertainment options, recreational opportunities, traffic, noise, pollution, flooding, and the quality and cost of housing.

The costs of local government also differ from place to place, sometimes quite significantly. Taxes in a region typically vary among its municipalities, counties, and special purpose districts. For example, although a lower rate was charged for food, the general sales tax in Tennessee in 2017 was 7 percent. Yet local sales taxes on top of this varied from place to place and were as high as 2.75 percent, so it really mattered where a consumer bought something. Indeed, the sales tax in Hamilton County (Chattanooga) was 9.25 percent. Perhaps not surprisingly, there is a major outlet mall forty-five minutes south in Calhoun County, Georgia, where the sales tax rate is "only" 7 percent.[18] Differences in property taxes and fees like water rates, business licenses, inspections, and building permits also exist among communities.

The procedures and structure of local governments also vary substantially, including how and when various officials are elected. Most counties elect their officials on ballots with party labels. On the other hand, most cities, especially smaller ones, have nonpartisan elections. The dates of local elections also cover a wide range, with most county offices on the ballot in even-numbered years but many cities holding elections in odd-numbered years. City councils and county boards vary in size; few are as large as Chicago's fifty-member city council. Some are elected at large, while others are chosen from districts, and many serve only part time. Elections in smaller constituencies cost little and involve a personal style of campaigning, while running for office in larger cities can be extremely expensive with paid staff and costly media efforts. All of these differences in organization and procedures affect things like voter turnout, the role of political parties and interest groups in campaigns, the information voters have about candidates, and the types of candidates who tend to run for office and win.

Local governments may elect an executive such as a mayor or have the council hire someone as city manager to run the government on a day-to-day basis—an arrangement not used at the state or national level. Many communities also permit direct democracy—procedures that allow or require citizens to vote on proposed policies and that often allow citizens to circulate petitions to force a vote on a policy or remove an elected official.

Variety might be "the spice of life," but it is also at the core of urban politics. The United States is an urbanized country, but local history and development patterns are quite different from place to place. Similarly, the structure of local governments, their election procedures, their relationships with other governments, the services they provide and how they pay for them, and the impacts of their policies all vary widely and have significant connections to local politics. However, there are patterns and tendencies among the nation's urban areas. A core task of this book is to describe and explain those patterns, focus on the role of political participation, and prompt you to do research to see how your community is similar or different.

TYPES OF US LOCAL GOVERNMENTS AND WHAT THEY DO

Local governments are not mentioned anywhere in the US Constitution, so each state decides how to set up its own. These systems have changed over the years, as have the number of local governments, with approximately 90,000 today.

Local governments are usually divided into two categories based on the functions they perform. First are **general-purpose governments**, which perform a range of public services. These include counties, municipalities, and (in some states) towns. Counties (called boroughs in Alaska and parishes in Louisiana) are traditionally viewed as administrative arms of state governments. Historically, counties kept vital records (birth, death, property, marriage, etc.), enforced state laws (prosecuted crimes, provided law enforcement, maintained jails), and provided essential services on behalf of the state (e.g., public health, welfare programs, roads). In the South and West in particular, counties have provided a wide range of services in rural areas, which do not have the townships common in areas like the Midwest. In many states, constitutions require election of a sheriff, district attorney, county clerk, and other county officials. During the period after World War II, many states allowed counties, especially those in suburban areas adjoining major cities, to provide services that might be considered urban, such as water, sewers, parks, trash collection, fire protection, and public transportation.

The other type of general-purpose government is municipalities (cities and villages in most states). Much like a business, they receive a charter from the state to incorporate and are then allowed or required to provide a range of services. Also, creating a municipality gives the new government significant control over development through the use of zoning, building codes, and similar regulations.

The second category consists of **special-purpose governments**, which are normally established to provide a single service, usually with their own governing board and revenue sources. The special-purpose government most visible to most Americans is their local public school district. Others range from hospital districts to airport authorities to community colleges and water and sewer districts. Many of these special-purpose districts rely on fees (tuition, water bills, parking, etc.).

The US Census Bureau conducts a "Census of Governments" in years ending in 2 and 7, with the first of the 2017 data released in April 2019. Table 1.2 displays census data for the different types of local governments from 1962 through 2017. During this period, the number of counties remained virtually unchanged while the number of townships and municipalities shifted modestly. In contrast, the number of school districts plummeted by two-thirds while the number of special districts more than doubled.

Table 1.2 reflects pressure by state governments to consolidate many small and rural school districts into larger ones that could provide a wider array of classes and programs. Colorado, for instance, went from more than 2,100 school districts in 1935 to 967 in 1956, dropped sharply to 275 in 1961, and declined again to 178 by 2000. States have continued to address this issue, including efforts accompanying the onset of the Great Recession in 2007.[19] Merging school districts is not easy, though, as communities can resist in order to avoid losing a local school or their own high school football team.[20]

TABLE 1.2	Number of Local Governments in the US, 1962–2017											
Government	1962	1967	1972	1977	1982	1987	1992	1997	2002	2007	2012	2017
Counties	3,043	3,049	3,044	3,042	3,041	3,042	3,043	3,043	3,034	3,033	3,031	3,091
Municipalities	17,997	18,048	18,517	18,862	19,076	19,200	19,279	19,372	19,429	19,492	19,519	19,495
Townships	17,144	17,105	16,991	16,822	16,734	16,691	16,656	16,629	16,504	16,519	16,360	16,253
School Districts	34,678	21,782	15,781	15,174	14,851	14,721	14,422	13,726	13,506	13,051	12,880	12,754
Special Districts	18,323	21,264	23,855	25,962	28,078	29,532	31,555	34,683	35,052	37,381	38,266	38,542
TOTAL	91,185	81,248	78,218	79,862	81,780	83,186	84,955	87,453	87,525	89,476	90,056	90,075

Source: US Census Bureau, *2012 Census of Governments,* "List and Structure of Governments: Number of Governments," tables 4 and 5, https://www.census.gov/govs/go/index.html; *2017 Census of Governments—Organization,* table 2, https://census.gov/data/tables/2017/econ/gus/2017-governments.html.

A Really Special District: The Port Authority of New York and New Jersey

Brooklyn Piers Operated by the Port Authority of New York and New Jersey.

Rapid growth in and around New York City during the 1800s was phenomenal, but it resulted in frequent conflict.[a] Although New York and New Jersey signed an interstate compact in 1834 to smooth relations, battles continued over railroad freight rates, water pollution, and port congestion. In 1921, the two states signed another agreement, creating what is now the Port Authority of New York and New Jersey, to build, buy, and lease facilities within twenty-five miles of the Statue of Liberty. Each governor appoints half of the twelve-member board.[b]

The Port Authority built or took over bridges and tunnels spanning the Hudson River in the

Special districts are sometimes truly regional in nature, providing services that encompass multiple cities or counties (see box 1.1). They also permit cities and counties to shift services—and financial obligations—to independent local governments. Special-purpose governments at times even provide a way for private interests to shift their costs to a public entity, as when developers create water districts to service their subdivisions.[21]

A simple way to compare what local, state, and federal governments do is to compare how they raise and spend money. The US Census Bureau gathers such data, but information on state and local finances lags behind federal budget data by a year or two, so table 1.3 covers finances for all three levels of government through the 2017 fiscal year. A **fiscal year** is the twelve-month period covered by a budget and is named after the calendar year in which it ends. Fiscal years are not uniform, however, and most governments do not follow a regular calendar year.[22]

The largest share of the federal government's $3.98 trillion in spending in fiscal 2017 went to Social Security and Medicare, with another 16-plus percent allocated for both defense and intergovernmental aid. States allocated the largest portion of their spending (over one-fourth) to social welfare programs, with a slightly smaller share as aid to local governments. In contrast, over one-third of the $1.9 trillion in local expenditures was for education, overwhelmingly for public school systems, with almost 15 percent for utility services, 10 percent for public safety, and nearly 9 percent for health and hospitals. As a whole, this picture shows the degree to which the three levels of government specialize in doing different things, with local governments shouldering responsibility for most day-to-day services on which the public relies.

1930s. It gained control of three airports (Newark, LaGuardia, and what is now Kennedy) and the Port of Newark in the 1940s, took over commuter rail from New Jersey, erected a massive bus terminal in Manhattan, opened the world's first container port, added two more airports, and built the World Trade Center.[c]

The Authority has about 8,000 employees.[d] Its budget is comparable to states like Idaho, Montana, New Hampshire, South Dakota, and Vermont.[e] Its performance remains political—and often controversial.[f]

[a] This included the landmark US Supreme Court case over boat traffic on the Hudson River, *Gibbons v. Ogden*, 22 US 1 (1824).

[b] Jameson W. Doig, *Empire on the Hudson: Entrepreneurial Vision and Political Power at the Port of New York Authority* (New York: Columbia University Press, 2001), 70–73, 363.

[c] Doig, *Empire on the Hudson*, especially chapters 3, 7, 11–14.

[d] Port Authority of New York and New Jersey, December 2017, *Proposed 2018 Budget*, 18, http://corpinfo.panynj.gov/documents/Proposed-2018-Budget/.

[e] The budget for fiscal 2018 was $3.2 billion for operating expenses and $3.4 billion for capital expenses. See Port Authority of New York and New Jersey, December 7, 2017, "Port Authority Board Adopts 2018 Budget," press release no. 220–2017, http://www.panynj.gov/press-room/press-item.cfm?headLine_id=2835 Council of State Governments (CSG), *The Book of the States 2017* (Lexington: CSG), table 7.5.

[f] Marc Santora, "Some See Biden's 'Third World' Description of LaGuardia as Too Kind," *New York Times*, February 7, 2014, https://www.nytimes.com/2014/02/08/nyregion/some-see-third-world-as-too-kind-for-laguardia.html; Aria Bendix, "'Bridgegate' Mastermind Avoids Prison Sentence," *The Atlantic*, July 12, 2017, https://www.theatlantic.com/news/archive/2017/07/bridgegate-mastermind-avoids-prison-sentence/533493/.

Another way to compare the three levels of government is seeing how they get their money. As table 1.3 indicates, local revenue sources are quite different from those of the federal or state governments. Local governments depend on states for over one-fourth of their revenue—a situation that can be threatening based on changes in state finances and the whims of governors and legislatures. Another 26 percent of local government money comes from taxes on property, primarily land and buildings. They also rely on charges, fees, and utility revenue: residents pay for such things as water, tuition, parking and traffic fines, bus fares, parking meters, rent for public facilities, and similar services at the local level. Local government services are covered in greater depth in chapter 10, and chapter 11 examines local finances.

As urban areas expanded in the United States, so did the numbers and types of local governments. These changes led to complex interactions among the three levels of government, usually referred to as intergovernmental relations. One type of relationship involves governments at the same level, usually labeled *horizontal relationships*. In contrast, *vertical relationships* involve local governments' dealings with those above them—the state and national governments. The next section provides a short overview of intergovernmental relations, which is covered more thoroughly in chapter 4.

THE WORLD OF LOCAL GOVERNMENTS

Local governments operate in an extremely complex environment. They interact with each other and with higher-level governments in several ways. They are also expected to respond to residents, employers, and other interests.

TABLE 1.3 / Government Finances, Fiscal Year 2017

	Federal	State	Local
Expenditures ($billion)	$3,981.6	$2,314.8	$1,912.1
Major Functions			
Defense and International Affairs	16.2%	N/A	N/A
Intergovernmental Expenditures	16.9%[a]	23.8%	0.9%
Education	3.6%	13.6%	36.4%
Public Welfare/Income Security	12.6%	26.6%	3.0%
Health and Hospitals	13.4%	5.6%	8.6%
Law Enforcement, Fire, Corrections	1.5%	3.2%	9.7%
Transportation	2.3%	4.9%	5.3%
Natural Resources, Parks, Recreation	1.0%	1.2%	2.6%
Utilities, Sewerage, Solid Waste	—	1.3%	14.7%
Insurance Trust Expenditures[b]	38.7%	12.8%	2.8%
Net Interest on Debt	6.6%	1.9%	3.3%
Revenue ($billion)	$3,316.2	$2,548.6	$1,938.2
Major Sources			
Federal Intergovernmental Revenue	N/A	25.1%	3.6%
State Intergovernmental Revenue	N/A	N/A	27.5%
Social Insurance and Retirement[b]	35.0%	—	—
Individual Income Taxes	47.9%	13.8%	1.7%
Corporate Income Taxes	9.0%	1.8%	0.4%
Sales/Excise Taxes	2.5%	17.7%	6.4%
Property Taxes	—	0.6%	26.3%
Charges and Fees	—	8.9%	15.5%
Utility Revenue	—	0.5%	8.0%
Insurance Trust Revenue[b]	—	21.8%	4.6%

[a] Grants to state and local governments of $674.7 billion are included in the other functional categories in the table. The largest share (76%) went to income security and health.

[b] The federal social insurance entry includes Medicare and Social Security. Trust categories involve items such as retirement, unemployment compensation, and workers' compensation.

Source: US Census Bureau, "Annual Survey of State and Local Government Finances: Datasets and Tables," 2017, "US Summary and Alabama-Mississippi," https://www.census.gov/data/datasets/2017/econ/local/public-use-datasets.html; US Office of Management and Budget, "Historical Tables," 2.1, 2.2, 3.2, 12.2, https://www.whitehouse.gov/omb/historical-tables.

Competition and Cooperation with Other Governments

Local governments do not exist in isolation. In fact, they often compete with others from across the country, in the same state, and even the same urban area for residents, businesses, state and federal money, and other resources. This was highlighted vividly by the scramble to "win" Amazon's second corporate head-quarters (see box 1.2).

Bidding wars like those for HQ2 are nothing new. Cities competed in the 1800s for roads, river ports, canals, and railroads. In the 1930s, they also began competing for manufacturing plants with financial incentives—an "arms race" that continues to this day.[23] This includes the huge deal that Wisconsin struck with the Taiwanese manufacturer Foxconn in 2017, which could cost state and local taxpayers $4 billion; the incentives include free land for the factory, which might employ up to 13,000 workers producing flat-screen televisions and other electronics products.[24]

Local governments also engage in several forms of cooperation. Common, but not necessarily visible, are the many agreements between police and fire departments to provide support to neighboring communities, including the shar-ing of 911 centers. Some governments even buy services from one another, as when a city hires its county sheriff's department to provide law enforcement or contracts with a neighboring community for water or sewer services.

Cooperation can also be vertical in nature. States provide multiple types of support for local governments. For example, Arizona, Georgia, and Indiana are among the states that maintain a training center or academy to provide basic and advanced training for police officers, which is especially difficult for smaller com-munities to do on their own.[25] Also common are state and federal **grants-in-aid**, funds made available to local governments for specified purposes and under guidelines set by the higher-level government. Such grants take many forms and can be very broad or quite narrow. They sometimes require local governments to put up some of their own money to "match" the state or federal funds. Grants-in-aid are often used to make transportation improvements, administer health programs, and bolster programs in public schools.

Conflicts with Other Governments

Local governments also have frequent conflicts. Horizontal conflicts with other local governments can sometimes end up in court. For instance, the city of Erie, Pennsylvania, and Erie County battled in and out of court during much of 2015 and 2016 over governance of the region's transit agency—a conflict that threat-ened to shut down the bus service.[26] Similarly, after approving a development, Orange County, California, was sued in late 2017 by the city of Irvine and others that considered the project both a violation of an agreement and a stimulant for traffic and other problems.[27]

Vertical conflicts occur when higher-level governments impose unwanted policies on lower-level ones. Local governments are often described as "crea-tures of the state," and state legislatures unhappy with local policy decisions

BOX 1.2

Selling Your Soul for Amazon's Second Headquarters?

Map 1.1 The Twenty HQ2 Finalist Cities, January 2018

Source: MarketWatch, January 18, 2018.

In September 2017, Amazon announced that it was seeking bids for a second headquarters, HQ2, to complement its Seattle operations. It was looking for a metropolitan area of at least one million, mass transit and an international airport, a "business-friendly" environment, technical talent, and certain building specifications. Other preferences included a diverse population, excellent universities, and "elected officials eager and willing to work with the company."[a] Amazon claimed that it would invest $5 billion and create up to 50,000 jobs.

Amazon received 238 bids, at least one from every state except Arkansas (the home of Wal-Mart), which included billions of dollars in incentives to reduce company costs.

increasingly undercut local actions through **preemption**, laws or administrative rules that remove or restrict the authority of lower-level governments over certain policies. Preemption has occurred in multiple states, with some forbidding local governments from banning plastic bags, prohibiting fracking, or adopting nondiscrimination and other policies favored by their residents.[28]

Such control also extends to **mandates**, orders by a higher-level government to a lower-level government to meet a certain standard or follow a specific procedure. For example, states generally require city councils to conduct business, with a few exceptions, in meetings open to the public. States also set minimum qualifications for local employees such as teachers, police officers, city clerks, and magistrates.

The federal government also adopts mandates that limit state and local governments. One is the Americans with Disabilities Act, with requirements

Newark and the state of New Jersey reportedly offered $7 billion, Maryland $5 billion, and St. Louis up to $3.8 billion, with multi-billion-dollar offers from Chicago and Philadelphia. There was pushback toward Amazon because of the competition's secrecy and the company's history of getting subsidies.[b] Some called for the finalists (see Map 1.1) to demand more from Amazon. Critics also questioned the legality of subsidies or called for changes in federal law to curtail them.[c]

Early on, a *New York Times* team did a simulated selection and cut the list to twenty-five based on job growth, then to fourteen and nine after considering labor pool, amenities, transit, and housing. The *Times'* finalists were Boston, Denver, Portland, and Metropolitan Washington. Portland seemed too close to Seattle, and the cost of land eliminated Washington and Boston—so Denver was the guess.[d] Instead, Amazon split HQ2 between New York City and Washington's Virginia suburbs and added an operations center in Nashville. Critics saw this as a scam in which Amazon had already made a choice but got information from states and cities for future use. In the face of local opposition, Amazon dropped New York—on Valentine's Day, 2019.[e]

[a] For Amazon's brief guidance for applicants, see https://images-na.ssl-images-amazon.com/images/G/01/Anything/test/images/usa/RFP_3._V516043504_.pdf.

[b] Sarah Holder wrote a number of articles on the Amazon sweepstakes in *CityLab*: "How Far Will Cities Go to Win Amazon's HQ2?" October 4, 2017, https://www.citylab.com/life/2017/10/how-far-will-cities-go-to-win-amazon-hq2/541551/;

"The Extreme Amazon Bidder Just Got Real," November 28, 2017, https://www.citylab.com/life/2017/11/the-extreme-amazon-bidder-just-got-real/546857/; "Amazon Whittles Down List of HQ2 Contenders to 20 Finalists," January 18, 2018, https://www.citylab.com/life/2018/01/omg-amazon/550763/. Also see Tamara Chuang, "Just How Far Should Colorado Go to Lure Amazon's HQ2? Debate over Incentives, Transparency Intensifies," *Denver Post*, February 24, 2018, https://www.denverpost.com/2018/02/24/amazon-headquarters-colorado-incentives/; J. Scott Trubey and Greg Bluestein, "Amazon Secrecy Keeps Georgians in Dark," *Atlanta Journal-Constitution*, February 22, 2018, A1.

[c] Richard Florida, "The Disturbing Part about Amazon's HQ2 Competition" (editorial), *CNN*, January 21, 2018, https://www.cnn.com/2018/01/20/opinions/amazon-headquarters-competition-disturbing-richard-florida-opinion/index.html; Andre M. Perry and Martha Ross, "Here's What Happens When Inclusion Is Factored into Amazon's List of 20 HQ2 Finalists," *The Avenue* (Brookings Institution blog), January 18, 2018, https://www.brookings.edu/blog/the-avenue/2018/01/18/jeff-bezos-will-value-inclusion-amazon-hq2/; Amy Liu, "How Cities Can Strike a Win-Win Deal for Amazon HQ2," *The Avenue* (Brookings Institution blog), February 6, 2018, https://www.brookings.edu/blog/the-avenue/2018/02/06/how-cities-can-strike-a-win-win-deal-for-amazon-hq2; Sarah Holder, "The (Legal) Case against Bidding Wars Like Amazon's," *CityLab*, January 17, 2018, https://www.citylab.com/life/2018/01/the-case-for-the-case-against-economic-incentives/549632.

[d] Emily Badger, Quoctrung Bui, and Claire Cain Miller, "Dear Amazon, We Picked Your Headquarters for You," *New York Times*, September 9, 2017, https://www.nytimes.com/interactive/2017/09/09/upshot/where-should-amazon-new-headquarters-be.html.

[e] Shane Goldmacher, "Amazon Scraps New York Campus," *New York Times*, February 15, 2019, A1; J. David Goodman, "An Abrupt Retreat Follows an Uproar over Incentives," *New York Times*, February 15, 2019, A1; Vivian Wang, "What People Are Saying about the Breakup," *New York Times*, February 15, 2019, A23.

including disabled access to public buildings, sidewalks, parking, and public transportation. Mandates are sometimes a bit more indirect. For example, Congress has not set a national drinking age. Instead, it passed a law in 1984 that leaves the decision to the states; however, states that set the drinking age lower than 21 stood to lose 5 percent of their share of millions in federal highway money. Some considered this blackmail, but the US Supreme Court has decided that it is constitutional.[29]

What Do We Mean by Politics?

Political scientists have defined **politics** in many different ways. The struggle for who gets what, when, and how is a classic definition created by Harold Lasswell in 1936.[30] "Who" refers to the beneficiaries of government decisions. "What" refers to the substance or benefits and costs of policy decisions. "When" and "how" refer to the timing of decisions and the process by which they are made. Had Lasswell been focused on urban politics, he might have added "where" to his definition because the effects of local government policies often depend on where people live or work. Another, more recent, definition is "The process through which individuals and groups reach agreement on a course of common, or collective action—even as they disagree on the intended goals of that action."[31] A third one refers to the "conflicts/struggles over the leadership, structure, and policies of government."[32] According to the latter definition, the goal of politics is to have a share or say in the composition of the government's leadership, how the government is organized, or what its policies are going to be.

Choice and decision making are key elements in all of these definitions. These are relevant not only for leaders, who face numerous, complex, and repeated decision-making situations every day, but also to voters, candidates, interest groups, and others who attempt to influence the direction of cities. Conflict and struggle are also central to politics. If everyone felt and thought the same way about the opportunities and challenges faced by government, politics would be easy. Because people do not think the same, they engage in politics to deal with different opinions, values, and preferences, and possibly to compromise and negotiate a path forward.

People are a critical element of what happens in *urban* politics. "People" includes voters and their elected representatives, public sector workers and managers, and a wide range of political parties and interest groups. The role of the people is explored most thoroughly in chapters 6–9, which cover city councils, mayors and other executives, elections, candidates and campaigns, and other forms of participation like protest politics, interest group lobbying, and citizen contacting. Central to any discussion of the people in democracy is representation.

Representation

In a broad sense, **representation** means to speak or act for others, and it is what we expect our elected officials to do. More specifically, scholars, especially those who study local government, focus on **descriptive representation**, or whether those who serve in government look like, in demographic, political, and ideological terms, the people they are supposed to represent. Another type of representation critical to the approach taken in this text is **substantive representation**, which refers to whether the processes and decisions of government are in actuality representative of the different perspectives in the community.[33] This text returns consistently to the concept, practice, and implementation of representation in modern urban America.

Representative government involves collective action at every level and in nearly every situation. **Collective action** is action taken by a group in pursuit of a common objective. The people who lead and are employed by government are expected to act collectively to make policy and to provide services. Groups act collectively to pursue their interests in the political process. Campaigns act collectively to support a candidate or cause. Politics at any level—federal, state, or local—and really in any other situation (work or family life) involves collective action. A major paradox in urban politics is that voter turnout is lowest for local elections, the level of government closest to people.

Successful collective action is rarely easy, however. Consider an assignment for a group project. One of the reasons these can be so frustrating and provoke angst, especially among the hardest-working students, is because preferences among the group's members vary. Some want an A grade and will work like crazy to achieve it, while others are happy to just complete the project and will be fine with a C. The latter group member is unlikely to contribute much to the effort, leaving those who desire an A to do all the work. If everyone slacks off or free rides on the work of others, hoping to benefit from the group's product but contributing very little to it, nothing will get done. **Free riding** is a situation in which a member of a group fails to contribute to the group effort but nevertheless derives a benefit because someone else steps up to do the work. The same is true in politics and government, which is considerably more complex than a class project.

A guiding assumption throughout this text is that people and political actors behave rationally to achieve their goals, responding to incentives in their environments. The nature of incentives helps us understand why collective action succeeds or fails. Institutions help structure collective action because they affect people's incentives to act.

Institutions

In representative democracy, an **institution** can be defined as "an organization that manages potential conflicts between political rivals, helps them find mutually acceptable solutions, and makes and enforces the society's collective agreements."[34] Decisions of government are made by institutional actors—local legislators, mayors and executives, and bureaucracies. Institutions establish the rules of the governmental game. The effects of the rules, however, are rarely neutral, no more so than in shaping who or what interests get represented in government. For example, at-large election systems hinder the representation of racial and ethnic groups in a community because those groups often constitute a minority of the population concentrated in specific areas and struggle to achieve representation when candidates have to run citywide.[35] Whether a local election is timed with state or national elections will influence voter turnout in city elections—lower when held on separate dates—affecting local democracy.[36] Institutions, of course, not only structure how actors interact; the rules require that certain things take place. Budgets have to be passed and required services have to be provided. Because the institutional arrangements of cities vary considerably, the local government arena is a great place to consider their effects.

The rules of the game can only get us so far. Politics usually requires success in persuasion. Campaigns must convince voters to vote for them and not another candidate. Mayors must convince city councilors to follow their policy agenda. Department heads must convince public employees to follow the rules guiding policy implementation. Given the myriad incentives to act in contradictory ways in any area of local government—voting, campaigning, policy making, and implementation—it is a small wonder that anything gets done at all. We explore these dynamics throughout this text.

Our approach is not a narrow exercise in the application of rational choice concepts (the idea that individuals seek always to maximize their own goals and/or favored outcomes). Although such concepts are useful for explicating the nature of urban politics, other motivations besides individual gain drive people to participate in the political process. The desire to serve the community is one such motivation, as is the desire to act symbolically (in voting, for example) as a sign of support for democratic ideals.

We must also appreciate that politics and governance occurs within a particular historical and social context and that things change over time, especially those things essential to understanding urban politics. Preferences change, modes of politics change, society and the economy change, and institutions change. Thus, although it is easy to assume that people behave with their goals in mind, that institutions structure interactions among political actors, and that collective action is at the center of it, all of this present-day activity remains connected to institutional, societal, economic, technological, and demographic changes that are the stuff of history. Because history matters, the next two chapters provide a relatively comprehensive treatment of urban American development (without turning this into a history text).

Policy Making

As the preceding discussion suggests, much of what local governments do is adopt and carry out policies in response to public pressure, which is the focus of chapters 10–13. It is important at this stage, though, to define **policy** as a government's course of action about a perceived problem. It has two key characteristics. First, policies can at times seem to clash or be contradictory. For example, a city may try to preserve historic buildings or neighborhoods while also attempting to promote business development, or promote public transit at the same time as it is building parking decks to benefit drivers who commute to work. Second, government *in*action can also be a policy. Say that a city does little to enforce building code violations by major landlords in poor neighborhoods or ignores complaints about police practices. Inaction serves to maintain the status quo.

Is Local Politics Really Different?

Government and politics at the local level are also different from government and politics at higher levels; therefore, we need a different lens to understand why things happen the way they do. First, local government is focused primarily on the day-to-day delivery of basic goods and services to local residents—police, firefighting, water, solid waste disposal, infrastructure, parks and recreation, education, etc. Most of these issues are also not part of the broader ideological struggles that dominate the attention of officials at higher levels, nor do they often generate national media headlines. Nevertheless, ideology is not irrelevant in city politics, especially as it relates to policy (see chapters 10–13).[37]

Second, local governments are also limited by what states say they can do. Third, as Paul Peterson in *City Limits* so elegantly states and box 1.2 demonstrates, unlike the national government, cities have a severely limited range of tools they can use to grow and manage their economies. Fourth, for the most part, local officeholders are elected on a nonpartisan ballot, and most are not professional politicians as is the case at higher levels.

Although this text shares much in common with leading texts in American politics, it rejects the idea that local government can be studied in exactly the same way. That important assumption guides the chapters that follow.

SUMMARY

Laying out important background for the remainder of the book, this chapter includes alternative definitions of *urban* and gives a brief overview of the history of US urbanization. It also provides a brief comparison of the three levels of government, explains the different types of general-purpose and special-purpose local governments, and describes the ways that local governments interact with one another and with higher-level governments. Finally, the chapter defines the key terms of *politics*, *representation*, *institution*, and *policy* and explains why collective action and location are instrumental in distributing costs and benefits to those in urban areas.

Key Terms

collective action *(18)*
Combined Statistical Areas (CSAs) *(4)*
Core Based Statistical Area (CBSA) *(3)*
descriptive representation *(18)*
fiscal year *(12)*
free riding *(19)*
general-purpose governments *(10)*
grants-in-aid *(15)*
institution *(19)*
mandates *(16)*

Metropolitan Statistical
   Areas (MSAs) *(3)*
Micropolitan Statistical Areas *(3)*
policy *(20)*
politics *(17)*
preemption *(16)*
representation *(18)*
special-purpose governments *(10)*
substantive representation *(18)*
urban area *(3)*

Discussion Questions

1. To what extent is your county urbanized? Are there areas within it that do not seem to fit that label? What differentiates them? You can explore these questions with data from your regional planning agency or the US Census Bureau: https://www.census.gov/en.html.

2. If you were a local official, would you ever consider hiring another government to provide services in your community? Which services? Under what conditions?

3. Imagine that you are a local official in one of the final twenty communities bidding for Amazon HQ2

as outlined in box 1.2. How would you decide what to "give" Amazon to locate in your community? What would you ask for in return?

4. What would it take to produce a dramatic increase or decrease in the level of residents' trust in your city or county government?

Exercises

1. Use the *Census of Governments* to determine the number and types of local governments in your state and compare those totals to national patterns. Determine how these totals have changed over time. Your best source is to go to the "Tables" section and work with those under "Organization": https://www.census.gov/programs-surveys/cog/data/tables.html. You can also get more detail from the "Individual State Descriptions" link under "List and Structure of Governments": https://www.census.gov/govs/. Consult major newspapers and other media, government websites, and other sources to try explaining the changes.

2. Determine the number of different types of local governments in your county (or one assigned to you).

Choose a sample of these governments and determine from their websites or other sources how they differ in the services they provide or how much money they are spending this year.

3. Search local news sources for stories about a major company expanding, coming to, or leaving your area. How did local officials and interest groups get involved in this process? What factors seem to have influenced the company's decisions? How thorough was the media coverage?

4. Identify examples of your state legislature preempting the decisions of cities and counties. Describe the participants on both sides of one or two of these issues, explain who "won" the conflict, and analyze the impact on local governments.

Practice and Review Online
https://textbooks.rowman.com/understanding-urban-politics

2

THE DEVELOPMENT
OF URBAN AMERICA
THROUGH WORLD WAR II

GUIDING QUESTIONS

1. How did economic and transportation changes shape American cities in the 19th and early 20th centuries?

2. How did domestic migration and immigration influence US preindustrial cities?

3. How did changing urban conditions, political machines, and political reform influence urban development from the 1870s to World War I?

4. In what ways have the Great Migration, suburbanization, and government policies—both local and national—affected the ways that American cities developed following World War I?

WHEN TIMOTHY SULLIVAN died in 1913, a reported 75,000 mourners participated in his New York City funeral procession.[1] The grieving were thankful for all that Sullivan and his ilk had done for them. Sullivan epitomized the political bosses who came to dominate many big cities beginning in the late 1800s. These men rose through the ranks of local political party (usually Democratic) organizations. The party "machines" they served flourished in the days before the US had major social welfare programs by helping immigrants adjust to life in urban America, finding jobs for party loyalists, providing food or other relief to the unlucky, and steering government work to favored contractors. All the beneficiaries had to do was support the party's candidates, although opponents had to be wary. This system was known for corruption, and middle-class and business "reformers" took steps to undermine party machines in the early 20th century. These competing forces and their legacies are key parts of this chapter.

HISTORY AS A LENS FOR UNDERSTANDING URBAN POLITICS

Urban development does not just happen. It is the result of millions of decisions by individuals and businesses about where—and where not—to locate. Urban development is also shaped by political decisions at the local, state, and national levels. Few of these decisions represent a "fresh start." Rather, they are constrained by important legacies, including the cumulative effects of an area's population movements; development of its economic base; natural features such as water, topography, and weather; and the built environment of buildings and projects such as roads and water systems.

Urban areas have changed in many ways over the years and have figured prominently in every century of US history. This is not a book about urban history, but we include two chapters on history because it is hard to understand where we are and where we might be headed if you do not understand where we've been. This chapter and the next one are designed to provide sufficient grounding in the development of urban America to link past and present. This chapter emphasizes major economic, population, and political changes through World War II: early cities and competition among them, industrialization, European immigration, political party machines and efforts to displace them, the first wave of suburbanization after World War I, the Great Migration, segregation, and the federal government's growing influence on urban development beginning during the Great Depression. Chapter 3 picks up the story after World War II.

The timeline in table 2.1 is intended as a quick reference to some milestones in US urban development prior to the end of World War II and to complement the chapter narrative. Entries in the first column highlight events at the national level, such as policies adopted by Congress, landmark decisions by the US Supreme Court, and notable dates in the US Census. The third column identifies events that represent a break from the past or affect perceptions of urban trends or issues. The sections that follow are also organized chronologically but should not be seen as hard and fast historical periods.

PRE-INDUSTRIAL CITIES

This section describes the key role of port cities in the early development of the US. As the country expanded westward, canals and railroads aided the development of new cities. These places benefited from migration from rural areas and the immigrants who arrived before the Civil War and the postwar boom in manufacturing.

TABLE 2.1	Timeline of American Urban Development, 1790–1945

National Milestones	Dates	Local Milestones
First Census: US is 5% urban	1790	
	1825	Erie Canal opens connecting New York City to the Great Lakes via the Hudson River
	1830s–1850s	Railroad networks are developed, helping transform Chicago into a major city
	1848	California Gold Rush helps launch San Francisco as a boom town
	1840s–1850s	Cities increasingly create professional fire and police departments
	1840–1920	More than fourteen million immigrants come to the US, mainly from Europe
	1858–1860	Central Park opens in New York City
	1873	San Francisco cable cars begin operating
Tenth Census: New York is first city to reach one million population	1880	
	1880s	First electric streetcar lines in US cities
Congress adopts Chinese Exclusion Act	1882	
	1904	Subway service begins in New York City
	1910–1970	More than sixteen million southerners move to the North and West in "The Great Migration"
	1914	Dayton is first large city to adopt the council-manager form of government
	1919	Race riots in multiple cities, mainly led by white mobs, left more than 150 dead, most of them black
Fourteenth Census: First time the US has an urban majority	1920	
Ratification of the 19th Amendment gives women the right to vote	1920	
	1920s	First major suburbanization, bolstered by streetcars and proliferation of cars
Congress passes law limiting immigrants based on country quotas	1924	
	1926	Supreme Court upholds zoning in an Ohio case, *Euclid v. Ambler Realty*, launching widespread use of local land-use regulation
Congress creates federal public housing and mortgage support programs	1930s	Cities face large-scale unemployment and budgetary problems during Great Depression
Congress passes the GI Bill to aid veterans returning from World War II	1944	

Westward Expansion and Economic Change

Even though Britain's American colonies were overwhelmingly rural, key events during the Revolution occurred in economically important ports like Boston, Philadelphia, and New York. The country expanded aggressively to the west after independence, including the 1803 Louisiana Purchase, the annexation of Texas in 1845, and statehood for California in 1850. New territory was largely rural, but westward growth was also powered by the development of commercial centers. Table 2.2 lists the ten most populous cities from 1820 to 1920.

Several things stand out during the period prior to the Civil War. First, many of these places seem "small." That is true of their population compared to today, of course. The nation was still rural in 1820, and only sixty-one places met the

TABLE 2.2	Ten Largest US Cities in 1820–1920				
1820		**1840**		**1860**	
New York	123,706	New York	312,710	New York	813,669
Philadelphia	63,802	Baltimore	102,313	Philadelphia	565,529
Baltimore	62,738	New Orleans	102,193	Brooklyn	266,661
Boston	43,298	Philadelphia	93,665	Baltimore	212,418
New Orleans	27,176	Boston	93,383	Boston	177,840
Charleston, SC	24,780	Cincinnati	46,338	New Orleans	168,675
N. Liberties, PA[a]	19,678	Brooklyn	36,233	Cincinnati	161,044
Southwark, PA[a]	14,713	N. Liberties, PA[a]	34,474	St. Louis	160,773
Washington, DC	13,247	Albany	33,721	Chicago	112,172
Salem	12,731	Charleston	29,261	Buffalo	81,129
1880		**1900**		**1920**	
New York	1,206,299	New York[b]	3,437,202	New York	5,620,048
Philadelphia	847,170	Chicago	1,698,575	Chicago	2,701,705
Brooklyn[b]	566,663	Philadelphia	1,293,697	Philadelphia	1,823,779
Chicago	503,185	St. Louis	575,238	Detroit	993,078
Boston	362,839	Boston	560,892	Cleveland	796,841
St. Louis	350,518	Baltimore	508,957	St. Louis	772,897
Baltimore	332,313	Cleveland	381,768	Boston	748,060
Cincinnati	255,139	Buffalo	352,387	Baltimore	733,826
San Francisco	233,959	San Francisco	342,782	Pittsburgh	588,343
New Orleans	216,090	Cincinnati	325,902	Los Angeles	576,673

[a] Became part of Philadelphia in 1854.

[b] Brooklyn joined four other boroughs in 1898 to form present-day New York City.

Source: US Census Bureau, "Population of the 100 Largest Cities and Other Urban Places in the United States: 1790 to 1990," https://www.census.gov/population/www/documentation/twps0027/twps0027.html.

census definition of urban with a population of at least 2,500. Second, cities were indeed small in terms of being compact—not more than two miles from the center—because people generally got around by walking.

Third, a commonality among the early cities in table 2.2 is water. Several began during the colonial era as part of the mercantile economy, which concentrated on shipping raw materials to Europe in exchange for finished goods. Others reflect the continued reliance on water as the primary shipping mode before the mass building of railroads. That includes places like Albany and Buffalo, which benefitted from the opening of the Erie Canal in 1825. Smaller cities not in the table were mill towns that relied on rivers to power factories before the use of steam.[2]

Much of the development prior to the Civil War was fueled by what historian Sam Bass Warner called privatism, an American tradition in which "the first purpose of the citizen is the search for private wealth; the goal of a city is to be a community of private money makers."[3] For example, early Philadelphia had limited regulation of features like street widths and setbacks. Many public services were purchased from private sellers or provided collectively in different parts of the city. Housing and other land uses were mixed together haphazardly; this changed later in the 1800s, when home and work became separate places as the factory system developed and cities expanded rapidly. As table 2.2 indicates, some of these cities tripled their population or even expanded nine-fold between 1820 and 1860. Adjusting to this growth was not easy given the lack of paved streets, sanitation, quality water, building standards, and other necessities. It took much of the 1840s and 1850s to centralize many core services in communities, including provision of citywide professional police forces.[4]

Eastern seaports still dominated in 1860, although New Orleans retained a prominent position. Note that Brooklyn was a separate city until 1898, when Manhattan, Brooklyn, Queens, the Bronx, and Staten Island merged to create the modern boundaries of New York City. The factory and rail systems expanded before the Civil War, primarily in the North. Investors and local boosters promoted railroads, which helped Chicago surpass other midwestern cities that continued to rely on water. Railroads had advantages in dealing with weather compared to water-borne travel and often had telegraph lines running alongside their tracks.[5]

Early Immigration

In addition to people moving from rural to urban areas, the period before the Civil War saw the first noticeable arrival of immigrants, mainly from England, Germany, and Ireland. The Census Bureau did not systematically gather data about immigrants until the 1850 census. Table 2.3 displays key features of foreign-born residents counted in censuses between then and 1930.

The table captures the overall significance of immigration, as well as the timing of the arrival of different groups. British immigration fluctuated, but the Irish and Germans were early arrivals whose presence diminished after 1870. At least 20,000 Germans and Irish arrived annually, beginning in the mid-1830s. The key exodus from Ireland was in the 1840s, the era of the notorious potato famine. Indeed, numbers of Irish immigrants first reached 30,000 in 1836, exceeded 50,000 in 1846, and then accelerated to more than 100,000 annually from 1847 to 1854; almost 1.2 million arrived during the latter period, including over 221,000 in 1854. With political upheaval in Continental Europe in the 1840s, German immigration accelerated, reaching 215,000 in 1854.[6]

Table 2.3 also displays the timing of the "late arrivals" from Scandinavia, Italy, Poland, Russia, and Mexico, plus Canadian immigration, the importance of which is often ignored. Overall, tables 2.2 and 2.3 demonstrate the impact of **push and pull factors**. "Push" includes conditions that prompt households to pack up and move away, while "pull" covers factors that attract people to a particular place. Movement can include migration within a country, as well as attempts to escape an unsafe country or move to a nation with better opportunities. For example, many Americans in rural areas during the 1800s were drawn to jobs and the hoped-for benefits of urban life. Similarly, many Europeans were pulled to this country because they saw the United States as "the land of opportunity" but also experienced the push factors of poor economic conditions and warfare. African Americans sought to escape oppressive racial segregation in the South during the early 1900s ("push") and saw the industrial North as offering greater economic opportunities ("pull").

TABLE 2.3	Foreign-Born Residents of the US, 1850–1930				
	1850	1870	1890	1910	1930
US Population	23,191,876	38,558,371	62,979,766	92,228,496	123,202,624
Foreign-Born	2,244,602	5,567,229	9,249,547	13,515,886	14,204,149
Foreign-Born %	9.7%	14.4%	14.7%	14.7%	11.5%
Origin					
Great Britain	379,093	770,414	1,251,402	1,221,283	1,402,923
Ireland	961,719	1,855,827	1,871,509	1,352,251	744,810
Germany	583,774	1,690,533	2,784,894	2,311,237	1,608,814
Scandinavia[a]	18,075	241,685	933,249	1,380,413	1,267,818
Italy	3,679	17,157	182,580	1,343,125	1,790,429
Poland	N/A	14,436	147,440	937,864	1,268,583
Russia	1,414	4,644	182,644	1,184,412	1,153,628
Mexico	13,317	42,435	77,853	221,915	641,462
Canada	147,711	493,464	980,938	1,209,717	1,310,369
China	758	63,042	106,688	56,756	46,129

[a] Denmark, Finland, Iceland, Norway, Sweden.

Source: Campbell J. Gibson and Emily Lennon, *Historical Census Statistics on the Foreign-Born Population of the United States: 1850–1990* (Washington, DC: US Census Bureau, 1999), table 4, https://www.census.gov/population/www/documentation/twps0029/twps0029.html.

Most immigrants settled in cities, where newcomers often faced bias or outright hostility. One early target was the Irish, who were the first "different" immigrant group to come to the United States in large numbers. They were unskilled and Catholic in a largely Protestant country, and they primarily spoke Gaelic rather than English. Before the Civil War, the city of Boston experienced anti-Catholic riots, the burning of a convent, and the bombing of a Catholic church.[7] Philadelphia's riots between 1834 and 1849 included some aimed at blacks, others between followers of different political parties, a number involving labor strikes, and several targeted at Catholics.[8] Nativist elements and the Know Nothing Party, which strongly opposed immigrants and followers of the Catholic Church, were active in New York during the 1840s.[9]

Immigration was not a major force in the growth of southern cities. Instead, they relied on people moving from rural areas.[10] The Civil War also took its toll. Atlanta, Richmond, Savannah, Charleston, New Orleans, and Mobile were among the places attacked by Union armies. Much of the South's infrastructure was damaged or destroyed. Plus, the South remained a largely agricultural region as the North industrialized. Seven of the nation's fifty largest cities were in the eleven states of the future Confederacy in 1860. That number shrank to six in 1870 and five in 1880. Some cities recovered, with Atlanta becoming both a railroad center and a new state capital. In the meantime, there was major growth in northern industrial cities such as Cleveland, Jersey City, Kansas City, and Toledo.[11]

URBAN DEVELOPMENT FROM THE 1870s TO WORLD WAR I

After the Civil War, the expansion of railroads and factories boosted interior regions and urban centers. As in the earlier 1800s, growth was associated with advertising and other forms of promotion, entrepreneurship, substantial government investments (and defaults), company bankruptcies, and frequent incidents of corruption.[12] This period included more and larger cities, industrialization, transportation improvements, an acceleration in immigration, the emergence of political machines, and the hardening of legalized racial segregation in the South.

One way to look at urbanization in the post-Civil War era is to examine the largest urban centers (see the second half of table 2.2). By the turn of the century, the list of the largest cities captures the dynamism in the industrial North. Chicago added a million residents between 1880 and 1900 and grew by another million people from 1900 to 1920. Detroit, Cleveland, Buffalo, and Pittsburgh rose as major urban centers during this period, and Los Angeles vaulted to the Top Ten in 1920 with its mild weather, booming oil industry, and emergence of movie studios. Union control of the South during Reconstruction did not end until the political bargain resolving the 1876 presidential election, and the South was largely left behind during the rise of manufacturing.

Figure 2.1 Number of Cities in Different Population Groups, 1850–1940 Censuses

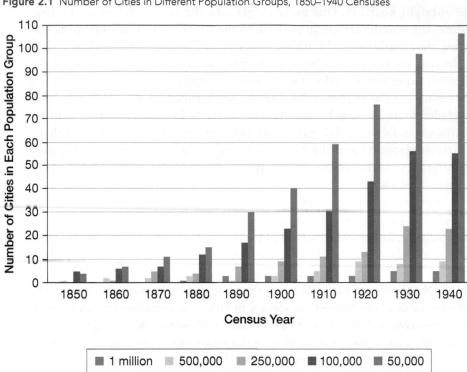

Source: US Census Bureau, *Census of Population: 1950, Volume 1: Number of Inhabitants*, table 5b, https://www2.census.gov/library/publications/decennial/1950/population-volume-1/vol-01-04.pdf; *Statistical Abstract of the United States: 2012*, table 28, https://www.census.gov/library/publications/2011/compendia/statab/131ed/population.html.

Another way to look at urbanization is to examine the proliferation of cities of different sizes. Figure 2.1 demonstrates that being "big" means very different things at different points in time. For example, the 1800 census (not shown) had just one city that reached 50,000 population and two with at least 25,000. Although these were major places at the time, people got around by walking, on horseback, or in wagons pulled by animals. Following improvements in construction, transportation, sanitation, steam power, and electrification, by 1890, twenty-eight cities had at least 100,000 residents, including three with a population exceeding one million. By the eve of World War II, cities of 100,000 were common, and over 100 cities had at least 50,000 residents. In 2010 (not shown in figure 2.1), there were over 400 such places, which by today's standards are considered "small" urban centers.

Late 19th- and Early 20th-Century Immigration

In addition to the internal movement of native-born Americans, immigrants who arrived during the 1800s and early 1900s tended to settle in cities. Promoters encouraged immigration through advertising and recruiting campaigns in Europe and by targeting those getting off ships in New York after crossing the Atlantic.[13]

As shown in table 2.3, the wave of immigrants just before the outbreak of World War I in 1914 was mainly from Poland, Italy, Russia, and Mexico.

Although 39 percent of the foreign-born population lived in rural areas in 1890, they made up only 9 percent of the rural population. In contrast, 25 percent of the urban population was foreign-born, including 31 percent of the six million living in cities of 100,000 or more.[14] The languages spoken by the immigrant population were also very diverse. Of the more than 13 million foreign-born people in the 1910 census, 2.8 million reported German as their "mother tongue," almost 1.4 million cited Italian, 1 million spoke Yiddish, 943,000 were native Polish speakers, and nearly 700,000 spoke Swedish.[15]

Different ethnic groups frequently clashed. Nonnative groups turned on one another to protect their gains against the next wave of immigrants, as the Irish did in response to the influx of Poles, Italians, and Jews beginning in the 1880s.[16] Conflict even existed among immigrants practicing the same religion. For example, Poles and Italians found the Catholic Church in the US dominated by the Irish and the Germans, which led to a proliferation of parishes and schools tied to each ethnic group.[17] Yet opposition to immigration never disappeared. In the late 1840s, immigrants began arriving on the West Coast during the California Gold Rush, many ending up in low-wage jobs. Hostility toward the Chinese led to efforts at the state and national levels to limit their presence, leading to passage by Congress of the Chinese Exclusion Act in 1882 to prohibit immigration from China; the effects of that legislation show up in the last two columns of table 2.3.[18] After several decades of effort, advocates got Congress to set immigration quotas by country in 1924, thereby reducing substantially the numbers of Jews, Italians, and others from southern and eastern Europe coming to the US.[19]

Industrialization and Changing Urban Conditions

It is almost impossible to separate the growth of cities in the 19th century from the rise of mass production in large factories. Manufacturing existed in early America, but it was conducted largely by individual artisans or guilds.[20] With the introduction of new technology that increased output, as well as innovations in organization and financing, the factory system began to take off during the 1830s and 1840s. This growth accelerated after the Civil War, aided by the development of railroads, steamships, urban transit systems, telegraph and telephone systems, and the postal service. Mass production was accompanied by wholesaling and mass distribution through such enterprises as the department store, mail-order house, and chain store.[21]

Factory work was difficult, dangerous, and largely unregulated. The precarious nature of wages and other factors stimulated the formation of working men's political parties in New York, Philadelphia, Milwaukee, and elsewhere during the early to mid-1800s.[22] Such political parties had limited success. Workers also formed trade unions. Organizing and protest by unions was difficult: Economic downturns weakened workers' bargaining power, employers often hired strike

breakers, and management often met strikers with force, including state militias.[23] Conflicts escalated after the 1886 Haymarket Square bombing in Chicago, in which a protestor threw a bomb at police during a labor demonstration, killing eight people.[24]

During the late 1800s, researcher Adna Ferrin Weber connected the growth of cities with increased agricultural productivity. Advances in farming required fewer workers, who could then better themselves economically in cities. Weber also observed that the "real checks upon the growth of population in previous centuries were war, famine, pestilence, and unsanitary cities involving particularly high infantile mortality."[25] With the taming of those problems, he argued, certain "social causes" also pulled people to cities: educational opportunity, amusements, a higher standard of living, intellectual associations, a level of social interaction not available in rural areas, and enhanced communication, including newspapers.[26]

The Shape of the City

The development of horse-drawn streetcars, which were usually privately owned and operated, made it easier for cities to spread more than a couple of miles beyond downtown. As the transit system developed in Boston, for instance, the middle-class families of doctors, lawyers, accountants, small merchants, and other professionals moved further out and commuted to the city center.[27] This separation by economic classes increased with electrified streetcars, which allowed development of neighborhoods even further from downtown.[28] The affluent did not completely abandon older parts of cities, however. As historian

Jon Teaford notes, "In every major city there was a mansion district" where the economic elite clustered their large, elegant homes. Perhaps the most famous is Fifth Avenue in New York, but there were similar areas in Boston, Buffalo, Chicago, Cleveland, Philadelphia, and St. Louis.[29]

In what might be considered another form of boosterism, local elites promoted "high culture" during the late 1800s and early 1900s, often mimicking the arts in Europe. This effort included orchestras, choral societies, opera houses, and concert halls in Boston, New York, Chicago, St. Louis, Philadelphia, Cincinnati, Pittsburgh, Cleveland, and elsewhere. Wealthy sponsors helped to import European conductors, composers, and performers (e.g., Czech composer Antonin Dvorak in the 1890s). Museums and libraries were built, often with large donations, to promote both art and knowledge. Examples include the Smithsonian Institution and hundreds of Carnegie libraries all over the country. Before 1900, cultural institutions in New York City included the American Museum of Natural History, Carnegie Hall, and the Metropolitan Museum of Art. Even small cities began competing to open a concert hall or opera house.[30]

Also during the late 1800s, the field of urban planning began to train professionals to lay out a vision, rules, and process for developing a city. By the early 1900s, cities began to adopt **zoning**, a set of regulations by local government for controlling the types of uses and structures permitted on a specific piece of property. Although intended to separate factories from residential areas, some of its early uses promoted racial segregation. Zoning was controversial because of its limits on owners' property rights, but the US Supreme Court ruled it constitutional in 1926.[31]

Few Americans owned homes in the late 1800s, and urban renters found housing crowded (see box 2.1). Working-class neighborhoods commonly became enclaves for immigrants from the same country, such as the Polish south side of Milwaukee, the preponderance of Czechs on the west side of Chicago, and Irish, Italian, and Jewish areas in most cities in the North.[32] Housing conditions in many ways matched the hazards of factory work, perhaps best remembered by the 1911 Triangle Shirtwaist Company factory fire in New York, which killed almost 150 workers, mainly young women.[33]

Beginning in the 1920s, the Chicago School, a group of sociologists at the University of Chicago, took a keen interest in the development of cities.[34] Looking at the history of their own city, they developed a model of urban development (see figure 2.2).

The model consists of five concentric zones rippling outward from the downtown. Land in Zone I ("the Loop") at the center is extremely expensive because of its concentration of offices, banking, and retail. In Zone II, the "in transition" zone, older dwellings and small commercial buildings stand in the path of downtown expansion; it is home to light manufacturing as well as *slums* (neighborhoods with high concentrations of poor residents in older, rundown housing) and *ethnic ghettos* (neighborhoods inhabited overwhelmingly by recent immigrants from the same country, usually practicing the same religion and relying on their native language). Zone III, generally referred to as the "second generation," houses factory workers who are the children of immigrants. Zone IV is inhabited

Figure 2.2 "Chicago School" Model of City Growth

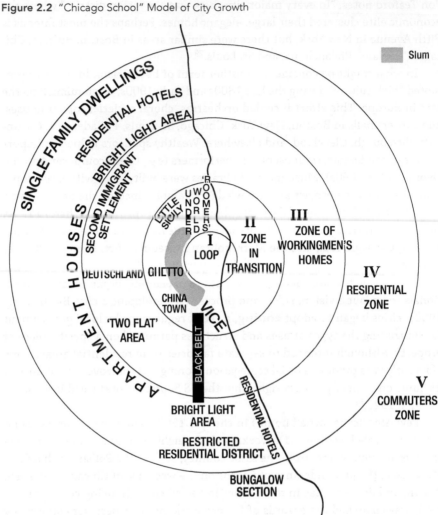

Slum

SINGLE FAMILY DWELLINGS

RESIDENTIAL HOTELS

BRIGHT LIGHT AREA

SECOND IMMIGRANT SETTLEMENT

APARTMENT HOUSES

LITTLE SICILY

ROOMERS'

UNDERWORLD

DEUTSCHLAND   GHETTO

CHINA TOWN

'TWO FLAT' AREA

BLACK BELT

VICE

I
LOOP

II
ZONE IN TRANSITION

III
ZONE OF WORKINGMEN'S HOMES

IV
RESIDENTIAL ZONE

V
COMMUTERS ZONE

RESIDENTIAL HOTELS

BRIGHT LIGHT AREA

RESTRICTED RESIDENTIAL DISTRICT

BUNGALOW SECTION

Source: Robert E. Park and Ernest W. Burgess, *The City* (Chicago: University of Chicago Press, 1925), 55.

by middle-class commuters residing in "high-class apartment buildings" or single-family homes. Living Zone V, the suburbs, requires a thirty- to sixty-minute commute to the Loop.[35]

This model captured the first wave of suburbanization, which occurred after World War I and was bolstered by mass production of the automobile.[36] The Chicago School model viewed cities as constantly in transition, including the notions of invasion and succession. New groups moved into ("invaded") an area as it aged, succeeding previous residents, who moved further out as they become more economically secure. In this way, ghettos could form and dissolve.[37]

The Chicago model makes development look quite uniform within each ring. However, it ignores the extent to which cities spread outward along streetcar lines likes spokes in a wheel, with development then spreading along streets crossing the spokes.[38] Nor did it anticipate the postwar development around freeways discussed in chapter 3.

The Chicago School also ignored institutional factors dividing cities. During the late 1800s and early 1900s, for example, southern states and cities created a system of **de jure segregation**, legally enforced racial segregation (*de jure* is Latin for "from law"). These arrangements involved multiple ways to limit where blacks could live. For example, after electoral defeats during the late 1800s in North Carolina, white elites controlling the Democratic Party were able to retake state government in part by dividing the coalition of poor whites and blacks against one another. This led to black disenfranchisement and de jure segregation after 1900 and allowed the city of Charlotte to create a system of housing segregation.[39] Louisville adopted a residential segregation ordinance in 1914, but the US Supreme Court declared it unconstitutional in 1917.[40] Atlanta adopted racial zoning in 1922, used roadways as barriers between black and white areas, and even changed the names of streets when they crossed from a white neighborhood into a black one.[41]

Even without race-based zoning, segregation was still enforced by restrictive covenants. A *covenant* is a requirement in deeds to property that limits how a property in a particular neighborhood can be used. Covenants are enforced like any contract: Neighbors with similar restrictions could sue homeowners they thought were in violation. Some covenants seem innocuous enough, such as prohibiting buildings other than a house on a lot or not permitting renting to boarders. **Restrictive covenants**, on the other hand, were a formal, legal way to keep "undesirables" out of a neighborhood by forbidding owners from selling their homes to members of certain groups, most notably blacks, Asians, Mexicans, and Jews. Such restrictions were not limited to the South. Indeed, they were used in a wide range of northern cities. It was not until 1948 that the US Supreme Court ruled that government enforcement of such covenants violated the equal protection guarantee of the 14th Amendment to the Constitution.[42]

Politics and Urbanization

Politics was an ever-present reality amid the population and economic dynamics of the 1800s and early 1900s. Local coalitions of political and business leaders engaged in **boosterism**, the enthusiastic promotion of a place to stimulate its growth and economic development. Efforts included projects like the Erie Canal, which connected upstate New York to the Hudson River and New York City. Other entrepreneurs saw the Ohio and Mississippi Rivers as gateways to financial success; Pittsburgh, Cincinnati, Lexington, Louisville, and St. Louis competed vigorously for water-borne trade before the Civil War. Their positions became stronger after the invention of the steamboat made two-way river traffic feasible. Although they began as commercial hubs, these cities also became strong in banking and manufacturing, including Pittsburgh's famous (but now-departed) steel industry.[43]

Boosters promoted Chicago relentlessly in the 1830s and 1840s, including attempts to strengthen its trading position with the construction of a canal connecting Lake Michigan to the Illinois River to provide access to the Mississippi. A private venture failed, but the state of Illinois finally completed the project in 1848. By the time of the Civil War, massive railroad building, often aided by eastern investors and federal land grants, connected Chicago to New York, the Gulf of Mexico, and areas west of the Mississippi River. This allowed Chicago to surpass St. Louis and other river towns as a commercial center.[44] The area developed as a major market for grain, lumber, and meat, and became a regional banking powerhouse and major manufacturing center. Perhaps the capstone to Chicago boosters' campaigns was reaching the one million mark in population in 1890 and winning the right to host the 1893 World's Fair, called the World's Columbian Exposition to commemorate Columbus's discovery of America.[45]

As urban scholar Amy Bridges explains, 1830–60 was a period when political parties were in flux, local politics took on a life distinct from national politics, a class of professional politicians arose, and local governments abandoned less formal arrangements in favor of professionals in services like police, fire, and education. It was in this context that political machines developed in New York, Chicago, and elsewhere by the late 1800s.[46]

A **political machine** is a local political party organization structured geographically and hierarchically to trade votes and other rewards for political favors in order to control local government. The head of the machine was usually referred to as "the boss." Geographically, the political machine was organized first at the level of the *precinct*, the neighborhoods assigned to a specific polling place where citizens went to vote. Precincts, in turn, were grouped into *wards*, which are sometimes called city council districts. Representatives from wards served on a committee (often at the county level) that governed each political party. The committee chose the party chairman, who could develop enormous power. The party organization paralleled the system for voting and representation on city councils. Each precinct had a captain who was responsible for mobilizing voters for the party's candidates and nurturing residents' party loyalty. The ward committeeman oversaw precinct captains and was tasked with making sure the party won the ward's seat on the city council.

The math driving the machine was that residents and neighborhoods received benefits based on their support for a party's candidates. Until the secret ballot was institutionalized in the early 1890s, party candidates were chosen in *caucuses*, meetings of party members where party leaders exerted pressure on voters to select their preferred candidates. Prior to the establishment of the modern social welfare system, the machine filled that role by helping people find jobs, gain citizenship, deal with crises, and obtain public services. The machine's influence also extended to land deals, the awarding of contracts, and similar types of government business.

Political machines built complex geographical relationships based on ethnicity and class. They also streamlined operations in city governments often run by multiple boards, weak mayors, and even city councils modeled after the bicameralism of the US Congress. On the flip side, machines often raised the level of corruption in city politics.

The most notorious political machines were Tammany Hall in New York and the Democratic machine in Chicago that reached its greatest power under Mayor Richard J. Daley from 1955 to 1976.[47] Others developed in cities such as New Orleans, Cincinnati, and Kansas City, and even in rural counties in Texas and Louisiana. Perhaps the ultimate image of the crooked machine politician was Tammany ward boss George Washington Plunkett in the early 1900s. Plunkett became famous for distinguishing "dishonest" graft—such as blackmail—from "honest" graft: "supposin' it's a new bridge they're goin' to build. I get tipped off and buy as much property as I can that has to be taken for approaches. I sell at my own price later and drop more money in the bank." Plunkett considered that honest graft, which he describes as "I seen my opportunities and I took 'em."[48]

Many of the early political machines were dominated by the Irish.[49] As local populations changed, machines had to adapt. For instance, Chicago's Democratic Party did not meddle in a ward composed primarily of Russian Jews during the 1920s and 1930s because of the cultural ties built by its alderman.[50] The machine also added Poles to the party's slate of candidates to garner their support as the Polish share of the population grew substantially. Maintaining Polish loyalty was not easy, however, as upwardly mobile Poles moved to more middle-class areas and could easily defect to support Polish candidates who were not backed by the Democratic political machine.[51]

There were several responses to the corruption and other perceived ills of American cities. In some places, local socialist parties campaigned against corruption and supported a more equitable distribution of public services, including public ownership of bus and trolley systems. They had some success in the early 1900s in Schenectady, Bridgeport, Milwaukee, and other cities.[52] The settlement house movement launched during the 1880s aided the poor with educational programs, shelter, public baths, and similar support; helped immigrants and others adjust to city life; and influenced the development of social work as a profession.[53]

Critics and Reformers

During the late 1800s and early 1900s, journalists and other writers known as *muckrakers* chronicled abuses of cities' economic and political systems. Upton Sinclair's novel *The Jungle* laid bare the extreme working conditions and health threats in the meat-packing industry. Investigative journalist Ida Tarbell took on the virtual monopoly of the Standard Oil Company in a series of articles for *McClure's Magazine* that eventually resulted in the prosecution and dismantling of the company.

Critics also zeroed in on bribery, embezzlement, and the questionable handling of contracts, licenses, inspections, law enforcement, and other practices. Lincoln Steffens wrote magazine articles about corruption in half a dozen local governments and turned his work into a book, *The Shame of the Cities*.[54] Such writing helped fuel the **urban reform movement**, an effort by middle-class and business leaders to undermine the power of political machines through changes in election procedures and the structure of local government.

Reformers often relied on organizations like the National Municipal League to advocate for their agenda and rural leaders in state government to enact it. Reformers promoted several means to weaken political parties. One was adoption of **nonpartisan elections**, in which ballots do not identify candidates with political parties, including only the names of people running for each office. Party is often an important cue, signaling to voters what a candidate might do while in office. With party labels removed, voters might surmise candidates' ethnicity or gender, but little else unless they were familiar with them from news reports or campaigns. Reformers also sought to make municipal elections "off cycle" so that they no longer overlapped state and national election dates, when political parties were already active in mobilizing voters. Today many elections for mayors and city councils are in odd-numbered years, when they receive limited media attention and are less visible compared to elections for president, Congress, or governor. This results in very low turnout, particularly among lower-income and less-educated voters. Reformers also proposed methods like literacy tests to make it harder for immigrants to vote, which also undermined support for political machines.

Attacks on political machines also included changes in representation. Rather than electing city council members from districts, reformers proposed **at-large elections**, which would require candidates to run citywide. At-large candidates needed to appeal to a broader range of voters than the smaller number in a ward; this made campaigning more expensive, as they had to cover more territory and communicate with more people. While racial and ethnic groups might be concentrated enough to dominate a ward, at-large elections made it difficult to get one of their own elected citywide (for more on electoral systems, see chapter 7).

Reformers were also strong advocates of **civil service**, a system of hiring and promotion based on certain qualifications, which usually included level of education and examination scores. This system was designed to undermine **patronage**, the practice of awarding government jobs and contracts to political supporters. Reformers also backed the **council-manager system**, a form of local government in which voters elect a city council, which in turn hires a professional manager to run city operations on a day-to-day basis. Most city managers hire and fire department heads and prepare the budget, functions otherwise performed by an elected mayor serving as chief executive. In council-manager systems, the council can normally fire a manager at will, and mayors preside over council meetings in a symbolic role, usually as just another voting council member. In many ways, this resembles a corporation: voters are like shareholders, and the city council resembles a board of directors that hires a chief executive (the city manager). Reformers were not able to impose this system in the nation's major cities in the early 1900s, but they succeeded in smaller cities and some that became much larger later in the 20th century.

Local government reformers were also active outside the traditional machine cities in the North. In the Southwest between the two world wars, political and business leaders eager to promote the growth of their cities implemented major political changes in what were then modest cities: Albuquerque, Austin, Dallas, Houston, Phoenix, San Antonio, San Diego, and San Jose.[55] There were other prominent issues besides local government reform during this era. Moral crusaders targeted gambling, prostitution, and alcohol. Their campaigns for "decency" zeroed in on saloons, which were popular gathering places often connected to machine politicians.[56]

THE 1920s THROUGH WORLD WAR II

The end of World War I in 1918 was a springboard for the first major wave of suburban development on the fringes of US cities. This was bolstered by increased prosperity, a growing middle class, improved transit, and the mass production and sale of automobiles. The era also witnessed significant population movements among regions, particularly African Americans leaving the South, and implementation of major federal policies adopted during the 1930s that have affected urban development to the present day.

Increased Prosperity and Suburbanization

After World War I, "streetcar suburbs" proliferated all over the country, much like those that Warner describes on the fringe of Boston beginning in the 1870s.[57] The 1920 census was the first when a majority of America's population lived in urban areas, albeit with the old definition of urban as 2,500 or more. Table 2.4 traces the development of "metropolitan districts" made up of large cities and their nearby suburbs. The definition of these districts changed over time until 1950, when the Census Bureau started using *Metropolitan Statistical Areas* (*MSAs*; see chapter 1) following county lines. In 1910, these twenty-five areas included central cities of at least 200,000 and had more than twenty-two million residents, almost one-fourth of the US population. Following the suburban boom of the 1920s, the number of districts nearly quadrupled and by 1930 had over fify-four million residents, or 44 percent of the nation.

The table also tracks the growing significance of suburbia. From 1910 to 1920, new residents of central cities grew by 26.1 percent, but those in their suburbs grew by 32.7 percent. These differences widened during the next 20 years, with cities growing by 44 percent and suburbs expanding by 75 percent during the 1920s. In the wake of the Great Depression, cities grew by only 6.1 percent between 1930 and 1940, but 17 percent more residents were added to the suburbs. Pittsburgh and Boston continued to be eclipsed by their suburbs during this period. From 1920 to 1940, Cleveland's suburbs added 270,000 residents, suburban St. Louis expanded by 400,000, and both Detroit and Philadelphia witnessed suburban growth of more than half a million people.

TABLE 2.4	City and Suburban Population for the US and Its Twelve Largest Metropolitan Districts, 1910–1940 Censuses

	1910		1920	
	Cities	Suburbs	Cities	Suburbs
United States	17,099,904	4,988,427	26,254,645	9,682,355
New York	4,766,883	1,707,685	5,620,048	2,290,367
Chicago	2,185,283	261,638	2,701,705	477,219
Philadelphia	1,549,008	423,334	1,823,770	583,455
Boston	670,585	849,885	748,060	1,024,194
Pittsburgh	533,905	508,950	588,343	619,161
St. Louis	687,029	141,704	772,807	179,115
San Francisco-Oakland	567,087	119,787	722,937	168,540
Baltimore	558,485	100,230	733,826	53,632
Cleveland	560,663	52,607	796,041	128,879
Cincinnati	363,591	200,213	401,247	205,603
Minneapolis-St. Paul	516,152	10,104	615,280	13,936
Detroit	465,766	35,216	993,678	171,475
	25 districts (23.9% of US)		58 districts (33.9% of US)	

	1930		1940	
	Cities	Suburbs	Cities	Suburbs
United States	37,814,610	16,939,035	42,796,170	20,169,603
New York	7,942,600	2,958,824	8,435,496	3,255,024
Chicago	3,376,438	988,317	3,396,808	1,102,318
Philadelphia	1,950,961	896,187	1,931,334	967,310
Boston	781,188	1,526,709	770,816	1,579,698
Pittsburgh	669,817	1,283,851	671,659	1,822,401
St. Louis	821,960	471,556	816,048	551,929
San Francisco-Oakland	918,457	371,637	936,699	491,826
Baltimore	804,874	144,373	859,100	187,592
Cleveland	900,429	294,560	878,336	336,607
Cincinnati	451,160	308,304	455,610	333,699
Minneapolis-St. Paul	736,962	96,296	780,106	130,971
Detroit	1,568,662	536,102	1,623,452	572,415
	96 districts (44.4% of US)		140 districts (47.6% of US)	

Note: the Census Bureau identified Metropolitan Districts as cities and their suburbs with density of at least 150 people per square mile. Originally, the district extended no more than ten miles from the central city (dropped in 1930), and the central city had to have a population of 100,000 (1920) or 200,000 (1910 and 1930, changed to 50,000 in 1940).

Source: US Census Bureau, *Abstract of the Thirteenth Census: 1910*, 61–62; *Fourteenth Census of the United States Taken in the Year 1920, Population 1920: Number and Distribution of Inhabitants*, 62–63, table 40, table 41; *Fifteenth Census of the United States: 1930, Metropolitan Districts: Population and Area*, table 11; *Sixteenth Census of the United States: 1940, Population, Volume 1: Number of Inhabitants*, "United States Summary," 11, table 17. All available in pdf: https://www.census.gov/programs-surveys/decennial-census/decade.html.

The Great Migration

The limited opportunities for African Americans under legalized segregation in the South were reinforced in rural areas by a system of tenant farming in which poor households leased land to raise crops to sell. Often dependent on credit from landowners, who also got a share of the crops, tenant farmers often ended up essentially indentured to them. Plus, there was always the threat of lynching and other race-based violence. One major study of lynching during 1882–1930 in the South found 284 cases in which white mobs lynched white people and another 148 cases in which black or mixed-race mobs lynched black people; 2,314 African Americans were lynched by white mobs during this same period, making the larger pattern quite clear. These incidents rose from about forty to fifty annually during the early 1880s to eighty to ninety in the mid-1890s before declining slowly to twenty or fewer in the late 1920s.[58] In many places, and not just in the South, African Americans were not safe after dark.[59] Although African Americans found ways to undermine the system of segregation in the South,[60] increased job opportunities in the North after World War I opened a virtual floodgate of departures.

Moving to the North did not free African Americans from white hostility, however. Segregation might not have been enforced by law, but just like the South, it persisted through the use of restrictive covenants, social pressure, and violence. Efforts included gang clashes and physical enforcement of informally demarcated public spaces. For example, in 1919, violence erupted in Chicago after a black youth was stoned to death for entering white space at a Lake Michigan beach. This was part of a wave of racial violence in both the North and South after World War I, in which nearly 370,000 black soldiers had served despite segregation. Most of the violence in 1919, with an official death count of 150, was initiated by white mobs and often abetted by local newspapers. In 1921, white rioters virtually leveled Tulsa's black section, with thirty-six square blocks burned down, several dozen killed, and several thousand left homeless.[61]

The movement of millions of southerners to the North and West (primarily black people relocating to cities) between World War I and the 1960s is commonly called the **Great Migration**. Although researchers vary in their estimates of the exact dates, population totals, and destinations of these migrants, they generally agree that the impact of the Great Migration was profound and long-lasting.

In *The Southern Diaspora*, James N. Gregory argues that movement to the North took off after the Civil War, with some leaving to farm in other regions. Migration accelerated in the 20th century, especially with the job opportunities that developed during the two world wars. Gregory discusses some of the problems with the decennial census and relies instead on data that follow the moves of people born in the South, arguing that white migrants outnumbered black ones. During the 1920s, over 800,000 African Americans and nearly 1.5 million whites left the South. During the 1950s, the migrants totaled 1.1 million blacks and 3.2 million whites. According to the 1970 census, the residual effect was that nearly 7 million white southerners and 3.3 million black southerners lived in other regions.[62]

Gregory concludes, "Over the course of the 20th century, more than 28 million southerners left their home region—28 percent were African Americans, 68 percent were non-Hispanic whites, and 4 percent southern-born Latinos."[63] He adds, however, that there was an almost constant churning of these numbers for whites, with fewer than half leaving for good. Although the *number* of white migrants was much higher, a much larger *percentage* of blacks left the South; 20–33 percent of African Americans departed between the 1940 and 1970 censuses compared with less than 20 percent of whites.[64]

Black migrants brought their existing culture with them; this, and an often-hostile press, at times made it difficult to adjust.[65] Threats and violence were also standard. During World War II, there were strikes by whites to protest against the hiring of black factory workers, attacks on blacks and Latinos in several cities, and a 1943 riot in Detroit that left thirty-four dead.[66] Movement of African Americans had a profound effect on the economy and culture of big cities like Chicago, Detroit, and New York, where the Harlem Renaissance of the 1920s and 1930s produced major literature and art, perhaps best rendered in Jacob Lawrence's Great Migration series of paintings.

The Expanded Role of the Federal Government

Urban development came to a near-standstill with the onset of the Great Depression in 1929.[67] After Franklin Roosevelt became president in 1933, his New Deal agenda included programs to put people to work, build improvements like roads and public buildings, and develop housing. Roosevelt's election also realigned the coalitions making up political parties, with the white working class, African Americans, and Jews shifting increasingly to the Democratic Party.[68] The physical, political, economic, and population changes of the 1930s shaped development after World War II and have left an imprint on cities today.

The Public Works Administration (PWA) and its successor, the Works Progress Administration (WPA), were among the "alphabet soup" of agencies created during the 1930s. The PWA and WPA put people to work, but they also built large numbers of airports, schools, libraries, bridges and viaducts, and other projects that benefitted cities.[69]

Federal housing initiatives proceeded along two often-competing tracks. One was to facilitate home ownership, which was actively supported by builders, lenders, and real estate agents. This coalition opposed the second track, rental housing that was publicly owned and managed. Both approaches ended up reinforcing racial segregation.

Publicly owned housing was not a new idea; the federal government had built housing for defense workers during World War I but sold it after the war. Several residential projects were built between 1933 and 1935 as part of federal development or jobs efforts. They were leased based on neighborhood demographic composition, but primarily for whites. In 1937, Congress required local governments to set up their own agencies to build and run rental units with federal subsidies. So a local government had to accept public housing before any was built inside its borders—and many cities did not participate. The private sector and congressional conservatives were hostile to such "intervention" in the housing market, and the number of units actually built fell short of the number authorized. Local housing authorities located buildings in ways that reinforced existing racial patterns in neighborhoods.[70]

Bolstering home ownership involved several policies and agencies, most notably the Home Owners Loan Corporation (HOLC) and the Federal Housing Administration (FHA).[71] The HOLC was established in 1933 to help stabilize housing markets, bailing out homeowners in danger of foreclosure by refinancing their mortgages. Obviously, this was popular with lenders as well.

In order to determine risk in lending, the HOLC, relying heavily on local real estate agents, adopted appraisal criteria grading neighborhoods on maps with a color-coded scheme: A (green) for "Best," B (blue) for "Still Desirable," C (yellow) for "Definitely Declining," and D (red) for "Hazardous."[72] This system was the origin of the term **redlining**, which is the practice of denying or limiting financial services to certain neighborhoods based on racial or ethnic composition without regard for individual qualifications or creditworthiness (see box 2.2). Each classification was supported by an observer's report on neighborhood characteristics, making it difficult for African Americans and immigrants to obtain mortgages. The form for describing neighborhoods included space for detail about buildings. It also had blanks to fill in about the area's population, including "% Foreign Families" and "% Negro," along with space for population details. The HOLC wound down operations beginning in 1936.

The FHA was created in 1934 to provide federal insurance for mortgages. This protected lenders, who began to offer mortgages at lower interest rates and over longer periods, usually with a lower down payment. Buyers also paid both principal and interest to build equity in their homes, as opposed to the previous pattern of interest only at the front end of a mortgage. However, the FHA followed HOLC criteria in insuring mortgages; it also insured developers for entire subdivisions. In one notorious case, a Detroit builder seeking to put in a subdivision for white people was unable to secure financing until he erected a wall in 1941 that was six feet high and half a mile long, separating the new homes from an existing black neighborhood.[73]

The FHA is often seen as the culprit in suburban sprawl and housing segregation. Economic historian Judge Glock argues that such complaints are overstated.[74] According to Glock, urban politicians pressured the agency to become an important backer of multi-family housing through the 1950s and a major insurer of loans to improve existing structures, both of which benefitted cities. He also maintains that politicians were joined by civil rights activists in getting the FHA to back off racially exclusionary policies earlier than other federal agencies and ahead of the private sector.[75] However, an analysis by David Freund concludes that, "The FHA treated housing for blacks as constituting a separate market."[76] It was not until 1962 that President Kennedy issued an executive order against use of federal funds to aid racial segregation in housing.

BOX 2.2

Redlining and the Federal Government

Map 2.1 Redlining Map of Los Angeles, 1939

The large white section on the right (east) is downtown. Almost everything around it is labeled "Hazardous," although a few areas are "Definitely Declining." Other white sections designate business and industrial areas, including working oil fields. The large swath of "Best" and "Still Desirable" land to the northwest (upper left) includes Beverly Hills and Hollywood, and the line dividing these areas and the "Definitely Declining" area to the south is Sunset Boulevard. Santa Monica is due west of downtown along the Pacific Ocean and is not rated highly, although further south along the Pacific (not on the map) is the highly affluent community of Palos Verdes. The evaluator described the poorly rated area east of downtown (D53) as "50% Foreign Families," specifically "Russian, Polish & Armenian Jews, Slavs, Greeks, American Mexicans, Japanese and Italians. Subversive racial elements increasing." The area just southwest of downtown (D52) was described as "the 'melting pot' area" of Los Angeles, with a population that was half black and 40 percent foreign, including "low class Italians," with the entire area considered "a fit location for a slum clearance project."

Source: Digital Scholarship Lab, "Mapping Inequality: Redlining in New Deal America," https://dsl.richmond.edu/panorama/redlining/#loc=11/34.0393/-118.3049&opacity=0.8&city=los-angeles-ca.

This still did not bring a sudden end to government or private practices that had long promoted segregation, however.[77]

Local governments, especially with their regulation of land use, also promoted segregated housing (for more, see chapter 12). The effects of government policies and restrictive covenants were exacerbated by the actions of private organizations. In 1924, for instance, the National Association of Real Estate Boards adopted a code of ethics requiring agents not to be involved with sales that would foster racial or ethnic change that could depress property values in a neighborhood.[78] Similar practices were followed up to the 1960s by other organizations, such as the Chicago Real Estate Board and American Institute of Real Estate Appraisers.[79]

As the Great Depression gave way to World War II, the federal government spent vast amounts on military bases and equipment, and companies built major facilities to support the war effort. Government efforts also included the forced relocation of Japanese Americans to internment camps between 1942 and 1945, which the Supreme Court held did not violate the Constitution in *Korematsu v. United States*.[80] Spending, construction, and population increases were especially prominent in coastal locations and inland areas in the South and West, including places like Albuquerque, Fort Worth, Los Angeles, Norfolk, Phoenix, Portland, San Diego, San Antonio, Seattle, Tucson, and Wichita. These changes set the stage for postwar urban development outside the traditional large cities of the Midwest and Northeast and in areas related to industries such as aerospace.[81]

SUMMARY

The United States began as an overwhelmingly rural country, but its cities have always been critical to the economy and politics. By the late 1800s, a series of push and pull factors had stimulated rural-to-urban migration and immigration from Europe as the industrial economy took off, dramatically changing the character of America's cities. New York was the first city to hit one million population in 1880, and by 1920, a majority of Americans lived in urban areas. From the 1910s through the 1960s, northern cities grew as the Great Migration attracted southern blacks in search of better jobs and an escape from the worst effects of government-imposed racial segregation.

The first wave of suburban development occurred after World War I but came to a virtual standstill during the Great Depression of the 1930s, when the federal government adopted policies that had major consequences for urban development. These included mortgage bailouts that prevented foreclosure against homeowners and stabilized lenders, publicly owned housing, and changes in mortgage policies that made it easier for Americans to buy homes. These policies reinforced private practices that promoted segregation and provided a basis for more federal involvement after World War II, which enhanced growth outside the traditional industrial centers in the North.

Key Terms

at-large elections *(38)*
boosterism *(35)*
civil service *(38)*
council-manager system *(38)*
de jure segregation *(35)*
Great Migration *(41)*
nonpartisan elections *(38)*

patronage *(38)*
political machine *(36)*
push and pull factors *(28)*
redlining *(43)*
restrictive covenants *(35)*
urban reform movement *(38)*
zoning *(33)*

Discussion Questions

1. How have population movements affected urban development in the United States?

2. How have American urban areas developed physically over time? How are present-day areas different from those in the industrial era of the 1880s to the 1920s?

3. How have federal government policies affected American urban development?

4. How did political machines function, and how did their opponents and reformers try to undermine their influence?

Exercises

1. Gather information from your library, local planning agency, and/or historical society to determine the extent to which your region or a place assigned by your instructor developed like the Chicago School model depicted in figure 2.2. Try to identify any government or private decisions that had a major impact on the patterns that you discover.

2. Examine the local government charter of your hometown or college/university city in light of this chapter's coverage of political machines and urban reformers. Research any major changes in the charter, especially in terms of form of government and methods for electing officials; identify when they occurred, who their proponents and opponents were, and any related public votes.

3. Analyze neighborhood change in a specific location since the federal government got involved in housing in the 1930s. This will require several steps.

    a. Go to the website Mapping Inequality (https://dsl.richmond. edu/panorama/redlining/# loc=4/36.71/-97.194) and select a city or use one assigned by your instructor. For a neighborhood on the map that you choose or are assigned, review the HOLC appraiser's "thumbnail" description.

    b. To compare the area to the 2010 census, go to http://www. usboundary.com/ in another window and select the "Areas" option. Pick the state and county where the city is located. Choose the "Tile Maps" tool in the box at the right to allow you to zoom in on the map and find a census tract (with a tract number) in the same area as in the HOLC map (which does not include tracts). If you are unsure of the county, you can match the city with it in http://statsamerica.org/CityCountyFinder/Default.aspx.

c. Click on the tract in the map and use the "Area Page" option to explore the area's population. You can get additional information by going to the US Census Bureau's website and using "American Fact Finder" to search for the tract number, although you will have to use the "Add/Remove Geographies" option, starting with the tract level. Alternatively, your instructor might want you to gather data for the zip code area: https://factfinder.census.gov/faces/tableservices/jsf/pages/productview.xhtml?pid=DEC_10_DP_DPDP1&src=pt. To find out more about the population and housing, you will need to go to the "Advanced Search" tab in the upper left and then choose from the "Other Topics" (e.g., education, income, poverty) and "Race and Ethnic Groups" to get the most recent data about your area.

d. To add perspective, you can zoom in on the HOLC map to a point where it will display a neighborhood today with things like freeways that did not exist in the 1930s. A site like Google Maps can also help, including providing a neighborhood's name. To put the HOLC financial figures into context, you can adjust for inflation and convert them to today's dollars: https://data.bls.gov/cgi-bin/cpicalc.pl. Finally, an online search of local sources in your library, newspapers, and historical societies can yield useful information about changes in the area.

e. The bottom line: write an analysis describing how the area's population has changed (or not) over the intervening decades, including suggested explanations for the change. Consult your instructor for format and style guidelines for writing or presenting your findings.

Practice and Review Online
https://textbooks.rowman.com/understanding-urban-politics

3

URBAN DEVELOPMENT AFTER WORLD WAR II

GUIDING QUESTIONS

1. How have suburbanization and minority concentration in cities since World War II shaped American urban areas?
2. In what ways did federal policies affect urban development after World War II?
3. How did population and social changes in the late 20th century influence politics at the local level?
4. How might economic and social changes affect the development of cities in the 21st century?

AS AMERICANS PURSUED the good life in suburbia after World War II, not everyone found a welcoming environment. In 1957, a black veteran and his wife purchased a suburban tract house in Levittown, Pennsylvania. Their postal carrier shouted their arrival, and soon 600 demonstrators appeared at their home. Law enforcement did nothing for two months as rocks were thrown at the property and crosses were burned on their front lawn. A white family supporting their move had their home vandalized. These actions continued with no help from authorities, and the family finally moved out in 1961.[1] This episode captures the tension that pervaded many postwar changes in neighborhoods, which is one of the major narratives of this chapter.

SUBURBANIZATION AND MINORITY CONCENTRATION IN CENTRAL CITIES

Urban development came to a virtual halt during the Great Depression and World War II. Yet the decades since have dramatically reshaped urban America. Northern metropolitan areas became highly segregated, with African Americans concentrated in cities and white people moving to suburbia—a pattern reinforced by federal policies and leading to the "urban crisis" of the 1960s and 1970s. Hispanics, Asians, and members of the LGBTQ community also brought major changes to urban areas. While millions moved to the so-called Sunbelt, many observers saw a resurgence in central cities in the 21st century. Like the one presented in chapter 2, a timeline highlights the major changes during this period (see table 3.1).

America faced a severe housing shortage in the late 1940s and early 1950s with the return of over twelve million troops at the end of World War II in 1945, the redeployment of civilian workers, the beginnings of the "baby boom," and limited residential construction during the war. The first major population shift was a huge wave of residential and commercial development outside the nation's large cities, usually labeled **suburbanization**. The postwar boom outside central cities covered vast swaths of raw land, due in part to easier rules for mortgage lending and an automobile-centered culture bolstered by the construction of thousands of miles of roadways.

Of the 168 metropolitan areas that existed in 1950, central city populations had expanded by 14 percent, but suburbs had grown by 35 percent during the 1940s. By 1950, a majority of the population in metropolitan Atlanta, Boston, Hartford, Los Angeles, Pittsburgh, and Providence already lived in suburbia. This pattern accelerated: Central cities grew by 10.8 percent during the 1950s, but their suburbs increased by 48.5 percent. Of the metropolitan statistical areas (MSAs) for 1960 included in table 3.2, the only central cities to add population during the 1950s were Los Angeles, Long Beach, and St. Paul. At the other extreme, Boston, Pittsburgh, and St. Louis lost more than 10 percent of their populations even as their metropolitan areas continued to grow.[2]

Housing developers led the suburban expansion. In addition to programs established in the 1930s that made home buying easier, the Veterans Administration assisted service members in purchasing homes after the war. These programs reduced the down payments for single-family homes, established the standard repayment period of 30 years, and guaranteed loans against default—substantial differences from pre-Depression practices. Suburbia offered amenities that many people would not have considered standard in the 1940s: backyards, garages, and kitchens with modern ranges and refrigerators (with freezers). Small household appliances and (then black-and-white) televisions were also available. Critics, however, saw suburbia as socially sterile with acre after acre of cookie-cutter homes on treeless streets and cul-de-sacs—perhaps best satirized in the 1998 movie *Pleasantville* (see box 3.1).

TABLE 3.1	Timeline of American Urban Development, 1945–Present	
National Milestones	Dates	Local Milestones
Shelley v. Kraemer holds that enforcing racial covenants violates equal protection guarantee in 14th Amendment	1948	
Federal "urban renewal" program created	1949	
Supreme Court issues decision in *Brown v. Board of Education*	1954	
Congress passes law establishing the Interstate Highway System	1956	First enclosed regional shopping mall opens in a Minneapolis suburb
Congress passes the Civil Rights Act	1964	Major riot in Harlem (New York City)
Congress passes the Voting Rights Act and a law making non-European immigration easier	1965	
US Department of Housing and Urban Development established	1965	Major riot in Watts (Los Angeles)
Model Cities Program and Department of Transportation established	1966	
	1967	Major riots in Newark and Detroit, plus more in dozens of other cities
	Late 1960s	First black mayors elected in major cities, with more in the 1970s
Congress passes the Fair Housing Act	1968	
Congress creates the Community Development Block Grant Program	1974	
	1975	New York bailed out of potential bankruptcy
	1990	Los Angeles passes Chicago in the census to become second-largest city in the US
	2001	Terrorist attacks on World Trade Center and Pentagon
	2005	Hurricane Katrina devastates New Orleans
	2007–2009	"Great Recession" and drop in home values lead to massive home foreclosures
	2011	Occupy Wall Street forms in New York City to protest against inequality
	2013	Detroit is largest municipal bankruptcy in US history
	2013	Black Lives Matter forms; grows in following years after police shootings of black residents
Congress overhauls the federal tax code, including the creation of "opportunity zones"	2017	White nationalist rally in Charlottesville leads to clashes among competing groups and death of one counter-protestor

TABLE 3.2	**Twenty Largest Metropolitan Statistical Areas (MSAs) in 1960 and 2018**				
	1960			**2018**	
Metropolitan Area	**Population**	**Central Cities**	**Metropolitan Area**	**Population**	**Central Cities**
New York	10,694,633	72.8%	New York-Newark-Jersey City	19,979,477	44.8%
Los Angeles-Long Beach	6,742,696	41.9%	Los Angeles-Long Beach-Anaheim	13,291,486	36.2%
Chicago	6,220,913	57.1%	Chicago-Naperville-Elgin	9,498,716	32.4%
Philadelphia	4,342,897	46.1%	Dallas-Fort Worth-Arlington	7,539,711	35.0%
Detroit	3,762,360	44.4%	Houston-The Woodlands-Sugar Land	6,997,384	36.5%
San Francisco-Oakland	2,783,359	39.8%	Washington-Arlington-Alexandria	6,249,950	17.6%
Boston	2,589,301	26.9%	Miami-Fort Lauderdale-West Palm Beach	6,198,782	12.6%
Pittsburgh	2,405,435	25.1%	Philadelphia-Camden-Wilmington	6,096,372	28.5%
St. Louis	2,060,103	36.4%	Atlanta-Sandy Springs-Roswell	5,949,951	12.1%
Washington	2,001,897	38.2%	Boston-Cambridge-Newton	4,875,390	18.8%
Cleveland	1,796,595	48.8%	Phoenix-Mesa-Scottsdale	4,857,962	51.8%
Baltimore	1,727,023	54.4%	San Francisco-Oakland-Hayward	4,729,484	31.36%
Newark	1,689,420	24.0%	Riverside-San Bernardino-Ontario	4,622,631	16.1%
Minneapolis-St. Paul	1,482,030	53.7%	Detroit-Warren-Dearborn	4,326,442	21.0%
Buffalo	1,306,957	40.8%	Seattle-Tacoma-Bellevue	3,939,363	29.2%
Cincinnati	1,071,624	46.9%	Minneapolis-St. Paul-Bloomington	3,629,190	23.1%
Houston	1,243,158	75.5%	San Diego-Carlsbad	3,343,364	46.5%
Milwaukee	1,194,290	62.1%	Tampa-St. Petersburg-Clearwater	3,142,663	25.5%
Paterson-Clifton-Passaic	1,186,873	23.6%	Denver-Aurora-Lakewood	2,932,415	43.7%
Seattle	1,107,213	50.3%	St. Louis	2,805,465	10.8%

Source: 1960 data based on the US Census Bureau's 1963 and 1964 *Statistical Abstract of the United States,* table 10, https://www.census.gov/library/publications/time-series/statistical_abstracts.html; 2018 data from US Census Bureau, "Metropolitan and Micropolitan Statistical Areas Population Totals: 2010–2018," and totals for central cities listed using the bureau's "American Fact Finder."

BOX 3.1

The Postwar Suburban Boom

By 1948, mass developers like Levitt put up tract houses at a rate of 150 per week on Long Island and in suburban Philadelphia. Such development was common in almost all US metropolitan areas.

Source: Jon C. Teaford, *City and Suburb: The Political Fragmentation of Metropolitan America, 1850–1970* (Baltimore: Johns Hopkins University Press, 1979), 100–103; Howard P. Chudacoff, Judith E. Smith, and Peter C. Baldwin, *The Evolution of American Urban Society*, 8th edition (Boston: Pearson, 2015), 193–97.

Levittown, New York, 1957

Between 1945 and 1965, automobile registrations climbed from twenty-six million to seventy-two million, far outstripping the 35 percent growth in population. In 1956, Congress authorized the **Interstate Highway System**, a network of over 40,000 miles of multi-lane roads connecting the nation's urban centers that permitted high speeds without traditional intersections. Federal support boosted state and local construction substantially.

Freeways made it easier for suburbanites to commute downtown to work. City leaders also hoped that they would bring shoppers downtown, but retailers followed the population, with several thousand suburban shopping centers popping up by the mid-1950s, with many more to come.[3] Building freeways was relatively easy in undeveloped areas. In cities, they were often built by tearing up poor and minority neighborhoods near downtown, and they often served as barriers between white and black areas. With major backing in Congress and from local officials, contractors, construction unions, and business leaders, many freeways took advantage of easily accessible land in parks or along waterways.

A backlash against freeway construction began during the 1960s, including visible clashes in New York City.[4] Neighborhood activists and historic preservationists decried the destruction and social disruption of neighborhoods. Environmentalists and mass transit promoters complained about the seeming devotion to the automobile. Other critics considered freeways simply ugly. It took some time, but federal policy eventually favored a more regional approach and more balanced funding for multiple modes of transportation.[5] Some cities began to tear down some freeways and either put them below ground or replace them with city streets. Efforts by San Francisco and Oakland were aided by a 1989 earthquake.[6] Nevertheless, freeways still cover huge chunks of US urban areas, often with dense traffic even in times outside "rush" hours.

Suburbanization accelerated during the 1960s, when many central cities experienced decades of population losses and other signs of "decline." Metropolitan areas became more segregated, and cities and suburbs often battled each other politically and economically. Table 3.2 captures these trends, as well as the rise of the Sunbelt (described later in the chapter), by comparing the twenty largest MSAs in 1960 and 2018. Old industrial centers like Pittsburgh, St. Louis, Cleveland, and Baltimore disappear from the list, while Metro Detroit drops from fifth to fourteenth. Twelve of the twenty largest MSAs in 2018 are in the South and West, compared to four in 1960. Also noteworthy is the share of the population in central cities. Only four MSAs in 2018 had 40 percent or more of their populations in central cities, and many had less than 25 percent. So by the 21st century, urban America looked decidedly different than 50 years earlier, with many of the largest metropolises in entirely new regions and most central cities becoming islands surrounded by a sea of suburbs.

While freeways and mass-built homes were key contributors to suburbanization, the other component was **white flight**, the movement of white residents from central cities to separate suburban communities. In addition to problems in obtaining mortgages, black homebuyers were often steered away from white neighborhoods by real estate agents. As noted in the chapter introduction, even after qualifying for a mortgage and purchasing a home, African Americans moving into white neighborhoods were frequently met with threats and violence, often without any protection from police.[7] Freund notes that leaders in the public and private sectors characterized segregation as a reaction to "market" forces not to be disrupted by integrating a neighborhood and harming property values: "methods of exclusion and rationales for exclusion would decisively shape whites' approach to the politics of race and housing in the decades after 1940, as the market imperative defense quickly became the standard explanation for racial segregation."[8]

The effects of freeway construction and white flight on cities were exacerbated by **urban renewal**. Authorized by the Housing Act of 1949, the urban renewal program combined federal money and local actions, including the use of eminent domain, to clear so-called "blight" for redevelopment. Although it varies by state, **eminent domain** allows government seizure of private property for a public purpose in exchange for "just compensation" to the property owner. If negotiations to acquire the property fail, the matter can usually be decided in court. Urban renewal often replaced housing near downtowns with stadiums, civic centers, and office buildings. The displacement caused by urban renewal eventually earned it the nickname "Negro removal."[9] In some places, there was public pressure to use federal law to deal with poor housing conditions, but state laws could make that difficult. Texas, for example, allowed consideration of local petitions to hold a referendum opposed to urban renewal, which meant that conservative opposition derailed the program in several cities.[10]

Coupled with a growing black population, highway construction, the expansion of segregated public housing, and actions by developers and other businesses, many cities created what Arnold Hirsch labeled "the second ghetto."[11] Table 3.3 reflects these trends by showing the black percentage of the population over time for the twenty largest cities in 1950. The biggest shifts occurred in northern cities landlocked by suburbs. The data also capture other, less obvious patterns. For example, the declining percentage of African Americans in Houston is linked to the city's extensive annexation of territory on its periphery, which was inhabited overwhelmingly by whites.[12] The declining presence of African Americans in cities like Seattle, Los Angeles, San Francisco, and Washington, DC by 2010 reflects white in-migration and the increasingly high cost of living.

TABLE 3.3	Black Share of the Population, 1950–2010, in the Twenty Largest Cities in 1950						
City	1950	1960	1970	1980	1990	2000	2010
Baltimore (6, 21)	23.7%	34.7%	46.4%	54.8%	59.2%	64.3%	63.7%
Boston (10, 22)	5.0%	9.1%	16.3%	22.4%	25.6%	25.3%	24.4%
Buffalo (15, 69)	6.3%	13.3%	20.4%	26.8%	30.7%	37.3%	38.6%
Chicago (2, 3)	13.6%	22.9%	32.7%	39.8%	39.1%	36.8%	32.9%
Cincinnati (18, 61)	15.5%	21.6%	27.6%	33.8%	37.9%	42.9%	44.8%
Cleveland (7, 45)	16.2%	28.6%	38.3%	43.8%	46.6%	51.0%	53.3%
Detroit (5, 18)	16.2%	28.9%	43.7%	63.1%	75.7%	81.6%	82.7%
Houston (14, 4)	20.9%	22.9%	25.7%	27.8%	28.1%	25.3%	23.7%
Kansas City, MO (20, 37)	12.2%	17.5%	22.1%	27.4%	29.6%	31.2%	29.9%
Los Angeles (4, 2)	8.7%	13.5%	17.9%	17.0%	14.0%	11.2%	9.6%
Milwaukee (13, 28)	3.4%	8.4%	14.7%	23.1%	30.5%	37.3%	40.0%
Minneapolis (17, 48)	1.3%	2.4%	4.4%	7.7%	13.0%	18.0%	18.6%
New Orleans (16, 52)	31.9%	37.2%	45.0%	55.3%	61.9%	67.2%	60.2%
New York (1, 1)	9.5%	14.0%	21.2%	25.2%	28.7%	26.6%	25.5%
Philadelphia (3, 5)	18.2%	26.4%	33.6%	37.8%	39.9%	43.2%	43.4%
Pittsburgh (12, 58)	12.2%	16.7%	20.2%	24.0%	25.8%	27.1%	26.1%
Saint Louis (8, 57)	17.9%	28.6%	40.9%	45.8%	47.5%	51.2%	49.2%
San Francisco (11, 13)	5.6%	10.0%	13.4%	12.7%	10.9%	7.8%	6.1%
Seattle (19, 23)	3.4%	4.8%	7.1%	9.5%	10.1%	8.4%	7.9%
Washington, DC (9, 24)	35.0%	53.9%	71.1%	70.3%	65.8%	60.0%	50.7%

Note: Numbers in parentheses are the city's rank in total population in 1950 and 2010.

Source: Jon Teaford, The Twentieth-Century American City, 116; US Census Bureau, 1970 Census of Population, Supplementary Report: Distribution of the Negro Population, by County, table 4; Statistical Abstract of the United States series for 1982–83 (table 26), 1993 (table 46), 2003 (table 34), and 2012 (table 27); "Census 2010 Interactive Population Map," http://www.census.gov/2010census/popmap/.

POSTWAR URBAN DEVELOPMENT AND POLITICS

After World War II, the rise in black electoral power at the local level was connected to the civil rights movement, national policy changes, and the increased concentration of African Americans in northern cities. Many of the earliest acts of civil disobedience occurred in white-controlled southern cities and targeted de jure segregation (racial segregation enacted by law and enforced by government; see chapter 2). In addition to the actions of Rosa Parks and the 1955–1956 Montgomery bus boycott, there were sit-ins at "whites only" lunch counters starting in Greensboro, North Carolina, in 1960, and a campaign of protests and boycotts in Birmingham, Alabama, that were met with violent attacks by police using water cannons and dogs. These and similar events focused on local conditions, but the growth of television news brought wider national attention to the civil rights movement.

Congress used its power over interstate commerce to pass the **Civil Rights Act of 1964**, which outlawed racial segregation in public places, including businesses, and banned employment discrimination based on race, national origin, religion, or sex. Its impact was not immediate in southern states, but it did survive an early court challenge.[13] In the wake of President Johnson's landslide reelection in 1964, Congress followed with the **Voting Rights Act of 1965 (VRA)**, which made voting in the South subject to review by the federal government; this included *racial gerrymandering*, the drawing of district lines to limit or eliminate the chances of black voters electing one of their own to city councils, county boards, and other legislative bodies. Renewals of the law expanded its scope to linguistic minorities, which had its greatest impact on states and local governments with large Hispanic populations. Implementation of the law, which often prompted litigation, forced many local governments to replace at-large elections with district elections, which improved minority representation.[14] However, in its 2013 decision in *Shelby County v. Holder*, the Supreme Court effectively ended federal oversight of electoral rules and procedures under the VRA.[15] The Johnson administration also launched initiatives that were thought to improve urban conditions, including two cabinet departments (Housing and Urban Development in 1965 and Transportation in 1966). Johnson announced the "War on Poverty" in 1964 and created the Model Cities program, created in 1966, which emphasized citizen participation and often pitted activists against city officials (for more on federal programs, see chapter 4).[16]

Legislation in response to the civil rights movement was aimed at de jure segregation in the South. In the North, however, the Great Migration and white flight had altered the racial composition of cities, creating black ghettos. There was also strong white resistance to change. This resistance is exemplified by **NIMBYism (Not In My Backyard)**, where neighbors organize to fight the introduction of unwanted land uses or residents in their area.

Groups opposed to public housing, urban renewal, nondiscrimination requirements such as fair housing laws, and school integration used *initiative campaigns* (petition drives to put policy questions up for a vote in an election) in states and communities to undermine such programs. One such campaign led to an amendment to the California Constitution requiring a local vote on publicly funded housing projects beginning in 1950. This strategy to limit low-income housing in suburbia was upheld in 1971 by the Supreme Court.[17] During the 1960s, voters repealed fair housing ordinances in Berkeley, Toledo, and several other cities. Voters in Akron, Ohio, amended their charter in 1964 to require voter approval of fair housing legislation, while efforts to "protect" property owners' rights in Detroit and Milwaukee were eventually thrown out by the courts. Similar campaigns targeted the busing of children to desegregate schools.[18]

Urban conditions led to riots during the 1960s, usually precipitated by police action. Riots in New York City's Harlem area in 1964 and the Watts section of Los Angeles in 1965 were followed by over 150 conflicts in 1967, including major riots in Detroit and Newark (see box 3.2). The disorder in Detroit lasted five days and included the mobilization of federal troops; it left forty-three killed, over 1,100 injured, more than 7,000 arrested, and several thousand buildings damaged or destroyed. President Johnson responded by appointing a National Advisory Commission on Civil Disorders. The commission pointed squarely at "white racism" as an underlying cause of the riots, but President Johnson never formally acknowledged its work. The commission released its report in March 1968, about a month ahead of incidents in over 100 cities following the assassination of Martin Luther King, Jr.[19]

White flight accelerated in the 1960s, but a growing black presence in cities, along with political mobilization and federal pressure in the South, helped elect more African American officials. Among the first black mayors in major cities were Richard Hatcher in Gary and Carl Stokes in Cleveland in 1967 and Kenneth Gibson in Newark, Coleman Young in Detroit, Maynard Jackson in Atlanta, and Ernest Morial in New Orleans during the 1970s (for more on electoral changes, see chapters 6, 7, and 8).[20]

BOX 3.2

Urban Unrest in the 1960s

Newark, July 1967

A confrontation with police on July 12, 1967 led to five days of unrest in Newark. The conflict left 26 dead and $26 million in property damage. A week later, another confrontation in Detroit produced another major rebellion.

Source: For a retrospective on the Newark riot, see Rick Rojas and Khorri Atkinson, "Five Days of Unrest That Shaped, and Haunted, Newark," *New York Times*, July 11, 2017, https://www.nytimes.com/2017/07/11/nyregion/newark-riots-50-years.html.

At the national level, the Johnson-era programs, coupled with urban violence and protests against the Vietnam war, generated a backlash captured in Richard Nixon's 1968 presidential campaign promoting "law and order." The Nixon administration scaled back or eliminated most of Johnson's domestic programs, preferring to turn money and decision making over to states. One example is the consolidation of several specific grants into the Community Development Block Grant Program (CDBG) in 1974. The Carter administration tried—but failed—to establish a national urban policy, and the Reagan administration returned to the Nixon-era policy of leaving urban issues up to the states.[21]

NEW URBAN REGIONS AND GROUPS IN THE LATE 20TH CENTURY

Several shifts during the last 25 years of the 20th century had long-term effects on urban areas. One was the growth of the Sunbelt. Another was the rising presence of other groups added to the traditional black-white mix of urban politics. Third were changes in the layout of urban areas. Not surprisingly, all of these trends had a political component.

The Rise of the Sunbelt

During the 1970s, observers began paying attention to the growth of the **Sunbelt**, the region extending across the southern tier of the United States from Florida to California. Analysts differ on the Sunbelt's boundaries, but most describe a region below the 37th parallel: Florida, Georgia, North Carolina, South Carolina, Tennessee, Alabama, Mississippi, Arkansas, Louisiana, Texas, Oklahoma, New Mexico, and Arizona, along with Las Vegas and some part of Southern California (see figure 3.1).[22]

Figure 3.1 Map of the Sunbelt

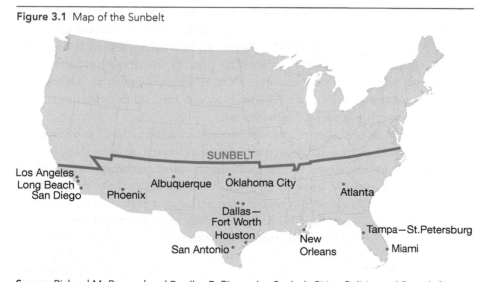

Source: Richard M. Bernard and Bradley R. Rice, eds., *Sunbelt Cities: Politics and Growth Since World War II* (Austin: University of Texas Press, 1983), 7.

Table 3.1 captures the dramatic growth of some of this region's metropolitan areas. Despite the image contrasting it with the "Frostbelt" North or the "Rust Belt" of the industrial Midwest, the Sunbelt has a diverse population and political mix. It includes the traditional Bible Belt of the conservative, religious South; it also extends through New Mexico and Arizona to more secular and liberal Southern California.

The Sunbelt benefitted substantially from defense spending during and after World War II and the economic stimulus from retirement and leisure. Boosterism (see chapter 2) also has a long history in the region. Southern states took the lead during the 1930s in offering incentives to manufacturers to build in or relocate to the region. Such incentives, along with strong opposition to labor unions, were often identified as a "good business climate."[23] These efforts expanded to include targeting corporate headquarters or US headquarters of foreign firms, with companies such as Kimberly-Clark, NCR, Mercedes-Benz USA, and UPS eventually relocating to the South.

In another form of boosterism, Sunbelt political and business leaders pursued professional sports teams to burnish their image. Franchises had been concentrated in the North for decades, but teams and leagues looked to tap new markets in the postwar years. In 1958, the Dodgers left Brooklyn for Los Angeles, and the Giants exited New York for San Francisco. By the 1970s, there were Major League Baseball teams in Anaheim, Atlanta, Dallas-Fort Worth, Houston, Oakland, San Diego, and Seattle. Denver, Miami, Phoenix, and Tampa-St. Petersburg fielded expansion teams in the 1990s.[24] A mix of relocations and expansion brought basketball to Dallas, Houston, Miami, Orlando, Phoenix, Sacramento, and other places,[25] producing some strange team names. "Lakers" made sense in Minneapolis, but the team kept the name when it moved to Los Angeles in 1960. Odder still, when the "Jazz" left New Orleans for Utah, they kept the nickname even though many might associate Salt Lake City musically with the Mormon Tabernacle Choir. Professional football expanded largely by awarding new franchises, starting with Dallas and Atlanta in the 1960s, but a few teams have relocated (some multiple times), including the Raiders' plan to leave Oakland a second time (they spent the 1982–94 seasons in Los Angeles) for Las Vegas.[26] The bottom line is that team owners often play off one city against another to get public subsidies for stadiums and arenas. However, the sales pitch sometimes fails: San Antonio still has no NFL team for a domed stadium that opened in 1993, where it has hosted NCAA basketball.

The growth of the South and West has also affected national and state politics. In the 1960 presidential election, California, Nevada, Arizona, New Mexico, Oklahoma, and the eleven former Confederate states combined for 179 of the 537 electoral votes (33 percent). In 2012, 2016, and 2020, those sixteen states had 244 of the 538 electoral votes (45 percent) because their number of seats in the US House of Representatives had grown along with their population.

The Democratic Party controlled the South for decades by promoting segregation. That changed with the civil rights movement in the 1960s, which helped to alter the makeup of the two major political parties. The South's dominant ideology has remained conservative, but white voters have migrated to the

Republican Party, which developed a virtual lock on the region's seats in Congress and their electoral votes.[27] Republicans have not completely won over the Sunbelt, however: California and New Mexico have voted Democratic in recent presidential elections, while Florida, North Carolina, and Virginia have been competitive.[28] In most of the South, Republicans became dominant in state governments. This increasingly left urban areas, which tend to vote Democratic, in conflict with state legislatures and governors (see chapter 4).

The Changing Look of Urban America

Urban politics has become far more complicated than differences between white suburbs and black cities.[29] Over time, members of the LGBTQ community, Hispanics, Asians, and recent immigrants have also become a major social and political presence in many urban areas. Minorities have also played a major part in suburban growth.

For LGBTQ people, cities became something of a sanctuary. Beginning in the 1940s, many gay men began concentrating in urban neighborhoods. Meeting other gay men in public spaces could lead to prosecution under state sodomy laws, often through police entrapment. In addition, homosexuality was considered a psychological disorder and was grounds for dismissal from the military and federal government jobs. It was even a focus during the anti-Communist crusades of the 1950s.[30]

Over time, neighborhoods deemed safe and welcoming were even referred to as "gay ghettos," including the Castro Street area in San Francisco, West Hollywood near Los Angeles, Christopher Street in New York, the Halstead Street "Boystown" in Chicago, Midtown Atlanta, and Montrose in Houston. These neighborhoods included social clubs and bars that served as gathering places, although they were often subject to police harassment and shakedowns by organized crime organizations. Especially after the gay liberation movement took off following the 1969 Stonewall Riot in New York, there were more efforts to strengthen gay and lesbian enclaves, much like the ethnic neighborhoods developed by immigrants. As the legal climate changed and homosexuality became more acceptable, these areas attracted a wider range of residents, became home to annual "Gay Pride" festivals, and often included active political and social organizations.[31] Also, gay men and lesbians increasingly lived in other areas, and activists questioned whether the gay ghetto was still viable or necessary. As one observer notes, "There goes the gayborhood."[32] Even though the LGBTQ population might be less geographically concentrated today, it can still be an influential voting bloc in many cities.

A change in federal law in 1965 facilitated immigration from countries outside Europe. As a result, Hispanic and Asian immigrants and their descendants have had a huge influence on urban development and politics. Both groups originally concentrated during the 1980s and 1990s in a limited number of states, particularly in the "gateway" metropolitan areas of New York, Los Angeles, San Francisco, Houston, Chicago, and Miami. In the 2000s, they dispersed, particularly to urban areas in the Southeast and West. In some areas, these changes are complemented by immigrants fleeing war zones such as Laos in the 1970s and Somalia more recently.[33]

The Hispanic population grew from just under 10 million in 1970 to 50.5 million in the 2010 census, when they outnumbered African Americans.[34] Hispanics are diverse in terms of national origin; almost thirty-two million in the 2010 census were Mexican. National groups congregate in different metropolitan areas: Mexicans primarily in California and Texas, Cubans in Miami, and Dominicans in New York, for example. Since 1990, though, the Hispanic population has dispersed throughout the country; those in newer destinations are more likely to be foreign born, less educated, and poorer. Metropolitan areas with especially rapid increases in Hispanic populations from 1990 to 2010 include Charlotte, Raleigh, Nashville, Indianapolis, and Atlanta.

Similarly, the Asian population has expanded significantly and is diverse in terms of national origin.[35] The Asian total grew from 1.5 million in the 1970 census to 14.7 million in 2010, with 3.3 million Chinese people, 2.8 million Indians, 2.6 million Filipinos, and roughly 1.5 million each Vietnamese people and Koreans. Most of the Asian population in the 2010 census was foreign born, college educated, and younger than the white population. The Los Angeles and New York MSAs were popular areas for most Asian groups; the largest concentration of Japanese people was in Honolulu, Vietnamese people were prominent in Houston and Dallas, and Indians were prominent in Chicago and Washington, DC (though not as common as in metropolitan New York).

In addition to the changes related to immigration, urban America was also affected by the reversal of the Great Migration—more blacks moving to the South than the number leaving. Demographer William Frey describes this shift as "a trickle that began in the 1970s, increased in the 1990s, and turned into a virtual evacuation from many northern areas in the first decade of the 2000s."[36] Between 1995 and 2000, Georgia gained nearly 130,000 African American residents, and New York lost 165,000. The Atlanta, Dallas, Charlotte, and Orlando MSAs experienced the biggest growth, and New York, Chicago, Los Angeles, San Francisco, and Detroit had the biggest losses.[37]

A Further Reshaping of Urban America?

Suburbanization might have started with housing, but it eventually included significant commercial, industrial, and warehouse space that reshaped urban areas quite differently from the Chicago School model described in chapter 2. As changes occurred during the 1980s and 1990s, Joel Garreau highlighted **edge cities**—outlying office, retail, and logistics clusters that challenged the role of the traditional downtown. Examples include Tyson's Corner outside Washington, at least four areas north of central Atlanta, and business centers around airports in many cities.[38] In some metropolitan areas, suburban residential and business centers grew rapidly to several hundred thousand residents and were called "boomburbs." These include Anaheim and other cities around Los Angeles; Scottsdale and Mesa near Phoenix; and Arlington and other large suburbs between Dallas and Fort Worth.[39] Rather than a series of concentric rings as imagined by the Chicago School in the 1920s (see figure 2.2) or a downtown with transportation corridors going out from it like spokes in a wheel, many metropolitan areas became dotted with what seemed like multiple "downtowns," usually centered on major freeways.

Another major spatial change was the emergence of **exurbs**, areas at the fringes of metropolitan areas that a Brookings Institution study defines as low density and high growth, with at least 20 percent of workers commuting to jobs in adjoining urbanized areas. In examining MSAs with at least 500,000 people in 2000, Brookings found that about 6 percent of residents lived in exurbs. In many ways, these areas could be seen as transitioning to suburban development in the future. They averaged fourteen acres per dwelling, and the largest share of workers were in construction, manufacturing, and farming. In the 1990s, exurbs grew twice as fast as the nation, were more common in the Midwest and South, and were disproportionately white and middle income. Residents were also more likely than the nation as a whole to be homeowners, which might reflect greater housing affordability and space on the fringe of metropolitan areas compared to cities and inner suburbs.[40]

Journalist Bill Bishop had another perspective on the way people are distributed across the American landscape that he called "the Big Sort."[41] Examining election results since the 1970s, Bishop suggested that people who are like-minded in terms of ideology and other characteristics have increasingly tended to cluster in the same communities, a pattern that feeds political polarization. This is not a universal view, however.[42]

URBAN DEVELOPMENT IN THE 21st CENTURY

Many observers see urban life in this century as potentially quite different from what emerged after World War II. The decline in manufacturing and rise of the service sector, the increasing global connections of the US economy, population shifts, and a new "pull" to central cities all suggest a different pattern of urban development—and maybe major changes in local politics.

The Service Sector and Globalization

The rise of the service economy and globalization have had dramatic impacts on urban development and continue to shape cities today. By the late 1800s, the US economy had already shifted from agriculture and extractive industries like mining and timber to manufacturing. In 1947, 53 percent of US economic output was still from goods-producing industries, including agriculture, forestry, mining, construction, and manufacturing. Service industries accounted for 39 percent, and government output accounted for the remaining 8 percent. By 1970, goods and services were each at about 44 percent, but services comprised the majority of economic output by 1986. This trend has continued: Services accounted for 63 percent of the more than $31 trillion in US economic output in 2015, while goods-producing industries had declined to 26 percent, including just 19 percent in manufacturing.[43]

The service sector is a rather broad category, however, including everything from janitorial jobs and low-wage work in fast food places to high-income earners in medicine and investment banking. The decline in manufacturing was telling for older cities in two ways. First, they were often left with abandoned factories and warehouses as operations moved overseas or to sites spread over more acreage in outlying areas. Second, people with limited skills or education could no longer count on factory jobs as a way to enter the workforce and build a middle-class life. That dilemma became worse as technology, especially robotics, reduced the need for production workers.

In addition to shifts among sectors of the US economy, **globalization**—the increasing interaction and integration of people, companies, and governments around the world—has had a tremendous impact. Technology, investment, and trade generally drive this process; for example, Apple designs its products in the United States, produces them in Asia, and distributes and sells them around the world. It is hard to find something made exclusively in the United States, as supply chains that provide the raw materials and parts to make a product extend across multiple countries.

Globalization has also reshaped what is often considered an **urban hierarchy**, a ranking of urban centers based on their central role in the economy and ability to withstand economic downturns. For most of the 20th century, leading cities were viewed as being within nations because of the limited economic linkages across nations. At the bottom today are places tied to a single industry extremely dependent on external forces, such as those connected to mining or lumbering. Headquarters and financial centers appear further up in the hierarchy. Business and political decisions in these "Global Giants" or "Mega-Regions" (including New York, London, Los Angeles, Paris, Tokyo, Hong King, Singapore, Seoul, and several other places) can have major consequences that are felt all over the world.[44] A city or region's rank in this hierarchy, along with its types of businesses and its population characteristics, affects the types of economic development policies it can implement successfully (see chapter 12).

The Great Recession

What has been termed the *Great Recession*, the worst downturn in the US economy since the 1930s, lasted officially from December 2007 through June 2009 (nineteen months), but its effects lingered much longer. It had a huge impact on urban areas. The earlier political and business push to increase home ownership in the US included millions of "sub-prime" mortgages—easy loans to high-risk buyers, often with misleading promotions. These mortgages were then bundled together and sold to investors. Plus, large numbers of people borrowed cash against the value of their homes during the mid-2000s to buy second homes or other items. The authors of *Reckless Endangerment* explain how the entire system was riddled by loose regulation, highly questionable actions by lenders, and inadequate analysis by the firms that rated the mortgage investments. By the mid-2000s, as increasing numbers of borrowers were failing to meet their payment obligations, investors began losing money.[45] The ensuing financial collapse meant that millions of borrowers saw the value of their homes drop precipitously. Many defaulted on their mortgages or failed to pay property taxes, and millions lost their homes to lenders or others.[46] The Federal Reserve Bank of St. Louis concluded that, with some regional variation, the foreclosure crisis was almost over at the end of 2016, but by then up to ten million borrowers had lost their homes.[47] All of this had devastating effects for neighborhoods, especially those with high numbers of minority sub-prime borrowers, and for the property tax base of many cities.

Major Population Changes in the 21st Century

Demographer William Frey sees four major trends reshaping the nation's population, including its urban areas:

- rapid growth in the Hispanic, Asian, and multiracial populations,
- sharply diminished growth and rapid aging of the white population,
- black economic advances and migration reversals, and
- a shift toward a nation in which no racial group is a majority.

Frey argues that "blacks and other racial minorities were historically subjected to blatant discrimination, whether through Jim Crow laws, the Chinese Exclusion Act, or any of the many other measures that that denied racial minorities access to jobs, education, housing, financial resources, and basic rights of civic participation." He adds, "What will be different going forward is the sheer size of the minority population in the United States."[48] Generational differences will also come into play, with the interests of the aging white majority population pitted against those of younger, more diverse generations. Taken together, these trends have brought the United States to a "pivotal period" in its development.[49]

These patterns are also associated with housing segregation. A standard measure of segregation is the *index of dissimilarity*, which ranges from 0 (complete integration) to 100 (complete segregation) and uses neighborhood data to calculate the percentage of a minority group that would have to move to be completely integrated with white people. In the 2010 census, the large metropolitan areas with the highest levels of black-white segregation remained in the North (Milwaukee, followed by New York, Chicago, Detroit, and Cleveland).[50] Although lower than in 1990 and much lower than in 1970, segregation levels for African Americans remained high in 2010. Much of the decline is due to black people moving to the suburbs, both from central cities and other parts of the country (see figure 3.2). Segregation indices were lower for Hispanics and Asians than for blacks in 2010 but slightly higher than in 1990 (see figure 3.3). The MSAs with an increase of 20–25 points in Hispanic-white segregation index between 1990 and 2010 were Miami, Nashville, Scranton, Indianapolis, and Tulsa. Another seven areas showed an increase of at least 15 points.

Many people have an image of abundance in suburbia and poverty in inner-city black neighborhoods. Such a view ignores the fact that a majority of those living in poverty are white, but they tend to be more dispersed geographically.

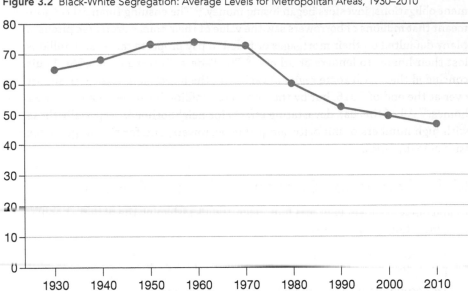

Figure 3.2 Black-White Segregation: Average Levels for Metropolitan Areas, 1930–2010

Source: William H. Frey, *Diversity Explosion*, revised edition (Washington, DC: Brookings Institution Press, 2018), 169.

Indeed, 52 percent of the 126 million people living in poverty in 2016 resided in suburbs of metropolitan areas.[51] Today, zoning decisions and NIMBYism still affect segregation through practices such as limiting the location of subsidized low-income housing. For example, it has been reported that members of Chicago's city council have blocked development in their districts to restrict affordable housing. In contrast, in 2018, Denver required all landlords to accept renters using low-income housing vouchers.[52]

The bottom line regarding racial and ethnic change is that whites are a declining share of the population and are increasingly concentrated in rural and suburban areas. Whites are also leaving large metropolitan areas for smaller ones—both the New York and Los Angeles MSAs lost over 1.1 million white residents between 1990 and 2010, and there still might be pockets of white flight.[53] In the 2010 census, whites were a minority in 22 of the 100 largest MSAs.[54] In addition, the minority population is younger, is growing more rapidly, and has an increased presence in more regions. These patterns have implications for the coalitions making up political parties, the pool of candidates for public office and the nature of their campaigns, and the types of issues and policies on the public agenda.[55]

A New Push and Pull?

Despite long-standing images of urban decline, some foresee a revival for cities, often led by **Millennials** (those born between 1980 and 1995; sometimes called Generation Y) abandoning the sterility of suburbia for urban amenities, including eliminating dependence on cars. This 21st-century urban revival has been bolstered by a drop in crime, fewer burdens of commuting, and cultural

Figure 3.3 Black, Hispanic, and Asian Segregation: Average Levels for 100 Largest Metropolitan Areas, 1990–2010

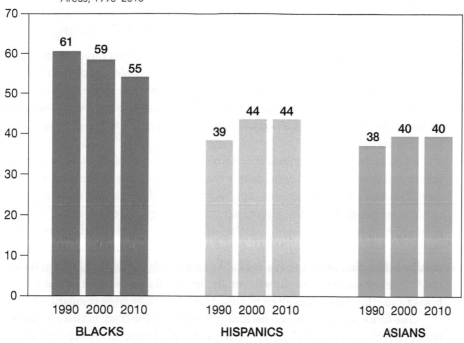

Source: William H. Frey, *Diversity Explosion*, revised edition (Washington, DC: Brookings Institution Press, 2018), 169.

attractions—all of which also lure many empty-nesters from suburbia back to the city.[56] Developers aware of these trends are even trying to replicate dense, mixed-use areas in suburbia, sometimes building walkable centers around the downtowns of older suburban areas.[57]

Related to an urban revival is a pattern labeled broadly as the rise of the **creative class**. Researcher and consultant Richard Florida describes the creative class as those who "engage in work whose function is to *create meaningful new forms*."[58] Members of this class are typically well educated and include engineers, scientists, designers, entertainers and artists, researchers, editors, knowledge-intensive workers in finance and business, and similar professionals. Florida argues that strong economic growth is not based on policies that subsidize firms to reduce costs. Instead, growth requires the development of urban areas where the creative class can function best, namely, the "three T's": technology, talent, and tolerance. Florida defines tolerance as "openness, inclusiveness, and diversity to all ethnicities, races, and walks of life."[59]

Florida is not without his critics, however. More recently he has lamented the extent to which the creative class has concentrated in certain areas, raising a host of issues regarding segregation, inequality, the future of the middle and working classes, and a growing gap between urban areas that are winners and those that are losers in the new economy.[60] Still, the reversal of the Great Migration, the expansion of the Asian and Hispanic populations, the seemingly unrelenting movement of Americans of all ages to the Sunbelt, and the rise of the creative class will all play important roles in determining the future of American metropolitan areas.[61]

Politics and Urban America in the 21st Century

Local political activism has seemed on the upswing since the onset of the Great Recession. As many Americans faced layoffs and the possible loss of their homes, public hostility to corporate bailouts intensified, perhaps most visibly with the launch of the Occupy Wall Street protests in 2011. Even though Detroit survived its bankruptcy, hundreds of local governments still face major financial problems (see chapter 11).

As individuals and communities recovered during the 2010s, local governments and their residents faced major conflicts over their economies and services. Growing cities and regions, especially those tied to the tech economy, have confronted issues about the affordability of housing.[62] In some cases, this has spawned battles over the seeming isolation of tech companies and workers from the community around them.[63] On the flip side are older industrial centers, mainly smaller MSAs, that seem to have been abandoned with the decline in manufacturing.[64] In many debates over growth and decline, local groups often deride the tax breaks and other incentives given to businesses, especially large companies.[65]

One focus of debate is the declining condition of infrastructure, including roads, bridges, transit, and water. Perhaps the most contentious conflicts over local services have surrounded policing and the criminal justice system. Initially formed in 2013, the Black Lives Matter movement grew in response to later police killings of African Americans, particularly unarmed teens (see chapter 13). Others raised concerns about patrols, frisking, and other practices, including the role of police and sheriffs' departments in stepped-up federal efforts to contain illegal immigration. The cash bail system, which can land the poor in jail for minor offenses, often costing them their jobs for missing work, was also criticized. Local officials have also had to deal with national issues, with some protests ending in violence, like the 2017 white nationalist rally and counter-protest in Charlottesville, Virginia.[66]

None of these issues will go away in the near future. Local officials will continue to face challenges in representing the needs and interests of their residents while dealing with economic, social, and political pressures from outside their communities.

SUMMARY

The return of millions of people from military to civilian life at the end of World War II in 1945 helped to launch a tidal wave of suburbanization outside cities, causing many cities to experience population and business losses. White flight to suburbia had a major effect on housing segregation and was accelerated in many areas by riots during the 1960s. By the beginning of the 21st century, suburbia had become more diverse and housed a large share of the nation's poor. The rise of the service economy, the growth of the Hispanic and Asian populations, globalization, and the changing values of younger generations of Americans provided the foundation for a revival of many central cities. Most metropolitan areas, though, faced problems of segregation and growing income inequality.

American urbanization has been shaped by substantial movements of people, major economic changes, and significant geographic modifications. These developments were the result of private decisions and government policies, and they have had long-lasting effects. Urban areas must live with these legacies; some would say that they are "stuck" with them. It takes decades to change attributes such as infrastructure, political institutions, economic base, racial and ethnic mix, and the ages and skills of the work force. The ongoing dilemma is determining how local actions can help cities adapt to change, much of which is well beyond their control.

Key Terms

Civil Rights Act of 1964 *(55)*
creative class *(65)*
edge cities *(60)*
eminent domain *(53)*
exurbs *(61)*
globalization *(62)*
Interstate Highway System *(52)*
Millennials *(64)*

NIMBYism (Not In My Backyard) *(55)*
suburbanization *(49)*
Sunbelt *(57)*
urban hierarchy *(62)*
urban renewal *(53)*
Voting Rights Act of 1965 *(55)*
white flight *(53)*

Discussion Questions

1. Describe how various population groups have moved into cities and to outlying suburbs. What are the effects of these patterns, both historically and for the future?

2. How have US urban areas changed since the 1940s, when much of the population was in larger cities in the Northeast and Midwest? What explains these changes, and what have their effects been?

3. What were the positive and negative effects of federal policies on the development of US urban areas in the late 20th century?

4. To what extent have economic changes and population movements reshaped urban development in the 21st century? What are the implications of these patterns?

Exercises

1. Identify the racial and ethnic changes since 2000 in your MSA or one assigned to you. Compare the MSA to its central city, your state, or the nation as a whole to see how "typical" the area is. To obtain data, search the US Census Bureau (https://www.census.

gov/en.html) or your regional planning agency (you can find it in the list of agencies in your state: http://narc.org/about-narc/state-associations/). Some changes can be summarized in tables or figures that you create. Suggest explanations for these population patterns and analyze their effects.

2. This exercise can be broken up into parts assigned to individuals or groups. The goal is to trace the physical development of a metropolitan or micropolitan area in your state after World War II. Your regional planning agency, local newspaper, historical society, or other organizations should have material available online. Focus on the history of key elements such as transportation (e.g., freeways, airports, public transit), major neighborhoods, downtown and other business centers, public facilities (e.g., arenas, dams, library or school systems), and major employers. For each element, identify when things were added (or eliminated), what prompted the action, and how it fit into the larger community.

Practice and Review Online
https://textbooks.rowman.com/understanding-urban-politics

PART II

LOCAL INSTITUTIONS

4

DEALING WITH OTHER GOVERNMENTS AT THE NATIONAL, STATE, AND LOCAL LEVELS

GUIDING QUESTIONS

1. What is the legal status of local governments in the American federal system?
2. How do state governments affect a city's government structure, powers, services, and finances?
3. In what ways does the federal government try to influence local governments?
4. How do local governments interact with one another and try to deal with higher-level governments?

IN 2015, the St. Louis Board of Aldermen (city council) adopted an ordinance raising the minimum wage in the city to $10 an hour in 2017, $11 in 2018, and increasing thereafter to keep pace with inflation. In response, Missouri's Republican legislature and governor passed a law prohibiting cities from adopting local minimum wages. This rolled back the St. Louis minimum wage to the state level of $7.70 per hour.[1] Local governments are not mentioned in the US Constitution, which effectively puts them at the mercy of their state legislatures. St. Louis was not alone: By 2018, a total of twenty-four states prohibited local minimum wage laws, forty-one had preempted local ride-sharing regulations, and twenty-three restricted local paid leave ordinances.[2] The relationships between local governments and their states—as well as with each other and the national government—are the focus of this chapter.

LOCAL GOVERNMENTS IN THE AMERICAN FEDERAL SYSTEM

Like any federal system, the US Constitution gives certain powers to the national government, others to the states, and some to both levels of government. Its 10th Amendment guarantees certain vague rights to the states. Certain limits on the states are included in the 13th, 14th, and 15th Amendments, which were added following the Civil War to free slaves and—their supporters hoped—to guarantee their rights and ability to participate in the political system. Most significant are three key provisions in the 14th Amendment. One holds that states cannot deny their citizens "the privileges and immunities of citizens of the United States." This essentially sets a floor below which a state cannot go in abridging a person's rights. A state can, however, guarantee *more* rights than those specified by the federal government. For example, the US Constitution says nothing about education, but the constitutions of all fifty states require the creation of public schools, often with detail on funding, requirements that the system be "uniform" or "efficient," and religious restrictions. Thirty state constitutions also include higher education.[3]

The other two 14th Amendment provisions are in a pair of consecutive clauses: "nor shall any State deprive any person of life, liberty, or property without *due process of law*; nor deny any person within its jurisdiction the *equal protection* of the laws" (italics added). The US Supreme Court has used a process called selective incorporation to interpret the fairly broad language of these clauses as applying the guarantees in the Bill of Rights at the state level. For example, the due process clause has been used to protect the rights of the accused by relying on the 4th, 5th, 6th, and 8th Amendments, such as the standard warning officers give during an arrest about self-incrimination and the right to an attorney. The equal protection clause has been the basis for significant cases dealing with discrimination. In addition, the 5th Amendment guarantees that states cannot seize private property "without just compensation."

Where does this leave local governments? Because they are created by states, the same constitutional limits applied to states extend to their local governments. On top of this are the powers and limits in each state's constitution. In the end, local governments are at the mercy of state legislatures and courts.

The majority of states follow Dillon's Rule, which comes from an 1865 Iowa case that treated local governments as doing no more and no less than the state specifies. In effect, they are "creatures of the state." Still, Dillon's Rule does not grant any authority to local governments; it is merely a guide for courts to use when there is a dispute over a local government's authority.[4]

There are over 90,000 local governments in the United States, and each of the fifty states has created a unique system of general- and special-purpose local governments. General-purpose local governments, which include counties, municipalities (usually cities or villages), and (in some states) townships, provide a range of services within their territories. Special-purpose governments, on the other hand, generally provide a single service. Examples include public school districts or special districts such as the authorities established to run hospitals, parks, airports, or water and sewer systems.[5]

Counties were established by the states as basic administrative units to handle functions such as official records for things like property and births, operation of law enforcement and jails, and road maintenance. This made a great deal of sense in the 1800s, when it was unimaginable for such things to be handled only at the state capital. States are not required to have counties. Connecticut and Rhode Island have none; the other states range from three counties in Delaware to 159 in Georgia and 254 in Texas. These units are called boroughs in Alaska and parishes in Louisiana. As noted in chapter 1, the number of counties has stayed at around 3,000 for more than 50 years.

Outside the South and West, states also have townships, which were originally rural governments smaller than counties. Historically, states allowed municipalities to be created in more densely populated areas with residents and/ or property owners who desired a wider range of services than was available from counties and townships. Townships in metropolitan areas have expanded their services, especially since the 1960s, and today seem much like cities. The largest changes in the governmental landscape have been in special-purpose governments. Starting in the 1950s, school districts merged or disappeared, their numbers dropping from almost 35,000 in 1962 to fewer than 13,000 today. On the flip side, states have allowed special districts to grow from just over 18,000 in 1962 to more than 38,500 today.

The American federal system also seems to be in flux. It is the focus of those who study intergovernmental relations—the many ways that governments within a political system interact with one another. That is the focus of the remainder of this chapter.

STATE LIMITS ON LOCAL GOVERNMENTS

State government essentially controls the destiny of its local governments. This includes things seemingly as simple as creating a city and specifying its authority. It ranges as far as prohibiting local governments from adopting certain policies and even having the state take over operation of cities and school districts.

Incorporation, Charters, and Home Rule

How do all of these changes occur? One way is **incorporation**, the process of creating a new municipal government under requirements set out in state law. Territory in counties without any other general-purpose government is considered unincorporated. Establishing cities (and villages and towns in some states) involves carving out a piece of unincorporated territory and establishing a municipal corporation. Much like a business, the city incorporates and generally gets a charter from the state. A **city charter** can be thought of as a city's constitution. Like all such documents, a charter lays out the structure of government; assigns authority among various officials and bodies; details procedures such as elections, lawmaking, and charter revision; and specifies certain rights or protections, such as open meetings and use of the **initiative**, a process that permits citizens to sign petitions to put a question before voters to accept or reject. This can include policy questions on matters like taxes and amendments to a city charter (for more, see chapter 7).

The area seeking incorporation normally has to meet state standards regarding population, land area, density, and similar factors; it must also follow an incorporation approval process and be prepared to provide certain services in the territory. A city's residents and businesses generally still pay for certain services provided by their overlapping county (e.g., courts), except in Virginia, where cities and counties are completely separate governments.

There were nearly 2,000 incorporations during the postwar suburban boom between 1950 and 1970. Over 1,000 municipalities were added during the next 20 years, followed by 263 during the 1990s and 148 during 2000–2009.[6] There were another fifty-nine incorporations during 2010–18.[7] Incorporating a new city is more than a bureaucratic exercise in following state law. Rather, self-interest is a constant, and incorporations can have significant political, social, and economic effects.

Why incorporate a new city government? Scholars have uncovered several motives based on case studies and statistical research that relied primarily on census data. In analyzing the 1950s through 1980s, Nancy Burns found that many of these efforts were initiated by businesses, especially developers and manufacturers seeking looser regulation, low taxes, and cheaper development costs. Other incorporations were led by citizens seeking better services or avoiding the higher taxes that would result from annexation by a neighboring city.[8] More on annexation appears later in the chapter.

Other research found that incorporation was initiated to provide residents with greater control over growth and land use, particularly through zoning. Still others were motivated by maintaining the racial or class status of areas.[9] When Rice et al. analyzed local newspaper stories to uncover the motives behind incorporations between 1997 and 2007, the main differences from earlier periods that they found were dissatisfaction with county government, efforts to control community revenues, and desire to maintain rural character.[10] Another analysis found that incorporations between 1980 and 2000 were more likely in areas with higher incomes than their counties.[11] There is some diversity in incorporations: one study found that 10 percent between 1990 and 2010 had majorities consisting of people of color.[12]

In Georgia, state law prohibits a new city from incorporating within a limited distance of an existing one, which for many years left much of suburban Atlanta under the jurisdiction of counties. That all changed after Republicans won control of state government in 2005, because the state constitution permits local laws covering a specific place, which could override the prohibition. The legislature passed a series of local laws allowing voters in several affluent, largely white suburbs to incorporate, essentially separating their new cities from a Fulton County government dominated by black Democrats. These efforts spread to nearby DeKalb County and included several areas dominated by African Americans. The general aim became incorporating rather than being part of county governments with ever-shrinking territories.[13]

States deal with charters in multiple ways. In some cases, proposed new cities have a process for drafting their own charter. Other states have a general law with a "boilerplate" charter for incorporating. Some states require the legislature to pass a special act (local law) for incorporating a new city or specify the conditions for doing so.

Those crusading against political machines in the late 1800s and early 1900s saw changes in city charters—usually enabled by supportive state legislatures—as a means to promote their political aims. In 1894, a group that included the president of Harvard, then–New-York politician Theodore Roosevelt, and others held a conference that led to what is now the National Civic League. The organization eventually produced a "model" city charter with the core elements of at-large elections, a nonpartisan ballot, a merit system of employment, and the council-manager form of government. Some revisions acknowledged situations where a strong mayor and district elections might be reasonable.[14] Because of the crucial role that a charter plays in setting the basic "rules of the game" for governing a city, many campaigns led by business and political elites to adopt or amend charters were laced with conflicts over race, ethnicity, and class.[15]

In addition to getting the type of charter they wanted, urban reformers in the early 1900s also pushed for **home rule**. In many ways, this was supposed to be the mirror image of local authority in Dillon's Rule: Cities would be permitted to do anything *not* prohibited by the state, usually including the ability to amend their charters. The goal was to thwart state legislatures from frequent involvement in issues that were seen as purely local. Backers of home rule expected that the protection would be stronger if it became part of the state constitution rather than being legislated. Forty states have some form of home rule, but that has not prevented state legislatures from undermining local policies.[16]

Many states group cities into classes, usually based on population, and then vary authority among the classes. In Washington State, for instance, first-class cities have a population of at least 10,000 and can have a charter. Seattle, Tacoma, and eight other cities are considered first-class cities. There are three other categories of municipal government in smaller places that almost universally follow state requirements without a charter. Minnesota has four classes of cities, and all can choose whether to have a charter or follow state law.[17]

Procedures

Most states require local governments to adhere to certain procedures. Perhaps the most basic is open meetings, often called "government in the sunshine," which allows only certain types of closed meetings, for instance, city councils discussing litigation, personnel actions, or the purchase or sale of real estate. Posting public notices about when and where meetings will be held often accompanies an open meetings requirement. Similarly, public access to government documents is usually covered under a state Freedom of Information Act (FOIA). Such openness has not always been expected, and it is still frequently contested and in some cases thwarted by expensive document fees.[18]

Cities, counties, and special districts make plenty of information available quickly in the digital age compared to the reliance on newspaper notices decades ago. Many broadcast public meetings on cable television or via the internet. Meeting agendas and minutes are also posted, along with information items like budget summaries, street closings, and job openings.

States also impose requirements regarding local elections. These include qualifications of candidates (e.g., residency requirements), election dates, designation of a partisan or nonpartisan ballot, outcome rules (e.g., runoff requirement or even the new instant runoff system used in some places), and the ability to use procedures like early voting. Cities and counties are also responsible for running elections in most states, including those held by mail and at local polling places.

Some states also empower citizens by allowing direct democracy at the local level. California cities have frequent ballot measures, both through the initiative process and submitted by local governing bodies, with many tax measures requiring voter approval by a two-thirds supermajority. There are generally between 100 and 200 ballot questions across the state in odd years and 500 to over 800 in even years. Complicating this deluge is that these campaigns can be spread across many election dates. In 2017, California had 122 local ballot measures, only eight of which were the result of citizen petitions. These votes occurred on eighteen different dates, with only the months of September and December free of ballot measures. November was the peak month, with sixty-two proposals on local ballots. Many votes covered local taxes, with cities seemingly eager to tax marijuana businesses following the state's legalization of the drug.[19]

Boundaries

In addition to rules for establishing boundaries when a local government is created, states set procedures for changing them, which can take multiple forms. It almost goes without saying that proposed changes can be highly controversial. The bottom line regarding local government boundaries is a fairly simple but harsh reality: Where you reside, work, or own property determines what you get—and don't get—in services, costs, and community conditions.

Annexation is the process of a city adding unincorporated territory to its city limits. Each state sets its own procedures for this process, and they vary widely. Some states require petitions from residents or homeowners seeking annexation. Cities are not passive, however. For much of the 1920s through 1950s, Milwaukee used city employees to circulate annexation petitions; more recently, Charleston and Columbia, South Carolina, have done the same. Some outlying property owners, especially businesses, will seek annexation if they can get better services, more favorable zoning, or even better regulation of alcohol sales. Some states require a referendum in an area that a city proposes to annex, which can be a formidable barrier. Until 2017, Texas allowed cities to annex territory within a certain distance simply by passing an ordinance (see box 4.1).

North Carolina law has also made this process relatively easy for cities. Virginia law has procedures for cities to annex outlying territory when it meets certain "urban" characteristics. The criteria are relatively specific, and the matter is decided in court by a judge applying the law to the annexation proposal.

Cities have occasionally merged, either with one another or with their overlapping county, in a process called **consolidation**. This is rare, largely because of the political minefields that must be traversed. Reformers pushed consolidation during the 1920s and 1930s as a way to promote the governance of metropolitan areas, but it meant combining cities with their suburbs—a daunting political task.

Consolidation was also promoted after World War II by advocates in academia and the business community as a way to deal with the "fragmentation" of metropolitan areas that resulted from suburbanizaton. Suburban residents and politicians were usually opponents. In central cities, public employees were

BOX 4.1

How Did Texas Cities Get So Big?

Map 4.1 Three Maps of Houston's Territorial Growth

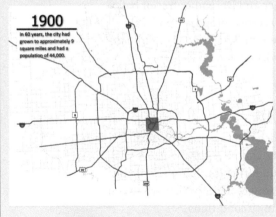

1900

In 60 years, the city had grown to approximately 9 square miles and had a population of 44,000.

1950s

By the end of the decade, Houston was 350 square miles with nearly 1 million residents.

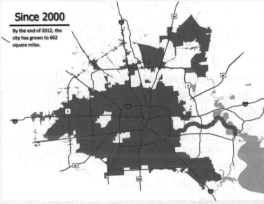

Since 2000

By the end of 2012, the city has grown to 662 square miles.

Source: City of Houston, "Annexations in Houston," http://www.houstontx.gov/planning/Annexation/docs_pdfs/HoustonAnnexationHistory.pdf.

skeptical because of possible job losses; politicians' positions varied by place and time.

Advocates were able to get city-county merger proposals to voters on multiple occasions, but the success rate has been dismal at best (see table 4.1). Many efforts after World War II were in the South, where there are no townships outside cities to oppose the proposals. However, several passed in western states like Montana and Nevada, plus seven in Alaska. As the data indicate, the chances of a successful consolidation are not good, but voter approval was more likely in small or medium-size communities. Still, there were some notable mergers, including Louisville and Nashville, as well as the state legislature's creation of modern-day New York City by combining Manhattan, Brooklyn, Queens, the Bronx, and Staten Island. Some places voted multiple times, including four failed attempts in Albuquerque and Chattanooga. In Macon, consolidation failed three times between 1960 and 1972 before voters in the city and Bibb County ratified a merger in 2012.[20]

People are often shocked that Houston spreads over 655 square miles. According to the local tourism office, this is enough area to contain Boston, Miami, Minneapolis, New York, San Francisco, Seattle, and Washington combined.[a] Just one of many large Texas cities, Houston is more than half the size of the smallest state, Rhode Island. In 2016, San Antonio covered 461 square miles, Dallas 341, Fort Worth 340, and Austin 298.[b] Adding territory translates into more residents. These cities, along with Houston, are among the fifteen most populous in the US.

Until recently, Texas has made annexation easy. In addition, new cities cannot incorporate in an existing city's *extraterritorial jurisdiction* (ETJ), an area adjoining the city limits over which the city exercises some control over development. City councils in Texas annexed simply by passing an ordinance—residents and landowners in the outlying area had no say in the matter, often calling these actions a "land grab."

From 1940 to 1981, San Antonio completed 257 annexations totaling almost 232 square miles. Some were done with little warning; one in 1952 took in eighty square miles and 32,000 residents. The state began restricting cities' annexation power beginning in the mid-1960s, but cities continued to add territory, often with the support of developers. Between 2000 and 2017, Fort Worth annexed twenty-eight areas totaling more than 11.5 square miles, and Austin added 16.6 square miles. Finally, during a 2017 special session, the state legislature passed a law giving residents within proposed annexations a vote on the matter.[c]

[a] Visit Houston, "Facts and Figures," https://www.visithous-tontexas.com/about-houston/facts-and-figures/.

[b] The available land areas from the US Census Bureau are from the 2010 census, although its "Boundary and Annexation Survey" does provide updates, but there are gaps in the acreage data. Land areas here are from the Open Data Network: https://www.opendatanetwork.com/.

[c] Arnold Fleischmann, "Sunbelt Boosterism: The Politics of Postwar Growth and Annexation in San Antonio," 151–68, in David C. Perry and Alfred J. Watkins, eds., *The Rise of the Sunbelt Cities* (Beverly Hills: Sage, 1977); Arnold Fleischmann, "The Politics of Annexation: A Preliminary Assessment of Competing Paradigms," *Social Science Quarterly* 67:1 (March 1986): 128–42; data downloaded from the US Census Bureau, "Legal Boundary Change/Annexation Data: Texas," https://www.census.gov/geographies/reference-files/time-series/geo/bas/annex.html; Taylor Goldenstein, "Abbott Signs Bill Limiting Annexation Powers of Cities," *Austin American-Statesman*, August 16, 2017, https://www.statesman.com/news/state–regional–govt–politics/abbott-signs-bill-limiting-annexation-powers-cities.

TABLE 4.1	City-County Consolidation Proposals	
Period	Adopted/Total	Major Consolidations
1800s	6/6	New Orleans-Orleans Parish
		Philadelphia-Philadelphia County
		New York City (current five boroughs merged by the state)
1900–1939	2/12	Denver-Denver County
		Honolulu-Honolulu County
1940–1959	3/15	
1960–1969	6/21	Nashville-Davidson County, TN
		Jacksonville-Duval County, FL
1970–1974	5/32	Columbus-Muscogee County, GA
		Lexington-Fayette County, KY
1975–1979	3/17	
1980–1984	1/12	
1985–1989	1/15	
1990–1994	3/14	Athens-Clarke County, GA
		Lafayette-Lafayette Parish, LA
1995–1999[a]	2/10	Augusta-Richmond County, GA
		Kansas City-Wyandotte County, KS
2000–2004	4/15	Louisville-Jefferson County, KY
2005–2009	5/6	
2010–2014	4/4	Macon-Bibb County, GA
GRAND TOTAL	45/179 (25.1%)	

[a] Does not include Colorado constitutional amendment allowing creation of Broomfield-Broomfield County from parts of four counties.

Source: Vincent L. Marando, "City-County Consolidation: Reform, Regionalism, Referenda, and Requiem," *Western Political Quarterly* 32:4 (December 1979): 409–21; Matthew Fellows, "City County-Consolidation Proposals through 2010," National Association of Counties, 2011, http://www.naco.org/sites/default/files/documents/City%20County%20Consolidations.01.01.2011.pdf; National Association of Counties, "NACo County Explorer," http://explorer.naco.org/index.html?dset=City-County%20Consolidations&ind=Consolidation.

In some cases, consolidation was forced. In Indianapolis, business and political leaders got the state legislature to pass a law in 1969 merging the city and Marion County to form what is popularly known as Unigov. Notably, the law left some suburbs intact and did not merge some city and county departments or any school districts. The merger "grew" the city so that its population has been in the Top Twenty nationally, aided Republican control of Unigov, and helped boosters promote the city, including adding the NCAA headquarters and an NFL franchise. In the end, the old city school system has seen its enrollment drop precipitously and become increasingly segregated, and there have been calls for further consolidation of services that remain scattered throughout the county.[21]

In Battle Creek, Michigan, Kellogg threatened to pack up its cereal boxes and move its headquarters if the city did not merge with the outlying, more affluent township. Voters in both jurisdictions approved the measure in November 1982, adding 20,000 to Battle Creek's 35,000 population and more than doubling the property tax base. Kellogg employment has since grown from 700 to more than 2,000, and the company joined others in creating an economic development fund and supporting the rebirth of downtown.[22]

Consolidation votes during the mid-1970s in Montana were "nudged" rather than forced. The state's new constitution in 1972 required local government study commissions to be established in every city and county every 10 years. This led to a wide range of proposals being placed before local voters in the first iteration. Voters tended to maintain the status quo, approving changes in only 31 of 182 local governments, although voters approved city-county consolidations in Anaconda and Butte.[23]

The bottom line on the effects of consolidation is mixed. One major study compared nine consolidated governments with counties that did not merge. Many backers of consolidation promised more efficient local government. In examining per capita spending, both generally and for several key services, the research team found that consolidation led to lower expenditure in only about half the cases. The record on economic growth and development in the consolidated governments was much stronger, however. The consolidated governments also delivered on more specific promises in some areas about preventing annexation by neighboring jurisdictions, cleaning up a history of corruption, improving services, and enhancing infrastructure and other public improvements.[24] Consolidation of small cities also fails to show major declines in taxes and spending. Proponents did not push mergers only for efficiency; they had multiple goals related to improving their communities, including spending on infrastructure.[25]

At the other extreme, cities and counties have sometimes cast off existing territory to improve their perceived economic, political, or social position. In the mid-1800s, St. Louis viewed the rest of the county as living off the wealth of the city and separated in 1875. Today, St. Louis County is a generally affluent suburban area with no legal connection to the city of St. Louis. In San Francisco, reformers targeting governance and corruption were able to get San Francisco restructured in 1856 as a combined city-county separate from modern San Mateo County to the south, which is the heart of Silicon Valley.[26]

In the 20th century, residents in areas who saw themselves as slighted by city hall failed in efforts to secede from Los Angeles and New York City.[27] The Birmingham suburb of Gardendale, Alabama, was allowed to split from the Jefferson County schools in 2017 to form its own school district. Gardendale was 84 percent white, while the Jefferson County schools were 47.5 percent black and 43.5 percent white.[28] Similarly, the Georgia legislature passed a local law in 2018 permitting an affluent area south of Atlanta to vote on seceding from its existing city to form a new one; the effort failed, however.[29]

A more radical way to transform local boundaries is to eliminate them. In Maine, some small rural towns have disbanded in favor of being overseen by the state and their county rather than shouldering tax and service burdens on their own.[30] In Georgia, a 1993 law required municipalities to provide at least three services from a list of over a dozen options, hold at least six regular meetings annually, and be able to conduct elections. Within 2 years of its passage, almost 200 municipalities were declared inactive and dissolved, mainly in rural areas.[31]

Service Mandates

Critics often focus on **mandates** imposed by the federal government, for example, standards for clean air and water. States impose mandates on local governments, often with the argument that citizens should be able to expect certain minimum service standards no matter where they live within the state.

States impose service requirements in three ways. First, they can specify the services that a city or county must provide, as well as those it is permitted to provide. In Pennsylvania, counties are responsible for most human services programs, property records and assessment, voter registration and elections, and courts and jails. Many have taken on other services such as 911 call centers, roads and bridges, and mass transit.[32]

Most states assign responsibilities to certain county officials in their constitutions. These so-called constitutional officers that every county must elect usually include a sheriff, a prosecutor, one or more officials related to revenue and taxation, someone responsible for the administration of courts, and often a county clerk. Many state constitutions also require electing a register/recorder of deeds to handle property records, and some still mandate electing a county coroner to investigate causes of death, usually without demanding that the person have medical training.[33] Requiring a specific elected official to be responsible for these functions might have made great sense in the 1800s, but not in the 21st century. Counties are stuck with these offices today whether they want them or not, since eliminating them would require state constitutional amendments, an uphill political battle. Cities typically have much more flexibility than counties about the structure of their executive branches.

Second, states can require certain credentials or training for workers providing services. Perhaps the most obvious are licensing standards for professionals such as teachers working in local school districts or nurses employed by public hospitals, who typically must have certain college degrees and pass qualifying exams. Also common are requirements for bus drivers, operators of water treatment plants, employees at day care centers, and many more.

Training requirements often extend to public officials, many of whom do not have a degree or specific training to prepare them for their jobs. For instance, city/municipal clerks can be appointed or elected, depending on the state and city, and have responsibilities regarding government records, public notices, some financial functions, and (in some states) election administration. Qualifications vary, but the International Institute of Municipal Clerks has programs for different levels of certification, and state associations of clerks and others provide training. In South Carolina, this consists of two half-week sessions in three consecutive years, while California offers four week-long programs in conjunction with a university.[34] In Arizona, judges in limited-jurisdiction courts that handle misdemeanors, traffic, minor financial disputes, and similar matters are not all required to be attorneys.[35] Like most states, though, Arizona does require orientation, training, and continuing education for judges, including those in city courts and justices of the peace.[36] Some states also run orientation programs for newly elected members of city councils and county boards.

Third, states impose service standards on both local governments and private or nonprofit providers in communities. This has become increasingly common—and controversial—with emphasis on student test scores and other indicators in public schools and scrutiny of the finances of entire school districts.[37] The states often specify city and county measures in terms of water quality, street mainte-nance, and building codes.

Finances

State influence over local government finances includes a long list of restrictions and a few rewards (see chapter 10 for more detail). The starting point for most local governments is a state requirement for a balanced budget; in other words, the spending approved for the year must match the projected revenues. This is quite different from the federal government, which almost routinely runs an annual deficit and borrows extensively. Other common state limits cover local governments' allowable revenue sources. Property taxes are almost universally permitted, but states place many restrictions on how they may be used. Some states allow local governments to adopt sales taxes of various types, and a few permit local governments to levy an income tax, usually one rate for residents and a lower rate for those who work in the city or county but live elsewhere. This is seen as a way to tax commuters for the extra services a government must pro-vide during the work day. States often permit specialized taxes—like those on motel rooms, rental cars, and other sources—and set requirements about tax rates, what items can be taxed, and how real estate is assessed for property taxes. Most also impose limits on how far into debt a city or county can go. All of these things affect local governments' revenue streams and budgeting.

States also employ different forms of oversight. Perhaps the most common is requiring local governments to have an audit, either annually or on some fixed schedule. An *audit* is a review conducted by an outside accounting firm of the gov-ernment's books, ordinances, documents, vouchers, and other records to make sure that money was spent in compliance with an approved budget and estab-lished policies.

On the plus side for local governments is revenue from the state; however, it is often based on formulas to encourage certain policies or behavior. Many aid programs are based on population. One of the most common is the "head count" that school districts conduct to secure state money based on enrollment. South Carolina does this three times each school year, Wisconsin does its primary count on the third Friday of September and another on the second Friday in January, and Washington State has a count day each month between September and May.[38] A similar approach applies to highway aid in most states. For example, Minnesota has funded county roads with a formula that includes vehicle registrations, total roadway lane miles, and need.[39] In addition to formula-driven funding, states also have many grants for which local governments can apply, as with specific infrastructure projects like bridges.

Figure 4.1 captures local government revenue trends since 1992. The data are in current dollars, which means that they are not adjusted for inflation. Several patterns are significant. One is the steady growth in local government revenue to almost $1.8 billion by 2015. Another is the limited amount of federal money going directly to local governments. Third is the flattening of state aid. It was 30 percent in 1992, helped local governments during the Great Recession that began in 2007, but has been below 30 percent since 2010. This suggests that local governments are increasingly going it alone financially.

Figure 4.1 focuses on overall levels of state and federal support and masks differences among different types of local governments. The US Census Bureau publishes more detailed breakdowns of local government revenue every 5 years (see chapter 11). Those data show that the major distinction over the past 20 years is the dependence of school districts on state aid, which has averaged just over half of their revenue; hardly any of their revenue came from the federal government. The biggest recipients of state aid after schools are counties, which get about 30 percent of their funds from states. Cities and townships get less than one-fourth of their revenue from states, while special district support from states

Figure 4.1 Local Government Revenue, 1992–2017 (Millions of Current Dollars)

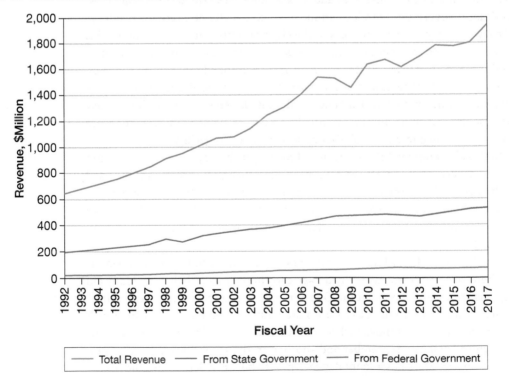

Source: US Census Bureau, "State and Local Government Finance: State and Local Summary Tables by Level of Government," annual, https://www.census.gov/programs-surveys/gov-finances/data/datasets.html.

hovers in the high single digits. Federal support for local governments remains below 5 percent with the exception of special districts, which are in the double-digit range. This makes sense given that such districts include those providing health and transportation, which are covered by major federal programs. These are general patterns, and funding can vary from state to state. For instance, only 4 percent of school revenue is raised locally in Vermont, but over 60 percent is raised locally in neighboring New Hampshire.[40]

A Big Hammer: Preemption

A blunt method for states to control—some would say punish—their local governments is through preemption, which limits or removes local officials' policy discretion (see chapter 1). To many, this can look like state legislatures second-guessing or overruling local decisions that they dislike no matter how popular an action might be in a given community.

Conflicts over preemption became increasingly controversial, beginning in the 2000s. This was due in part to partisanship, with Republican-controlled states reining in Democratic-leaning cities. Examples include states prohibiting cities and counties from banning plastic bags, prohibiting fracking, and limiting firearms.[41] In some cases, preemption can even be done in anticipation of local action. For example, the Alabama legislature passed a law prohibiting cities from removing most monuments that were at least 20 years old.[42] That action followed removal of Confederate memorials in other cities, where those who opposed the monuments described them as having been erected in the late 19th and early 20th centuries to celebrate white supremacy.[43]

Perhaps the most attention-grabbing preemption in recent years was the 2016 North Carolina law repealing a Charlotte nondiscrimination ordinance that included gender identity—which allowed people to use a bathroom other than their gender assigned at birth—and other restrictions. There was a quick and strong backlash; other states banned nonessential travel by their employees to North Carolina, college and professional sports events relocated (including the NBA All Star Game to New Orleans from Charlotte), multiple conventions were cancelled or went to other states, businesses threatened to abandon investments in the state, and performers as big as Bruce Springsteen dropped events. The controversy helped a Democrat defeat the incumbent Republican governor, and the state adopted a partial repeal of the so-called "bathroom bill" in 2017.[44]

The Ultimate Sanction: State Takeover

In some cases, states have taken over local institutions. Most common have been takeovers of individual public schools based on standardized test performance. In some cases, entire school districts, in response to either student performance or financial problems, have come under state oversight or takeover, and states have created new districts from existing ones. State takeovers have increased with the growing emphasis on metrics, including federal mandates in the No Child Left Behind Act passed by Congress in 2001 and the

Every Student Succeeds Act in 2015. After Hurricane Katrina, New Orleans ended up with an entirely new district built around charter schools. Tennessee, Michigan, and New Jersey have also tried this strategy. Kentucky has moved to take over Jefferson County schools (Louisville).[45] Some states have also allowed local schools to be controlled by a city's mayor, as in Boston, Chicago, and New York City.[46]

States have also increasingly monitored and taken over municipal governments due to financial distress, especially since the Great Recession and its aftermath. Still, although their approaches vary, one study found that only twenty-two states make even some effort to monitor the financial condition of their local governments. North Carolina has an extensive monitoring and benchmarking system for local governments, which can be especially helpful for small cities. A few states require permission for local governments to issue debt or raise taxes above certain levels. Most states have ways to provide technical and other assistance, but twenty-one do not allow local governments to declare bankruptcy as a way out of their problems. New Jersey allows state intervention in the day-to-day running of cities, but little has seemed to help the poor cities of Atlantic City and Camden. Michigan can assign an emergency manager to run cities with broad powers and little input from elected officials.[47] Not all takeover moves are based on distress—some Republicans in the Georgia legislature failed in 2018 to exert more state control over Atlanta's airport, which has been run by the city since the 1920s.[48]

FEDERAL EFFORTS TO INFLUENCE LOCAL GOVERNMENTS

In many ways, the national government mimics the states in using commands and money to influence local governments. It often does this indirectly, though, because local governments are not mentioned in the US Constitution.

Federal Mandates

Federal mandates have come in many forms, especially since the 1960s and 1970s. Some of these are conditions for receiving any form of federal aid. The first one was part of the 1964 Civil Rights Act, which Congress adopted to prohibit discrimination based on its power to regulate interstate commerce in Article I of the Constitution. The 13th, 14th, and 15th Amendments adopted after the Civil War also allowed Congress to deal with racial discrimination. The Voting Rights Act (VRA), which was signed into law in 1965, imposed federal supervision over state and local election procedures. The VRA was the basis for challenges to redistricting, the movement of polling places, the use of at-large elections that produced underrepresentation of minorities on city councils and county boards, and other practices. The Supreme Court largely voided the law, however, in its 2015 decision, *Shelby County v. Holder*.[49] Another major mandate was the Americans with Disabilities Act adopted in 1990, which forced many local governments to modify infrastructure like sidewalks, make public buildings more accessible, add parking for people with disabilities, and make changes in transit systems such as buses. In addition, school districts have made major changes in resource allocation to boys' and girls' programs, especially sports, as a result of Title 9 of the Education Amendments of 1972.

Mandates also cover employment, the environment, and other policy areas. Those most often cited by state and local officials are connected to federal highway money. Congress used a threat of cutting funding to states that did not adopt a drinking age of 21 in 1984 and a 55-mph speed limit in 1974. States challenged this "blackmail" by the feds, but the Supreme Court validated the strategy when it upheld the speed limit requirement in *South Dakota v. Dole* in 1987.[50] As an alternative, the federal government offered extra money to states requiring mandatory use of seat belts.[51]

The federal government also moves beyond mandates to sue local governments. For example, the US Department of Justice took action against police conduct in Baltimore, Chicago, Milwaukee, Seattle, and other cities.[52] Similarly, the Environmental Protection Agency sues under various federal laws, including against local governments over pollution caused by their water and sewer systems.[53]

Financial Support

Like the states, the federal government has used money to help state and local governments, often with strings attached. Over the years, the feds have used categorical grants, block grants, and revenue sharing.[54] **Categorical grants** are funds that must be used for specific purposes, usually with a required application and often along with local matching funds. The federal agency administering the grant has significant discretion in imposing standards on the "winners" selected to receive the funds. Categorical grants began during the 1930s, with new programs after World War II supporting airport construction, urban planning, urban renewal, and the Interstate Highway System. The number and types of grants increased substantially in beginning in the 1960s. By 2018, Congress had created nearly 1,300 categorical grant programs, many tied to specific types of projects.

Block grants are funds for a range of activities that are usually awarded based on formulas, and they give local officials more discretion and less federal oversight than categorical grants. The number of block grants has ranged between twenty and twenty-six since 1996.

More generous still for local officials is **revenue sharing**, which gives them almost unlimited discretion in spending federal money. Money was generally distributed based on measures like population. Federal revenue sharing was begun under President Nixon in 1972. It ended in 1986, when the Reagan administration saw its elimination as one way to deal with federal budget deficits.

In 2018, federal grants to state and local governments totaled an estimated $728 billion, with almost 60 percent of funds going to health programs such as Medicaid grants to states. At the local level, almost $21 billion went for Section 8 housing vouchers, $16.3 billion supported education programs for the disadvantaged, and $9.8 billion assisted urban mass transportation.

An argument in favor of these grants is that they allow the federal government to put national standards in place for such things as water treatment plants and highway bridges. Federal oversight also means that money goes for the intended purpose. Critics complain about categorical grant processes being slow and burdensome, especially for smaller local governments. Perhaps a more cynical view is that Congress loves these grants because they allow senators and representatives to take credit for projects back home, including attendance at ribbon-cutting ceremonies.

The first major block grant was the Community Development Block Grant (CDBG), which was created in 1974 by consolidating eight existing categorical grants.[55] Much of the argument for these grants was to give more discretion to locals, who were presumably more knowledgeable about their communities' needs. Proponents argued that they might encourage experimentation and permit more variation from place to place. The formulas and streamlined procedures also made the amount and timing of funds more predictable. Skeptics noted that the Nixon administration's push for block grants made funds more readily available to suburbs—part of Nixon's electoral coalition.

Two major concerns with block grants are biases in aid formulas and how local officials exercise their discretion. One dilemma for local officials using CDBG is that while funding has remained steady over the years, it has fallen far short of keeping up with inflation, as the dual formulas have added more jurisdictions entitled to the pool of recipients. In addition, the grant's procedures and areas of emphasis have varied from one administration to another. The Trump administration's first budget proposed eliminating CDBG funding, although Congress did not agree.[56] Critics say that the formula for CDBG funding does not focus on need, singling out its use of age of housing stock, which can advantage older, wealthier suburbs.[57] Local spending priorities have shifted over the years, and it remains unclear how much the program actually benefits low- and moderate-income residents. There is also concern about the extent to which communities incorporate public participation and include CDBG as part of comprehensive plans to improve housing and community development.[58]

In the end, federal money is not a large part of most local government budgets, but it can support certain types of projects. Given that incentive, federal grants show no signs of going away, and local government does everything possible to get its share.

DEALING WITH OTHER GOVERNMENTS

Scholars of intergovernmental relations focus on both vertical and horizontal relationships. Vertical includes governments at different levels, such as states and their cities. Horizontal covers governments at the same level, such as a county interacting with the cities, school districts, and special districts within its borders. Local relationships involve a mix of competition and cooperation. Local governments also face calls to promote their regions rather than going it alone.

Local Strategies to Deal with Higher-Level Governments

As already noted, local governments are not passive in their dealings with states or the federal government. They have organizations promoting their interests in Washington and at state capitals. In addition to lobbying, these groups provide training, conferences, research, and other forms of advocacy. At times, they even file lawsuits.

Major entities promoting cities and counties at the national level are the US Conference of Mayors (USCM), the National League of Cities (NLC), the International City/County Management Association (ICMA), and the National Association of Counties (NACo). These groups all lobbied heavily in 2017 as Congress considered and passed a major overhaul of the federal income tax. They are also members of the State and Local Legal Center, which files *amicus curiae* (friend of the court) briefs in appeals to the US Supreme Court and provides other support.[59] For instance, the Center filed a brief in a 2017 case supporting the ability of state and local governments to tax internet sales of companies not within their borders (see box 4.2). Local governments have also tangled with the Trump administration over immigration, including declaring themselves sanctuary cities that would not aid arrest or deportation of the undocumented, and many adopted local strategies on climate both before and after the 2017 US withdrawal from the 2015 Paris agreement.[60] Cities also lobby on their own at the national level, usually when Congress experiences a change in party control or when the city experiences major fiscal problems.[61]

While local officials generally believe that they have lost authority at the hands of states, there are organizations that represent local governments at the state level.[62] Larger cities, counties, and special districts also promote their interests individually. For example, the County Commissioners Association of Pennsylvania represents the interests of county governments, while another organization, the Pennsylvania Municipal League (PML), promotes the interests of cities, boroughs, and towns in the commonwealth. PML reported spending almost $50,000 on lobbying during 2017; separately, the city of Philadelphia spent over $90,000 that same year.[63]

Similar arrays of local government interests exist in other states. Each state, for instance, has a school board association affiliated with the National School Boards Association.[64] Many local special districts also organize statewide to promote their interests, as with the Special District Association of Colorado.[65] Efforts to promote local interests extend beyond governments to include professional associations and unions representing public school teachers, police chiefs, sheriffs, firefighters, city clerks, prosecutors, judges, and many more. There are even organizations representing volunteer-based groups. For example, groups in each state promote the collective interests of their many local Parent Teachers Associations (PTAs).

Competition among Local Governments

Perhaps the most visible competition among places is economic development. Cities and counties offer tax breaks, land, and other incentives to attract investment, often to the chagrin of local residents and businesses questioning how they benefit from such deals. While the scramble to win Amazon's second headquarters attracted huge media coverage (see box 1.2), it is similar to many other efforts, just on a bigger scale. A bidding war ensued in 2011 when Boeing announced a search for a new headquarters and then left Seattle for Chicago, passing over Dallas and Denver. In 2015, GE announced plans to move from a Connecticut suburb of New York, eventually selecting Boston.[66] The same dynamic was even more intense when foreign automakers, including BMW, Honda, Hyundai, Kia, Mercedes-Benz, Nissan, Subaru, Toyota, Volkswagen, and Volvo, began building factories in the United States. This competition extends to sports, where cities strive for a "big league" image. Aside from corporate headquarters, manufacturing facilities, and teams, cities also compete for "temporary" attractions, including the presidential nominating conventions held every 4 years, major trade shows and conventions, and sporting events like college playoffs and the Olympics, which Los Angeles won for the summer games in 2028 (for more on economic development, see chapter 12).

Cities and counties also compete in a more "local" way within metropolitan areas. They try to attract not only businesses and residents, but also government and foundation grants, facilities like federal research centers and branch campuses of colleges and technical schools, and infrastructure like highway and airport improvements.

Cooperation among Local Governments

Perhaps the most basic form of cooperation among local governments is the mutual aid agreement. The classic case is fire, police, or EMS agreements between cities to back up one another in a major emergency. Smaller cities and counties have found it beneficial to share services, including local health departments. One national study found savings and enhanced services in using a shared executive and combining services such as finance, accounting, purchasing, communications, and outreach.[67] While collaboration is often sold in terms of reduced costs, that does not always happen. However, there can be benefits in terms of improved expertise, quality and scope of services, and effectiveness. Such agreements can be difficult, and there is concern about how effectively they are monitored.[68]

Both the federal government and some states require or encourage some degree of cooperation among local governments. In the 1960s and 1970s, the

BOX 4.2

Why Am I Paying Sales Tax When I Buy Something Online?

Every state except Alaska, Delaware, Montana, New Hampshire, and Oregon has a sales tax. Of the remaining forty-five states, thirty-eight plus Alaska allow local governments to levy some kind of sales tax. In decisions in 1967 and 1992, the Supreme Court held that states could not tax purchases shipped to residents unless the seller had a physical presence in the state. This was thought to impede interstate commerce. The spread of electronic sales put traditional retailers at a price disadvantage because they had to collect the tax. This also cost state and local governments billions in potential tax revenue.

Companies like Amazon and eBay initially did not collect tax on shipments from third-party vendors, and Amazon at one time avoided locating shipment centers in certain states. South Dakota passed a law in 2016 to tax out-of-state vendors, but small entities were exempt. Several firms challenged the law. In *South Dakota v. Wayfair*, a 5–4 Supreme Court majority overturned its earlier precedents in 2018 and upheld the South Dakota law.

Source: For background, oral arguments, and the justices' opinions in the case, see *South Dakota v. Wayfair, Inc.*, 585 US (2018), https://www.oyez.org/cases/2017/17-494. On the concerns of state and local governments, see Jon Kuhl, "States Have a $23 Billion Sales Tax Loophole and Congress Is Considering a Bill to Close It," *Tapping Into Online* (National Conference of State Legislatures newsletter), March 2012, http://www.ncsl.org/research/fiscal-policy/tapping-into-online.aspx.

federal government promoted the creation of regional planning bodies commonly called councils of government (COGs). These voluntary bodies are made up of representatives from member local governments.[69] They include more than 400 metropolitan planning organizations (MPOs) required to develop and oversee regional transportation plans tied to federal funding for urbanized areas of 50,000 or more population.[70] Some regional planning crosses state lines, as with the Duluth-Superior MPO, which covers areas in both Minnesota and Wisconsin, and the MPO for the Kansas City area, which extends over nine counties in Missouri and Kansas.[71]

At the state level, Montana is unique; its constitution requires cities and counties to give voters the option every 10 years of establishing a study commission to submit proposals on restructuring their government, some of which have led to government mergers.[72] City officials in Georgia complained for years that county governments were collecting taxes county-wide to provide services such as law enforcement and trash collection in unincorporated territory (all the area outside the county's cities). This was labeled "double taxation" for city residents, who paid for both their own services and those in the unincorporated part of their county that they did not use. The legislature responded to this pressure in the late 1990s by requiring counties and the cities within them to negotiate agreements regarding service provision and distribution of certain revenues under a process overseen by the state's Department of Community Affairs.[73]

The Long-Standing Calls for Regionalism

The push for regional problem solving began in earnest during the suburbanization of the 1920s. Some form of regional governance might seem obvious to many, but the dilemma is creating institutions to meet this need. After all, movements of air and water are unconcerned with local government boundaries. Labor markets also cross over multiple jurisdictions as employers and workers function within broad regions. Plus, there are actual government services that serve regions, like airports. Others, such as highways and railroads, stretch across and between regions. The political challenge is finding a way to generate the support to create regional institutions.

Early advocates suggested several alternatives. One was to add a regional layer of government on top of existing cities and counties. A second option was to consolidate (merge) local governments so that a new government would be regional in nature. The third option was to create a regional government with limited powers and services. Little came of these efforts, although the discussion has remained alive.[74]

Modern advocates of regional governance have argued that expanding the boundaries of central cities keeps them from being encircled by wealthy suburbs and becoming the site of concentrated poverty and other problems, and that expanding cities makes it easier to address problems that are truly regional in nature.[75] Opponents often treat metropolitan areas as a market in which residents "vote with their feet" by picking the location to live based on the mix of high-quality services and low taxes. In this view, cities compete with one another for residents and businesses, rendering the system more efficient compared to being under the umbrella of a single large government.[76] However, opponents generally ignore the extent to which local governments can use zoning and other policies to keep out certain land uses and residents, usually the less affluent.[77]

At this point in time, advocates for regionalism have generally moved past pushing for annexation and consolidation in favor of leaving existing boundaries alone and either adding a metropolitan-wide government to perform certain functions or creating large special districts that cross city and county lines to produce certain services. There are regional governments in the Portland, Oregon, and Minneapolis-St. Paul metropolitan areas,[78] and a large number of areas use special districts for services such as water, sewers, public transit, and even destinations such as convention centers, museums, and sports facilities. In some cases, these have required enabling laws from the state legislature.[79] The presence of very large suburbs or counties as service providers can also avoid balkanization, or fragmenting metropolitan areas into many small cities.[80] Some states, including California and Minnesota, have established regional or statewide agencies for reviewing, approving, or modifying local boundary changes.[81] In the end, it is the states that must devise ways to deal with regional issues, which might be even harder than in the past because of today's polarized political environment.

SUMMARY

Describing the US federal system as "complex" might be an understatement. Local governments are not mentioned in the US Constitution and are seemingly under the thumb of their state governments. States control the creation, boundaries, finances, and powers of local governments through a wide range of restrictions. They have preempted local governments from adopting certain policies favored by their residents and, in some cases, have taken over schools, school districts, and city governments.

Both the federal and state governments have used mandates and financial support to influence local policy making. Cities, counties, school systems, and special districts have all developed state and national organizations to promote their interests. Local governments also deal with one another in both competitive and cooperative relationships. Cooperating on regional issues always has been difficult and might be even more so in today's polarized environment.

Key Terms

annexation *(75)*

block grants *(85)*

categorical grants *(85)*

city charter *(73)*

consolidation *(76)*

home rule *(74)*

incorporation *(72)*

initiative *(73)*

revenue sharing *(85)*

Discussion Questions

1. How does the state limit the ability of your city or county elected officials to represent the interests of their constituents?

2. What are the advantages and disadvantages of categorical grants, block grants, and revenue sharing?

3. What would you identify as regional issues in your area? How prepared are local governments to address them?

Exercises

1. Search online to see if a new city has incorporated in your county during the past decade. If so, search on your regional planning agency's website or use the Census Bureau "Quick Facts" to describe how this new city compares to the rest of the county. Identify whether local media coverage explains who supported and opposed the incorporation and why.

2. Use the Census of Governments or your regional planning agency's website to identify the number and types of general-purpose and special-purpose local governments in your county. Describe how they differ in terms of purpose, budget, and government structure (this could be summarized in a table).

3. To what extent does your city or county budget include funds from the state and federal governments? Can you identify any limitations on the use of this money?

Practice and Review Online
https://textbooks.rowman.com/understanding-urban-politics

5

LOCAL LEGISLATURES

GUIDING QUESTIONS

1. How do institutional rules affect key functions of local legislatures in the areas of representation and lawmaking?
2. What are the main functions of local governments in the US and how do they influence governance?
3. Are local legislatures capable of providing adequate representation to city residents?

IN SPRING 2018, the Albuquerque **City Council** approved a 3/8th percent increase in the gross receipts tax rate to close a $40 million budget deficit and provide critical support for public safety in a city with the nation's highest rate of car thefts and a spiking murder rate.[1] Although its newly elected Democratic mayor had pledged to support tax increases only as a last resort, and only if they were approved by voters, the severity of the budget deficit and crime problems he inherited caused him to backtrack on a major campaign promise, which he did in signing the bill.

The nine-member city council voted 8–1 to raise the tax rate on local goods and services. In this show of bipartisan support, two of the three Republican council members sided with the council's six Democrats to support the legislation. The lone dissenting vote was cast by the council's third Republican member. At the same meeting, the council voted 5–4 to support an amendment requiring that 60 percent of the money generated by the tax be dedicated to public safety. Four of the council's six Democrats voted against the amendment, while the remaining councilors—two Democrats and three Republicans—voted to support it. Public comment at the meeting was against the tax increase, with residents noting an uncompleted and mismanaged transit project cutting through the heart of downtown as an example of city government wasting tax resources.

This vignette illustrates a number of key things about local legislatures. First, city councils make critical decisions on local issues (e.g., public safety and how to pay for it). Second, although the vote on the amendment was divided somewhat by party, with three Republicans joining with two Democrats to constrain how the new money would be used, in the end Democrats and Republicans voted with each other to support both pieces of legislation. The party affiliation of city councilors, even in a nonpartisan city like Albuquerque, can be an important guide to how it might behave, but it is unlikely to cause the kind of gridlock that party polarization causes at higher levels.[2] Third, although councils function according to majority rule, there is no need to send legislative proposals through to a second chamber. Unicameralism, or one-chamber legislatures, is the rule at the local level, not the exception. And fourth, city councils make their decisions in public with active involvement from members of the community.

INSTITUTIONAL CONTEXT OF LOCAL LEGISLATURES

Local legislatures dot the American political landscape, and the decisions they make are critically important for day-to-day quality of life in our cities and counties. In addition, because local governments directly affect the built environment—roads, bridges, public transportation, water and sewage systems, zoning and building codes—more than any other level of government, many local decisions set in motion processes that are, for the most part, irreversible. Service at the local level entails great sacrifice. Candidates must win elections, and once sworn in, they are subject to intense public scrutiny and work pressures—because council or commission positions are most often part time, councilors do not give up their day jobs—all in service to their fellow citizens.

Service on local legislatures has launched the careers of many notable current or former elected officials. Former President Harry S. Truman got his start as an elected official in Jackson County, Missouri, with the help of Kansas City Democratic Party boss Tom Pendergast.[3] Barry Goldwater, the Republican presidential nominee in 1964 and long-time senator from Arizona, got his start on the Phoenix City Council. Joe Biden, vice president under President Barack Obama and US Senator from Delaware, began his career on the New Castle County Council, as did his Senate replacement, Christopher Coons. Other officials who started locally include Dianne Feinstein, the senior Senator from California (San Francisco Board of Supervisors); Martin Heinrich, Senator from New Mexico (Albuquerque City Council); Tim Kaine, Senator from Virginia (Alexandria City Council); and Cory Booker, Senator from New Jersey (Newark City Council). In the US House of Representatives, forty-nine current members (11.3 percent) had served on their local city council or county board prior to winning their House seat.[4]

This chapter focuses on local legislatures, specifically city councils and **county boards**. (There is actually a third, school boards, which are not addressed in this chapter.) These institutions represent city or county residents in the governing process, make laws covering their jurisdictions, and oversee those responsible for executing the laws. They also serve as an important training ground, giving those who serve experience in the art of governance and the practicalities of public administration. Although they share many functions with higher-level legislatures, they are, for a variety of reasons, quite different. This chapter explores these similarities and differences, with an eye to understanding the role of institutions, representation, and policy making in local legislatures.

Before beginning, one caveat is in order. Research on county commissions is inadequate to the task of comparing them to city councils, making it impossible to give them equal time. When available, research based on the descriptive information pertaining to county commissions will be cited to give you a sense of differences and similarities, but for the most part, attention is focused on US city councils. Because they represent a "higher" level of government, this discussion begins with a general overview of county commissions.

County Commissions/Boards of Supervisors

In the forty-eight states that use them, counties are agents of state government, implementing state services in the areas of health, welfare and criminal justice. According to the US Census, there are 3,144 counties in the US, each of which has a legislature, typically referred to as a commission or board of supervisors. Like legislatures generally, county commission or boards represent constituents, make laws, and oversee policy implementation. These commissions or boards are part of the broader governing system at the county level.

A survey prepared by the International City/County Management Association (ICMA) in 2014 identifies three main forms of county government in the US: county commission, commission-administrator, and commission-elected executive.[5]

The **county commission** is the most traditional form of county government and is often considered *unreformed*. Under this system, commissioners perform both legislative and executive functions by serving as elected representatives who craft policy and as executives who direct departments (e.g., public safety, public works, etc.) and implement policy. According to the survey, 26 percent of counties used the county commission form of government. One oddity among the fifty states is Georgia, which is unique in permitting a *sole commissioner* form in which a single elected official has all executive *and* legislative authority. Such governments, once common in rural parts of the state, are rapidly disappearing, though. As late as 1988, 24 of Georgia's 159 counties used this system. By 2015, only eight remained.[6]

The **commission-administrator** form is similar to the council-manager system found in a majority of American cities. Commissioners appoint a chief executive who is responsible for executing county services, preparing and implementing the budget, overseeing department heads, and making policy recommendations to the commission. According to the ICMA survey, approximately 64 percent of counties in the US use this form of government.[7]

Under the third major form, the **commission-elected executive**, the executive is elected countywide, and there is a clear separation of powers between the county commission and the executive branch. The elected executive implements policy, prepares the budget, has veto power (in most cases), and is the political figurehead in the county. This form most closely resembles the separation of powers system at the national level, among the fifty states, and the strong mayor council form often found in large cities. The commission-administrator and commission-elected executive are considered *reformed.*

Most commissioners (58 percent) are elected by ward or district. Only 28 percent of counties report that commissioners are elected at large, while 13 percent use mixed systems of representation, composed of district and at-large commissioners.[8] In mixed systems, on average, two of seven commissioners are elected at large. Eighty-one percent of US counties elect commissioners on the basis of partisan elections where candidates are listed and designated by their party affiliation, the exact opposite of what is found in cities. This is most likely an outgrowth of the closer connection to and control of counties by state governments, which elect officials on a partisan basis.[9] Only 6 percent of counties limit the terms of commissioners.[10] In terms of demographics, most county commissioners are white and male.[11]

Counties have begun to modernize in response to growing demands for services, however. Moving away from the traditional county commission form, they have embraced greater professionalism in the commission-administrator and commission-elected executive forms. Compared to the past, county governments today are considerably more involved in the delivery of urban services, especially in the areas of economic development, planning and zoning, infrastructure, and public safety. In many cases, they have increased their powers, professionalized their governments, and diversified their policy agendas to meet the service demands of county residents and metropolitan regions.[12] Much of this shift is a function of suburban sprawl and the growing necessity to expand services to settlements on the outskirts of central cities.

But do counties effectively *represent* the will of the people in the policy process? On one hand, we expect the connection between the people and elected officials at the local level to be closer than that at the national level. On the other, because local government tends to be less salient in the lives of residents, it is possible that few signals are sent from voters to representatives, and perhaps only from the most politically active residents. According to one study, however, the answer to the representation question would appear to be yes. Garrick Percival, Martin Johnson, and Max Neiman studied counties in California to assess the connection between a county's ideological profile and its policy outputs. They found that the greater the correlation between these two variables, the more responsive county governments were to citizen preferences. More liberal counties spent more than conservative counties on social welfare and education, and more conservative counties spent more than liberal counties on economic development (narrowly defined as infrastructure).[13] While the study did not delve into the role of commissions in these decisions per se, it did indicate that the connection between ideology and spending in counties with home rule charters was stronger than in counties without home rule charters.

City Councils

Cities are both more numerous and more studied than county governments. According to the US Census, there are 19,354 incorporated places (i.e., municipalities) in the US. An **incorporated place** is a settlement of people that is legally recognized as a municipal corporation, or municipality. Each of these municipalities has a city or town council,[14] with an average size of six members.[15]

Unlike state politics scholars who study state legislatures through the lens of legislative professionaliam, or congressional scholars who study Congress through the lens of the *electoral connection*, there is no agreed-upon framework or lens through which to study city councils.[16] However, according to public administration scholar James Svara, local governance involves four main components: mission, policy, administration, and management. **Mission** is a statement of broad policy goals and should be established by a city's elected officials. **Policy** represents the decisions and actions of government that, ideally, support its effort to accomplish its mission.[17] **Administration** refers to the execution of policy, while **management** concerns organizational matters, such as overseeing the personnel needs of city government. In theory, city councils should take the lead in mission and policy, while chief executives (city managers and mayors) should play a stronger role in administration and management.

In practice, however, councils exercise very little authority or even presence in any of these roles.[18] Comparing executive-legislative interaction in six mayor-council and six council-manager cities, Svara found that city councils tend to focus more on representational items, such as dealing with constituents and responding to group demands, than on their policy-making responsibilities, especially in council-manager and strong mayor-council cities. An exception to this might be the council in a city with a weak mayor-council form of government. Because such councils have both legislative and executive powers, especially in appointing top executive officials and overseeing policy execution, they may pay more attention to their lawmaking duties. In general, though, while city councils tend to represent constituents well, they are weak policy makers.

City institutions influence who serves on the city council and the kind of representation its residents can expect. The power and visibility of city councils depends on the form of government. Most cities use either the council-manager or mayor-council form. The council-manager system is clearly more popular; 59 percent of cities employ the council-manager form, while 33 percent use the mayor-council system. The other 8 percent use either the commission or town meeting form, both of which are popular among small towns in the Northeast.[19]

The council-manager system does away with the traditional system of separation of powers largely preserved by the mayor-council system. In council-manager cities, an elected city council appoints a manager to run the day-to-day operations of city government. While the manager is institutionally separate from the city council, he or she is not independent from it, however. These systems empower elected officials in the formation of policy but give professional administrators power over implementation.

By contrast, mayor-council systems are designed to empower elected officials in both legislative and executive functions. The voters select the city council and mayor, who collectively make policy. In some cities, especially larger ones, the mayor is institutionally strong, meaning that they have extensive powers over the executive branch of local government and can play a powerful role in setting the city's agenda via the budgetary process and/or their veto power. In the weak mayor variation of the mayor-council system, in which city councils are strongest, the mayor may have some appointment powers and will preside over council meetings but is weak in terms of executive powers. Table 5.1 presents descriptive data on the institutional features of city government relevant to city councils.

To illustrate the variations in the practical challenges of representation, table 5.2 shows council size in the nation's ten largest cities. Although city population size is a good predictor of council size, the two are not perfectly correlated. New York City, which has a population of 8.5 million, has only fifty-one council members, while Chicago, a city one-third the size of New York, has fifty. Los Angeles, the nation's second largest city at almost four million people, has only fifteen members. On average, then, New York City councilors represent 167,655 residents, while in Los Angeles and Chicago the numbers are 264,792 and 54,411 respectively. So the challenge of representing constituents in these three cities is considerably different.

The form of government, ballot structure, and size of city councils are regionally based. In comparison to older cities in the Northeast and Midwest, cities in the Sunbelt region of the US favored a *reformed* system of local government, which resulted in smaller city councils. As Sunbelt cities have grown, the number of constituents represented by each councilor has grown as well. Other factors influencing the size of city councils are "the complexity of services provided, the council's workload, the diversity and size of the population, the political dynamics and preferences of the city."[20]

TABLE 5.1	Institutional Features of US City Councils
Institutional Feature	Percentage/Average
Council-Manager Form	59%
Mayor-Council Form	33%
Council Size	6
At-Large Representation	66%
District	17%
Mixed	17%
Nonpartisan Ballots	80%
Staggered Terms	85%
Committee Use	66%
Council Staff	16%

Note: Data are from the 2011 International City/County Management Association Form of Government Survey.

The Functions of City Councils | 99

TABLE 5.2	Representation in Top Ten US Cities, 2017				
City	Population	Number of City Council Seats	Avg. Residents per District	Number of Committees	Salary
New York City	8,550,405	51	167,655	35	$148,500
Los Angeles	3,971,883	15	264,792	17	$184,610
Chicago	2,720,546	50	54,411	17	$115,000
Houston	2,296,224	11 districts	208,748	10	$ 62,983
		5 at-large	2,296,224		
Philadelphia	1,567,442	10 districts	156,774	24	$129,632
		7 at-large	1,567,442		
Phoenix	1,563,025	8	195,378	5	$ 61,599
San Antonio	1,469,845	10	146,985	10	$45,722[a]
San Diego	1,394,928	9	154,992	10	$ 75,000
Dallas	1,300,092	14	92,864	6	$ 60,000
San Jose	1,026,908	10	102,691	7	$ 97,204

Note: Population data are from the US Census. Number of seats information was gathered from relevant city websites. [a]This salary was set by voters in 2015 through an amendment to the city charter. Before the charter amendment, the salary for San Antonio councilors was $20 per meeting, or about $1,040 per year.

Source: Ballotpedia, "City of San Antonio Council and Mayor Salaries, Amendment 2 (May 2015)," https://ballotpedia.org/City_of_San_Antonio_Council_and_Mayor_Salaries,_Amendment_2_(May_2015), accessed October 17, 2018.

THE FUNCTIONS OF CITY COUNCILS

The nature and scope of what city councils do are shaped by form of government and state law.[21] City councils make laws, represent constituents, and oversee executives. *Lawmaking* refers to the formulation and adoption of ordinances, or city laws. Table 5.3 summarizes the main city council functions and gives examples of activities that fall within each category.[22]

TABLE 5.3	Functions of US City Councils
Function	Examples
Representation	Communicating policies and programs to constituents; responding to constituent complaints and needs; helping to represent city to other levels of government
Lawmaking	Approving budgets; establishing tax rates; borrowing funds; modifying city charters; passing ordinances and resolutions; regulating land use through zoning codes; regulating local businesses through licensing and regulations; regulating health and safety; exercising eminent domain powers
Oversight and Management	Establishing long- and short-term objectives; overseeing performance of local public employees; entering into legal contracts

Note: Information is from National League of Cities, "City Councils," http://www.nlc.org/city-councils, accessed June 19, 2017. Row categories defined by the authors.

City councils are *political* bodies, elected by voters to serve as the public's representatives in city government. As indicated in the opening vignette, their deliberations and actions are public, and therefore subject to intense public scrutiny, especially from local media.[23] They must frequently balance competing differences of opinion, whether the action under consideration is an economic initiative, police reform, or enactment of the city budget. In contrast to members of Congress, city councilors live and work among those they serve on a daily basis, and many, if not most, are contacted around the clock by constituents (e.g., at the local grocery store or a child's sporting event) to address some concern or another.

While Congress, state legislatures, county commissions, and city councils share some similarities, essential differences are important to bear in mind. Unlike Congress, forty-nine out of fifty state legislatures, and most county commissions, roughly 80 percent of councils are elected on a nonpartisan basis. In addition, service is typically part time. Like the US Senate, but unlike the US House and state legislatures, most city councils (85%) use **staggered terms**, meaning that roughly half of the seats are up for election in any given election cycle. This is done to ensure continuity and institutional memory. The larger the city, the more likely that a seat on the city council will resemble legislative service in larger states; the smaller the city, the more likely that it will resemble a form of civic duty.[24]

Another difference from higher-level governments is pay and service. Members of Congress serve full time and earn an average annual salary of $174,000. State legislative salaries vary tremendously, with legislators in New Mexico earning $0 in salary for their service and legislators in California earning $100,113 each year.[25] Some states link salary to number of days in service, and most also pay a per diem during legislative sessions (plus mileage reimbursement for travel to the legislature). According to the ICMA municipal government survey, 83 percent of cities pay their city councilors for their service. Average pay for full-time councils is $8,000 per year, while the average for part-time councils is $5,156. Obviously, city councilors cannot make a living as elected officials in most places. This, however, conceals significant variation based on city size. In the ten cities over one million population in the US, average pay for full-time councilors is $56,298, while average pay for part-time councilors is $40,500. Another way to examine this is to consider that city councilors in San Mateo, California (population 102,893) are paid $7,200 annually for *part-time* service, while those in Los Angeles (population 3.9 million) are paid $184,610 for *full-time* service, which is more than what members of the US Congress earn.

REPRESENTING CONSTITUENTS

In general, representation means to speak or to act for others (see chapter 1). In the US, we live in a representative democracy, which means that we elect others to represent our interests in government. Our expectation is that elected officials will faithfully serve our interests; in other words, we expect them to be accountable.

But how do we know when this is happening? The short answer is that we do not, in part because of the **principal-agent problem**.[26] This challenge of self-government requires that principals, or those with power (in the US system, the people), monitor the behavior of agents (e.g., elected officials) to ensure that they do what principals want. As you might imagine, this is a very difficult challenge, even at the local level. City residents rely on local media and organizations to point out what is happening in the city so that they can be better informed. During elections, challengers point out flaws in incumbents' (agents') records of service and explain to principals how they would do a better job. In the governing process, policy debates can provide information about what is at stake so that the public can effectively evaluate each side of an issue. Anticipating public reactions, elected officials modify their behavior in ways that will be met with satisfaction.

These are all imperfect mechanisms to ensure *accountability*, or the idea that elected officials must answer to the voters in regular elections to determine whether they will continue their service. Two other contextual factors make accountability even more difficult. First, as noted throughout this text, local government, somewhat ironically, is often the level that people follow and/or participate in the least. Second, the media landscape is changing. Although newspapers cover local government more than most other news outlets, fewer people are reading them.[27] Together, these factors threaten the promise of urban democracy in the US because they make holding elected officials accountable considerably more difficult.

Descriptive Representation: Election System, Ballot Structure, and City Council Professionalism

As noted in chapter 1, there are two main types of representation: descriptive and substantive. Descriptive representation examines the connection between characteristics of a population and the composition of its governing institutions, while substantive representation asks whether the diversity present in a community is reflected in the community's policy process.[28] These types relate to the principal-agent problem in the following way. By electing a set of leaders that, in demographic and political terms, is reflective of the population it serves, the people will have greater confidence that government actions will be in their interests. In the absence of descriptive representation, substantive representation is still possible, but monitoring elected officials is more complicated. (On the flip side, it is entirely possible that descriptively representative officials will not substantively represent the voters.)

Cities with large concentrations of minority residents are likely to have more representatives on the city council, as demographic strength translates to seats.[29] Representation systems affect descriptive representation above and beyond population characteristics, however. Three different systems are used to choose city councilors: **single-member districts**, at-large representation systems, and **mixed-representation systems**. Under single-member districts, councilors represent a subset of the city's population in what are referred to as districts or wards. Single-member districts focus representation on a particular set of neighborhoods and areas within a city, helping to personalize the link between residents and representatives. In at-large systems, councilors are elected by the city as a whole; consequently, their representational focus is on citywide issues. Cities with mixed-representation systems combine these two formats in order to derive the benefits of both representation systems.[30] Early-20th-century reformers argued that at-large systems were more effective than single-member districts because councilors elected at large would represent the interests of the entire city as opposed to a subset of city residents, eliminating district-based turf battles and ensuring that the interests of all would be considered first in council decisions. At-large systems are used in 66 percent of cities, while 34 percent (split evenly) use ward/district or mixed systems (see tables 5.1 and 5.2).[31] The trend is away from at-large systems and toward single-member districts and mixed systems.[32]

Scholars explore descriptive representation by examining the relationship between representation system type, population characteristics (e.g., proportions of particular racial and ethnic groups), and composition of governing institutions (e.g., presence; number/percentage of black, Latino, and female councilors).[33] A city council that "looks" like the population it serves can be identified as descriptively representative.

How can descriptive representation be measured? One way is by examining the **parity ratio**, the ratio between the percentage of a particular group in the population and the percentage represented on the city council. If, say, the percentage of one group in the population (e.g., Latinos) is 25 and the percentage of that same group on the city council is 25, then the ratio is 1:1, or at parity. If the ratio is greater than this, say 2:1, a group is overrepresented; less, and a group is underrepresented. Say that women are 10 percent of the council but half the population. The parity ratio would be 0.2. This can be applied to all groups (gender, race/ethnicity, occupation, party affiliation, etc.) as a way of helping to determine the descriptive representation of not only city councils, but all governmental bodies.[34]

Institutional arrangements affect the ability of minority groups to gain representation on city councils. As noted earlier, in single-member districts, councilors represent a particular territory within the city. Map 5.1 shows city council district lines in the city of Seattle, which elects seven members from districts and two at large. By contrast, at-large systems require each city council candidate to compete citywide for a seat, and selection is often based on the number of seats on the council, not where the candidates live. Visualize map 5.1 without the lines separating the nine council districts.

Because groups tend to be residentially concentrated and because subgroups by definition lack the voting power of the majority, it is difficult for them to win a seat on the city council in a municipality with at-large representation.[35] District representation systems solve this problem (see box 5.1). Given patterns of residential segregation, district mapmakers—in most cases city councilors—can draw boundaries around minority communities, essentially guaranteeing that people within those borders will be able to elect someone of their choosing. In contrast, at-large elections harm the ability of minority groups to achieve representation, resulting in considerable litigation about their constitutionality.[36] All things being equal, however, at-large systems are not by definition

Map 5.1 Map of Seattle City Council Districts

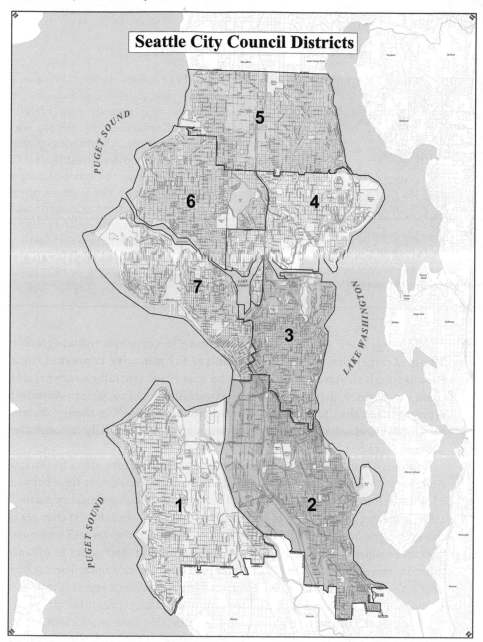

Source: King County, "Seattle City Council Districts," https://www.kingcounty.gov/~/media/depts/
elections/elections/maps/seattle-city-council-maps/seattle-city-council-districts.ashx?la=en

unconstitutional. It is only when they are combined with a sufficiently large and
residentially concentrated minority community, racialized campaigns, and patterns of racial bloc voting (such as majority white voters voting as a bloc against
black candidates and vice versa) that these systems become legally dubious and
harmful to minority interests.[37]

BOX 5.1

Harvey Milk Launches a Political Movement

Harvey Milk Celebrates His Election Victory. Campaign Manager Anne Kronenburg on Motorcycle

In November 1977, when Harvey Milk won a seat on the San Francisco Board of Supervisors, he became the first openly gay official ever elected in California. His victory was significant because it brought political power to a community that had been subjected to years of discrimination on the basis of sexual orientation. Often lost in the discussion of Milk's ascension to power as spokesperson for San Francisco's gay community is that it probably would not have happened were it not for the city's shift from at-large to single-member district elections. In fact, in 1975 when Milk first ran, the city used an at-large system,

The degree of residential concentration is key when thinking about single-member districts as a mechanism for minority representation. Because African Americans tend to be more residentially concentrated than, say, Latinos, districts are more powerfully linked to African American representation than to Hispanic representation in cities.[38] In theory, district elections should enhance the representation of any residentially concentrated subgroup (see box 5.2).[39]

Research from the early 1980s suggested that the negative effect for African Americans of at-large systems appeared to have diminished over time because of three factors: (1) changes in the law that expanded black political opportunities; (2) greater acceptability of black political involvement; and (3) changes in the campaigns of black candidates.[40] More recent data, however, call into question the conclusion that single-member districts have lost their power to enhance minority representation. One study examined over 300 city council and school board elections to determine the effect of districts on black representation. It found that districts remain critical for producing black representation—especially in crossing the representational hurdle of electing even one African American councilor—but that the size and concentration of the black population are critical as well. The number of seats on the council is also key for increasing the number of black councilors.[41]

Representation systems have more limited effects on the representation of women, who comprise only 29 percent of city councilors in the typical city.[42] Although women are generally underrepresented in legislatures, at the city level this is not because of the nature of council representation systems. Indeed, because they are not residentially concentrated, women have tended to be and Milk lost. By 1977, the city had created a single-member district that encompassed The Castro, an area at the heart of San Francisco's gay community. With more favorable political geography, Milk used his name recognition from previous campaigns, his experience as a small businessman, and his status as a gay activist to secure victory.

Milk's story ended in tragedy, however. He and Mayor George Moscone were assassinated in City Hall by Dan White, who, as a former member of the San Francisco Board of Supervisors, had served alongside Milk. Ironically, the person who announced the news on the night of the assassinations was newly sworn-in Mayor Diane Feinstein, who prior to the assassinations was president of the board on which Milk and White had served (and who is now the senior US Senator from California).

White claimed during his trial that he had diminished capacity as a result of eating too much junk food, in what became known derisively as the "Twinkie Defense." Although he escaped a life sentence, White later committed suicide in prison.

Source: History, "Harvey Milk," http://www.history.com/topics/harvey-milk, accessed June 16, 2017.

more *fairly* represented in cities with at-large systems.[43] The argument was that women were more successful in at-large systems because voters have more than one option in these contests.

Does this apply to women of color? Some research shows that at-large systems improve the electoral chances of white women only, not all female candidates.[44] Other work indicates no relationship at all between election structure and female representation.[45] The representation of women is greater in larger cities, where more women in professions (e.g., law and business) that lead to political involvement and success are likely to be found, perhaps along with more tolerant attitudes toward female political leadership.[46] In sum, districts matter less for groups that are either (a) not geographically concentrated, or (b) so large that they would be advantaged by at-large systems.[47] And when *national* minority groups constitute *local* majorities, district systems may actually enhance the representation of whites in city governments at the expense of nonwhites. The type of representation system is only part of the explanation of what produces greater descriptive representation in cities. City demographic factors such as minority population size, minority residential concentration, voting age population, and education and income levels create the essential building blocks of political success.[48]

Representation systems and the structure of the ballot, whether it is partisan or nonpartisan, may also effect what interests are represented on city councils. People with higher incomes and higher levels of education are more likely to be elected in cities with at-large election systems compared to district systems. Upper-income people are also more likely to be elected in cities with nonpartisan ballots.[49] The connection between the socioeconomic and

BOX 5.2

Arab American Representation in Dearborn, Michigan

In 2013, voters in Dearborn, Michigan, a city of 95,535 residents and a local political system long dominated by Irish, Italians, and Poles, elected an Arab American majority to its city council for the first time in its history.[a] At 40 percent of the population, this large minority group was poised to achieve representational parity, or representation in line with its population size. It did one better, though. By winning four of the seven council seats, or 57 percent, Arab Americans are now overrepresented on the council by 17 percentage points.

The case of Dearborn illustrates a number of key ideas about descriptive representation. First, local legislatures should represent the population as a whole. Second, once a group in the population reaches a certain percentage, district election systems cease to be the most effective route for maximizing representation. Under Dearborn's charter, or

demographic characteristics of officeholders and how interests are represented is discussed more fully below.

The relationship between ballot type and party representation has also been studied extensively. By examining the partisan characteristics of a community and the partisan identification of those elected, scholars have sought to understand whether nonpartisan ballots generate a Republican bias in local officeholding. Early research supported the conclusion that Republicans were advantaged in nonpartisan cities. This was due to higher voter turnout among Republican voters active in the kinds of business and civic organizations from which local candidates were recruited in cities with nonpartisan ballots.[50] Later research showed that the Republican advantage in nonpartisan cities was weak and limited to smaller cities in the West that also used at-large systems of representation.[51] Most recently, Brian Schaffner, Matthew Streb, and Gerald Wright show that Republican candidates are not advantaged when nonpartisan ballots are used to select officials. Instead, candidates from the minority party in a jurisdiction, be it a city or a state, are advantaged because partisan ballots exaggerate the effects of party affiliation in the minds of voters. When this cue is absent, voters are forced to assess candidates on the basis of other criteria, which more often than not gives an advantage to candidates who would otherwise be disadvantaged if their party *was* officially disclosed on the ballot. Put simply, nonpartisan ballots level the playing field for candidates who would otherwise be disadvantaged.[52] It is not clear whether women are disadvantaged in nonpartisan systems, however. The argument in favor of nonpartisan ballots boosting women's electoral prospects in city council elections focused on the idea that women would not have to compete in party primary elections dominated by male party leaders and voters. Nonpartisan ballots, in other words, were seen as more open and hospitable to female candidacies. However, studies employing varied samples and methodologies indicate that the nature of the ballot has no effect on the proportion of women on city councils.[53]

local constitution, councilors are chosen at large. Had they used districts as the basis of representation, depending on how the lines were drawn, Dearborn's Arab Americans may have been underrepresented. As one group gets near 50 percent of the population, district systems do not yield the representational gains that might be had in at-large systems. Third, it illustrates the dilemma for newcomer groups in politics. According to newspaper coverage, there was concern about whether this minority group would govern on behalf of the entire community or seek to use power to advance causes near and dear to them. These latter concerns are the stuff of substantive representation. Susan Dabaja, Michael Sareini, David Bazzy, and Robert Abraham were all reelected in 2017.

[a] Niraj Warikoo, "Arab Americans Become Majority on Dearborn Council," *USA Today*, https://www.usatoday.com/story/news/nation/2013/11/06/arab-americans-become-majority-on-dearborn-mich-council/3460591/, accessed June 16, 2017.

Source: Jessica Strachan, "Taking the Oath: Dearborn's Elected Officials Sworn in to Serve City," *The Press & Guide*, January 10, 2018, http://www.pressandguide.com/news/taking-the-oath-dearborn-s-elected-officials-sworn-in-to/article_4a6f5074-dcb1-5286-b321-405630ac699d.html, accessed June 17, 2019.

Variation in city councilor occupational background is another way to examine representation. Unlike the narrow jurisdictions of special-purpose government (e.g., school districts, water authorities, cemetery districts, fire districts, and mosquito abatement districts), city councils are a part of general-purpose governments, so, as explained in chapter 1, they have general jurisdiction to address a broader scope of issues. However, certain issues, such as economic development, capture most of their time and energy. Research by Timothy Bledsoe, therefore, showed, not surprisingly, that more city councilors came from the business community than from any other occupation, including the legal profession.[54] He also found that the types of occupations represented on a city council are related to its *stature*, or professionalism, measured by the salary paid to councilors and the amount of staff and office space provided to them. Full-time councilors, lawyers, professionals, and entrepreneurs were more likely to serve on city councils with greater statures, whereas homemakers, students, and blue-collar workers were more likely to serve on city councils with low stature. The same patterns generally held in larger cities and in cities with a greater scope of duties (measured as mayor-council government).[55] Not surprisingly, a large majority of councilors do not have experience in government or community service prior to running for office, but among those who do, positions on city boards or commissions or leadership roles in community organizations are common. This is especially the case for female city councilors.[56]

Substantive Representation: Constituency Service and Lawmaking

The public also expects substantive representation from city councils to reflect the diverse views and interests of a community in the governing process.[57] They also expect the action of local government to reflect the will of the people.

Therefore, an important starting point in thinking about this form of representation is how city councilors view their constituencies.

A city's system of representation affects the *focus* of representation among those who serve. Representatives must decide at any given moment who they speak for: the collective interests of the larger entity, the city as a whole, or the narrower interests of those who live within their districts. This holds true even for city councilors elected at large. While they will tend to see the entire city as their main constituency, their neighborhood interests may take precedence on particular issues. Cross-pressure arises if a council member's political base in a certain part of the city is pitted against the interests of the city as a whole on a particular issue. Whose interests get protected? Similarly, there will be times when pressure from the broader community will cause a district councilor to consider voting against the interests of his or her constituency. In general, district councilors view their districts as their focal points, whereas those elected at large perceive theirs as the city as a whole.[58]

Constituency Service

Constituency service, or the practice of representing and responding to constituent demands, is a key form of substantive representation. In contrast to our knowledge about the US Congress, we know little about the role city councilors play in responding to public demands for action. We do know that the type of election system (at-large or district system) influences how council members perceive their role in constituency service. District councilors tend to devote more time and energy to constituency service than members elected at large, whose connections to particular constituents, areas, or groups and willingness to work on specific problems are weaker.[59]

According to one study, demand and supply come into play regarding constituency service at the council level, at least in the area of economic development.[60] Personal characteristics, institutional factors, and electoral politics influence *demand* from constituents. Councilors who devote a greater portion of their time to council work receive more requests for service on economic development issues than councilors who commit less time to council duties. The same goes for district councilors when compared to those elected at large. District councilors represent smaller areas than at-large councilors, therefore they are more in tune with district concerns and more accessible when constituents ask for service. District councilors with more diverse campaign support networks receive more calls for service than those with less diverse campaign support networks and those elected at large, suggesting that the seeds of substantive representation are sown in council campaigns. Despite these influences, media coverage of economic development issues has the largest effect on demand for constituency service.[61] Not surprisingly, when things are covered in the news, councilors hear about them.

A combination of personal characteristics, institutional variables, and political factors also influence the *supply* of constituency service.[62] The supply of constituency service refers to whether city councilors are acting on the demands they receive from constituents. More senior councilors and those who devote more time to council duties intervene more regularly on behalf of constituents concerned about economic development issues compared to less senior members and those who devote fewer hours to their council duties. Like demand, the supply of constituency service is affected by the nature of their campaign support networks; those with diverse campaign support are more likely to contact economic development agencies on behalf of constituents than those with less diverse networks. This research shows not only that city councilors use constituency service as a means of providing substantive representation but that they provide it in proportion to the demand they receive for it.

City councilors also provide substantive representation in their dealings with the city bureaucracy. Minority council representation translates into more black and Latino job applicants being hired, as they use their power to modify hiring policies and practices and alter the composition of the city workforce. Examining numerous categories of municipal employment, scholars have generally concluded that black and Latino representation on city councils, measured in relation to the local minority population, leads to greater diversity in city hiring.[63] This does not apply to the representation of women, however; one study examining a number of cities over several years showed little impact from having more female council representation.[64]

Lawmaking

Substantive representation is perhaps most important in lawmaking. The basic process of lawmaking at the city level is fairly straightforward. Legislative proposals are drafted, often in committees, then voted on by the full chamber. If the local governing body does not have a separately elected chief executive (e.g., council-manager system at the city level and county commission or commission-administrator form at the county level), most proposals become law with a simple majority. If the local government executive has veto power, the proposal must get their signature before it becomes law. About three-quarters of city mayors have the power to veto legislation. In almost all cases, city councils can override a veto with a super-majority vote.[65]

To consider legislation, city councils meet in formal session. Sixty-six percent of the city councils meet in formal session twice per month, while 26 percent meet once per month.[66] Meetings are usually held in the evenings and can go on for many hours. City councilors also meet in committee sessions; about two-thirds of city councils have standing committees to help them craft policy proposals. What is unique about council meetings that distinguishes them from other legislatures is the degree to which ordinary citizens become involved in the process of local self-governance they make suggestions, offer criticism, and, on occasion, praise the council.[67] Unlike legislatures at higher levels, councilors conduct their business with their bosses (i.e., taxpayers and voters) watching and asking questions about what they are doing.

Two questions have guided scholarly inquiry into council policy making: (1) How independently can councils act from city executives who have both legal and informational advantages and make policies backed by sufficient expertise? and (2) How do institutional features of city government influence levels of conflict and cooperation among councilors and between councilors and city executives? Councils in all but the largest cities tend to be weak policy makers, in part because they lack the institutionalization that will allow them to respond effectively to policy challenges. As noted previously, they are typically part time and have little staff support, an essential element of legislative professionalization and independence. Only 16 percent of city councils have staff resources available to aid them in policy and constituency relations.[68] Because they function as collective bodies but get elected as individuals, there may be little incentive to prioritize policy making over serving constituents important to reelection. City councils are less institutionalized than the city's chief executive, a feature of urban politics that can negatively affect their ability to function independently as lawmaking bodies.

Legislative committees allow councils to strengthen their policy-making role. Committees allow legislatures to manage their workloads, enable policy making to be more efficient, and provide information valuable in formulating policy. Committees are used to make proposals and study policy alternatives, conduct public hearings, oversee the chief executive, and evaluate the effectiveness and efficiency of existing programs.[69] Their use may also help cities attract intergovernmental aid to support local spending and policy efforts.[70] In general, committees enhance the lawmaking capacity of city councils.

Constituent pressures and needs influence policy making as well. District systems are expected to engage in turf battles, in which councilors defend one another's prerogatives over matters in their districts, and in **logrolling**, or vote-trading at the expense of the interests of the city as a whole. This, of course, was the argument of urban reformers in the early 20th century (see chapter 2).[71] Districts create incentives for this kind of behavior, especially given the motivation of elected officials to be reelected,[72] but has it resulted in practice? One study showed that district representatives and minority councilors are more likely to favor economic development programs targeted to particular groups or constituencies than other councilors, in part because of their desire to serve constituents.[73] However, district systems may not always lead to the kind of logrolling in which councilors vote for one another's proposals with the expectation that the favor will be returned. In Los Angeles, city councilors often defer to other councilors on routine issues facing their own districts but not on those with the potential for citywide impact.[74] In Chicago, councilors respect one another's prerogative to determine what is in the best interests of their districts in the realm of historic preservation (and other matters) so long as such initiatives are solely contained within a single district; they cooperate less when such initiatives include multiple community areas and multiple council wards.[75] In general, then, logrolling and turf-based forms of behavior are context-specific.

Lawmaking involves conflict.[76] Like the other aspects of city councils discussed in this chapter, the amount of conflict present in a city council is rooted in its governing and electoral institutions.[77] In general, reformed institutions—council-manager government, nonpartisan ballots, and at-large elections—are thought to promote greater policy cooperation. A survey of mayors, councilors, and chief administrative officers showed that perceptions of conflict were significantly greater in mayor-council systems than in council-manager systems.[78] And while the amount of conflict is not different, city councils with district systems tend to have more turf-based conflicts than cities with at-large elections.[79] Similarly, city councils selected on the basis of partisan ballots tend to have more partisan conflicts.[80]

Council policy making and policy decisions are also affected by the agendas of mayors and managers. If the city council and the mayor generally agree, then the process is likely to be smooth and policy outcomes easier to achieve. If they do not, things may break down.[81] City councils must deal with managers and bureaucrats as well. The nature of each of these relationships affects how well city government is able to respond to the policy challenges they face and to represent the interests of city residents.[82] The roles of mayors, managers, and bureaucrats are addressed more fully in chapter 6.

Beyond institutions, demographic factors, such as age and race, and party affiliation may increase policy conflict on city councils. Political scientist Susan MacManus's study of Florida city councilors showed that different age cohorts differed in their assessments of the importance of crime, police, welfare, moral issues, and transportation, with older council members identifying greater generational differences on these issues.[83] Regardless of age, council members agreed that different generations have different policy preferences on issues such as taxes, growth, parks and recreation, education, and economic issues.

Race and ethnicity may also be a source of conflict on city councils. In the 1980s, after Chicago elected its first African American mayor, Harold Washington, the council entered a period of gridlock, known locally as "Council Wars" (after the *Star Wars* movies), in which its white majority sided against Washington's legislative program and against the African American and Hispanic councilors who supported him. Whether city councils more generally are polarized on racial or ethnic grounds is not clear, however. Rory Austin compared roll-call voting patterns in three northern cities (New Haven, Connecticut; Rochester, New York; and Springfield, Massachusetts) to three southern cities (Huntsville, Alabama; Raleigh, North Carolina; and Alexandria, Virginia) from 1987 to 1996. He found little evidence that legislative minorities composed of African American councilors were consistently outvoted by legislative majorities composed of white councilors. Only in Alexandria was there any evidence of racially polarized voting.[84]

Party loyalty is another dimension on which city councils might experience conflict. Studying 2 years' worth of roll-call votes on a range of issues in San Diego, Craig Burnett discovered that despite the city's official nonpartisanship, the party affiliations of councilors was indeed a significant source of lawmaking conflict, especially on budget and land use matters (compared to general policy questions). In other words, members of the Democratic Party tended to side with one another against members of the Republican Party—and on some of the most important issues facing the city. However, despite its importance in national and state politics, whether the party affiliation of councilors constitutes a consistent source of conflict on city councils more generally is an open question.

Do City Councils Deliver Substantive Representation?

There are a couple of ways to look at this question. One is to examine the connection between descriptive representation and substantive representation. The other is whether substantive representation fits the policy preferences of the community in general.

The benefits of descriptive representation are both substantive and symbolic. Adequate representation enhances the ability of local government to respond effectively to the diverse policy interests of the community. It leads to greater diversity within city bureaucracies that can influence local government policies and delivery of services to city residents. For example, police-community relations often improve when the ranks of city leaders, both elected and appointed, are more diverse. In addition, more diverse council representation produces more diverse appointments to city boards and commissions, allowing a broader range of voices to be heard in local policy making.[85] Minority representation, often a function of greater voter turnout in city elections, is associated with greater spending on social services, something that opinion surveys suggest minorities prefer more than whites.[86] When political institutions are more diverse, local residents' attitudes about race relations and government service generally improve.[87]

Do city councils represent the policy interests of their cities as a whole? Scholars commonly examine this by attempting to connect indicators of a city's policy preferences to revenue and spending priorities of city government. One study, for example, found that Democratic-leaning cities spend more overall— and more on public safety, public transportation, public worker salaries, and parks and recreation—than Republican-leaning cities. It also found that Democratic-leaning cities received more funding from state and federal governments.[88] Research also shows that city governments respond to the ideological preferences of their residents. More conservative cities produce more conservative policies, spend and tax less, and rely more on sales taxes than on property and income taxes—resulting in a more regressive tax structure—than cities with more liberal populations.[89] Although party and ideology may be important sources of conflict on city councils, scholars have not examined the direct connection between these factors and city council policy decisions. Nevertheless, in general, it would appear that cities—and their elected representatives—do a good job of accurately representing residents' policy interests.

SUMMARY

City councils and county commissions are the most common forms of legislatures in the US. The largest area of study, and the one that has generated the most controversy, is the effect of electoral institutions—in particular, representation systems (district versus at-large)—on the composition of city councils and the behavior of legislators. The controversy stems from the impact of systems on the ability of racial and minority ethnic groups to achieve representation in the local political arena. The legacy of discrimination, especially in housing, and the natural tendency of people to self-segregate on the basis of racial and ethnic identification creates entire neighborhoods and great swaths of our largest cities composed of a single racial or ethnic group. Because of this concentration, at-large representation systems put minority groups at a natural political disadvantage, and at risk, when combined with racial bloc voting and racially charged campaigns, of violating the US Constitution's one person, one vote principle.

Governing and electoral institutions affect many other aspects of local legislatures. Everything from orientation toward representational role to legislation to overseeing the executive is significantly affected by what institutions are in place. Unlike the US Congress, or even a professionalized state legislature, the powers of most local legislatures are limited, not only by the governing charter but also by state law. And while city councils in our nation's largest cities are full time, well staffed, and well compensated, all councils (and county commissions) are greatly affected by the "rules of the game," a core theme of this text.

The rules can be changed, of course, which is why scholars and practitioners seek to understand their effects. Changing the rules is far easier than changing citizens' attitudes about racial and ethnic minorities or women serving in public office. That said, change to governing institutions is more frequent than you might imagine. Although the Progressive Reform Era was more than 100 years ago, city and county governments change governing systems often. The most common change is one that enhances the power of chief executives in city governance, the subject of chapter 6.[90]

Key Terms

administration *(97)*

city council *(93)*

commission-administrator *(95)*

commission-elected executive *(96)*

constituency service *(108)*

county board *(95)*

county commission *(95)*

incorporated place *(97)*

logrolling *(110)*

management *(97)*

mission *(97)*

mixed-representation system *(101)*

parity ratio *(102)*

principal-agent problem *(101)*

single-member districts *(101)*

staggered terms *(100)*

Discussion Questions

1. In what way(s) do the institutional contexts of county commissions and city councils differ?

2. In general, what is meant by representation? More specifically, what is the difference between descriptive and substantive representation?

3. In practical terms, how do councilors represent constituent interests?

How is this affected by institutional arrangements in cities?

4. Why are city councils thought of as weak policy makers but strong advocates for their constituents?

5. Does descriptive representation lead to substantive representation in city government? Why or why not?

Exercises

1. Choose a county in your state and identify its largest city (aka the "county seat"). Compare and contrast the forms of government and electoral institutions at both levels of government. Make a note of the number of legislators at each level, the number of people they represent, and the demographic compositions of the constituencies.

2. Choose a sample of cities in your state. Collect census information on the demographics of each city. Then compare the city's

demographics to the demographics of those serving in council positions. What is the parity ratio?

3. Interview a member of your city council or county board to learn more about the legislative process in local legislatures. In what ways is the process shaped by institutional factors? Also ask them about the role they play in representing constituent interests through constituency casework and in policy debates (e.g., over zoning disputes, police protection, city government services).

Practice and Review Online
https://textbooks.rowman.com/understanding-urban-politics

6

MAYORS AND EXECUTIVES

GUIDING QUESTIONS

1. What is the context of mayoral leadership and why are some mayors considered more successful than others?
2. How do formal and informal powers influence a mayor's ability to lead?
3. What are the main elements of the political environment of urban managers and administrators?
4. How do institutions and representation affect the ability of managers and administrators to lead urban bureaucracies?
5. What are the main types of constitutional officers in city and county government?

THE CITY MAYOR is the most visible and influential figure in local politics. Whether the city is small, medium, or large, the point-person for action on city problems is the mayor, or, as they like to say in Chicago, "Da Mayor," or in New York City, "Hizzoner."

When you arrive at an airport, you are likely to see a picture of the city's mayor welcoming you as you head to pick up your bags and a similar message as you leave the airport parking lot. In a small but important way, this highlights the mayor's role as community promoter. Visitors are often a key part of a city's economic development plan, helping to pump up the local economy by spending money in restaurants, at cultural attractions, and at professional sporting events, so mayors thank them for coming to town. Mayors also promote the city through their efforts to recruit and retain well-paying jobs and when they deal with state or federal officials over money for urban needs. At times, however, mayors are called upon to defend cities against unwanted actions of higher-level governments. States may seek to preempt local governments from doing things they otherwise wish to do (e.g., raise the local minimum wage) or the federal government might want to reduce funding in critical areas (e.g., law enforcement or infrastructure).[1]

In addition to the president and the nation's governors, mayors and local government managers constitute a third layer of executive leadership in the US.[2] As you will see, the chief executive may be elected or appointed, but each type of executive functions in a highly political environment. Because the mayor's job is the most prominent of all elected positions in local government, this chapter begins there before moving on to a discussion of elected and appointed administrators and local constitutional officers.

THE CONTEXT OF MAYORAL LEADERSHIP

Mayors are first and foremost political leaders. Among other things, what distinguishes them from their counterparts at the state and federal levels is that the problems and political challenges they confront are right outside their front door every single day. There is no hiding from local political challenges.

To get a feel for the mayoralty in American cities it is instructive to establish its place in US political history. Almost two decades ago, historian Melvin Holli published a book called *The American Mayor: The Best and the Worst Big City Leaders*.[3] In it, he catalogued for the first time the opinions of political scientists and historians on the best and worst mayors in American history.

Among the best were Republican Fiorella LaGuardia of New York City (1933–45) and Democrats Richard J. Daley of Chicago (1955–76) and Tom Bradley of Los Angeles (1973–93). These mayors were noted for longevity in office and the ability to grow their economies and stimulate investment. They were also known for the power they wielded beyond their cities and for the representation they provided and the political coalitions they built. Among the worst were Philadelphia mayors Frank Rizzo (a Republican) and Wilson Goode (a Democrat) and Cleveland mayor Dennis Kucinich (a Democrat). (Note that in recent decades Philadelphia has had many good mayors.) The worst mayors shared policy disasters, disinvestment, and an inability to effectively represent the people or use their power to build enduring political coalitions.

The success of mayors, like presidents and governors, is a function of many factors. At the heart of it is the idea that mayors must overcome myriad challenges to successful collective action.[4] In other words, to implement their vision they must get others to do things they might not want to do or that they might be openly hostile to doing—an easy task if mayors were all-powerful, but (as you might have guessed) they are not.

Public safety, economic development, zoning, parks and recreation, and city personnel are usually within the policy jurisdiction of city governments. What about issues that cross jurisdictional lines, such as education, transportation, poverty, immigration, or the environment? Other types and levels of government often handle these policy areas, but each directly affects city residents.

Unfortunately, mayors lack the ability to command others to do what they want, especially those actors and entities outside their jurisdiction. Mayors, for example, cannot command the federal government to fix immigration or the local school district to fix education. They can only try to persuade them to do so.

According to Douglas Yates, who wrote about mayors and urban governance in the 1960s and 1970s, the American city mayor was the leader of an "eight-ring circus." Beyond the formal structure of city government lies "community groups, urban bureaucrats, taxpayers and citizens, higher level governments, business, other local governments, and public employee unions."[5] Then of course there is the city council, with which mayors must negotiate all manner of policy issues confronting the city each year. Successful orchestration of the "circus" is a mark of effective leadership. Yates, however, was not optimistic in his assessment of mayors' ability to lead their cities, as indicated by the title of a book he wrote on the subject: *The Ungovernable City*.

MAYORAL LEADERSHIP: FORMAL AND INFORMAL SOURCES OF POWERS

The ability of mayors to lead their cities effectively depends on a number of factors. Presidential scholars who study leadership focus on the institutional rules of the game or **formal powers**, the legal authority given to elected officials to act in their official capacities. Examples are the president's role as Commander-in-Chief and the president's ability to veto acts of Congress. They also focus on the ability of presidents to persuade others through the use of **informal powers**, conditions in the environment that enhance a political leader's power. This category includes public approval, reputation, and the ability to rally the public through careful use of speeches, major addresses, and travel.[6] This chapter examines mayoral leadership according to this framework to help you organize the study of the mayoralty and provide a lens through which you can view mayoral leadership.

A city's form of government or *system* (see chapter 5) establishes the institutional parameters of a mayor's formal power, assigning them tasks, responsibilities, and authority. Think of it as a toolbox. Formal powers that are well defined, numerous, and focused on consequential areas of governance provide some of the tools mayors need to achieve success. In a strong mayor-council system, the mayor typically enjoys the full complement of executive powers, including appointment of department heads and other executive branch officials, drafting of the budget, implementation of policy, delivery of services, and vetoing laws passed by the city council. Strong mayors also manage *intergovernmental relationships* (relationships with counties, special districts, and state and federal governments). City councils, courts, and state government can check a mayor's use of formal authority, so these powers are not absolute.

Weak mayor-council and council-manager systems provide few, if any, of these formal powers to mayors. The mayor in a weak mayor-council system may have the ability to recommend people for appointments, but that power is usually shared with the city council. The mayor may preside over the city council while it is in session (which gives them agenda power) but usually does not have veto authority. The mayor in a weak mayor-council system is more of a political figure-head than an elected executive.

Mayors in council-manager cities are also weak relative to strong mayors. In contrast to the separation of powers logic of both variants of mayor-council systems, the mayor is an elected member of the city council, and an appointed city manager executes policy and provides services. Because the mayor is a member of the council, he or she cannot also veto ordinances passed by it. Mayors in this type of system usually lack appointment and budget power. And in smaller council-manager cities, the mayor is selected by the other councilors, the position rotates, and the role is largely ceremonial. Mayors in council-manager systems, however, are "first among equals" and are charged with running council meetings, which gives them somewhat greater leverage to shape the council's legislative agenda and the public's expectations about the role of city government in solving local policy challenges.

City forms of government have evolved over time, however, making the clear distinction between form or type difficult to maintain. Public administration scholars George Frederickson and Gary Alan Johnson refer to these places as "adapted cities."[7] For example, mayor-council systems are increasingly utilizing a chief administrative officer (CAO) to derive the benefits of professional city management embedded within the council-manager structure. Council manager systems, especially in larger cities, are increasingly selecting their mayors in separate, citywide elections to advance the goal of stronger political leadership. This affords the mayor a higher profile—a bigger "bully pulpit" or megaphone, if you will—and greatly increases public expectations that the person selected will provide strong leadership. These mayors are also in a privileged position with respect to working with the city manager to develop a city's policy priorities. In the end, the major distinction between formally strong and formally weak mayors is their degree of executive authority.[8]

Aside from a mayor's toolbox of formal powers, a mayor's policy responsibilities can change as well. In recent decades, the policy responsibilities of mayors in certain cities have been augmented to include public education in an effort to improve struggling urban school systems. Mayors have total or partial control of public education in Boston, Baltimore, Chicago, Cleveland, Detroit, Harrisburg (Pennsylvania), Hartford (Connecticut), Indianapolis, Jackson (Mississippi), Los Angeles, New Haven (Connecticut), New York City, Oakland (California), Philadelphia, Providence (Rhode Island), Trenton (New Jersey), Washington, DC and Yonkers (New York).[9] Whether or not mayor-led education systems are more successful than traditional school systems remains an open question, but there is some evidence of improved student outcomes.[10] Table 6.1 summarizes information on the formal powers and responsibilities of mayors in the nation's ten largest cities.

The highly fragmented system of governance in the United States ensures that a mayor's formal institutional power is only part of the story of how mayors attempt to lead. Informal powers constitute a second toolbox for mayoral leadership. Informal powers can be described as circumstances in the environment and/or unique individual characteristics that support a mayor's ability to persuade others to do what they might not otherwise be inclined to do.[11]

TABLE 6.1	Formal Powers of Mayors in Top Ten Largest US Cities									
City	Budget	Appoint	Veto	Line-Item	Term Length	Succession	Mgr. or CAO	Presides	Education	Salary
New York Pop. 8,622,698 FOG: SMC	Yes	Yes	Yes	Yes	4 years	2-term limit	No[a]	No	Yes	$225,000
Los Angeles Pop. 3,999,759 FOG: SMC	Yes	Yes	Yes	Yes	4 years	2-term limit	Yes	No	No	$238,000
Chicago Pop. 2,716,450 FOG: SMC	Yes	Yes	Yes	No	4 years	No term limit	No	Yes	Yes	$216,210
Houston Pop. 2,312,717 FOG: SMC	Yes	Yes	No	No	4 years	2-term limit	Yes	Yes	No	$235,000
Phoenix Pop. 1,626,078 FOG: CM	No	No	No	No	4 years	2-term limit	Yes	Yes	No	$88,000
Philadelphia Pop. 1,580,863 FOG: SMC	Yes	Yes	Yes	No	4 years	2-term limit	Yes	No	Yes	$218,000
San Antonio Pop. 1,511,946 FOG: CM	No	No	No	No	2 years	2-term limit	Yes	Yes	No	$61,725

(Continued)

TABLE 6.1 (Continued)

City	Budget	Appoint	Veto	Line-Item	Term Length	Succession	Mgr. or CAO	Presides	Education	Salary
San Diego Pop. 1,419,516 FOG: SMC	Yes	Yes	Yes	Yes	4 years	2-term limit	Yes	No	No	$100,464
Dallas Pop. 1,341,075 FOG: CM	No	Yes[b]	No	No	4 years	2-term limit	Yes	Yes	No	$80,000
San Jose Pop. 1,035,317 FOG: CM	No	No	No	No	4 years	2-term limit	Yes	Yes	No	$114,000

Note: FOG=Form of government. SMC=Strong Mayor-Council, WMC=Weak Mayor-Council, CM=Council-Manager. All mayors are directly elected in separate mayoral election. *Presides* means that the mayor presides during city council meetings. [a] New York City Mayor has broad powers and can appoint deputy mayors to aid in administration; [b] City Council committees and chairs only.

Source: Source information for this table is contained in an online appendix.

In a classic article on mayoral leadership, Jeffrey Pressman argued that mayors can effectively lead their communities by "pyramiding resources,"[12] which include formal powers as well the prestige of their office, their relationships with powerful interest groups and political parties, and media attention, to advance their agendas.[13] Brokering disputes among competing factions, building strong coalitions, and aggressively promoting the mayor's agenda are keys to mayoral leadership. Indeed, this hallmark of Mayor Henry Cisneros's leadership in San Antonio put him on the list of the nation's best mayors. Los Angeles mayor Tom Bradley, also one of the nation's best, exhibited similar strengths. Functioning in a weak mayor-council system, Bradley achieved success by building a strong bi- and multiracial electoral coalition, sustaining a strong and working majority on the city council, and appointing officials sympathetic to his agenda to key policy positions.[14]

Leadership Styles

Depending on context, personality, and political objectives, mayors approach their jobs in different ways. Over time, scholars have identified a number of different **mayoral leadership styles**, each of which can be an important informal source of power. Styles should not be divorced from context; particular eras tend to produce particular styles. As noted urban scholar Dennis Judd writes: "In sum, urban leadership arises from local contexts, but it responds to both local and external forces."[15]

City boss, entrepreneur, and crusader were styles found most often between the 1950s and 1970s.[16] *City bosses* used **patronage**—which, as defined in chapter 2, is a system of hiring local employees that is based on the political support provided by a job-seeker—to advance their agendas and maintain their positions. As courts moved to limit patronage, this style of leadership is less evident today.[17] *Entrepreneurial mayors* sought to redevelop their downtowns at a time when industrial production was slowing in the US and residents began vacating cities for the suburbs. Mayor Richard Lee of New Haven, Connecticut, in the 1950s and 1960s, is a classic example. He helped rebuild his downtown by establishing a strong coalition with the downtown business community and using federal grant dollars to support his objectives.[18] *Crusader mayors* emerged in the 1960s Civil Rights Era. Their focus was on highlighting and bringing attention to challenges faced by their cities in the areas of housing, neighborhood conditions, education, jobs, and crime. The first African American mayors of major cities, such as Carl Stokes in Cleveland, Kenneth Gibson in Newark, and Richard Hatcher in Gary, adopted this strategy. White liberal mayors such as John Lindsay of New York City are also included in this group.

Leadership styles during this era also included brokers and managers.[19] *Broker mayors* are somewhat passive in their leadership style, often waiting for competing interests to set the parameters of debate—say over a redevelopment project or mass transit initiative—and work to build consensus among the different interests.[20] Broker mayors are often found in cities with council-manager systems. Lacking executive authority, they influence outcomes through negotiation and compromise. *Manager mayors* focus narrowly on the effective administration of local government.

In the 1990s, following waves of federal cutbacks in aid to cities and the taxpayer revolts of the 1970s and 1980s, a new generation of mayors turned their attention to more effective management and administration of scarce city government resources, in some cases—such as Philadelphia—to forestall a municipal bankruptcy.[21] A reboot of the earlier manager style, these mayors were more innovative, focusing more on "reinventing government" to improve the quality of urban services and to deliver more and better services at lower cost.[22] Privatization of city services such as garbage collection, street light maintenance, tree trimming, and legal services became a go-to strategy for mayors seeking to make local government more efficient, less costly, and less beholden to public employee unions. With federal aid declining, populations and businesses leaving central cities for the suburbs, and taxpayers hungry for greater efficiency, mayors in this period—such as Rudolph Giuliani of New York City, Ed Rendell of Philadelphia, Richard M. Daley of Chicago, Stephen Goldschmidt of Indianapolis, Richard Riordan of Los Angeles, and John Norquist of Milwaukee—arguably had fewer options but to seek to do more with less. Interestingly, but reflective of the more conservative mood of the time, three of these big city mayors were Republicans (Giuliani, Riordan, and Goldschmidt), and two (Giuliani and Riordan) served in heavily Democratic and liberal cities.[23]

According to media and even scholarly expectations, mayors should aspire to strong executive leadership. This style, though, may not be welcome in council-manager cities, which are better suited to a *facilitative leadership* style. Because the toolbox of formal powers is largely absent in council-manager systems, James

BOX 6.1

Mayor of Oakland Clashes with Trump Administration over Sanctuary Cities

Oakland Mayor Elizabeth "Libby" Schaff and Former US Attorney General Jeff Sessions

Svara argues that effective leadership can occur when mayors facilitate interactions between elected officials and managers, and between elected officials and the public, in a way that enhances and acknowledges the positive contributions of each in the process. Facilitative leadership focuses less on a mayor's use of formal powers to broker conflicts among groups or manage policy implementation and more on fostering cooperation among governmental actors. Because formal powers are lacking, personal leadership skills are paramount. Facilitative leadership can also work to reduce conflict and gridlock associated with mayor-council systems modeled on a separation of powers arrangement, but it is most effective in council-manager systems that lack a more formal separation of powers.[24]

What about mayors today? What styles of leadership are they adopting? Although none of the leadership styles described thus far is completely irrelevant, a number of adjectives might be used to describe today's mayors: innovative, progressive, inclusive, impatient, and frustrated. They embrace technology to make cities "smarter" and more responsive to citizen needs, and they are more data-driven in their approaches than past mayors. They promote urban sustainability by advancing alternative means of transportation and renewable energy. They embrace inclusivity and globalization as a way to strengthen—not weaken—cities. They are impatient with Washington gridlock and frustrated with state government interference in local decisions. Instead of waiting for Washington to act, and in defiance of state governments, cities are adopting a DIY (do-it-yourself) ethos.[25] Not surprisingly, many are unafraid to speak out against higher-level elected officials they feel are harming city interests. See box 6.1 for a description of Oakland Mayor Elizabeth Schaff's leadership style on the issue of federal immigration policy and local policing.

After getting word that federal Immigration and Customs Enforcement (ICE) agents were preparing to conduct a sweep of undocumented immigrants across Northern California, Oakland Mayor Elizabeth "Libby" Schaaf released a statement warning her community about the impending raids. The source of her information was unclear, but her efforts placed her squarely in the sights of the Trump administration. "I will not back down," Schaaf said. "I'm very clear about what the values of the people of Oakland are, and I believe it is my job to stand up for those values."[a]

This episode is part of a broader controversy involving so-called *sanctuary cities*. On one side are Mayor Schaff and other liberal mayors who think that inclusivity, not threats and intimidation, help local police do their jobs. On the other is the Trump administration, which has actively sought to use the power of the Department of Justice (DOJ) to force local police agencies to identify and report illegal aliens.[b] A June 2018 Gallup Poll showed that 50 percent of the nation supports a ban on sanctuary cities while 46 percent oppose it, an indication that the tug of war will continue until a comprehensive immigration plan is in place.[c]

[a] Kimberly Veklerov, "Oakland Mayor Libby Schaaf 'preparing for the worst' in Federal ICE Warning Investigation," *San Francisco Chronicle*, June 28, 2018, https://www.sfchronicle.com/bayarea/article/Oakland-Mayor-Libby-Schaaf-preparing-for-the-13035252.php, accessed July 29, 2018.

[b] US Department of Justice, Office of Public Affairs, "Justice Department Demands Documents and Threatens to Subpoena 23 Jurisdictions as Part of 8 USC 1373 Compliance Review," press release, January 24, 2018, https://www.justice.gov/opa/pr/justice-department-demands-documents-and-threatens-subpoena-23-jurisdictions-part-8-usc-1373, accessed July 29, 2018.

[c] Frank Newport, "Americans Oppose Border Walls, Favor Dealing With DACA," June 20, 2018, https://news.gallup.com/poll/235775/americans-oppose-border-walls-favor-dealing-daca.aspx, accessed July 29, 2018.

Representation and Governing Coalitions

Both the symbolic and substantive components of representation can enhance a mayor's ability to lead. A major symbolic component of representation is the race and ethnicity of mayors. Minority mayors bring a sense of pride and accomplishment and a hope that minority voters will be more effectively represented in City Hall.[26] Indeed, it is hard to underestimate this symbolic component, especially if it is a first for a group. It also applies to those who represent other groups historically subject to discrimination besides racial and ethnic minorities, such as women or the LGBTQ community. The mayor's role as representative of the people is complicated by the need to represent all of the people, not just one subset. Balancing these competing demands takes a great deal of political skill, and mayors who lack these skills are less effective than those who do not. Table 6.2 lists "mayoral firsts" in the history of descriptive representation in major American cities.

TABLE 6.2	Elected "Mayoral Firsts" in Top Ten Largest US Cities				
City	African American	Latino	Asian	Female	LGBTQ
Chicago	Harold Washington 1983–87			Jane Byrne 1979–83	Lori Lightfoot 2019–
Dallas	Ron Kirk 1995–2001			Annette Strauss 1987–91	
Houston	Lee Patrick Brown 1982–90			Kathryn Whitmire 1982–92	Annise Parker 2010–16
Los Angeles	Tom Bradley 1973–93	Christobal Aguilar 1866–1868, 1870–1872			
New York City	David Dinkins 1990–93				
Philadelphia	Wilson Goode 1984–92				
Phoenix				Margaret Hance 1977–83	
San Antonio	Ivy Taylor 2014–17	Henry Cisneros 1981–89	Ron Nirenberg 2017–	Lila Cockrell 1975–81, 1989–91	
San Diego				Maureen O'Connor 1986–92	
San Jose		Ron Gonzales 1989–96	Norman Mineta 1971–75	Janet Gray Hayes 1975–83	

Note: Blank cell indicates that no such person has even been elected.

Complete documentation for the contents of this table is available online, as is a table with "mayoral firsts" in cities greater than 250,000 since the mid-20th century.

According to Marion Orr and Domingo Morel, mayoral patterns in racial or ethnic representation track distinct periods of economic change in the US. During the industrial period, when European immigrants were coming to US cities in great numbers, mayors often came from the ranks of Irish (or Italian) populations that dominated big city populations.[27] These leaders produced electoral coalitions based on immigrant solidarity, voting strength, and patronage.[28] In the redevelopment period, from roughly 1940 to 1980, African American migration to Northeast and Midwest cities provided the foundation for African American mayoralties. In the postindustrial period (1980 to the present), characterized by massive immigration from Latin America and Asia, Latino mayors are emerging in many of the nation's largest and most important cities.[29] There are currently more than 250 Hispanic mayors in the US, a roughly 81 percent increase since 1984.[30]

More important than the symbolic act of winning an election is the construction of a stable **governing coalition**, or the coalition of groups and political leaders that effectively govern a community toward a set of policy goals. The coalition should be devoted to the idea of full **political incorporation** of minority groups. At the risk of oversimplification, greater *descriptive representation* (see chapter 5) should include incorporating minorities in top-level administrative positions, increasing diversity in city hiring, and improving police-community relations.[31] The longer-term goal should include improving the economic outlook of minority communities by enhancing education and career opportunities.[32] This latter goal is an extremely tall order for any mayor, however, given the myriad economic, political, and social forces standing in its way. While minority administrations are successful at diversifying the city workforce—especially in the police department—and improving police-community relations, research shows that minority mayors struggle to produce economic gains for minority communities or to alter city spending priorities in ways essential for addressing core urban problems.[33]

Women represent a unique voice in US urban politics and are expected to lead on issues such as affordable housing, social welfare, domestic violence, and those related to children.[34] According to the Center for American Women in Politics, female mayors lead 19 percent of the nation's top 100 cities, including San Antonio, Fort Worth, Charlotte, Washington, DC, Nashville, Baltimore, Las Vegas, Fresno (California), Omaha (Nebraska), Raleigh (North Carolina), Minneapolis, and Oakland. Six of these women are African American, one is Hispanic, and two are Asian American. Women constitute 17.5 percent of mayors in cities with populations greater than 100,000 and 19.3 percent in cities of more than 30,000.[35]

Research on the effect that female mayors have on their cities is somewhat mixed but suggests that it results in greater female political incorporation into city politics. Female mayors improve gender balance in the city bureaucracy, especially in policy-making positions, which then affects city government employment opportunities.[36] Female mayors tend to be more flexible and inclusive in their governing style, and their cities are more likely than those with male mayors to discuss and deal with issues of importance to women, especially in the areas of domestic and sexual violence.[37] However, female mayors do not affect the size of city government (as indicated by spending) or its priorities (indicated by how money is spent). Nor do female mayors handle major issues like crime any better or promote women's issues over core concerns of cities such as economic development when compared to men.[38] Women do, however, enjoy a larger incumbency advantage, suggesting that their impact on city politics goes beyond policy differences.[39]

Electoral Mandates and Public Approval

Electoral mandates and public approval are two additional sources of informal power for mayors. In general, an **electoral mandate** means that the message sent by the results of the mayoral election is clear enough to guide the agenda of the winning candidate, empowering them to act aggressively on their platform. Mayors with strong mandates can move others to follow their lead on policy more effectively, especially other elected officials like city councilors. The margin of victory is an important barometer, but how it is interpreted with respect to what key voting blocs want is also important. While tricky to assess, a clear mandate can be a major source of informal power.

One way to examine electoral mandates is to study whether *change* in the position of mayor affects policy outputs. Political scientists Harold Wolman, John Strate, and Alan Melchior analyzed the effect of mayoral change on the policy outputs of cities. They found that election of a new mayor had a significantly larger effect on city spending than the reelection of an incumbent (i.e., maintaining the status quo). The effect of a new mayor on spending was significantly greater in cities with mayor-council governments, which are more open to political influence compared to those with council-manager governments. So electing a new mayor can change a city's policy direction, but effects appear contingent on institutional arrangements.

A related source of power for mayors is **public approval**, the share of the public that approves of the job a mayor is doing. In theory, mayors can be evaluated on virtually any local condition or service—poverty levels, economic prosperity, trash collection, flooding, snow removal, educational performance, crime, number and quality of parks, availability of parking, you name it. Like a popular president or governor, popular mayors are more powerful than unpopular mayors. This is important not only for reelection but also for advancing a mayor's policy agenda.[40]

Douglas Arnold and Nicholas Carnes studied mayoral approval in New York City between 1984 and 2009. They found that the health of the economy and crime were the conditions most likely to affect mayoral approval. When crime increased, mayors got blamed; when it decreased, they got credit. Likewise, an improving economic outlook increased mayoral approval, while a sagging one decreased it. Race creates a baseline for residents' evaluations of mayors, however, as white residents evaluate white mayors more favorably and black residents evaluate black mayors more favorably. Nevertheless, the evaluations of white and black mayors respond similarly to changes in performance.[41] Strong public approval, then, can be used as a tool to move others to action, especially other elected officials who do not want to buck a popular mayor.

Agenda Setting

Agenda setting refers to the act of establishing the policy priorities of the city. Mayors are in a unique position to shape the local policy agenda by influencing what and how people think about the problems confronting the city and suggesting solutions. Mayors also target their persuasion efforts to other elected officials, including the city council and state and federal officials. Like governors and presidents, mayors can use the power of the bully pulpit to rally the public and political elites behind a particular policy. Mayors can use their access to media coverage to shape public perceptions and highlight policy challenges and solutions. Speeches before local interest groups, annual "State of the City" addresses, press conferences, and public appearances are examples of what presidential scholar Samuel Kernell refers to as "going public."[42] The end goal of going public is to mold opinions and frame issues in ways that enhance a mayor's ability to persuade.

"State of the City" or inaugural addresses present opportunities to highlight policy challenges, successes, and future goals, helping mayors shape the public agenda. Starting in 2015, researchers from the National League of Cities (NLC), a major professional advocacy association for the nation's municipalities, began coding and analyzing "State of the City" speeches delivered by mayors across the country.[43] In 2018 they coded 160 such speeches to determine what was on the minds and agendas of the nation's mayors. Fifty-eight percent of the speeches delivered by mayors in these annual addresses gave significant attention, measured as three or more paragraphs, to economic development, followed by infrastructure (56%) and budgeting of city resources (49%). Next in importance were housing (39%), public safety (36%), health and human services (34%), education (28%), energy and environment (25%), government data and tech (14%), and demographics (12%). (The percentages do not add up to 100 because more than one topic area could get significant attention.) Economic development issues included downtown redevelopment, arts and culture, neighborhood revitalization, and jobs. Infrastructure topics covered roads, streets and street signs, water and sewer improvements, public transit, pedestrian infrastructure, and how to fund these improvements. Budget and management concerns included intergovernmental relations, property taxes, fiscal transparency, leadership, and fiscal conditions.

Although basic, each of these topics is essential to our daily lives, and many have captured the interests of the millennial generation. Walkable communities, art- and culture-led development, downtown development, energy and environment, and, of course, jobs are the main concerns of young people today, large percentages of whom are flocking to big cities and surrounding metro areas.[44] Social welfare is prominently discussed in state and national politics but rarely mentioned in "State of the City" speeches.[45] Nevertheless, a fair number of mayors claim that social welfare, or redistributive services, is high on their agenda.[46]

Party and Group Influences

As party and ideological polarization have advanced in national politics,[47] urban scholars have turned their attention to studying the connection between a mayor's party affiliation and city policy outputs. In most places, local politics is officially "nonpartisan," but even without the backing of party organizations, in theory at least, mayors should be guided by their own party and ideological preferences.

Research about the influence of a mayor's party on the direction of city policy is complicated by the fact that Democratic mayors tend to be elected in cities dominated by Democratic voters and Republican mayors tend to be elected in cities dominated by Republican voters. These are not random distributions; liberals tend to live in big cities and conservatives tend to live in suburban and rural locations.[48] Some research suggests that the mayor's party affiliation has no effect on revenue (i.e., taxes and fees) and spending policies, or the size of city government (measured by the number of employees),[49] but may affect spending on police; for example, GOP-mayor-led cities spend more on police than cities with Democratic mayors.[50]

Others have uncovered broader policy effects of party affiliation. According to these studies, cities with Democratic mayors generally spend more than cities with Republican mayors, much of it financed through debt.[51] Democratic mayors also prioritize and act on policies to address income inequality and poverty more than their Republican counterparts.[52] Katherine Einstein and David Glick, the authors of research on mayors and poverty, suggest that their results "offer evidence of a broader story about the nationalization of local politics. A significant segment of mayors are actively promoting initiatives in a salient policy arena previously thought to be outside their purview. What's more, their preferences for initiatives in this sphere are consistent with the national parties' positions."[53] This argument is also consistent with the finding about GOP mayors and police spending. For decades national Republicans have positioned themselves as the party that is "tough on crime" to a point where they now "own" that issue relative to Democrats.[54]

City interest groups can also help advance a mayor's policy agenda. The heart of regime theory argues that the electoral coalition that emerges to support a successful mayoral candidate forms the foundation of that mayor's governing coalition. This coalition of interests might be centered in the city's corporate community and devoted to sustained economic development, or it might be focused on progressive objectives like improving neighborhoods and using government to advance the needs of the poor. The governing coalition might also be devoted to simply maintaining the status quo, keeping taxes low, and protecting homeowner interests.[55] In each of these cases, mayors are at the top of the governing coalition, drawing support and power from its core members and the direction it takes. A more detailed discussion of regime theory is included in chapter 9.

CITY MANAGERS AND ADMINISTRATORS

As you learned in chapter 5, in council-manager cities, the city council appoints a city manager to carry out the executive function of city government. This system emerged in the US during the Progressive Era in response to reformers' efforts to enhance the quality of local government, which at that time was beset with mismanagement and corruption. By strictly separating politics—what mayors and councilors engage in during policy making—from administration—what executives do—reformers reasoned that the quality of local government would improve.[56]

According to the most recent International City and County Management Association survey, approximately 59 percent of American cities use the council-manager form of government. [57] City managers have the executive powers of strong mayors. They formulate policy and prepare and execute the budget following approval by the city council. They appoint and can remove most major city department heads. They also create and maintain formal relationships with other governments, both within the immediate metropolitan area (e.g., special districts, school boards, county governments), and with state and federal governments. City managers also execute city services such as police and fire protection, solid waste, parks and recreation, land use planning, and human resources.[58]

City managers are well educated, usually having attained a master's degree in public administration. Most have several years' experience running a city department or serving as an assistant city manager. This is a far cry from when this form of government was first adopted in US cities in the early decades of the 20th century. In those days, city managers were often engineers who worked in city water or public works departments. Today's city managers are trained in financial administration, personnel systems, service delivery, information systems, land use planning, and urban politics and policy administration.[59] Although their training has changed, the demographic profile of city managers in the US has not, at least not much. Although minorities and women have penetrated the US workforce in great numbers, the city management profession remains decidedly white, male, and middle-aged. Only about 12 percent are women.[60] This lack of descriptive representation affects the nature of city management, as female managers tend to be more inclusive and democratic in how they approach their jobs.[61]

City managers function in an inherently political environment,[62] serving at the pleasure of city councils. Their work environments are often defined by the principal-agent problem (defined in chapter 4), because elected principals with authority (council members) choose and oversee the work of their agents in government (city managers). It is not unlike the relationship that exists between voters and city elected officials, in which voters are the principals and elected officials are their agents. Although it is often very difficult for voters to monitor and oversee elected officials—an essential function of citizenship—it is far easier for city councilors and mayors to monitor and oversee the role of city managers. More importantly, city managers can be fired for cause through a simple majority vote, so understanding city council political dynamics is essential to their survival. Even the most politically savvy manager can provoke the ire of city councilors, however. Indeed, turnover among city managers is common; the average time that a manager stays in any one city is a little over 6 years.[63]

Scholars have identified a number of "push" and "pull" factors at the core of city manager turnover.[64] Not surprisingly, one push factor is conflict with or among city councilors about the manager's role, especially in policy making, which can lead to firing or early departure.[65] (Election-induced turnover on the city council may also lead to turnover in the manager's office.) Chief administrative officers in mayor-council cities are usually appointed by mayors, so they have a single principal to please. Nevertheless, poor performance, a bad working relationship with the mayor, or an electoral defeat can lead to turnover.[66] City managers in places experiencing economic and population decline tend not to stay as long as those in cities with strong economies and population growth.[67] County managers serving in the commission-administrator form of government face similar pressures and are often pushed out by political conflict.[68] Pull factors include the desire for career advancement in a bigger city, with better pay and a larger organization to run, or family considerations.[69]

Two implications of this discussion stand out. First, managers, at both the city and county levels, are often in a precarious position. To keep their jobs, they must maintain majority support from the elected officials who appointed them. At the same time, managers have policy expertise that part-time elected officials with few staff resources often lack. Elected officials are at the mercy of appointed managers who know more than they do about policy and its implementation. Managers, however, are loath to enter controversial policy debates for fear of alienating a particular faction on the city council and jeopardizing their employment status. In the end, a leadership vacuum may occur, leaving a city (or county) directionless.[70]

A second implication relates to careers in city management. Being the chief executive of a city is an attractive career track for those interested in the practical work of government. The pay is good, especially for those in larger cities such as Austin, Dallas, San Antonio, and San Jose, who easily command six-figure salaries given the scale and scope of responsibilities, but political uncertainty creates inherent risk for managers and the governments they serve. Consequently, cities experiencing conflict on the city council find it harder to attract talented managers than those with less conflict. Increasingly, managers are structuring employment contracts to guard against uncertainty through guaranteed severance packages or employment guarantees immediately before or after city elections. The bigger theoretical problem is a principal-agent one: The expectations of elected officials and managers rarely align completely. City councilors delegate administrative power to a city manager whose incentives are to act in accord with their wishes to maintain a positive working relationship. The problem emerges when a manager's professional training and experience run counter to the political desires of popularly elected officials.[71]

THE URBAN BUREAUCRACY

Elected and appointed chief executives in city government oversee a **government bureaucracy**, a group of departments instituted to enforce laws and deliver services, including police and fire services, housing, economic development, parks and recreation, solid waste pick-up, zoning, infrastructure, and other services. As noted previously, some cities even oversee public education. For the most part, executives of these departments are appointed officials. In mayor-council cities, either the mayor or some combination of the mayor and city council will appoint individuals to serve as department heads. In council-manager cities, appointments are made by the city manager. A central part of urban bureaucracies are the people employed to work for city government.

Patronage, Merit Systems, and Municipal Unions

Historically, city employees were chosen on the basis of patronage. Starting in the 1970s, however, courts have consistently ruled against patronage systems of filling positions in the city bureaucracy, so today, most city employees are hired according to **merit systems**, in which hiring is based on merit rather than on politics.[72] The First Amendment protects free speech, which patronage systems violate by linking government employment to private political behaviors. In contrast to patronage systems, which link who gets what job to political support in a **quid pro quo** ("this for that") relationship, merit systems make the selection of city employees conditional on qualifications. The goal of this Progressive Era reform was to change local government by improving the capacity and quality of the workforce hired to deliver government goods and services.

Public employee unions also protect local government employees from unfair treatment. Data from 2017 indicate that unions represent about 44 percent of local government workers. In contrast, about 38 percent of all public employees, and only 7.3 percent of all private sector employees, are union members. The total percentage of workers in the United States represented by a union is 10.7 percent, down from 20.1 percent in 1983.[73]

Unions offer workers an opportunity to negotiate better salary, benefits, and working conditions through **collective bargaining**, the act of negotiating with management via a legally recognized organization of workers. The American Federation of State, County and Municipal Employees (AFSCME) is the largest union representing city and county employees. Because unions represent more than 40 percent of local government employees, they are a powerful political force. From a collective action standpoint, unions, as a relatively small group with a narrow interest (i.e., protecting the interests of government workers), have an advantage over other, more diffuse, interests, such as those promoting environmental protection.[74]

Although mayors bear the brunt of failed contract talks, city managers and CAOs typically take the lead in negotiating for the city when existing union contracts end. This can be a politically fraught exercise, as each side seeks to protect its interests. As noted previously, union interests include increased pay and benefits and improvements to working conditions. Management's interest is to protect the short- and long-term fiscal health of the city by limiting these increases and altering working conditions to make local government more effective and efficient. The most powerful tool unions have in their negotiating arsenal is the threat of a work stoppage, which can seriously disrupt a community if executed by sanitation workers or teachers. Not all local public employee unions are able to strike, however, including police and firefighters.[75] From an electoral perspective, unions (especially those representing public safety workers) often play a central role in city campaigns and elections supporting candidates favorable to their interests.

From an economic perspective, public-sector unions are stronger than private-sector unions because local governments have a monopoly on the services they provide.[76] Public workers can go on strike, stop work, or otherwise pressure officials to give them what they want, and the public has nowhere else to go to replace the services they provide. This dynamic can put otherwise sympathetic politicians and administrators in a bind. Most big cities have Democratic mayors, who are friends of labor, *and* powerful unions, who are major Democratic Party allies. Mayors and executives, however, must consider short- and long-term implications of negotiations given the need to balance budgets and remain fiscally competitive with neighboring cities and regions.

In 2018, the United States Supreme Court dealt what many consider a blow to organized labor in *Janus v. AFSCME*.[77] In this case the court ruled that nonunion employees covered by collective bargaining agreements could no longer be forced to pay union dues to support union efforts. The Court reasoned that to do so is a violation of a worker's free speech rights. The problem for public employees is how to keep people from free riding, or getting the benefits of collective bargaining

BOX 6.2

NYC Mayor Bill de Blasio and the NYPD Go Head to Head

New York City Mayor Bill de Blasio Speaking at a Rally for Union Labor

In 2017, New York City's mayor Bill de Blasio cruised to reelection with strong union backing. His prolabor administration, which supported increasing the city's minimum wage to $15 per hour, also successfully negotiated new contracts with 99 percent of unionized city employees, a remarkable achievement given that *none* of the unions were working under contract when de Blasio became mayor in January 2014.[a]

Shortly after his reelection, however, the Police Benevolent Association (PBA), the union representing the city's police officers, started to complain that they were working without a contract and that the mayor's most recent proposal failed to increase officers' take-home

without paying the costs (dues). In the past, unions charged *everyone* dues to support the group's efforts regardless of union status. This ruling will probably hurt union finances and their ability to negotiate better union contracts, as well as their power in local campaigns. Box 6.2 describes New York City mayor Bill de Blasio's contract negotiations with the New York Police Department (NYPD).

Street-Level Bureaucrats

The vast majority of the public's interaction with city and county government is through **street-level bureaucrats** including police officers, sheriff's deputies, firefighters, teachers and administrators, county health and welfare department staff, and virtually anyone with the responsibility of providing public services to local residents face to face.[78] The main challenge confronted by street-level bureaucrats is how to deliver services in an environment that is ambiguous, from both contextual and policy standpoints. Should a police officer arrest a suspect? Should a teacher discipline a student? Because situations are often unclear and because policy is imprecise, street-level bureaucrats are free to use **discretion** to do their jobs. Add to discretion a lack of resources—including low pay, the threat of physical or psychological stress or injury, and conflicting demands from the public and elected officials—and you get a significant dilemma often dealt with through **short cutting**, or failure to treat each case as a unique situation.

Short cutting may be a good short-term coping mechanism, but the long-term effects can be quite negative. Indeed, one of the major issues in service delivery involving street-level bureaucrats is bias, often seen in the delivery of public safety. A critical issue is whether people of color are treated differently from whites in their interactions with local government, especially police. To give a broad pay. As part of their public strategy, the PBA even went so far as to confront the mayor and his wife as they left a coffee shop on their way to their neighborhood Y to exercise.[b]

Negotiations followed a familiar path, with each side saying that the other was negotiating in bad faith and refusing to sit down and hammer out a deal.[c] The irony is that Mayor de Blasio is prolabor. However, this is a case in which ideology and the practicality of city politics clash. The mayor's obligation is to city taxpayers as well as unions; therefore, he must balance these competing demands. It also illustrates the up-close and personal nature of city politics. Mayors cannot hide from issues, even if they just want some even ise and a cup of coffee.

[a] Jeffrey C. Mays, "De Blasio, A Pro-labor Mayor, Is Sued over Bargaining Tactics," *New York Times*, January 31, 2018, https://www.nytimes.com/2018/01/31/nyregion/nyc-labor-de-blasio-contract-carpenters.html, accessed August 4, 2018.

[b] Alison Fox, "NYPD Union Tells de Blasio to 'Go to Work' on Contract Negotiations," *AM New York*, March 26, 2018, https://www.amny.com/news/nypd-union-de-bla-sio-1.17680527, accessed August 4, 2018.

[c] Richard Steier, "PBA Seeks Arbitration, City Accuses Union of Refusing to Negotiate," *The Chief Leader*, April 2, 2018, http://thechiefleader.com/news/open_articles/pba-seeks-arbitration-city-accuses-union-of-refusing-to-negotiate/article_b8ccc954-3367-11e8-897e-4bf80049159f.html, accessed August 4, 2018.

overview of the problem in public safety, a recent national study published in the *Journal of Epidemiology and Community Health* indicated that between 2015 and 2016, African American residents comprised 25.6 percent of deaths resulting from police violence despite being only 12.4 percent of the population.[79] Hispanics were 16.9 percent of deaths and 17.8 percent of the population, while whites were 51.7 percent of deaths and 61.5 percent of the population. According to the study, the average years of life lost was 56,064, with blacks making up more than half of this total (51.5 percent). The years of life lost was greater for blacks, American Indians/Alaskan Natives, and Hispanics than for whites, but lower for Asians/Pacific Islanders. These numbers indicate that people of color, especially black Americans, are disproportionately affected by police violence compared to whites.

The issue of police-community relations, violence by police, and violence against police, is a significant policy challenge that directly affects cities and their police departments, who are on the front lines defending American communities. In another principal-agent problem, it is difficult, if not impossible, for principals (police chiefs) to monitor the behavior of their agents (officers) on the street. Things happen in real time, and officers must make snap judgments.

Representative Bureaucracy

If the problem of police shootings is perceived as a question of bias, or—in the worst-case scenario—racism on the part of police officers, one response might be to make cultural sensitivity a larger part of the training officers receive. The question may also be a problem of political representation (see chapter 1). If the views of the minority community are not adequately addressed because city government demographics—of its mayor, city council, executives, and employees—do not reflect those of the community it serves, the question becomes how to make the government more representative. This is most adequately achieved by changing the personnel involved, a political exercise that begins with mayors and city councilors.

Scholars refer to this issue more generally as **representative bureaucracy**.[80] Bureaucracies that "look like" or represent in demographic terms the cities they serve are more likely to do a better (i.e., less biased) job of delivering services. Changing the bureaucracy involves changing the top executives, which is something that elected officials can do. Therefore, to make bureaucracy more representative and, theoretically, more effective, political leadership must be representative. As the ranks of elected officials become more diverse, so too do city departments, which results in less bias and greater trust among constituencies regarding the quality of local services and government.[81]

LOCAL CONSTITUTIONAL OFFICERS

Being mayor of a city, especially one with a large and diverse population with competing interests and demands, is a tough job. Indeed, being mayor is the probably the toughest political job in America. Unlike the federal government, which has a unitary executive, meaning a single chief executive (i.e., the president) with the power to appoint others to help execute policy, cities and counties often have numerous other elected officials with city or countywide jurisdiction over service delivery and policy execution.

Depending on location, cities may elect a clerk, a comptroller, and an attorney, or any number of other citywide officials. For example, in addition to the mayor, New York City voters choose a comptroller to audit and oversee the finances of the city, as well as a public advocate, an ombudsman who ensures that New York City residents are receiving their fair share of services and who advocates for those whose interests might be overlooked by city government. Current New York City mayor Bill de Blasio was Public Advocate before he won the mayoralty.[82] In California, each of the state's 482 municipalities has a city clerk, who administers local elections, maintains records of city council proceedings, and manages public records.[83] Of these, approximately 154 are elected. City attorneys in California are usually appointed, but in eleven cities, including the state's three largest (Los Angeles, San Diego, and San Francisco), they are elected. City attorneys provide legal advice to city councils and assist councils with legislative proposals, among other duties.[84] Chicago voters elect not only a city clerk (whose duties include issuing dog licenses) but also a city treasurer to manage investments for the city, especially those related to city worker pensions.[85]

County voters also elect a range of countywide officials. In addition to county commissioners—in some places called supervisors—in 10 percent of counties voters elect a County Executive.[86] Counties with the commission-elected executive form of government separate the legislative and executive functions, and the county executive's role is similar to the mayor of a strong mayor-council city. Like strong mayors, elected county executives have budget, appointment, and veto power and are expected to provide policy leadership to county government.

Current Democratic US senator Chris Coons of Delaware and former Wisconsin governor Republican Scott Walker both served as elected chief executives of their home counties before seeking higher office. In contrast to strong mayors elected on a nonpartisan basis, most county executives are elected on partisan ballots.

County voters also elect a range of other executive positions, specialized offices that deliver a narrow range of services. These include offices such as Sheriff, Clerk, Recorder of Deeds, Assessor, and Treasurer. Assessors are responsible for assessing property values for the purpose of levying taxes. This often generates controversy, but it is outside the purview of county executives, both elected and appointed. Treasurers may mismanage a county's investments, but county officials cannot remove them; only voters can do that. Clerks manage elections as well as vital public records, such as marriage and birth certificates, and records related to property. When a county clerk fails to abide by the law of the land it can spark a national controversy, as happened in Rowan County, Kentucky, when clerk Kim Davis refused to issue marriage licenses to same-sex couples. Local sheriff Joe Arpaio of Maricopa County, Arizona, may have become a national embarrassment (or hero, depending on your perspective) for his treatment of immigrants, but county supervisors were powerless to remove him from office. In both cases, they had to wait until the next election for voters to decide their futures (they were both voted out of office, Arpaio in 2016 and Davis in 2018).[87] As you might imagine given the number of county executives and the separation of roles, leading counties is difficult.

SUMMARY

This chapter has explained how city mayors exercise leadership. It also focused on local government executives, especially city managers. One of the key insights of mayoral leadership is that it is a function of the formal or institutional powers of the office as well as the mayor's ability to persuade others, which is supported by a host of informal sources of power. Mayoral authority is greatest in strong mayor-council systems and weakest in council-manager systems. Informal sources of power relate to things a mayor might control directly—such as how they use media, interest groups, and parties to advance their agendas—and conditions in the environment—such as public approval of the mayor's performance, especially on the economy and crime. The combination of formal and informal power directly shapes a mayor's ability to lead.

This chapter also addressed the topic of urban executives, both appointed and elected. This group includes city managers and local constitutional officers. Although the roles of managers and constitutional officers are primarily administrative in nature, the environment in which they function can be highly political. Managers and other urban executives oversee the work of street-level bureaucrats who are on the front lines of urban service delivery. Given their day-to-day engagement with the public, sensitivity to equity concerns and the representation of diverse interests is paramount to modern city administration. In sum, institutions, representation, and politics are at the core of our understanding of how mayors and executives function in urban politics.

Key Terms

agenda setting *(126)*
collective bargaining *(131)*
discretion *(132)*
electoral mandate *(126)*
formal powers *(117)*
governing coalition *(125)*
government bureaucracy *(130)*
informal powers *(117)*

mayoral leadership styles *(121)*
merit system *(130)*
political incorporation *(125)*
public approval *(126)*
quid pro quo *(130)*
representative bureaucracy *(134)*
short cutting *(132)*
street-level bureaucrats *(132)*

Discussion Questions

1. How do formal and informal powers of mayors influence their ability to provide political leadership to a community?

2. Why is political leadership a necessity in council-manager governments? How might mayors provide this?

3. What are the main causes of city manager turnover?

4. How might political incorporation affect the ability of local government to behave in a way that is more representative?

5. Is city government really nonpartisan? Explain your answer.

Exercises

1. Examine your city's charter to determine its form of government. (a) If it uses the council-manager form, list the powers given to the manager and compare to those given to the mayor. Research the identity of the city manager over the past three decades. What was the average length of service? What was the reason for the turnover? (b) If your city uses a mayor-council form, determine whether it is a strong mayor or weak mayor system. List the powers given to the mayor.

2. Looking over the previous 5 years, choose a controversial political issue in your community. What role did the mayor play in addressing it? What role did other actors in the political system play? Who exercised leadership?

3. Using census data (www.census.gov), determine the size of your city and county government as measured by total personnel. Then locate data on the distribution of street-level bureaucrats at the city and county levels.

Practice and Review Online
https://textbooks.rowman.com/understanding-urban-politics

PART III

PARTICIPATION AND REPRESENTATION IN LOCAL POLITICS

7

ELECTIONS AND VOTING

GUIDING QUESTIONS

1. What are the main elements of the urban electoral process and how does it differ from state and national elections?
2. What are the factors that influence voter turnout, and what are the representational implications of low voter turnout?
3. What factors influence voter choice in urban elections?

IN DECEMBER 2017, voters in Atlanta headed to the polls to select their next mayor. The election was the first legitimate opportunity for Atlanta to select a white mayor since 1973, when Maynard Jackson broke the color barrier by becoming the city's first African American mayor in a city and region long accustomed to racial hostility and oppression. The seat was open due to term limits, which forced the incumbent mayor, Kasim Reed, an African American Democrat, out of office. The contest pitted Mary Norwood, a white Independent, against Keisha Lance Bottoms, a black Democrat. Both were members of the Atlanta City Council, on which Norwood represented an at-large seat and Bottoms a district seat. Like most cities, Atlanta uses nonpartisan ballots in the selection of local officials.

Demographics and questions of representation were critical to the outcome. Throughout the 1990s, Atlanta's population was two-thirds black, but this has been changing. According to the 2010 census, Atlanta's population is now only 54 percent black, down 13 points from its high-water mark of 67 percent. In 2017, these demographic trends created a political opening for a white candidate in a city used to choosing between a moderate black Democrat or a more progressive black Democrat with political roots in Atlanta's lower-class neighborhoods. In the past, more conservative whites would vote for the most pro-business (i.e., moderate) black candidate, all of whom were members of the Democratic Party, while blacks would split their votes between moderates and more progressive candidates. Black voters split according to class, with higher-income blacks supporting moderate black candidates and lower-income blacks supporting more progressive black candidates, who would advocate more aggressive policies to combat poverty, lack of affordable housing, and community development.

After the final tally, Bottoms won the election by a few hundred votes. The election was marked by cross-cutting loyalties. Shirley Franklin, the city's first black female mayor, endorsed Norwood, who was accused by her rival of being a closet Republican, while the state's Democratic Party aggressively supported Bottoms.

This contest illustrates the core themes of this chapter: that representation and institutions significantly influence outcomes in city elections. It describes and explains the main features of urban elections, identifies and explains the key variables that help you understand patterns of voter turnout in urban elections, and presents findings from research on voter choice. An understanding of the urban electoral process, voter turnout, and voter choice will shed light on the importance of representation and institutions at the local level. Urban elections are vitally important because they have significant consequences for who is represented, what cities do, and how they do it.[1]

The main topic covered in this chapter is voting in city elections, but people get involved in local politics in many other ways. They contact government officials to express their opinion or request services, contribute to campaigns volunteer, join political parties and interest groups,[2] protest and rebel, and even "vote with their feet" by leaving an area because of dissatisfaction with the quality, level, or cost of local government services.[3] Although noted here, these alternative forms of participation will be covered more extensively in chapter 9.

URBAN ELECTORAL PROCESS

Cities hold elections for city council, mayor, other citywide officeholders (such as city attorney, city comptroller, and city clerk), and for initiatives, referenda, and recalls, all of which fall into the category of direct democracy. The exact mix of elections and offices varies from place to place and from election cycle to election cycle. Mayoral and city council elections have received the most attention from local election scholars, which is not surprising given that they are the most frequent and have the greatest direct effect on representation and policy. Before explaining voter turnout and voter choice, it is important to understand several key features of city elections: ballot structure, election timing, mayoral selection, and direct democracy.

Ballot Structure, Election Systems, and Election Timing

Local elections are officially nonpartisan in about 80 percent of American cities.[4] Nonpartisan elections, ones in which the ballot does not list the candidate's party affiliation (see chapter 2), is a key institutional feature that distinguishes urban elections from state and national elections. They do not exist at the federal level, and only the state of Nebraska uses nonpartisan ballots in the selection of state officials. This does not mean that city elections lack partisan influence, but that the ballots used in choosing leaders in the vast majority of cities exclude any mention of political party.

In cities with nonpartisan ballots, all candidates for office, regardless of their party affiliation, compete in a **nonpartisan general election**, a preliminary contest in which all candidates for an office compete against each other without reference to party affiliation. If one candidate wins a number of votes in excess of a legally determined threshold, usually 50 percent, they are declared the winner. Candidates for mayor compete against each other in this first contest, as do city council candidates who are running for district council seats. If no one reaches the designated threshold of votes, the top two candidates compete in a **runoff election**, typically held four to six weeks after the first election. The winner of this second election wins the seat.[5]

In at-large elections, the process is different, and it is hard to categorize, as a number of different methods for selecting at-large councilors exist. In some cities, voters have as many votes to cast as there are seats available, so if there are seven at-large seats and more than seven candidates running, the top seven would win the seats. In others, candidates must declare for a *position* or *place*, then compete against others with the same designation. The election is still city-wide, but voter choices are constrained to candidates competing for each place. In Houston's mixed representation system, for example, there are five at-large members on the city's sixteen-member city council.[6] In order to win an at-large seat, candidates must first declare for numbered positions from one through five, then compete against others who declare for the same position.[7] If no one wins a majority in the first election, a runoff is held between the top candidates. These are not districts, mind you; rather, they serve as a way for cities to narrow the available choices and make the process more manageable. Politically, they help to clarify the choices and contests for voters. Seattle and Atlanta, both of which have mixed-representation systems, also use numbered positions to select at-large councilors,[8] but voters cast a separate vote for their district councilor.

Philadelphia's and Tucson's methods of at-large selection are different still. Both cities use partisan ballots, but in Philadelphia the top seven candidates win the seven at-large seats, with one twist: The maximum number of seats any one party can hold is five. Therefore, because Philadelphia is overwhelmingly Democratic and because party affiliation is a key predictor of how people vote, the city usually ends up with five Democrats and two Republicans serving at large on the city council.[9] Tucson's system of electing councilors is truly unique. The city council has seven members (six councilors plus a mayor), each of whom represents a district. To win a seat, however, candidates must pass two hurdles: (1) a partisan primary in their district, and (2) a citywide general election. In other words, primary voters select their nominees at the district level, then those nominees run citywide. Consequently, because Tucson, like Philadelphia, is a Democratic-majority city, Republicans cannot even elect their nominee to the one council district dominated by Republican voters![10]

About a dozen cities in the US use a **ranked choice voting/instant-runoff voting** system (San Francisco, Oakland, Berkeley, Minneapolis, St. Paul, Santa Fe, and Memphis, among others). Voters rank candidates according to their preferences, and if no one wins a majority of first-place votes in the first round of balloting, the candidate with the fewest first-place votes is eliminated. Then the votes of those who ranked the losing candidate first are reallocated to their second-choice candidate. This process is repeated until a candidate wins a majority.

Santa Fe, the capital of New Mexico, has a population of about 84,000 people. In 2018, it held its first mayoral election under instant-runoff voting, and it took four rounds of counting to determine that Allan Webber, an entrepreneur and journalist, had won. Five candidates had entered the race (Figure 7.1). In Round 1, Peter Ives came in last place with only 6 percent of the first-choice votes. At that point, he was eliminated from the running, and his second-place votes were reallocated to those voters' second-place candidates. In Round 2, Joseph Maestas finished last, and his votes were reallocated. In Round 3, Kate Noble was eliminated, and by Round 4, Webber was chosen with 66 percent of the votes cast.

Allowing voters to rank candidates, as opposed to casting their ballots for just one person, eliminates the need for a traditional runoff election between the top two vote-getters from the first round, saving the costs associated with managing a second election. By giving voters the opportunity to rank the candidates, they are also less likely to feel they wasted their vote on a preferred but ultimately less viable candidate. Instant runoffs might also reduce negative campaigning, giving each candidate an incentive to attract their rivals' supporters and stay positive.

On the downside, because they reward candidates who do not finish last, instant-runoff elections are likely to inspire more candidates to run. This may have significant information costs for voters. News coverage of those not considered front runners is likely to be minimal, making it harder for voters to cast informed choices. Larger fields of candidates also make it harder for campaigns to cut through the clutter of campaign noise to get their messages heard, potentially obscuring the stakes of the election for racial and ethnic groups.[11] The added complexity may also invite more errors in the voter process.[12]

In the 20 percent of municipalities that use **partisan ballots**, the party affiliation of the candidate is listed directly on the ballot, and the process of selecting candidates is like that used in the selection of governors, state legislators, and members of Congress. Candidates must first win their party's nomination before competing against the other party's nominee in a general election. Partisan ballots in city elections are used most frequently in municipalities located in the Mid-Atlantic and Northeast regions of the country. New York City, Philadelphia, and Baltimore are the most prominent examples.

City elections can also be distinguished from state and national elections in terms of their timing. Most urban elections are held at times when state and/or

Figure 7.1 Sample Ballot for City of Santa Fe, District 1, 2018

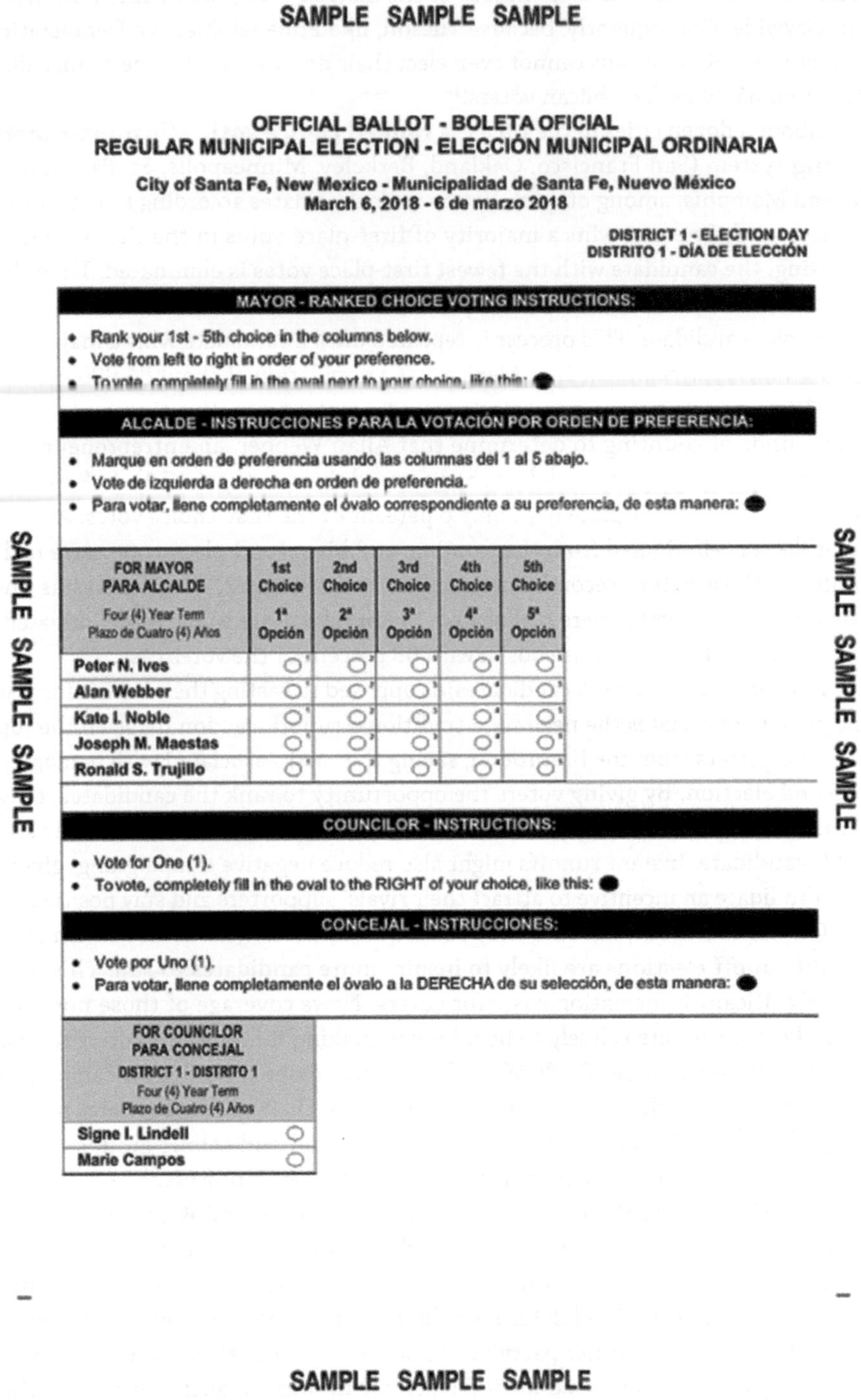

SAMPLE SAMPLE SAMPLE

OFFICIAL BALLOT - BOLETA OFICIAL
REGULAR MUNICIPAL ELECTION - ELECCIÓN MUNICIPAL ORDINARIA
City of Santa Fe, New Mexico - Municipalidad de Santa Fe, Nuevo México
March 6, 2018 - 6 de marzo 2018

DISTRICT 1 - ELECTION DAY
DISTRITO 1 - DÍA DE ELECCIÓN

MAYOR - RANKED CHOICE VOTING INSTRUCTIONS:

- Rank your 1st - 5th choice in the columns below.
- Vote from left to right in order of your preference.
- To vote, completely fill in the oval next to your choice, like this: ●

ALCALDE - INSTRUCCIONES PARA LA VOTACIÓN POR ORDEN DE PREFERENCIA:

- Marque en orden de preferencia usando las columnas del 1 al 5 abajo.
- Vote de izquierda a derecha en orden de preferencia.
- Para votar, llene completamente el óvalo correspondiente a su preferencia, de esta manera: ●

SAMPLE SAMPLE SAMPLE

FOR MAYOR PARA ALCALDE Four (4) Year Term Plazo de Cuatro (4) Años	1st Choice 1ª Opción	2nd Choice 2ª Opción	3rd Choice 3ª Opción	4th Choice 4ª Opción	5th Choice 5ª Opción
Peter N. Ives	○	○	○	○	○
Alan Webber	○	○	○	○	○
Kate I. Noble	○	○	○	○	○
Joseph M. Maestas	○	○	○	○	○
Ronald S. Trujillo	○	○	○	○	○

SAMPLE SAMPLE SAMPLE

COUNCILOR - INSTRUCTIONS:

- Vote for One (1).
- To vote, completely fill in the oval to the RIGHT of your choice, like this: ●

CONCEJAL - INSTRUCCIONES:

- Vote por Uno (1).
- Para votar, llene completamente el óvalo a la DERECHA de su selección, de esta manera: ●

FOR COUNCILOR PARA CONCEJAL DISTRICT 1 - DISTRITO 1 Four (4) Year Term Plazo de Cuatro (4) Años	
Signe I. Lindell	○
Marie Campos	○

SAMPLE SAMPLE SAMPLE

Source: City of Santa Fe, "Sample Ballots: March 6, 2018 Regular Municipal Election," https://www.santafenm.gov/sample_ballots_-_march_6_2018_regular_municipal_election

national elections are *not* held. So-called **off-cycle elections** are often associated with the same reformers who promoted nonpartisan ballots. Reformers in the early 20th century argued in favor of off-cycle elections as a way to force city residents to focus only on *local* issues when casting ballots in city elections and as a means to weaken immigrant-based party machines.[13]

Mayoral Selection

In addition to a city council, every city has a presiding elected official, most often called a mayor.[14] The method of selecting the mayor varies. According to a 2011 survey by the International City/County Management Association (ICMA), voters directly elect the mayor in approximately 76 percent of cities.[15] About 23 percent are selected by their city councils or they simply rotate through the position. (This was the method of mayoral selection favored by reformers, who advocated this as part of the council-manager system [see chapter 2].) Approximately two-thirds of cities with council-manager systems now directly elect their mayor. Direct election in a citywide contest increases the chances that the mayor will represent the city as a whole in his or her official capacity. This trend away from council selection shifts attention to the mayor as *the* political focal point within the community. The citizenry is more likely to attribute credit or blame for local conditions to a directly elected mayor.

Table 7.1 presents information on term lengths for city councilors and mayors, as well as the different kinds of mayoral selection methods.

TABLE 7.1 / Election Structures by Institution	
City Councils	
Term Length:	
Two-Year Term	22.5%
Three-Year Term	12%
Four-Year Term	63.5%
Mayors	
Method of Selection:	
Directly Elected	76%
Council Selection	21%
Council Rotation	2%
Term Length:	
One-Year Term	13%
Two-Year Term	33%
Three-Year Term	7%
Four-Year Term	46%

Note: ICMA 2011 Municipal Form of Government Survey Summary (Washington, DC: International City/County Management Association, 2012).

Direct Democracy

Voters also get involved in local elections through **direct democracy**, which allows citizens to make policy decisions or remove elected officials directly through the balloting process. Participation through direct democracy is not really an option at the federal level, but it is very prominent at the subnational level, especially in the western US.

Forms of direct democracy include initiatives, referenda, and recalls. According to a 2011 ICMA survey, 54 percent of cities allow the initiative (see chapter 4), in which citizens place policy matters directly on the ballot following successful signature petition drives, and 70 percent allow their city council to present policy matters to voters via legislative **referendum**.[16] Initiatives and referenda are similar in that a policy proposal (legislation, charter amendment, or advisory matter) is placed on the ballot for voters' consideration. The difference is the origin of the policy. As the term implies, initiatives require local residents to take the *initiative* to place a policy matter before the city as a whole. By contrast, it is elected officials who place a referendum on the ballot to seek the public's input on a policy proposal. Only 38 percent of cities have what is called a **popular referendum**, a referendum requiring a public vote on policy changes adopted by elected officials prior to implementation. Finally, citizens in 56 percent of cities have the ability to **recall** or remove an elected official before his or her term of office has expired.[17] In sum, citizens in at least 50 percent of cities have the ability to engage in direct democracy, which is roughly equivalent to the percentage of states with some element of direct democracy.[18]

Bond referendum elections are perhaps the most common form of direct democracy elections in which voters are asked to participate. Through local bond referenda, cities and other subnational governments can raise money—via the sale of bonds to investors—to build and improve parking lots, libraries, parks, community centers, educational facilities, police and fire equipment, solid waste infrastructure, transportation systems, etc. In most places, general obligation bonds—financial instruments that local residents agree to sell and pay back with interest from the city's general operating fund—must be put to a vote. Another type of bond is a revenue bond, a financial instrument that local residents agree to sell and pay back with revenue generated from a specific project. (See chapter 11 for more information on bonds.) Revenue bonds do not have to be put to a vote because city taxpayers generally are not on the hook for repaying the principal and interest. Instead, users of the facility—a parking structure is a classic example—pay fees to generate the revenue that the city then uses to repay bondholders. Approximately 64 percent of municipalities with a referendum provision in their charter report using it for bond measures.[19]

Issuing bonds through a public vote can be difficult because city residents have different preferences for public goods provision. If one group wants one thing and another group wants another, or if one group wants one thing that another does not want to pay for, stalemate may ensue. Reflecting this collective action dynamic, research on municipal bond elections supports the idea that fewer bonds are issued in more racially diverse communities, as different voter groups withhold support for bonds from which they do not directly benefit.[20] To overcome this problem, leaders in diverse municipalities include *multiple* spending items benefitting different groups in a single bond election, making it politically harder to oppose. Leaders in cities with diverse communities often schedule bond elections during general elections when they know that turnout will be larger and more diverse. Strategic behavior on the part of local leaders therefore helps to keep public goods funded in cities prone to undersupplying them.[21]

VOTER TURNOUT IN URBAN ELECTIONS

The most common form of political participation is voting. **Voter turnout** is most often measured as the number of ballots cast divided by the voting-age population (18 years or older) in a jurisdiction. Others use voting-eligible population, which is, by definition, a lower number as it excludes those who are older than 18 years of age but who are nonetheless ineligible to vote for some reason (e.g., a felony conviction).[22] A third way to measure turnout is by calculating the number of ballots cast as a percentage of registered voters. Turnout figures increase as the size of potential universe (i.e., the denominator) decreases.

Turnout should be most vibrant at the city level. People are closer in proximity to their local governments and more directly affected by their decisions and actions. Moreover, the impact of a single vote on the outcome of a local election is greater than the impact of one vote in a presidential election. There were 136,466,197 votes cast in the 2016 presidential election, with most of the focus on a few battleground states, and 190,397 votes cast in the 2015 San Francisco mayoral election. So each vote cast for president is far less important to the outcome than a vote cast for mayor of San Francisco.[23] Given these conditions, you might think that local politics would be a hotbed of citizen participation and activism, but this is not the case.

According to Neal Caren, only about 25–27 percent of voting-age residents (those 18 years old and older) vote in city elections.[24] While this represents an average *across* cities, it is still remarkably low given the impact of city leaders and institutions on our everyday lives and the potential consequence of low turnout for the quality of representation that city residents receive. The range of turnout in large US cities is also striking. According to Caren's research, Chicago's average turnout was 48 percent between 1970 and 2003 compared to an average turnout of 5 percent in Fort Worth, Texas. By contrast, average turnout in US presidential elections from 1970 to 2004 was 53 percent.[25] More alarmingly, elections in Los Angeles, New York City, Dallas, and Washington, DC between 2011 and 2015 saw record numbers of people *failing* to cast ballots in elections for the most important elected offices in city government.[26] Voter turnout in US mayoral elections has declined to a point where commentators and scholars are beginning to question the very foundation of urban democracy in the 21st century. Figure 7.2 presents information on turnout of voting-age residents in the thirty largest US cities.

Although turnout numbers and trends are important as general indicators of the health of urban democracy, the more important consideration is who votes and who does not, as this sets the stage for which interests get represented in decision making. Elected officials focus on those who vote, and in some cases

Figure 7.2 Voter Turnout in Mayoral Elections, Thirty Largest US Cities, 2011 and 2015

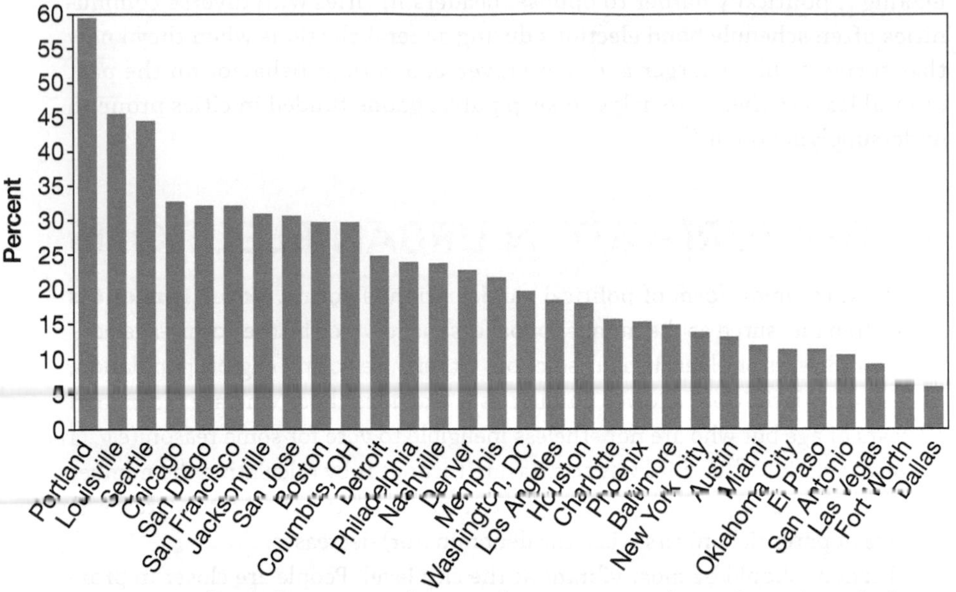

Note: Percentages reflect ballots cast as a fraction of voting-age population. Rates shown for last election held between 2011 and 2015 for either primary, general, or last election of runoff, whichever was considered most important in deciding outcome.

Source: Portland State University "Who Votes for Mayor?" report, http://www.whovotesformayor. org/.

they may have little incentive to encourage broad-based turnout. If a candidate assumes that higher voter turnout will imperil their electoral chances, they are unlikely to encourage voting. Officials and parties may even change how aggressively they encourage turnout from one election cycle to the next, even within the same city, in an effort to stay in office.[27] Although they cannot, of course, keep people from voting, not all officials, political parties, or interest groups support the notion that more participation is better. Nevertheless, voting is power, and those most involved in the political process have more power than those on the sidelines. Voter turnout is shaped by a number of factors, including individual-level demographic factors, institutional features of city government, and election context.

Class, Age, Race, and Ethnicity

In general, there is a pronounced class bias to participation in politics. This is a baseline condition of voluntary participation in politics in the United States.[28] Individuals can be divided on the basis of **socioeconomic status (SES)**, the combined levels of income and education that divide society by economic class. **Class bias** is the degree to which electoral participation is skewed in the direction of particular economic groups. Individuals with higher SES have greater capacity to engage in politics; they have more knowledge of the political process and the issues at stake; and they are often better equipped to deal with the process of voting. In sum, they have greater civic skills than those with lower SES.

This pattern is especially pronounced at the local level, where home owner-ship is a powerful element of class bias. Homeowners tend to participate more than renters, all else being equal. They have a clear interest in the policy choices of cities—on property taxes, zoning, the siting of new housing developments, public safety, and parks and recreation—because they directly impact the value of their most important asset, their home.[29] If wealthy individuals participate more, cities may focus more attention on issues relevant to them.

Turnout in local elections is also affected by age. Older voters have greater incentives to participate in local elections. They are more likely to have careers, families, property, and longer-term residential stability—in sum, a larger stake in the decisions of local government than younger voters. They are also more prac-ticed at voting and being a part of the electoral system, and thus have greater civic skills. Numerous studies document the significant effect of a voter's age on propensity to vote (see box 7.1).[30]

In addition to wealth, education, and age gaps, there is a significant turnout gap among voters of different races or ethnicities. Whites are substantially more likely to vote in local elections than all other demographic groups, including Afri-can Americans, Latinos, and Asian Americans. African Americans are more likely to vote than Hispanics, who in turn are slightly more likely to vote than Asian Americans. Because racial and ethnic groups are often engaged in intense com-petition over the benefits of local government, who votes has important implica-tions for substantive representation.

In sum, participation at the local level is driven primarily by wealthier, bet-ter-educated, older white individuals (see figure 7.4),[31] making the chances that city government can represent adequately the needs of lower-income, minority, and younger residents highly questionable.

Institutional Rules

A second category of variables that influences voter turnout is local institutional rules. Institutions advocated by municipal reformers, including council-manager government, nonpartisan ballots, and the timing of local elections, have been linked to low voter turnout in city elections.[32]

Municipal institutions are important because they influence the *incentives* that people have to participate. When the individual responsible for the deliv-ery of city services is an unelected administrator—as in the council-manager system—the salience of city politics and the perceived consequences for urban administration can seem beyond the control of ordinary citizens.[33] Many resi-dents may feel that there is no reason to participate. Similarly, nonpartisan bal-lots raise the cost of gathering information about local candidates and issues, as voters cannot rely simply on political party cues to "tell" them how to vote.[34] In addition, when city elections are separated from state and national elections, they fly so far under the radar that they are invisible to the mass public. As explained shortly, however, they are not as invisible to local stakeholders, which was exactly the motivation behind reformers' efforts.[35] As urban scholar Amy Bridges argues, they "wrote the rules to win the game" and to keep poor and nonwhite residents out of the political process, a legacy that exists to this day.[36]

BOX 7.1

When It Comes to Turnout, Older Voters Crush Younger Voters

Senior Citizens Participate in Early Voting at an Assisted Living Center in Austin, Texas

A report produced by researchers at Portland State University clearly illustrates the divide between older and younger voters. This study of thirty large US cities found that the median age of voters in city elections was 57, and ranged from 68 in Miami to 46 in Portland. Voters aged 65 and older were fifteen times more likely to vote in city elections than voters between the ages of 18 and 34. Fewer than one in ten younger voters cast ballots in mayoral elections, but 46.1 percent of them cast ballots in the 2016 presidential election.[a] A *Governing* magazine article on the study, entitled "Millennials Let Their Grandparents Decide Local Elections," notes that in order to encourage turnout among younger voters and to foster stronger democratic habits, Takoma Park and Hyattsville, Maryland and Berkeley, California all lowered the voting age to 16.[b] (If 16-year-olds can drive, perhaps they should be able to vote as well.) See figure 7.3 for age-related differences in voter turnout across the thirty cities in the Portland State study.

[a] "Too Few People Choose Our Local Leaders," http://www. whovotesformayor.org, accessed September 30, 2018.

[b] Mike Maciag, "Millennials Let Their Grandparents Decide Local Elections," http://www.governing.com/topics/elections/ gov-voter-turnout-generations-millennials.html, accessed September 30, 2018.

Not all reform-era institutions lower voter turnout. Research on California cities showed that places that allow for direct democracy, where local residents can legislate policy changes through the ballot box, usually have higher turnout than those that do not. But this research also indicated that the degree to which a city privatizes local services may lower turnout. Both of these institutional features create greater incentives for voters to be engaged. Where people are empowered to legislate directly, and where more public services are provided by the government, turnout should be higher.[37] In sum, cities oriented toward

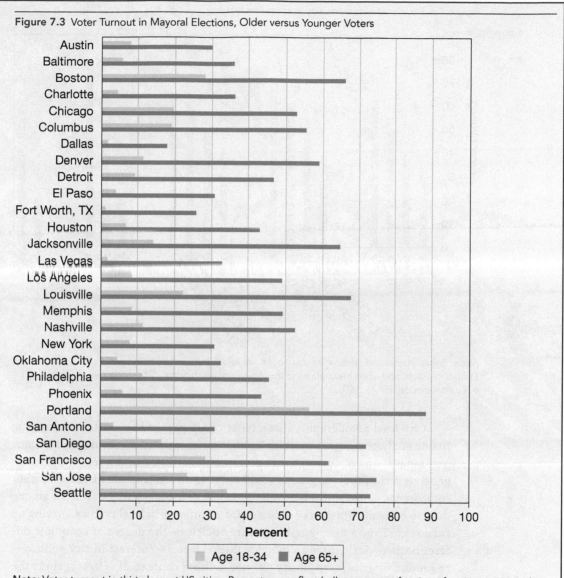

Figure 7.3 Voter Turnout in Mayoral Elections, Older versus Younger Voters

Note: Voter turnout in thirty largest US cities. Percentages reflect ballots cast as a fraction of voting-age population. Rates shown for last election held between 2011 and 2015 for either primary, general, or last election of runoff, whichever was considered most important in deciding outcome.

Source: Portland State University "Who Votes for Mayor?" report, http://www.whovotesformayor.org.

political engagement have higher turnout compared to those oriented toward administrative efficiency.[38]

Election Context

Election context also affects voter turnout in municipal elections. Individuals cast votes at a particular time and place—in other words, in a particular context. **Contextual effects** are features of the environment that affect voter turnout.

Figure 7.4 Race and Class Inequality in Local Electorates

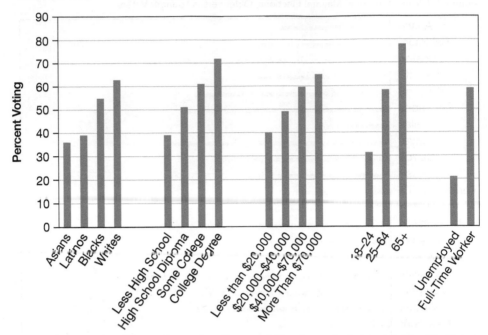

Note: Zoltan Hajnal and Jessica Trounstine, "Race and Class Inequality in Local Politics," in *The Politics of Racial and Class Inequalities in the Americas* (Washington, DC: American Political Science Association, 2016), 140.

City-level demographic characteristics are part of this context. According to one study, the degree to which a city is differentiated on the basis of income groupings is one feature of the electoral context. Cities with a relatively homogeneous mix of income groups are likely to have lower levels of voter turnout compared to those with a heterogeneous mix of income groups. Conflict among diverse economic interests produces greater interest in local politics, driving up turnout.[39] Thus a demographic feature of cities—the degree of economic differentiation—influences an individual-level factor—interest in city politics—to predict voter turnout in city elections. Other contextual effects include the level of neighborhood poverty and the existence of *social capital*, the amount of social connectedness within a community. Social capital is often measured as the amount of time neighbors spend interacting with one another socially and/or in groups, as well as the degree to which they discuss social, political, and civic affairs.[40]

A significant and unresolved question concerns the effect of city size on turnout. Some studies show that city size has a direct bearing on the debate concerning effects of *metropolitan fragmentation* (the proliferation of suburbs within metro areas) on democratic citizenship. Residents of smaller cities are more likely to know and be mobilized by their neighbors to participate in city elections.[41] In contrast, other research suggests that interest in city politics and community discourse about local civic affairs may be more important in determining how many show up at the polls. According to this line of reasoning, areas of high population density, characteristic of larger cities, generate substantially more discourse and interest, which stimulates greater turnout.[42]

Electoral competition significantly affects turnout and may be more important than institutional factors such as election timing.[43] If outcomes are not in doubt, there is little incentive for voters to get involved. It is like watching a sporting event with a known outcome; because there is no suspense, you are likely to stop watching. When campaign spending (an indicator of competitiveness) is greater, so is turnout.[44] Spending in an election is a sign of campaign effort and increases the amount of information available to voters. However, the type of information that relates most directly to voter turnout is unclear. One study of local elections in Florida indicates that negative campaign information actually *stimulates* voter turnout.[45] Certain candidate characteristics may also influence turnout among particular groups. For example, when minority candidates are on the ballot, minority voter turnout is usually greater.[46] The involvement of party organizations and nonpartisan civic groups can also influence overall voter turnout.[47]

And last but not least, campaign tactics can affect the number of people who cast ballots. Self-starting individuals create their own campaign organizations and decide when to run for mayor or city council. Candidates who spend significant amounts of time walking door to door, formulating campaign literature and messages, and meeting with local groups in an effort to increase turnout and sway the vote their way are not wasting effort. Research shows that turnout is greater in cities where candidates and organizations aggressively engage in door-to-door canvassing.[48] In general, then, although voter turnout is class-biased, a number of other factors—institutional, demographic, and context-related—can diminish that bias.

The Importance of Voter Turnout

Turnout is important not just because of what it tells us about the relative health of democracy—that is, that in theory more participation is healthier than less—but because of its substantive impact on governing. When the electorate is significantly biased in a particular direction, it is important to question the effects on election outcomes and local policies. Of course, if nonvoters feel exactly the same way as voters, there should be no bias in either election results or policy outputs. In such cases, voter turnout is directly linked to representation.

According to multiple studies, however, the number and characteristics of those who turn out on Election Day affect both election outcomes and the direction of city policy, suggesting a significant gap between the preferences of voters and nonvoters. For example, research on voter turnout and mayoral vote choice in ten large US cities indicates that had whites and minorities voted at similar rates, election outcomes would have been different in three of the ten elections.[49] Latino voters would have gained the most from proportional turnout; in each of the three cases, the candidate favored by Latinos would have won. Based on a sample of nearly 1,700 cities, researchers also found that higher actual turnout is linked to significantly greater levels of city council representation by Hispanics and Asian Americans. As discussed more fully in the discussion of bureaucracy in

BOX 7.2

Voters Have Their Say in Ferguson

A Woman Takes Part in a Protest against a Grand Jury's Decision Not to Charge Police Officer Darren Wilson in the Fatal Shooting of African American Youth Michael Brown, in Ferguson, Missouri

On April 7, 2015, voters in Ferguson, Missouri, elected two African Americans to the city council, bringing to three the number of African Americans on the seven-member council. Recall that Ferguson is the St. Louis suburb where unarmed 18-year-old African American Michael Brown was shot and killed by Darren Wilson, a white police officer. Days of protest, rioting, and media coverage followed, sparking a national debate about police-community relations in America.[a] It also resulted in a blistering US Department of Justice report and the resignation of the Ferguson city manager and police chief, both of whom are white.[b]

chapter 5, minority representation in elected positions leads to greater representation in policy-making roles, making government more responsive to the needs of minority communities.

Prolonged declines in voter turnout can also produce domination of local politics by one party or group. Low-turnout elections are typically dominated by major stakeholders in city government such as municipal workers and homeowners, who benefit from favorable city spending and tax policies.[50] This narrows the policy benefits of city government to those supporters and neighborhoods most supportive of the prevailing or dominant coalition, thus distorting basic notions of representation and **democratic accountability**, or the ability of the citizenry to hold the government accountable for policy decisions and outcomes.[51] See box 7.2 for a description of these issues in the city of Ferguson, Missouri.

VOTER CHOICE IN URBAN ELECTIONS

After deciding to cast a ballot in city elections, voters must choose. Similar to voter turnout, a number of variables influence voter decisions. These include party and ideology, race and ethnicity, and incumbency, candidate experience, and endorsements.

Party and Ideology

In general, party and ideology serve as a standing decision for most voters, and thus are important "cues" or cognitive shortcuts that help people make choices in

According to the US Census, Ferguson is a city of 21,059 people, 67.4 percent of whom are African American. Yet until this election only one member of the city council was African American.[c] What pushed the city toward greater representation of African Americans was greater than average turnout among black voters on Election Day. Indeed, turnout was more than double the previous election (29 percent versus 12 percent).[d] Until 2015, the city's white population had constituted 50–55 percent of the city's registered voters but only 29 percent of the population.[e] In short, with effective political organizing and voter turnout, greater representation can be achieved.

[a] Lawrence Ross, "2 Years after Ferguson, MO, the Fight Grows and Goes On for Black Lives Matter," http://www.theroot.com/articles/culture/2016/08/2-years-after-ferguson-mo-the-fight-grows-goes-on-for-black-lives-matter/, accessed January 23, 2017.

[b] John Eligon, "Ferguson City Manager Cited in Justice Department Report Resigns," New York Times, https://www.nytimes.com/2015/03/11/us/ferguson-city-manager-resigns.html, accessed October 21, 2018; Sara Sidner, Catherine E. Shoichet, and Julian Cummings, "Ferguson Police Chief Resigns, Gets One Year of Pay," CNN, https://www.cnn.com/2015/03/11/us/ferguson-police-chief/index.html, accessed October 21, 2018.

[c] Moni Basu, "Ferguson Election Makes History, Adds More Blacks to City Council," CNN, http://www.cnn.com/2015/04/08/us/ferguson-election/, accessed January 23, 2017.

[d] Yamiche Alcindor, "Ferguson Voters Make History and Increase Turnout," USA Today, http://www.usatoday.com/story/news/2015/04/07/ferguson-voters-head-to-polls/25401037/, accessed January 23, 2017.

[e] See Terry Jones's comment in Matt Pearce, "A Chance for Change as Ferguson Votes for 3 Council Seats," LA Times, http://www.latimes.com/nation/la-na-ferguson-election-20150406-story.html, accessed January 23, 2017.

complex information environments. Liberal voters are more likely to select more liberal candidates (i.e., Democrats), while conservative voters are more likely to select more conservative candidates (i.e., Republicans). Ideologically moderate voters will typically fall somewhere in between the extremes. This is fairly straightforward in cities that use partisan ballots, as candidates' party affiliation typically provides much of the information a voter needs to make an appropriate choice.

How does this work in the nonpartisan elections that are generally the rule at the local level? Without the party label, **information costs**—the time and effort required by voters to gather information on candidates and policy proposals—are certainly greater. Local candidates are reluctant to inject party politics into their campaigns for fear of alienating independent voters and those inclined to support a different party.[52] Although city elections cannot be viewed simply through the prism of "normal" party politics, party and ideology can still be important in understanding the choices that local voters make.

Voters learn about a candidate's issue positions and (perhaps) ideological perspective through media coverage, candidates' websites, efforts such as door-to-door canvassing, and advertising. Elections for prominent positions, such as the mayoralty in a large city, often attract experienced candidates who have served in a partisan office at the state or national level, making them known quantities. Learning about candidates' backgrounds helps voters locate them in terms of party and ideology. Thus, even if "party" is never mentioned in a "nonpartisan" campaign, the voters can employ information tools to figure this out. Because voters in city politics tend to have high levels of interest, they are likely to know something about the candidates well before campaigns and media coverage begin.

Political science research supports the idea that candidates' parties and ideologies influence voters' choices in urban elections. One study of *exit polls* (interviews with voters about their choices) conducted in mayoral elections in New York City and Los Angeles over a number of election cycles suggests that, indeed, voters can and do select candidates that fit their ideological and partisan preferences.[53] A more recent study of the 2011 San Francisco mayoral election provides experimental evidence that voters, even in a nonpartisan contest with a crowded candidate field, can position candidates on an ideological, issue-based continuum and effectively match their preferences to their choices.[54] Research on suburban elections also suggests that voters' choices are significantly affected by issue positions and party affiliations. These findings indicate that democratic accountability, predicated on voters knowing what politicians represent and being able to reward or punish them for the actions on the issues, is a real possibility at the local level.

Race and Ethnicity

Party and ideology may not be the most relevant factors shaping voter choice at the city level, however. Indeed, depending on the city and the kinds of candidates who run, it may not be important at all. In a multiracial election in a Democratic-majority city, it is likely that all of the viable candidates will be Democrats. Where they might vary, however, is in racial or ethnic identification. In terms of effect on the vote, demographic characteristics may trump party and ideology. This may be particularly true for partisan primary elections (especially in cities where one party dominates), in which the influence of party or ideology is muted.

As with turnout, race or ethnicity plays a considerable role in determining voter choice in local politics as demographic groups compete for power and influence. Signaling to voters that candidates are either like them or unlike them in terms of goals, values, and life experiences, a candidate's race or ethnicity is a powerful cue. Indeed, this has been a consistent theme of urban politics scholarship over several decades. As Joel Lieske concludes following his study of voting in Cincinnati elections in the late 1980s: "In sum, there is nothing in this body of research on Cincinnati, a city noted for its progressive political climate, to alter our ethnocultural interpretation of urban electoral politics. If anything, the results of this research provide support to a growing body of thought that is reinterpreting American electoral politics within a framework of racial, ethnic, and cultural conflict."[55] In other words, voters' expectations about candidates—what they might do, how they might represent—are often based on race, ethnicity, or cultural factors.

Other scholarship paints a similar picture. Political scientists Zoltan Hajnal and Jessica Trounstine analyzed exit poll data over a 20-year period (1985–2005) in five major cities: New York, Los Angeles, Chicago, Houston, and Detroit. They tested competing hypotheses regarding voter choice grounded in racial and ethnic identification, economic class, party, and ideology, and they studied voting in mayoral, city council, and citywide elections. When they added data on the twenty-five largest US cities and tested the influence of race in mayoral election outcomes, they found that voter choices are significantly affected by racial and ethnic identification (i.e., that groups tend to vote as a bloc), that racial and ethnic groups compete with one another in urban politics, and that the difference between African Americans and all other groups—whites, Latinos, and Asians— is largest. In other words, the preferences of specific racial groups are of paramount importance in urban politics; however, it is a mistake to assume that these groups are natural allies who will automatically coalesce behind candidates who happen to represent a minority group.[56]

There are both representation-based and policy-related reasons for the influence of race and ethnicity on vote choice. Because racial and ethnic minority groups tend to settle in the nation's major urban centers, minority groups are most likely to achieve political representation at this level of government. In other words, the concentration of minorities in central cities gives these groups a shot at power that is often out of range in congressional or gubernatorial elections, where population demographics tend to favor the white majority. On the policy side, minority candidates and officials often support the kinds of policies in housing, public safety, and social services desired by minority residents.

In racially and ethnically diverse contexts, a central issue is the circumstances under which voters of one race will cross over to support candidates of another race. Some argue that crossover voting is a function of context; voters who reside in diverse neighborhoods are likely to come into contact with one another, share information about local problems, and learn to trust one another, making them more likely to support candidates of a different race.[57] Others suggest the exact opposite: that racial competition produces racially polarized voting and that crossover voting is more likely when one group is dominant.[58]

The influence of race and ethnicity has been studied most consistently in mayoral elections. According to Karen Kaufmann's group conflict theory, racial considerations are *most* important when race explicitly enters the campaign or issue environment. A high-profile racial incident acts like a trigger, polarizing the community along racial or ethnic lines, but under "normal" conditions, party and ideology will matter more to local voters.[59] Racial influence also appears to be most relevant when a minority candidate is the first to run for the office or is challenging a white incumbent. One study of multiethnic Houston found that race mattered more in minority candidates' first bids for office; after winning, white and African American voters evaluated incumbents on the basis of performance, but Hispanics continued to vote based on ethnicity.[60]

Other research shows that, in contests involving black incumbent mayors against white challengers, the quality of the white challenger—measured by experience as well as newspaper and party endorsements—is more important than race in explaining the support of white voters. However, these same considerations were statistically unrelated to white voter support for black challengers running against white incumbents; in other words, white voters mostly opposed black challengers to white incumbents on racial grounds. Race, therefore, is frequently more important to white voters than qualifications or experience when black candidates make their first bid for an office and less important when they run as incumbents.[61] In general, performance or public approval of minority officeholders might reduce the effect of race in urban elections.

Incumbency, Experience, and Endorsements

Voters' decisions in urban elections are influenced by a candidate's political resources as well as their achieved characteristics. Political resources include incumbency, endorsements, and campaign spending, while achieved characteristics include education and occupational background.[62]

Like elections to higher office, incumbency exerts a profound effect on who wins and who loses city council and mayoral elections. Current officeholders enjoy an **incumbency advantage** that gives them a substantial edge with voters, helping them win most of the time they seek reelection.[63] Survey data from 1986 to 2001 indicate that approximately 86 percent of council incumbents who seek reelection win.[64] Research demonstrates that simply serving one term as a city councilor increases the odds of seeking reelection by 39 percentage points and the odds of winning by 32 percentage points.[65]

The incumbent advantage relates to the command of political and office-related resources. Incumbents are better known, raise more money, have established voter coalitions, and gather more endorsements than their challengers.[66] The ability to deliver favors and benefits to constituents is also a critical resource.[67] Examples abound of incumbent mayors, city councilors, and school board members using their positions to provide policy benefits (such as public improvements or policy representation) to specific constituency groups, be they minority communities,[68] women,[69] or members of the LGBTQ community.[70]

Much like US presidents derive an electoral benefit from a strong national economy, local incumbents also derive a benefit from favorable local conditions. Christopher Berry and William Howell show that improvements in test scores are linked to reelection prospects of school board incumbents.[71] At the city level, Craig Burnett and Vladimir Kogan show that improvements to local roads enhance the reelection prospects of both city councilors and mayors.[72] Cumulatively, these political and performance advantages generate goodwill and help cement voter loyalty.

Institutional features of local government exacerbate the advantage held by incumbents. County commissioners representing larger districts face less competition than those representing smaller ones.[73] City council incumbents benefit from the low-information and low-turnout environments that often characterize city politics.[74] Institutional variables are a critical part of this. City council incumbents are more likely to run for reelection and win in cities with institutional arrangements that reduce turnout, such as failure to identify polling place locations, lengthy preelection voter registration requirements, and nonconcurrent (i.e., off-cycle) elections. Together, these insulate city council incumbents from electoral competition and reduce their incentives to provide broad policy representation while in office.[75]

Election timing may affect voter choice and turnout in mayoral elections as well. Research indicates that mayoral elections timed with national elections—as opposed to being *off* cycle—further the advantage that mayoral incumbents enjoy.[76] Mayors in cities with elections timed to coincide with national ones are more likely to seek to reelection and win. Although voter turnout is lower in off-cycle elections, those who do vote are more knowledgeable and thus more likely to vote out incumbents. The incumbent advantage might also relate to the length of the ballot in off- versus on-cycle elections. In the former, ballots tend to be shorter. In the latter, voters are asked to decide a range of matters at different levels of government, with the city-level questions lowest on the ballot. Voters might become fatigued by long ballots and vote for the most recognizable name.

More generally, **quality challengers**—those with high levels of political, civic, occupational, and/or educational experience—are necessary to effectively challenge incumbents.[77] Challengers with some political experience, familiarity, and legitimacy do better among voters.[78] Candidates with high-status occupations (such as attorneys) and experience in nonpartisan and civic organizations also perform better in city elections than those who lack such experience.[79] The effect of experience may vary depending on the partisanship of the voter; Republican voters are more likely to support candidates on the basis of occupation classification, and Democratic voters cast ballots on the basis of political experience.[80] Quality challengers are also in a better position to raise money, an essential feature of elections in large cities, especially those for mayor. Because challengers are less well known than incumbents, every dollar spent increases their name recognition to a much greater degree than funds spent by incumbents, who are already more widely known and therefore enjoy less bang for their buck.[81] These dollars are hard to come by, though, given the strategic behavior of donors who hedge their bets and protect their interests by giving disproportionately to incumbents and candidates in open-seat elections.[82] Not only that, the strongest challengers are *unlikely* to emerge to run against entrenched incumbents, creating a downward spiral that often allows incumbents a free pass.[83]

Incumbent advantages are lower in the suburbs. Research by J. Eric Oliver and Shang Ha shows that support for challengers among voters in suburban communities is high, a function of greater interest in and knowledge of local issues and candidates. Among these voters, the decision is a function of candidate traits (e.g., likeability), issue agreement, shared partisan affiliation, and perceptions of local government performance.[84] Nevertheless, incumbents in suburban city council elections still tend to be reelected at very high rates.[85]

The larger implication of the incumbent advantage and electoral competition is democratic accountability. After all, if "we, the people" cannot hold elected officials accountable at the ballot box, elections may be irrelevant to governance. Put another way, if the same people are returned to office regardless of government performance or official representation of the needs of the community, elections are meaningless. To counter the lack of electoral competition, some cities have imposed term limitations on local officials. Although this is a popular idea at the state and federal levels, its adoption at the municipal level is not widespread and occurs mainly in larger municipalities. Mayoral term limits have been adopted in only 10 percent of American cities.[86]

Endorsements are a final resource that shapes vote outcomes in urban elections. Endorsements from party organizations, interest groups, or local newspapers are a stamp of legitimacy.[87] Party and interest group endorsements signal to voters that a candidate stands for something they value. A candidate endorsed by the Republican Party in a nonpartisan election is a signal to Republican voters that they will, in general, stand for the party's main principles.[88] Candidates endorsed by the police union or a local chapter of the Sierra Club will be seen as tough on crime or a friend of the environment, respectively.[89] Newspaper endorsements are also cherished by candidates because they send a broad signal of support and suitability for office to the electorate.

The effects of endorsements are difficult to assess empirically, however, given that the endorsing entity is likely to support candidates who are already strong. Interestingly, the study of the 2011 San Francisco elections noted previously shows that party and newspaper endorsements may *weaken* the ideological connection between voters and candidates, suggesting that this information is less an ideological cue and more about shared party identification (in the case of party endorsements) or candidate legitimacy (in the case of newspaper endorsements).[90] This latter effect is particularly strong among self-identified independents.[91]

SUMMARY

What do we know about voter participation in urban politics? Ironically, the government closest to the people experiences the lowest voter turnout. Voter turnout in urban elections is quite low compared to that in higher-level elections. Not only that, it is not representative of the general population, resulting in significant bias. Better-educated people vote more than less-educated people, and those with higher incomes vote more than those with lower incomes. Beyond that, older people vote more than younger people, those who own property vote more regularly than those who do not, and whites vote more frequently than nonwhites.

Voting in urban elections is also a function of the institutions and the incentives for individual involvement. In general, cities with reformed institutions tend to have lower turnouts. One of the key predictors of turnout among those eligible to vote is *when* the election is held. When local elections are held separately from state and national elections, turnout declines. Turnout is also a function of context; electoral competition, candidates, and mobilization efforts positively affect citizen engagement as evidenced through voting.

Racial competition is a critical factor in shaping voter decisions, especially in larger cities where elections, especially those for mayor, involve both large concentrations of minority voters and racially diverse groups of candidates. Large gaps in turnout between minority and nonminority voters affect who gets elected and whose interests are represented. Incumbency is also a key variable that influences voters' decisions. This is unsurprising given voters' aversion to risk and their desire to stick with the official they know rather than choose someone new. An incumbent who has done something good for the community while in office is often rewarded with another term. For nonincumbents, experience, group support, and the ability to communicate are keys to success. Candidates are key to elections, and elections are key to representation and governance. We turn in chapter 8 to a discussion of these and other important issues related to candidates and campaigns.

Key Terms

class bias *(146)*
contextual effects *(149)*
democratic accountability *(152)*
direct democracy *(144)*
incumbency advantage *(156)*
information cost *(153)*
nonpartisan general election *(140)*
off-cycle election *(143)*
partisan ballot *(141)*

popular referendum *(144)*
quality challenger *(157)*
ranked choice voting/instant-runoff voting *(141)*
recall *(144)*
referendum *(144)*
runoff election *(140)*
socioeconomic status (SES) *(146)*
voter turnout *(145)*

Discussion Questions

1. How do urban elections differ from state or national elections?

2. How do electoral institutions, the "rules of the game," influence voter turnout and voter choice?

3. How do voter turnout and voter choice advantage some groups over others? What are the policy implications of this electoral bias?

4. How do other noninstitutional factors influence electoral politics at the urban level?

5. Under what conditions would at-large systems do a better job of representing citizen preferences than district elections?

6. Have you ever voted in a local election? What do think explains the turnout gap between older and younger voters in urban elections?

Exercises

1. Collect data on voter turnout for the most recent elections held in a sample of cities in your state. Describe any differences in turnout based on institutional differences, population demographics, or the closeness of the elections.

2. Collect data on the candidates who ran in the last two competitive mayoral elections in your state's largest city. Make note of the candidates' sex, race/ethnicity, occupation, incumbency status, and

endorsements. Which candidate(s) were most successful and why?

3. Choose a sample of cities in your state. Create an issue profile of candidates based on social media pages, newspaper coverage, and

endorsements. Then create an issue profile of the community. Discuss how closely the winning candidate's profile matches the community's profile.

Practice and Review Online
https://textbooks.rowman.com/understanding-urban-politics

8

CANDIDATES AND CAMPAIGNS

GUIDING QUESTIONS

1. In what ways have campaigns and candidates in urban politics evolved over time? What are the implications of these changes?

2. How does the institutional context of local elections shape campaign strategy?

3. What are the key considerations in effectively utilizing a campaign's three main resources: the candidate, the money, and the message?

IN THE 2011 CHICAGO MAYORAL ELECTION, the eventual winner of the first open seat for that position in several decades, Rahm Emanuel, raised over $14 million, far outpacing his rivals. Interestingly, most of this money was raised in the ten weeks after he announced his candidacy and before a new state law kicked in limiting donations in Illinois elections. Emanuel had many of the characteristics that define a quality candidate. A member of Congress, Chief of Staff to President Barack Obama, and advisor to President Bill Clinton, he was also endorsed by both of the city's major newspapers and by both of his former bosses. Nevertheless, we must ask whether the election would have turned out the way it did if the candidates were subject to contributions limits throughout from start to finish. After the limits went into effect, Emanuel's average contribution declined from $7,987 to $1,414. His main rival, Geri Chico, saw his average contribution decline only a bit from $1,385 to $1,272. Moreover, the difference in each candidate's total number of donations, 3,246 and 3,174 respectively, was hardly significant.[1]

This case illustrates three important insights about mayoral campaigns addressed in this chapter. First, institutions matter. Had the campaign finance reform law been in place throughout the campaign, it might have had a significant effect on the outcome. Emanuel would have been forced to generate significantly more *donations* to match his fundraising total prior to the legal change. Had his average donation in the first weeks of the campaign equaled his average after the law changed, Chico would have outraised him by about $400,000.

Second, experience and endorsements legitimize candidates and can help produce financial and voter support in a campaign. Experience gives voters confidence about a candidate's ability to deliver on promises, knowledge of how to exercise power, and competence. Newspaper, interest group, and personal endorsements legitimize candidates and signal to voters what a candidate's positions and actions might be on key issues confronting the city. Third, in big-city mayoral elections, money is critical. The bigger issue, though, is whether substantive representation is affected by campaign finance.[2] If campaigns are financed primarily through the donations of wealthy interests capable of affecting election outcomes, what might that mean for those average city residents who either never contribute to campaigns or who make even small contributions?[3]

In this chapter you will learn about **campaigns**, or organized efforts to persuade and mobilize voters to support or oppose a candidate or cause, the historical transition from organization-based to candidate-centered elections, the kinds of people who run for local offices such as city council, mayor, and school board, and how institutional features of local governments (i.e., the rules) influence the strategies candidates employ. The chapter also illuminates the roles of race, ethnicity, and gender in campaign messages, as well as the role of money and media, especially in the nation's largest municipalities. Finally, you will learn how campaigns affect election outcomes. As the chapter title suggests, the heart of the discussion is candidates and campaigns. This deceptively simple title, however, masks a complex set of institutional, representational, and political factors that affect the strategic choices of candidates and the outcomes of local elections.

FROM GROUP- TO CANDIDATE-CENTERED ELECTIONS

One of the major trends at the state and national levels is the transition from party-centered campaigns to candidate-centered campaigns.[4] Over time, the connection of state and national campaigns to party platforms and party organizations gave way to an individualized style of campaigning focused more on individual candidates targeting specific types of voters. A similar shift happened at the local level, when local parties and groups yielded to individual candidates.

Group-centered elections are ones in which local party machines and nonpartisan slating groups are the dominant actors. In **candidate-centered systems**, candidates run largely on their own. This is not to suggest that party organizations and groups are irrelevant in local politics today; however, the pendulum has swung in the direction of individual candidates creating their own organizations and campaign strategies.[5]

In the group-centered era, the urban political machines were expert at winning elections. The strongest urban machines were organized at each level of the elections and voting process. Party workers at the block, precinct, ward or district, and city or countywide levels "delivered" the votes in their territory for the party and its candidates. And delivering the vote did not mean *maximizing* it, unless of course you had to in order to win a close election.[6] Rather, it meant delivering the number of votes that were needed and the number that one predicted would be delivered before the election.[7] Regular contacts between party officials and voters allowed officials to survey voters' sentiments and assess their needs. Satisfying voters' needs would cement their loyalty, ease mobilization on Election Day, and keep the machine humming.

Political machines were associated with corruption and anti-democratic practices, which helped trigger the urban reform movement of the early 20th century (see chapter 2). However, according to political scientist Jessica Trounstine, machine bosses and urban reformers, although focused on different supporters and different policy goals, had much more in common with each other than was once believed.[8] To secure victory and electoral dominance, reformers in places like Dallas, Austin, San Antonio, San Diego, and San Jose created powerful nonpartisan slating organizations that recruited and endorsed candidates and provided them with financial backing and key business elite supporters.[9] At the heart of their success was an ability to deliver votes to their endorsed candidates on Election Day.

Like machines, reform organizations and their elected leaders supported institutions and policies designed to produce an electorate favorable to their interests. Holding elections separately from state and national elections and using nonpartisan ballots ensured that upper-status voters were more likely to turn out to support the reform ticket. Similarly, poll taxes and government annexation policies (where poor neighborhoods were not annexed to cities but remained part of unincorporated counties) produced a far wealthier electorate, further solidifying the reform ticket's electoral dominance.[10] While cities with powerful machines elected tough-talking immigrants, reform cities elected smooth-talking white businessmen.

In today's **candidate-centered elections**, candidates are less likely to be recruited to run by a party or an organization, and they bear the burden for developing their own strategies and volunteer network. Organization is still a key factor in city elections, but it is harder to produce given that the centrifugal forces inherent in all campaigns are much stronger when parties and groups are less prominent. Although their role has changed, parties and groups remain important to election outcomes in many cities. Candidates actively seek the endorsement of local parties and groups and then use endorsements to demonstrate credibility on issues of greatest importance to them. For example, local environmental, civic, business, and civil rights groups often endorse candidates. Endorsements can open doors to campaign money, but more importantly they provide shorthand information to voters about the likely issue positions of candidates. In a nonpartisan environment, the cue sent by the group can be vitally important.[11]

INSTITUTIONAL CONTEXT OF URBAN CANDIDATES AND CAMPAIGNS

The institution of nonpartisanship affects campaign strategy very directly. To understand this, consider its opposite, or *partisan* elections. In cities with partisan ballots, candidates must first win their party's nomination before they can compete against the nominees of the other parties. Assuming a *closed primary* (i.e., one where only those registered with the party can vote), candidates face a powerful incentive to appeal to the party's activists, who are the ones most likely to vote in this initial contest. (Especially in low-turnout elections like city primaries, the votes of party activists will be key to victory even in *open primaries*.) In the general election, median voter theory predicts that rational candidates will move to the middle of the political spectrum to win because all voters, not just those affiliated with a party, are able to vote.[12]

What about nonpartisan elections, in which candidates of all political parties and ideologies are able to participate? In these cities, there is one contest with all candidates competing against each other (see chapter 7). One candidate can win an office outright if she or he is able to surpass a particular threshold percentage of votes—50 percent in most cases. If not, the top two finishers will compete in a runoff to determine the winner of the election. Unlike partisan primaries, in which most of the voters will come from one party, in nonpartisan elections the full range of the ideological spectrum could be represented among voters. In addition, a candidate could face one or more opponents from the opposite party, from the same party, or from minor parties.

An added complication is that coming in second is meaningful if the top candidate can be kept under the 50 percent threshold. In that case, the top two finishers advance to the runoff. How does a candidate campaign in this context? What is the right strategy to adopt? It might make sense to attempt to beat out a close rival or similar candidates. If there are three candidates in the race, say, two from the liberal side of the spectrum and one more toward the middle, the two on the liberal side are likely to split the liberal vote, thus creating an opening for the middle-of-the-road candidate to make the runoff. For a description of how this might work in practice, see box 8.1.

BOX 8.1

Democrats Split the Vote in Albuquerque

Former Albuquerque Mayor Richard Berry Speaking at a Press Conference on October 23, 2015

In the 2009 Albuquerque mayoral election, local Democrats split the vote between two moderate Democratic candidates, allowing Republican state representative Richard Berry to win outright in the city's nonpartisan general election. The election included two centrist Democrats, incumbent mayor Martin Chavez and Richard Romero, a former state senator, both of whom were ideologically to the left of Berry, if only marginally. In the end, the combination of Democrats splitting the vote and a very effective campaign by Berry made him the winner without a runoff. Interestingly, another institutional rule, Albuquerque's 40 percent threshold for avoiding a runoff, aided the candidate whose core support was among Republicans. Had the rule been 50 percent, as in most cities, Berry would have been in a runoff with Chavez, the second-place finisher, who would probably have consolidated Democratic votes to win another term.

Feeling burned, before the 2013 mayoral election, local Democrats pushed through an initiative to increase the threshold for victory to 50 percent. Unfortunately for them, Mayor Berry was popular and the lone Democrat was relatively weak. Berry cruised to victory with 68 percent of the vote. Navigating this combination of institutional rules—nonpartisan ballots and the vote threshold to win outright—becomes infinitely more complicated as the number and political diversity of candidates grows. Imagine what happens when demographic diversity such as race, ethnicity, and gender is added to the political and ideological diversity of candidates.

URBAN CAMPAIGNS

Campaigns are about getting people to vote for their candidate, thus candidates' organizations will **get-out-the-vote (GOTV)** by lining up volunteers to knock on doors, make phone calls, register voters, and get people to the polls. (Because there is also early or all-mail voting in thirty-seven states, depending on local rules, campaigns must plan accordingly to reach people *before* the first ballots can be cast.)[13] Strategy involves determining which areas of the community to hit the hardest and which ones to ignore, and identifying community groups to work with on behalf of the candidate. Campaigns with large budgets will survey voters to test particular campaign themes and discern pressing issues. All of this activity is designed to mobilize voters to support the favored candidate. The goal of a campaign, of course, is to win the election. In practice, this means making the most of its three main resources: the candidate, the money, and the message.[14]

Who Runs for Local Office?

Campaigns are first and foremost about candidates. Who takes the difficult step to declare their candidacies for local public office? Perhaps it would be better to start by asking who can run. Not surprisingly, given the variety of rules and institutions that govern local elections in the United States, there is not one place to go to answer this question. The US Constitution, of course, specifies a three-tiered age structure for national offices, where candidates must be at least 25 years old to run for the House of Representatives, 30 to run for the US Senate, and 35 to run for president. (Presidents must also be natural-born citizens.) State-level age requirements range anywhere from 18 to 30. At the local level a candidate can run for mayor in New York City, Chicago, and Los Angeles at age 18.[15] In theory, mayors with a combined 54 years of life experience between them could represent approximately 15.3 million people as mayors of world-class cities.

Local officials are usually older. Survey data gathered by the International City/County Management Association indicate that city councilors tend to be middle-aged and over. They asked city clerks in cities with more than 2,500 residents to report the number of city councilors that fell into specific age ranges (under 22, 22–29, 30–39, 40–49, 50–59, and 60 and older). On average, city councils had zero members under 22, one between 22 and 29, one between 30 and 39, two between 40 and 49, two between 50 and 59, and three members 60 and older.[16] Evidence from Florida suggests that city councilors are more likely to be older and retired. Because the US population in general is aging, Florida is a bellwether given its status as a leading state for retirees. Older people are more inclined to serve at the local level, and to have the time and financial independence to do so, while younger people are less interested in serving at the local level and are discouraged by the costs of running, particularly the required time commitment, media scrutiny, and public pressure.[17]

This may be changing, however. A 2017 *Time* magazine story featured a number of millennials who are currently leading American cities.[18] Among these are Michael Tubbs, who at age 26 became mayor of Stockton, California, a city of roughly 315,000 people; Svante Myrick, who at 24 became mayor of Ithaca, New York; Pete Buttigieg, who at 30 became mayor of South Bend, Indiana; Aja Brown, who at 31 became mayor of Compton, California; and Erin Stewart, who at 26 was elected mayor of New Britain, Connecticut. According to the article, millennials are attracted to service in local government because they feel they can make their mark sooner, and because local government is more directly accountable to the people and less partisan than state- or national-level politics. Age-related differences in who serves are important because people of different generations often have different policy preferences, which affects representation.[19]

Apart from their age, candidates for local office, like political candidates generally, tend to be better educated and to have higher incomes than the average person, reflecting the class bias of participation discussed in chapter 7. In terms of occupation, city council candidates often come from the business community and, according to one survey, from the ranks of retirees and homemakers.[20] School board members tend to work in or have backgrounds in the education system, but female school board members are significantly more likely than men to have this occupational background.[21]

So there appears to be some sorting among candidates by occupation and office type, with businesspeople running more for city office—not surprising given the intimate connection between city government and local business growth—and educators running more frequently for school board. Unlike elections for higher offices, where political experience is essential, city councilors and school board members also enter office with little or no previous public office experience.[22] If you think of political offices as a career ladder, local office would be the bottom rung.

Initial research into motivations of city councilors in the Bay Area by Kenneth Prewitt showed that a high percentage were initially appointed to office after having been recruited and groomed by local business organizations; most voluntarily resigned their positions, and most viewed their service as a form of civic **volunteerism**, with the emphasis on doing their civic duty.[23] Later research showed that the motivations of city councilors were more varied. According to Timothy Bledsoe, there were four motivations underlying individuals' decisions to seek a seat on the city council:[24]

- **particularism**: those with a desire to advance a cause or issue
- **localism**: those with a desire to help people or a political party
- **self-regarding**: those seeking to advance their self-interest
- **politico**: those entering politics for the sheer enjoyment of it

What motivates people to serve on councils may change over time, be shaped by issue concerns, and reflect particular contexts. For example, in Concord, California, the emphasis on volunteerism uncovered by Prewitt gave way in the 1980s to the emergence of **policy entrepreneurs**, who were devoted full-time to advancing strongly ideological solutions and nonincremental changes to local policy issues.[25] Policy entrepreneurs intent on responding to controversies over the pace of growth in their communities have also been found in suburbia, once the home of caretaker governments governed by citizen-volunteers.[26]

Deckman's research on school board candidates indicates that they are motivated by a desire to learn about local government, influence policy, work with people who share their ideals, and move schools toward more traditional values. Gaining political experience in order to run for higher office is not a primary motivation, suggesting a strong norm of volunteerism.[27] Men are more likely than women, however, to say they were motivated to serve because of a desire to "return schools to traditional values" or to "apply my religious or moral beliefs to education policy."[28] Having children in the school is also a principal motivator for women, especially among those who are more ideologically conservative.[29] Deckman's survey also showed, somewhat surprisingly, that more female school board candidates reported being Republicans than Democrats, and more were moderate-to-conservative than liberal in their ideological leanings. Regardless, women generally take more moderate positions on hot-button school issues—for example, teaching evolution, discussing homosexuality, multiculturalism, prayer in school—than men do.[30]

Like most political candidates, school board candidates are self-starters, encouraged to run by family and friends or community leaders and not by parties or political elites.[31] Campaigns for school boards are relatively simple, with candidates spending very little money and relying on door-to-door campaigning.[32] Campaign spending and interest group involvement tends to be greatest in larger school districts given the attractiveness of those seats compared to seats on smaller school boards.[33]

A second important characteristic of people who seek office is their level of **political ambition**, a desire to make politics a career. This could be **static ambition**—desire to win a position at the local level and remain there—or **progressive ambition**—desire to move up the political ladder.[34] Ambition is important because if getting elected and reelected is not a concern to those who serve, they may not have the incentive to adequately represent the people.[35]

Progressive ambition is also important because those who want to use their current office as a stepping-stone to a higher one are likely to behave in the present with their future goals in mind. The political ambitions of mayors have received the most attention from scholars. But is the mayoralty a stepping-stone to higher office? Looking at the ranks of higher office, you might be tempted to say yes. Current national political figures who served as mayors or county elected executives include US Senators Cory Booker of New Jersey, James Inhofe of Oklahoma, and Bernie Sanders of Vermont. Governors who served as mayors include Ed Rendell of Pennsylvania, Martin O'Malley of Maryland, John Hickenlooper of Colorado, and Sarah Palin of Alaska. No mayor has ever gone on to win the presidency, however.

Despite these examples, systematic studies paint a portrait of mayors as lacking in progressive ambition; and when they do seek higher office, they rarely win.[36] The earliest research indicated that only between 9 and 10 percent of mayors moved on to higher office. A study of mayoral careers between 1820 and 1995 puts the figure at around 17 percent. More recent scholarship, which looked at mayors between 1992 and 2012, suggests that about 20 percent of politicians launch their careers from the mayor's office. Thus, high-profile examples aside, the mayor's position is not a particularly solid stepping-stone to higher office.

A key question is why. Some have suggested that mayors could not break through the anti-big-city bias of suburban and rural voters critical to success in statewide and national campaigns.[37] (This argument, however, was later debunked by studies showing that mayors did just as well as other kinds of candidates with these constituencies.[38]) It is more likely to be a function of preferences. The people who serve as mayor make that choice because they want to help their communities or want to build things and leave behind a legacy of moving their communities forward. They enjoy the challenge of urban politics and administration and want to remain close to home and family. Many are turned off by the idea of service in the highly partisan environment of national (and increasingly state) politics and want little to do with round-the-clock fundraising and campaigning. But when they do seek reelection to their current office, mayors are successful at rates comparable to other kinds of officeholders, such as US Senators and governors.[39] Job performance is key to reelection, especially a mayor's ability to handle the economy and crime.[40]

Those who do seek higher office are more likely to be male, younger, and nonblack. Democratic and Republican mayors are more likely than independents to attempt a bid for higher office. Less than half of mayors are successful when they do so.[41] Although the answer to whether the mayoralty is a jumping-off point for those seeking to build careers at higher levels is no, it is unclear that "higher" office is more attractive.[42] As Willie Brown, who had a long career in California state politics before becoming mayor of San Francisco, said: "There's nothing that compares to my eight years as mayor of San Francisco. It's been an incredible ride."[43]

It is also important to consider *when* candidates run. In general, this is a function of opportunities. Prime opportunities are those with the clearest path to victory. The strongest candidates behave strategically, running for office when the odds of success are greatest.[44] This explains why more candidates emerge to contest **open seat races** (those without an incumbent running) and why these contests are almost always more competitive than those involving incumbents.[45] Institutional features of local government also affect patterns of **candidate emergence**, the process that moves people to declare their candidacy. The power of the mayor's office has been linked to the emergence of *political entrepreneurs*, candidates focused on making broad, nonincremental changes to city policy. District election systems may have a similar effect on the emergence of these kinds of candidates (and candidates more generally), because overcoming collective action problems is easier when voters can be organized on the basis of smaller units (i.e., districts) rather than citywide.[46]

When candidates run has also been studied in connection with descriptive representation. Research by Paru Shah on decisions of black candidates to run for local office in Louisiana shows that the predictors of candidacies are not always the same as those that predict victory. Although black voter registration and the percentage of whites in the population were linked to both candidacies and victories in predictable ways (e.g., as black registration increased, so too did black candidacies and victories, while increases in the white population reduced both), the presence of well-educated whites in the population only affected candidacies, not victories. Black candidates were also more likely to emerge in places where black employment was greater and where blacks had run for office before, but they were less likely to run in places that held their elections off cycle as opposed to on cycle. Black candidates were also less likely to run (and win) for executive and judicial offices compared to legislative ones, but they were more likely to run for municipal offices compared to county offices. In this latter case they were no more likely to win, however. This research clearly demonstrates the core themes of the text: institutions and politics affect representation in local government.[47]

Campaign Finance

A second resource of campaigns is money. In order to campaign vigorously, candidates, especially those in big cities and in big counties, need to raise money. This is not to say that campaigns in these jurisdictions are more competitive. Indeed, it is likely that they are *less* competitive given that incumbents are likely to work harder to maintain their full-time jobs as local officials.[48] Candidates in smaller communities can most certainly get by without spending a lot of money. Their campaigning is door to door and at local supermarkets and civic clubs. It is unlikely, therefore, that campaigning for these offices will require a lot of money. Time and effort is another thing altogether, which local candidates clearly put in because of the need to maintain full-time jobs, manage families, and all the other responsibilities of life while campaigning.

At the mayoral level in the nation's largest cities, if a candidate cannot communicate on TV, the campaign may be lost before it begins. This is not to say that those who spend the most money will always win the election. Indeed, the relationship between spending and votes is a complex one.[49] It does mean, however, that the candidate must have an ability to communicate, and that means raising enough money to do so in a way that keeps the contest for donations close. Recent mayoral elections in San Diego, New York City, Chicago, Los Angeles, Philadelphia, and Washington, DC tell the story. In New York City, one candidate, Michael Bloomberg, spent $109 million to win a third term, and in Chicago, as noted earlier, Rahm Emanuel spent $14 million to win his first. In the other places listed, spending totals ranged from $4 to $8 million depending on the level of competition.[50]

Patterns in campaign finance observed in elections to higher offices also apply at the local level, especially in large cities. The ability to raise money is related to characteristics of the candidates. Are they current officeholders? Do they have experience in public or community affairs? Have they run for office before? Do they have lucrative occupations in law or business or medicine? Do they have a network of potential donors? Raising money is also related to dynamic aspects of the campaigns. Candidates that appear to be

BOX 8.2

New York City Mayor Michael Bloomberg: Institutions, Strategy, Money, Racial Politics, and Experience

Former New York City Mayor Michael Bloomberg Looks over an Exhibit Relating to 9/11

Although it was cancelled and rescheduled, few remember that September 11, 2001, was also primary election day in New York City. One of the candidates for mayor that day was Michael Bloomberg, founder of Bloomberg News and a multi-billionaire. Given his vast wealth, Bloomberg was ready to spend heavily out of his own pocket to win. A lifelong Democrat, Bloomberg switched his party registration to Republican before the primary to make his road to the general election easier. As an outsider he would never be able to compete with the career politicians running on the Democratic side. This proved to be true and set up the scenario he was hoping for: a one-on-one contest with a Democratic nominee.

Bloomberg was aided by three other factors. During the primary, while he was campaigning without interference, the Democratic candidates were tearing each other to shreds. At a critical moment, the campaign of Mark Green, the city's Public Advocate and eventual primary winner, circulated a flyer that depicted his opponent, Puerto Rican Bronx Borough president Fernando Ferrer, smooching the behind of Reverend Al Sharpton, a black religious leader and political activist in New York City. The implication was that Ferrer was willing to do anything to secure Sharpton's endorsement. The racial backlash caused by the flyer badly weakened Green, leaving his electoral coalition in tatters.

Capitalizing on the endorsement he received from outgoing mayor Rudy Giuliani, a Republican, whose poll numbers skyrocketed after the attack as voters rallied to him as the city's top leader, Bloomberg advertised heavily to inform voters of Giuliani's support. Finally, with lower Manhattan reduced to rubble, voters decided that this was not a time for politics as usual, and that a nonpolitician executive had the right experience for the job. Bloomberg won and proceeded to serve three terms.

headed to victory or who are experiencing a surge in the polls or winning debates may find it easier to raise money than those who are lagging behind or not performing as well.[51] In the end, candidates are selling themselves in the sense that they need to convince donors to support them. How hard they work at raising money, therefore, will also be important to fundraising success.

Like donors generally, donors to local campaigns are strategic in their behavior, meaning that money tends to flow to the most important executive offices and to incumbents and candidates in open seat races.[52] Well-heeled interests such as those in real estate, development, and finance are particularly keen to target those in positions of power (e.g., mayors, city council and county board presidents, legislative committee chairs), as these individuals have a larger say over the policies these donors care most about.[53] There is a similar pattern for nonincumbents; candidate resources such as background and experience, endorsements, and racial characteristics, to a large degree, explain fundraising success (see box 8.2).[54]

Messages and Media

Campaign money is directly connected to media strategy and a candidate's **campaign message**, the issues and themes that candidates create and run on to persuade voters to support them. Media in local campaigns is not unlike what you might find in campaigns for higher office. Local newspapers and television stations report on campaigns, with most coverage going toward the mayor's race. Candidates, especially those for mayor, do their best to generate favorable news coverage. The relationship is a symbiotic one, as the media need access to candidates to cover the race and candidates need coverage in order to deliver their messages.

Campaigns below the mayor's level—for city council, county commission, and school board—do not usually get much media coverage. These campaigns are not silent, but their "noise" is not covered extensively. Newspapers can raise awareness of city council and school board candidates and increase turnout in local elections.[55] One way is by endorsing candidates. In order to determine endorsements, newspapers conduct interviews or send out questionnaires, asking candidates about what they would do if elected and the approach they might take when dealing with key issues. They also consider their own reporting on the campaigns to help them decide.[56] Newspaper endorsements are not politically or ideologically neutral, as they tend to reflect the political preferences of the newspaper's editorial board and the paper's publisher. In the 2017 mayoral election in Albuquerque, the city's major newspaper endorsed *two* candidates for mayor; one was the more conservative of the two top Democrats and the other was a Republican. Interestingly, neither of the more conservative candidates won the election.

Research does indicate, however, that newspaper endorsements increase a candidate's chances of victory. Newspaper endorsements legitimize candidates, providing voters with a useful **heuristic** or cognitive shortcut that helps them make a choice in what are often low-information elections.[57] Understanding the exact causal effect of newspaper endorsements on vote outcomes is difficult, however, because newspapers tend to endorse strong candidates. Voter awareness of the endorsement is key, which is why candidates emphasize them heavily in their literature and ads.[58]

A second way to think about media in local campaigns is from the candidate's perspective. At the mayoral level, candidates who are not getting covered have little shot at winning, so they attempt to generate **earned media**, media coverage gained through campaign activities, such as public speeches and rallies, debate performances, and press releases on key campaign issues and themes. Candidates also utilize **paid media**, any kind of media designed to promote the candidate for which a campaign has to pay. Television, newspaper, billboard and internet ads, direct mail, bumper stickers, campaign buttons, and yard signs are all forms of paid media. Paid media is a big chunk of candidate spending.

To better understand candidates' paid media strategies, one might begin by establishing a logic for media use in different campaign contexts. In general, all candidates (city council, mayoral, school board, etc.) who can generate a little money will opt for *direct mail*, mail directly targeted to specific voters, usually in the form of glossy paper ads with pictures of the candidate, their families, and information candidates deem it important for voters to know. Candidates and volunteers also go door to door, distribute yard signs, develop candidate web-pages, maintain a presence on social media, and participate in candidate forums to get their messages out to voters. But not everyone will go on TV, and the reason has to do with the difference between TV markets and the market for voters.

Mayoral candidates compete citywide for votes, and in bigger cities television is the most efficient and effective way to do so. When the market for television viewers and the market for voters overlap, candidates can reach a substantial portion of voters by advertising on TV, making it both efficient and effective. Campaigns can target specific blocks of voters at specific times because they know which demographic groups watch which television programs. When TV and voter markets do not overlap, the incentive to be on TV vanishes. This helps explain why mayoral campaigns in bigger cities are heavily dependent on TV and why mayoral campaigns in smaller cities, and city council and school board campaigns nearly everywhere, avoid the expense of producing TV ads. In the nation's largest media markets, TV advertising can be very expensive, which explains, in part, the high cost of running for mayor in those places.

Campaign advertising comes in three forms: **positive advertising**, **negative advertising**, and **contrast advertising**. A positive ad extols the virtues of the sponsor or entity paying for it. A negative ad attacks an opponent and says nothing positive about the sponsor. A contrast ad is a combination of positive and negative messaging. Table 8.1 shows examples to illustrate each kind of ad. One is the text of a positive ad from the 2005 mayoral election in San Antonio. Notice how the sponsor of the ad, in this case the eventual winner Julian Castro, stays positive about his own plans and says nothing negative about his opponents. In the middle column is a negative ad from the 2001 Los Angeles mayoral election. There is no positive information whatsoever included in the ad, and the sponsor and eventual winner, James Hahn, conveys nothing positive about his own campaign or plans for office. The third ad is a contrast ad aired by Maura Hennigan in the 2005 Boston mayoral election. In this case, Hennigan was challenging long-time Boston mayor Tom Menino. With this ad, she was trying to make an issue of the city's level of preparedness against terrorism and other kinds of major disasters. The contrast, albeit faint and nonspecific, is that she would do a better job as mayor to protect the city's residents in the event of catastrophe.

The decision to use attack speech in a campaign is often thought to be a reflection of campaign strength, at least as reflected in polls. Generally speaking, **frontrunners**, or those leading in the campaign, are not expected to be as

TABLE 8.1	Examples of Positive, Negative, and Contrast Television Ads in San Antonio, Los Angeles, and Boston Mayoral Elections	
Positive Ad	Negative Ad	Contrast Ad
Ad Sponsor: Julian Castro for Mayor, San Antonio, 2005	Ad Sponsor: James Hahn for Mayor, Los Angeles, 2001	Ad Sponsor: Maura Hennigan for Mayor, Boston, 2005
[Julian Castro]: "San Antonio is on the move: the PGA Resort, the new Texas A&M campus and Toyota will create thousands of new jobs here.	**[Announcer]:** "Fact: The father of a convicted crack cocaine dealer contributed money to Antonio Villaraigosa.	**[Announcer]:** "After the Red Sox won the pennant, Boston was caught unprepared. As real threats gather on the horizon—epidemics, natural disasters, terrorist attacks—experts agree Boston is vulnerable and still unprepared.
That's good, but to fulfill our destiny we need more.	Fact: Villaraigosa wrote the White House Pardon Office for the drug dealer claiming he was wrongly convicted.	And now Tom Menino wants to put biological weapons in your backyard.
As we create better-paying jobs, we must retain them. When I am your mayor, I will create an office to attract and keep more of the good jobs that San Antonians deserve.	Fact: Villaraigosa falsely claimed that crack cocaine dealer had no prior record.	As mayor, Maura Hennigan will do what Menino has failed to do—create a real plan to protect our city."
It'll be a boon for small business too.	Fact: Villaraigosa accepted more money from the drug dealer's father.	
Want to know more? Visit my website: www.castro-formayor.com.	Fact: In February, Villaraigosa denied he wrote the White House until the LA Times confronted him with his letter.	
We are one city. We have one destiny."	Los Angeles can't trust Antonio Villaraigosa."	

Note: Data compiled by the authors.

negative as those who are trailing fairly closely behind.[59] Research at the city level indicates that this may not be the case in primary elections but is more likely when two candidates face each other in a runoff. Candidates may also be more likely to attack on issues salient to the voters and on questions of their opponents' character. Finally, decisions to attack may be linked to race, with minority candidates less likely to attack than nonminorities in their effort to project a nonthreatening image as part of a deracialized campaign.[60]

While few would admit that they like negative advertising, there is some agreement among political consultants that it works.[61] Among scholars, however, the view is more mixed, with some arguing that negative speech depresses voter participation and others saying that it stimulates participation and interest in the process.[62] Most research has focused on national-level politics to understand the dynamics involved. At the city level, a field experiment by David Niven involving eligible voters in the 2003 mayoral election in West Palm Beach, Florida, indicated that negative information as conveyed via direct mail stimulates turnout.[63] Moreover, the odds of voting increased when the emotional content of negative mail increased. Although you cannot generalize from one or two studies, the case for using local elections to study important questions related to campaign communications is a good one.

Minority and Female Campaigns

The racial and ethnic distribution of the population greatly affects the politics of cities, counties, school districts, and other local governments. Although whites are likely to remain powerful in national politics for some time to come, minorities are powerful right now in many of the communities they call home, especially in the nation's urban centers. African Americans are a majority of the population in cities such as Atlanta, Baltimore, Birmingham, Cleveland, and Detroit, while Latinos or Hispanics are a majority in cities such as El Paso, San Antonio, Miami, and Anaheim.[64] Campaigns, candidates, and elections are greatly affected by the high concentrations of these groups. In most larger cities, though, the balance of racial and ethnic minority groups is somewhere between the national figures and the cities where national minority groups constitute local majorities. This produces racially and ethnically competitive elections.

Because voting and candidate support is not color-blind, in order for minorities to win, they must at a minimum mobilize their own demographic group to vote.[65] This, of course, is nothing new in American urban politics, as the Irish political bosses of old knew that the wellspring of political power was demography and that the key to winning elections was to outmobilize and outvote competing groups. Today, for minority candidates to win in places where their group is also a *local* minority, they must reach beyond their core group and build cross-racial coalitions. Assuming a two-person contest, a candidate needs an **electoral majority**, 50 percent plus one vote, in order to win the seat. Latino or Hispanic candidates running in a city with a population that is 30 percent Latino will need to go beyond their natural base of supporters to draw support from other groups in order to get there. In a fair system, successfully converting population numbers into action and votes leads to winning elections, gaining power, and influencing local policy agendas.[66] And this is regardless of whether the election is for mayor, city council, school board, or county office.

Building cross-racial alliances is easier said than done. A minority group may be divided internally along issue, ideological, socioeconomic, or generational lines, causing a failure to close ranks behind a single candidate.[67] This, in part, explains why it took almost 25 years for residents to elect Memphis's first black mayor in 1991, even though the preconditions for success were long in place.[68] Even if internal disagreements are successfully overcome and the group settles on one candidate, he or she might not be able to bridge the gap between the group and others that are needed to reach a majority. If the candidate is not a particularly strong leader able to forge an electoral coalition with other groups, the group will falter. Institutional factors may also hinder minority representation. Machine-style politics in cities such as New York, Chicago, and Baltimore often split more progressive minority leaders from minority group leaders aligned with white ethnic machine officials, creating a barrier to successful minority politics.[69] African American mayors are also more likely to be elected in *reformed* systems (i.e., those that employ a council-manager form of government as opposed to the more politicized mayor-council form; see chapter 5) because these places often lack strong political organizations that limit the advancement of "outsider" candidates.[70] The upshot is that a lot of things have to go right in order for minority candidates to win local office in situations where the demographics are against them.

For minority candidates competing in white-dominant cities, an important strategic consideration is whether to deracialize their appeals in an effort to attract white crossover support, critical to overcoming the bad "political math" that minority candidates usually confront. According to Joseph McCormick II and Charles Jones, a **deracialized campaign** is one run by a minority candidate that seeks to "deemphasize those issues that may be viewed in explicitly racial terms, for example, minority set-asides, affirmative action, or the plight of the black underclass, while emphasizing those issues that appear to transcend the racial question," such as government management, public safety, and economic growth.[71] Christian Collet also lists "law and order," "tough on crime," "education," and "economic development/low taxes/jobs" as central messages in deracialized campaigns. Deracialized campaigns are not just about issue positions but also political style. Candidates who choose to deracialize their appeals stress traits such as "competence" and "character" and an ability to "bring people together."[72] Although most research on deracialization has focused on mayoral elections, if local demographics require it, deracialization may also apply at the city council level.[73]

In contrast, an **insurgent campaign** is designed to mobilize minority group members and other liberals, particularly whites, by stressing progressive messages on social issues like economic justice, discrimination, and civil rights. An insurgent campaign is bent on challenging the existing political order.[74] There is, of course, a fine line between the types of messages emphasized in each type of campaign, and each one has pros and cons. Deracialized campaigns may attract support from nongroup members and help the minority candidate win, albeit at the risk of demobilizing a base of supporters who feel disheartened that the candidate may not be an aggressive spokesperson for core group concerns.[75] An insurgent campaign may fire up core supporters at the risk of turning off more moderate (in most cases, white) voters otherwise inclined to support the candidate.

A second question is *when* a candidate should choose one or the other strategy. In theory, a city's demographic context should be connected to the choice to pursue a deracialized or insurgent strategy. Political scientists Baodong Liu and James Vanderleeuw argue that racially polarized voting is least likely in situations where a particular group (white, black, Latino) is either a very small or a very large percentage of the population.[76] Where a group is, say, 15 percent of the local population or a clear majority, you might expect more general appeals for support, making a deracialized strategy most effective. Where groups are competitive—say two groups, each somewhere in the neighborhood of 50 percent—racial politics is likely to be most intense. In this case, campaigns are likely to be more narrowly targeted to core constituency groups (i.e., to employ an insurgent strategy).

Women of color face the *additional* challenge of gender stereotypes.[77] Compared to men, women are generally perceived as stronger on social issues—housing, childcare, education, poverty, and healthcare—and are more likely to be perceived as "empathetic."[78] Compared to women, men are perceived as stronger on issues such as economic development, taxes, and crime, issues that are thought to require "toughness" and "executive" decision making.[79] Some have speculated that local politics represents a uniquely hospitable venue for female candidates because local policy agendas favor these social issues. But this may not be so at the city level, where the hearts of local agendas are centered on economic development, business recruitment, and public safety, and where the top prize in local government is the mayor's office—in many larger cities an executive position.[80]

Recent experimental research indicates that female candidates in local elections do not derive an advantage from either female stereotypes or the issue terrain of city government. Nor is highlighting feminine traits advantageous to winning in either nonpartisan or partisan contexts. Female candidates do, however, derive an advantage from emphasizing masculine traits such as "toughness" and "assertiveness." This is especially the case for female Republicans.[81] The campaigns of female candidates may therefore deem it necessary to trespass on their male opponents' terrain, at least as far as issues and traits are concerned.[82] In other words, female candidates may find it necessary to inoculate themselves against charges of weakness by playing up their toughness on crime and criminals and their decisiveness on economic development and taxes.

Election Outcomes: The Effects of Campaigns

When all doorbells have been rung, ads produced and aired, and lawn and street signs distributed, people vote. What, then, is the effect of all this campaigning? It might surprise you that political science is somewhat conflicted about the effects of campaigning on election outcomes. Some argue that campaigns matter to election outcomes, while others say they do not.

A series of recent studies by Thomas Holbrook and Aaron Weinschenk paint a picture of US mayoral campaigns as remarkably similar to those that occur at higher levels in the federal system. Incumbent mayors enjoy significant advantages over challengers; campaign spending is more effective for challengers, the vast majority of whom are outspent by incumbents; and incumbents do better in more diverse cities, as challengers struggle to construct viable rival voter coalitions.[83] Campaign spending, especially challenger spending, is a significant driver of voter turnout in mayoral elections.[84] These studies indicate that mayoral campaigns (a) are important to local politics and election outcomes, and (b) parallel in important ways what we know about state and federal elections.[85]

As noted in chapter 7, campaign spending by challengers is more effective than campaign spending by incumbents, a finding about local campaigns that parallels decades of research on spending in congressional campaigns.[86] Effectiveness is essentially a measure of votes received for each dollar spent. For incumbents, this number is relatively low compared to challengers. The reason for this finding is straightforward: Incumbents are already well known, so each dollar spent is designed to generate *new* supporters, meaning that their substantial spending is targeted toward a relatively small group. Because challengers are relatively unknown, each dollar spent potentially allows them to reach someone learning about them for the first time.

Incumbent spending is also often defensive in nature; that is, the stronger the challenge, the more they spend. In general, spending in mayoral campaigns is greater in open seat and runoff elections and when more politically experienced candidates are running. It is also related to institutional and demographic factors such as mayor-council government, mayoral term length, income inequality, and local cost of living.[87] As discussed in chapter 7, incumbent city councilors and mayors enjoy a multitude of advantages. For nonincumbents, whether they are challengers or candidates in open seat races, the key to performance is leveraging the strengths—experience, commitment, and authenticity—they bring to the race. But because luck figures in and because voters can be hard to predict, even the best candidates and the best campaigns may not bring victory.

In elections where a minority candidate competes against a white candidate, evidence indicates that deracialized campaigns are, if not determinative, certainly effective.[88] Initial research focused on African American candidates; now attention has turned to Latinos. Hispanic mayors, for example, have been elected in places such as San Antonio, Denver, Los Angeles, Hartford (Connecticut), and Providence (Rhode Island). In each case, the successful Latino candidate employed a deracialized campaign strategy to build a cross-racial coalition.[89]

SUMMARY

Democracy depends on a steady supply of candidates, so who runs and why they do so is important. The quality of local government is affected by the talents, experiences, and motivations of those who enter the process. Perhaps most importantly, who runs directly shapes who or what gets represented in local democracy.

Over time, electoral politics in cities has evolved from party- and group- to candidate-centered, with self-starting individuals organizing their own campaigns, raising their own money, and recruiting their own volunteers. The level of political ambition among candidates is also an important question for representation. Some local candidates desire to seek higher office and build a career in politics, but most are content to serve at the local level in a quasi-volunteer capacity. And some do make a "career" out of serving their local community.

Mayoral campaigns in big cities are the most high-profile affairs in local politics, generating copious amounts of media coverage, advertising, and campaign spending. To win at this level requires candidates to raise millions of dollars, often from powerful groups and interests with a clear stake in the decisions of city government. Institutions and demographics directly affect campaign strategy. Candidates in cities with nonpartisan ballots are likely to campaign differently from candidates in partisan cities. And rules governing runoff elections will influence messaging strategies as well. Demographic content influences campaign strategies as candidates seek to build winning cross-racial coalitions. Because of the role of race and ethnicity in local voting patterns, candidates in multiracial settings must reach beyond the interests of their core supporters and build a coalition that will incorporate more voices in the process in order to win.

Key Terms

campaign *(162)*

campaign message *(172)*

candidate-centered elections *(163)*

candidate emergence *(169)*

contrast advertising *(173)*

deracialized campaign *(176)*

earned media *(172)*

electoral majority *(175)*

frontrunner *(173)*

get-out-the-vote (GOTV) *(165)*

group-centered elections *(163)*

heuristic *(172)*

insurgent campaign *(176)*

localism *(167)*

negative advertising *(173)*

open seat race *(169)*

paid media *(173)*

particularism *(167)*

policy entrepreneur *(167)*

political ambition *(168)*

politico *(167)*

positive advertising *(173)*

progressive ambition *(168)*

self-regarding *(167)*

static ambition *(168)*

volunteerism *(167)*

Discussion Questions

1. How do institutional rules of cities affect campaigns waged by local candidates?

2. In what way(s) do(es) the demographic context of cities affect the strategies of minority candidates?

3. Who are the major contributors, and what are the dynamics of fundraising in local campaigns?

4. Do campaigns matter? Why or why not?

Exercises

1. Research recent local elections in your state by consulting online sources. Catalog the occupational backgrounds and political experience of candidates for city council, mayor, and school board. What do you notice?

2. Examine the demographic profiles of the largest one or two cities *and* counties in your state. Then compare the demographic profiles of the jurisdiction to the demographic profiles of the candidates seeking office.

3. Interview a member of your city council or county board to learn about their motivations for becoming involved in local government. What is their background in terms of education and occupation? Do they plan to seek higher office in the future?

4. Consult local newspapers and, if applicable, advertising in a recent local election in your state. What groups and/or parties appeared to be active in the campaign? Describe the nature of their activity. Is the activity independent of the campaigns or coordinated with them?

Practice and Review Online
https://textbooks.rowman.com/understanding-urban-politics

9

NONVOTING FORMS OF PARTICIPATION

GUIDING QUESTIONS

1. Why are nonvoting forms of participation considered responses to dissatisfaction?
2. What is citizen contacting and why is it a form of participation in urban politics?
3. How do people use parties and interest groups as a means of participation in local politics? What are the challenges of parties and interest groups for urban democracy?
4. Do campaigns advance or erode notions of local representative democracy?
5. What are the differences between protests and rebellions? How are they similar? Do they matter?
6. Why does "voting with your feet" constitute a form of behavior in urban politics?

IN THE AFTERMATH of the 2014 police shooting of Michael Brown in Ferguson, Missouri, protestors took to the streets. For weeks, the city faced protests and rioting over a white Ferguson police officer's shooting and killing of an unarmed black man. This incident sparked global protests against police violence and, as noted elsewhere in this text, helped to launch the Black Lives Matter movement.[1]

Protest and demonstration are considered nonvoting forms of participation. However, unlike voting, they do not result in leadership change, at least not directly. Recall from chapter 7 that the events in Ferguson caused a substantial increase in political activism among that city's black community, which culminated in the election of more African Americans to the city council and the election of an African American District Attorney.

This chapter focuses on nonvoting forms of participation in urban politics at both the individual and group levels. You will learn about citizen contacting as a form of political participation, political parties and interest groups, regulation of money in local campaigns, and extraordinary forms of participation such as protest and rebellion. The chapter concludes with a discussion of how exit behavior is affected by the market for public goods. Each of these behaviors constitutes an important mechanism by which citizen interests are *represented* in local government.

NONVOTING FORMS OF PARTICIPATION IN URBAN POLITICS

Like voting, nonvoting forms of participation are a function of individual-level characteristics, especially socioeconomic status, reflecting the inherent class bias to political participation. More generally, though, nonvoting forms of participation are often a function of *dissatisfaction*.

This method of examining participation in urban politics was advanced by William Lyons and David Lowery.[2] Building on the work of Albert Hirschman and Charles Tiebout, they identified four kinds of responses to dissatisfaction in local politics: exit, voice, loyalty, and neglect. **Exit** is when a person who is dissatisfied with policies or conditions in the current community leaves that community to take advantage of more favorable policies or conditions in another. Exit is often referred to as "voting with your feet." **Voice** is when a person attempts to change the status quo by speaking out to improve conditions, joining a protest or demonstration, contacting local officials, or being involved in an interest group or party with the goal of changing or influencing policy. **Loyalty** includes behaviors that suggest a more optimistic view, such as voting, speaking positively about the city, or attending community functions. **Neglect**, the opposite of loyalty, includes behaviors such as not voting and feelings of distrust toward those in power and hopelessness regarding the future of the city.

According to Lyons and Lowery, these behaviors and attitudes can be arrayed along two dimensions: passive-active and constructive-destructive (see figure 9.1). Exit is an active but destructive form of behavior, while voice is active and constructive. By contrast, loyalty is passive but constructive, while neglect is both passive *and* destructive. This chapter discusses a number of voice behaviors, including citizen contacting, parties and interest groups, campaign contributions, and protests and rebellions. The exit behavior of leaving a jurisdiction is discussed at the end of the chapter.

CITIZEN CONTACTING

The vast majority of nonvoting forms of participation are both active *and* constructive. They involve citizens acting in ways designed to improve city

Figure 9.1 Dimensions of Response to Dissatisfaction, Response Types, and Illustrative Behaviors

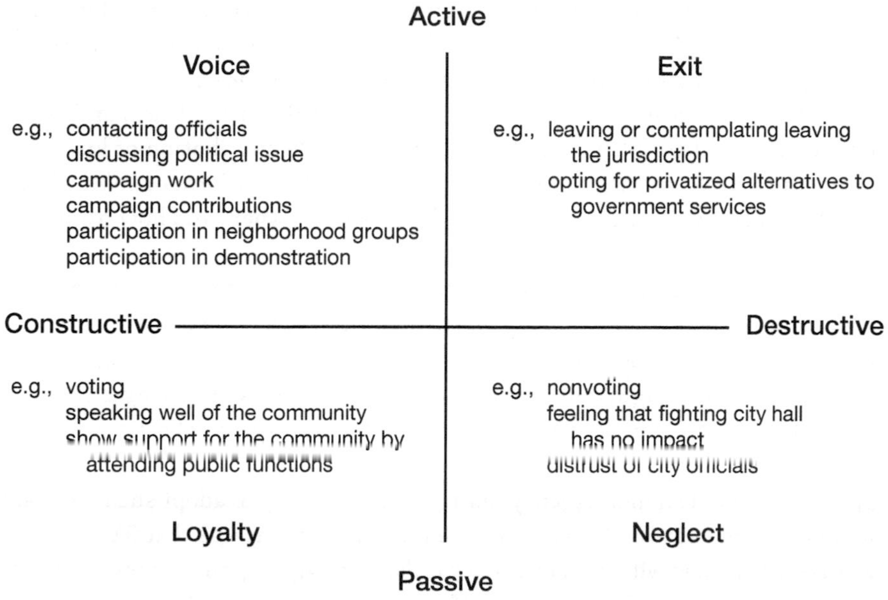

Active

Voice   Exit

e.g., contacting officials
       discussing political issue
       campaign work
       campaign contributions
       participation in neighborhood groups
       participation in demonstration

e.g., leaving or contemplating leaving
       the jurisdiction
       opting for privatized alternatives to
       government services

Constructive ——————————————————— Destructive

e.g., voting
       speaking well of the community
       show support for the community by
          attending public functions

e.g., nonvoting
       feeling that fighting city hall
          has no impact
       distrust of city officials

Loyalty   Neglect

Passive

Source: William E. Lyons and David Lowery, "The Organization of Political Space and Citizen Responses to Dissatisfaction in Urban Communities: An Integrative Model," The Journal of Politics, 48:2 (May 1986): 321–46, 331.

life and symbolize commitment to addressing challenges faced by local residents. One of these forms of behavior, called **citizen contacting**, involves actions by people to inform and therefore prompt government to do something. According to Michael Hirlinger there are two types of citizen contacts in urban politics. One, a **general referent contact**, is when someone contacts the city to express an opinion or address an issue of citywide importance. A second, called a **particularized contact**, is when someone contacts the city about an individual need or concern, for example, to fix a pothole on their street.[3]

Hirlinger's distinction between types of contacts has implications for patterns of contacting behavior. For general referent contacts, **political efficacy** (the belief that a person's participation is intrinsically valuable and that it matters) and political ties or connections (measured as a person's involvement in parties or electoral campaigns) largely determine whether a citizen contacts government on a matter of citywide concern. By contrast, particularized contact is explained by the interaction between *perceived need* for service and political ties. When people perceive a need and have connections, they are more likely to make contact.

In a representative democracy, people have the right to make their views heard. Because contacting is a critical means by which government is made aware of residents' needs, who contacts and why has clear implications for whose interests are substantively represented.[4] If poor neighborhoods with great needs do not get served because local residents have little faith that the government will respond to their complaints or because they lack political connections, that is a problem for democracy, which might only be addressed through greater descriptive representation where power is held from inside the system.[5] Consequently, *patterns* in contacting behavior have significant political and social implications and are a key ingredient in the equitable distribution of local government services. In short, city contacting is considered a form of *political* participation because it often determines who gets what, when, and how from local government.

Advances in technology have increased the ways that ways people can contact government. So-called e-government initiatives have made it far easier for people to inform local government about problems.[6] Besides calling, there is email and text messaging; in addition, almost all cities have webpages that can be used to register complaints, request a service, or process applications for jobs or services. Calling city government is now easier than ever in locales with 311 systems to handle nonemergency matters. The first city to adopt such a system was Baltimore in 1996.[7] The impetus behind 311 systems was that 911 systems were overwhelmed with *non*emergency calls, lowering response times for actual emergencies and burdening city staff. In 1997, the Federal Communications Commission (FCC) allowed police departments to use this system to alleviate pressure on their 911 systems. Since then, these circuits have been used by cities to more effectively receive and respond to citizen inquiries across a range of services.[8]

In addition to helping residents communicate with city government, 311 systems generate a wealth of information that can be used by researchers to analyze patterns in contacts and the responsiveness/effectiveness of local government. For example, in a recent study of New York City, Scott Minkoff studied where contacts come from within the city by aggregating census tract information on 311 calls.[9] He then studied contacts about government goods (e.g., street conditions, overgrown and dead trees, rodents, street signs, water quality, broken meters, snow removal, etc.), graffiti, and noise. He found that areas with older housing, higher volumes of foot and car traffic, and higher rates of population growth generate more contacts. Places with higher levels of owner-occupied housing (as opposed to rental units) also generated more contacts about government goods, suggesting neighborhood investment in a key factor in contacting. Areas with more owner-occupied housing units also had fewer graffiti- or noise-related contacts, and awareness of problems was only weakly related to contacting behavior. This suggests that 311 systems reduce a major barrier to contacting: knowing who to call about a particular issue.

The representational implications of contacting are clear: If government response and services are at least partially dependent on contacts from the citizenry, those in low-income neighborhoods with the greatest needs will experience a double whammy leading to both substandard services and substandard responses from city government. In contrast, those at the top of the economic ladder will enjoy the best of both worlds. Reforms that make it easier for people to contact city government should lessen this representational inequity.

POLITICAL PARTIES AND URBAN INTEREST GROUPS

People also get involved through political parties and interest groups, which are alike in many ways, but there are key differences. A **political party** is a group of like-minded individuals who share a common viewpoint of government and who organize to win elections and control the policy agenda.[10] By contrast, **interest groups** are groups of like-minded individuals who band together to influence the policy agenda. In practical terms, political parties focus on winning elections to control government and its policy direction, and interest groups focus primarily on influencing the policy agenda and outcomes. They both function at all levels of government, but for reasons related to institutional and political changes at the city level, the influence of parties has waned over the decades.[11] Interest groups, however, remain strong in local politics.

Political Parties

Party attachments motivate people to work for their local party organization as campaign volunteers, helping to produce mass mailings, going door to door to contact voters, or serving as precinct or district captains. In general, however, political parties are weak at the *city* level. One reason for this is the use of nonpartisan ballots. (This is not the case in US *counties*, where 81 percent of elections employ partisan ballots.) According to research in the early 1980s by political scientists Timothy Bledsoe and Susan Welch, nonpartisan ballots decrease the incentives of candidates to campaign on party issues and themes and substantially increase the costs in time and effort for local political parties to organize voter support. However, they also found that parties in larger cities and in the Northeast were more active than parties in smaller cities and cities in the South and West.[12] In more recent decades, the tendency of people to sort demographically into cities that "fit" their party preferences reduces the need for parties in the first place, which is to compete to win elections.[13]

Despite this weakness, there are several reasons why political parties still matter at the city level. First, as discussed in chapter 7, party (and ideological) attachments affect vote choices in urban elections.[14] Given a choice between a Republican or a Democrat, in most cases a Republican voter will support the Republican candidate. Second, there are exceptions to party weakness. Cincinnati, for example, is known for having strong local parties—Green, Charter,

Democrat, and Republican—that endorse candidates and organize voters.[15] In addition, although the powerful party machines of old are largely a thing of the past,[16] in almost every place where they once existed (Albany (New York), Chicago, New Haven (Connecticut), New York, Jersey City (New Jersey), and Pittsburgh), the remnants of those organizations remain, with the power to influence local politics.

Local party organizations have endured in machine-descendant cities because of the distinction between political machines and machine politics.[17] Recall from chapter 2 that *political machines* were local political party organizations structured geographically and hierarchically to trade votes for political favors in order to control local government. They were directed by a boss, who used *machine politics*—candidate endorsements, patronage workers, quid pro quo arrangements, and government favors for supporters—to wield power. However, machine politics *can* exist in the absence of a dominant political machine. People in machine-descendant cities often still orient their thinking about local politics in terms of "the machine." This is certainly true in Chicago and Cook County (Illinois). It is also true in Nassau County (New York), where a GOP machine dominates local politics by doling out patronage jobs and contracts to supporters and by intimidating rivals.[18] Because campaign money matters more than ever before, the legitimacy conferred on candidates by party endorsements can affect the flow of contributions.[19] However, like their more powerful ancestors, party power is threatened by two things: corruption and internal strife. Box 9.1 illustrates both of these points with a description of the 2019 election of Lori Lightfoot, who upset the Chicago political machine on her way to becoming mayor of that city.

Interest Groups

The involvement of interest groups in American politics is protected by the First Amendment to the Constitution, which, among other things, protects the "right of the people peaceably to assemble, and to petition the government for a redress of grievances."[20] Examples at the local level include business organizations, homeowner and neighborhood associations, public and private sector employee unions, racial and ethnic minority groups, environmental groups, the LGBTQ community, environmental and faith-based organizations, and local media.[21] Another powerful vehicle for citizen participation is *ad hoc groups*, groups that form to combat a particular issue, but then disband when the issue is resolved. [22]

Interest Group Theories

Numerous theories of urban interest groups exist. **Elitism** identifies a **community power structure**, dominated by social and economic elites, at the center of all major decisions in a community,[23] whereas **pluralism** suggests a more democratic and representative interest group structure wherein multiple

BOX 9.1

Lori Lightfoot Stomps on the Chicago Machine

Mayor Lori Lightfoot Giving Her Victory
Speech to Supporters at the Chicago Hilton.
Ms. Lightfoot is Chicago's First African American
Female Mayor

In localities with a strong party organization, competition often comes from *within* the party itself. In Chicago, the last American city to have a dominant Democratic machine, progressives have battled machine "regulars" for decades. The differences between the two factions are ideological, sociological, and political. Progressives are more liberal than regulars and more likely to have high-end occupations (i.e., regulars are more blue-collar). Progressives are also more likely than regulars to support political reforms that end insider deals and increase transparency, and to advance an ideological agenda. Regulars want to get and hold on to power, principles be damned.

With the election of Lori Lightfoot, the third African American, second female, and first LGBTQ mayor, Chicago progressives scored their most significant victory in decades. Lightfoot defeated another African American woman, Toni Preckwinkle, a long-time Chicago and Cook County officeholder and head of the powerful local Democratic Party organization. Although Preckwinkle had fought the machine when she first started her career nearly three decades earlier, and still claimed the progressive mantle, she could not help but be tarred with her connection to it, in particular her association with a long-time machine alderman accused by the FBI of extorting campaign contributions. This scandal buttressed the reform message, which Lightfoot delivered with a stinging anti–"politics-as-usual" ad that catapulted her to first place in the general election. Her first-round victory also jump-started her fundraising operation, allowing her to amass a $2 million advantage over Preckwinkle, whom she went on to defeat by a 3 to 1 margin in the runoff.

Source: Bill Ruthhart, "Lori Lightfoot Elected Chicago Mayor, Making Her the First African-American Woman to Lead the City," *Chicago Tribune*, April 2, 2019, https://www.chicagotribune.com/politics/elections/ct-met-chicago-election-results-mayors-race-lightfoot-preckwinkle-20190402-story.html, accessed June 9, 2019.

groups compete for power and influence.[24] According to **growth machine** theory, a constellation of interests in finance, real estate, banking, development, and media promote a growth agenda. The focus of local governance, with its emphasis on zoning and economic development, means that in all communities a growth machine is likely to dominate decision making.[25] Together this coalition of actors controls urban policy making in ways that promote growth, which benefits the respective financial interests of each actor in the growth machine.

Paul Peterson argued that city politics was largely devoid of interest group politics, at least in the area most important to the future of cities: economic development. For Peterson, all cities have a *unitary*, or singular, interest in promoting economic development, which provides the tax resources needed to provide the essential day-to-day goods and services of city government, without which urban life would be unsustainable. Therefore, policies that promote the economic (and social) prestige of a city are in its interest, and ones that do not (e.g., redistributive services) should be avoided. Interest groups play a role in city politics in an area that Peterson labeled "allocational policies," the basic services of cities. In this realm, neighborhoods, minority groups, and public sector unions will fight over who gets what from government.

Regime theory flatly rejects the notion that economic development is an apolitical, and therefore groupless, realm of city policy making. For those in this camp, city politics *matters*, and while the relationship between the local state (i.e., city) and the economy (i.e., market) is fundamentally important, it does not *determine* what cities do.

According to regime theory, a city's politics are fundamentally shaped by the political forces within it. The public and private sectors each control resources needed by the other. The public sector has legal authority, while the private sector controls wealth and investment decisions. At the heart of these forces is the **electoral coalition**, or the economic, racial/ethnic, and/or neighborhood-based alliance of groups that *prevail* behind the successful candidate or set of candidates in an election. This coalition of supporters, however, does not constitute a "regime."[26] For a regime to exist, the successful electoral coalition must develop into a stable **governing coalition**, which, as noted in chapter 6, is the coalition of groups and political leaders that effectively govern a community toward a set of policy goals.

A governing coalition or regime centered in the business community would pursue policies that, on balance, are beneficial to business. Atlanta and Dallas are classic examples of this kind of regime.[27] A regime centered in a city's homeowner associations and main street businesses might pursue policies beneficial to these groups, such as those that promote high-quality city services, low property taxes, and minimal regulation. Many suburban jurisdictions can be characterized in this way. Alternatively, a city's regime could revolve around progressive activists who want to see local government pursue policies that benefit the disadvantaged, enhance the quality of neighborhood life, and promote equality and inclusivity. Santa Monica and Berkeley, both California cities, fall into this category.[28] Critiques about the generalizability and use of regime theory suggest that the debate about urban interest groups will continue.[29]

Interest Group Activities and Influence

Interest groups use tactics such as lobbying, electioneering, and litigation to advance their objectives in the political process.[30] Lobbying is activity undertaken by groups to sway officials and/or voters to side with them on policy.[31] Electioneering encompasses campaign activities such as endorsements, making campaign donations, and providing campaign labor to both endorsed candidates and causes. Litigation involves the use of the courts to promote or block things anathema to group interests. These activities are often controversial because they appear to straddle the line between corruption and fair political advocacy.

The business community is a powerful lobby because it is instrumental to local job creation and because it can keep its agenda before city councils, mayors, and the general public and keep away from its agenda things it dislikes.[32] Nevertheless, does it represent an unchecked power in urban politics in ways often suggested by interest group theories? While privileged groups like business, civic, and professional organizations are thought of as more influential than nonprivileged groups such as women, minorities, and LGBTQ groups, government is not necessarily more responsive to their interests. According to one study, governmental responsiveness to groups is a function of their degree of organization, the amount of opposition they face, their activity, and the inclusivity of their goals; it is *not* a function of privileged or nonprivileged status. Urban decision makers are no more responsive (in general) to powerful interests than they are to less powerful interests, including poor and marginalized populations.[33]

Other research supports this conclusion.[34] Elisabeth Gerber and Justin Phillips, for example, show that voting on prodevelopment ballot initiatives in San Diego was *not* dominated by prodevelopment business groups, and that environmental groups and voter preferences also played a critical role in vote outcomes.[35] Another study of eight municipalities in the Boston metropolitan area shows that social service organizations are more active in more urbanized cities relative to business as a proportion of all groups, while citizen and neighborhood groups are more active in suburban communities.[36] In the city of Boston, economic development projects are driven as much by big nonprofits like universities and hospitals as they are by developers.[37] The lessening of business influence at the city level is a function of national and global economic shifts that separate production from front office operations in finance, marketing, human resources, and planning. Simply put, large local companies do not have quite the same interest in local politics as they once did.

The influence of business in local politics can be checked by local media, which can expose sweetheart deals, or those not in the interests of the general public, and other corrupt practices. (The role of media, especially newspapers, is complicated, however, by the fact that it is often considered a prodevelopment interest in its own right.[38]) Media can play the role of civic watchdog to hold interest groups and leaders accountable to the public. Unfortunately, local newspapers have fallen on hard times and are disappearing across the country, posing a serious threat to the health of urban democracy.[39] Citizen lobbyists may also play a role in checking powerful interests in local politics. Box 9.2 explains this form of local political participation.

Urban political campaigns involve a range of interest groups. Important among these are demographic minority groups. Research by Sarah Reckhow shows that African American, Latino, and Asian American interests rooted in local organizations (religious, business, labor, political, nonprofit service provider, and civic) are active in local elections.[40] They endorse candidates, raise money, distribute voter guides, and mobilize voters. The presence of these organizations in a city is a function of the percentage of the group in the population; as it increases, the number of organizations tends to increase as well. Interestingly, however, the density of these groups in a city (number of groups per 100,000 residents) is negatively related to minority representation in city government. In other words, as the number of minority advocacy groups relative to a city's population grows, their power and influence diminishes.

Labor unions representing municipal workers—such as the American Federation of State, County and Municipal Employees (AFSCME) and Fraternal Order of Police—and service and industrial unions often get involved in door-to-door canvassing to support endorsed candidates and causes important to them. They may also host candidate debates and town halls. And, of course, unions make campaign donations. By contrast, the business community's involvement in urban political campaigns is less in terms of "boots on the ground" mobilizing voters and more in terms of providing monetary campaign support.

Interest groups in school board elections have garnered a large amount of scholarly attention. Conventional wisdom suggests that teachers' unions, parent organizations, racial and ethnic groups, religious organizations, and the business community are the dominant actors in school board elections given their interests in the quality of local school systems. According to Frederick Hess and David Leal's national survey of school boards, however, teachers' unions and business contribute very little money in these contests, and "neither religious organizations nor race-based groups were thought by board members to wield much influence on board decisions or on elections."[41] Interestingly, teachers' unions were still considered influential despite their limited role in funding local political campaigns, suggesting that their power stems from nonmonetary activities such as recruiting campaign volunteers and working for endorsed candidates.[42]

Terry Moe, however, argues that the power of teachers' unions is greater in small school districts where they face less competition from other interest groups.[43] They also have greater impact in Democratic districts than in Republican ones and in open seat races compared to races involving incumbents. In addition, research by Sarah Anzia shows that teachers' unions are more successful in achieving policy goals in school districts that elect their board members in off-cycle elections (at times when state and national elections are not held).[44] Anzia's research shows that teacher pay is 3 percent greater in districts that hold off-cycle elections compared to those that time their elections with federal or statewide elections. This case shows that institutions affect the expression of interests; in

BOX 9.2

Citizen Lobbyists

Santa Ana, California, City Hall

According to Brian Adams, local residents often play the role of **citizen lobbyists** in their efforts to influence local policy. His case study of Santa Ana, California, an older, ethnically diverse suburb of Los Angeles, showed that citizen lobbyists are people who "identify issues of importance to them, develop a set of political goals, and lobby government to accomplish them."

While citizen lobbyists participating in city and school board politics perform similar functions to lobbyists at, say, the national level, such as compiling information, communicating with and mobilizing allies, and working with elected officials, at the local level they can do this informally via social networks. To coordinate group efforts, the scale of the state and national levels require a more formal process of outreach by interest group organizations and their lobbyists. It also requires more resources. Locally, this is accomplished by the citizen lobbyist.

Citizen lobbyists are more likely to have influence when policy decisions directly affect their interests, such as neighborhood transportation and zoning issues, but are less likely to be influential on citywide issues. Thus, although citizen lobbying efforts produce many positive benefits, including education about local government, working with others to build social capital, being the community's voice, and enhancing civic skills, they fail to add much to the city's *capacity* to solve problems because the issues on which they focus require little in the way of policy or technical expertise. Therefore, the substantive effects of citizen lobbyists are, in general, limited.

Source: Brian E. Adams, *Citizen Lobbyists: Local Efforts to Influence Public Policy* (Philadelphia: Temple University Press, 2007).

off-cycle elections the main voice being heard is the one that wants more pay and better benefits for interest group members.

Interest groups perform many important functions in local politics:

- They supply campaign labor and money to local candidates and campaigns.
- Through lobbying, they provide critical information without which elected leaders and administrators would not be able to function as effectively.

- They advocate through the court system. Groups have gone to court to protect the rights of people to be free from housing discrimination, to open suburbs to mixed-use housing, to protect the environment, to promote gun control, and to rid the nation of segregated schools.

For these reasons, interest groups are essential to political life at the local level.

POLITICAL CAMPAIGNING

People participate in local politics by getting involved in political campaigns, which is another form of voice in urban politics. Candidates need volunteers to go door to door and contributors to help them fund their campaigns. At the local level especially, candidates are most likely to recruit their own volunteers, many of whom might be friends and neighbors or family members. As the size of the city increases, campaigns become more professionalized as interest groups and political parties get more involved in supplying labor and money, and as campaign consultants are used more extensively to hone a candidate's message.

Campaign Finance

A significant way that people and groups make their voices heard is through campaign donations. The emphasis on fundraising has been substantial for decades in the largest places such as New York City, Los Angeles, and Chicago. Campaign spending is driven by the need for advertising, in particular television advertising, which is more expensive and more necessary in larger places. However, campaign fundraising is now becoming more important in mid-sized cities, such as Portland, Denver, and Baltimore, where campaigns for mayor can get into the millions of dollars. Spending by independent groups and individuals and the need to hire expensive media consultants to craft messages that can penetrate the clutter of the media environment are two other reasons why costs continue to escalate.[45]

Campaign contributing is dominated by people with disposable income sufficient to spend on politics—in reality only a tiny fraction of people overall—which means that this form of participation is severely *class biased*. Among groups, business, law, development, real estate, financial, retail, construction, homeowner, environmental, and social advocacy interests are some of the main players in city campaign finance.[46]

Where money comes from is also important because it hints at whose interests might be more effectively represented. Research by Jennifer Heerwig and Brian McCabe shows the considerable role of large donors and affluent neighborhoods in the 2013 Seattle mayoral election. In that contest, 20 percent of donors contributed the maximum amount ($500) allowed by local ordinance, but this accounted for over half of all money raised. About a quarter of all donations came from only 10 percent of the wealthiest neighborhoods.[47] This geographic pattern of campaign money may further bias city policy on the basis of neighborhood wealth. Because people and interests can donate money to any campaign anywhere, it is also common to see money from suburban locations show up in central city campaigns. The involvement of suburbanites in central city campaigns is a consequence of fragmented metropolitan areas where people have professional interests "downtown" but personal residences in the suburbs.[48] *National* advocacy groups also frequently become involved in local elections to support promising minority and LGBTQ candidates, especially at the mayoral level.

The coalitions of individuals and groups that support candidates also affect representation. A candidate may enter office with financial support from unions, neighborhood interests, liberal political groups, or downtown business interests. Once in office, though, that financial network or coalition is likely to change, as interests outside the network alter their strategies about who they support in order to get and maintain access to key decision makers.[49] The conundrum for representation is when candidates purport to represent one thing but then accept money from interests opposed to it.

Ultimately, candidates for office do not control their donors, who decide, independently from the campaign, who to support and when to do so. Sometimes donor decisions reflect their true preferences. This is the case for small donors and for those who support candidates representing a cause or ideological viewpoint or—especially at the city level—symbolizing the breaking of new ground for a racial or ethnic group or for the LGBTQ community. These kinds of supporters will often rally to their favored candidate in a display of **defensive contributing**, the tendency of committed followers to rally to protect their favored candidate in the face of negative information.[50] Many donors, though, are often more strategic, giving to those who are favored to win, such as incumbents or politically experienced candidates.[51] The flow of contributions in city campaigns is also a dynamic process prone to change as candidates move up or down in the polls or are subject to positive and negative information.[52] This affects electoral competition because fundraising is linked to candidates' perceived electoral strengths. Successful fundraising helps reinforce those strengths by allowing candidates an even greater ability to communicate with voters.

Campaign Finance Reforms

Who contributes, where money originates, and why people donate (i.e., their motivations) are three important sources of bias in local campaign finance. A fourth is how interest group money can affect the behavior of elected officials. Although it is not particularly well understood at the city level, the influence of campaign money on the behavior of elected officials is a major threat to representative democracy because it has the potential to sway outcomes in favor of special interests against the public interest. One study showed that critical votes on a living wage ordinance in the Chicago City Council were heavily influenced by labor unions' contributions.[53] A fifth form of bias is the effect that money has on electoral competition, in particular its effects on who runs and who wins. If good candidates are dissuaded from running because they cannot compete financially, electoral competition and therefore government accountability are threatened.

To address the different sources of bias inherent in campaign contributions, governments adopt regulations that must fit within parameters established by the US Supreme Court. If powerful interests are able to use money to wield disproportionate influence, then the voices of the general population are unlikely to be represented fairly. Indeed, this is the central debate about the US Supreme Court's decision in *Citizens United v. Federal Election Commission*, in which the Court upheld the argument of plaintiffs that any limitation on the ability of an organization or individuals to independently spend money for political purposes violated the Constitution's guarantee of free speech.[54] Furthermore, the ruling permitted unregulated money (i.e., undisclosed donations) to enter the political system at all levels. The broad grant of protection provided to groups by *Citizens United* raises the specter of independent expenditure groups entering local politics in ways not seen before. The concern is that "outsider" interests with national ideological or policy goals will attempt to influence local elections, biasing policy agendas in ways not favored by local residents. Research on this question is in its infancy, but early studies indicate that it may be happening already.[55]

Some cities will limit the amount of money that can be contributed to local campaigns, but per the US Supreme Court's decision in *Buckley v. Valeo*, limits cannot be imposed on candidate *spending* unless taxpayer money is involved.[56] So-called **public matching funds** are taxpayer dollars that "match" donations received by candidates from individuals and groups. For example, the government might provide a grant to candidates in the amount of $100 for every $200 a candidate raises from private sources. Both New York City and Los Angeles have systems that use public matching funds, but candidates cannot be forced into them. Reform proposals in Portland, Denver, and Baltimore are exploring contribution caps as well as public matching funds to reduce the monetary barrier for potential candidates.[57]

Some localities, such as Albuquerque, have a system of pure public financing of elections. In these systems, local taxpayer dollars are used by candidates. (Again, candidates cannot be forced to participate.) Public financing systems were dealt a blow, however, when so-called "wealthy candidate" provisions, which sought to supplement the grant given to publicly financed candidates running against wealthy privately funded candidates, were struck down by the US Supreme Court as an unconstitutional burden on free speech.[58] As you can see, federalism, in particular decisions of the Supreme Court, is critical to understanding the legal boundaries that local governments must follow in regulating campaign finance.

Another type of reform focuses on donors as opposed to candidates. In November 2015, voters in Seattle approved a ballot initiative to provide

democracy vouchers to local residents. Funded through a property tax levy, the city appropriates $3 million per year to the democracy vouchers program. Each resident eligible to vote in the election is entitled to $100 in vouchers, distributed in $25 increments, which they can use to support candidates of their choice. The idea behind the program is to provide a mechanism for regular citizens to support candidates via campaign donations; the larger objective is to democratize local campaign finance. However, research on contribution limits indicates that, while they may reduce the impact of wealthy donors, they have little effect on the competition for funds between incumbents and challengers, which is a key consideration in making elections more competitive.[59]

In general, reform efforts focus on increasing transparency in campaign finance disclosure and the ease with which citizens and media can access information about who is donating and to whom. They also focus on leveling the financial playing field among candidates and reducing the impact and corrupting influence of large donors.

PROTESTS AND REBELLIONS

A **protest** is a type of political participation in which a mass of people, acting collectively, makes demands on the political system. It is considered an active and constructive form of participation (see figure 9.1). **Rebellions**, often referred to as *riots*, are also a form of collective action designed to express dissatisfaction, but in this case the expression involves illegal activity, such as violence to people and property. Rebellions are not accounted for in figure 9.1, but they are clearly active and destructive. However, this does not mean that they are illegitimate expressions of dissatisfaction.

The Nature of Protest Activity

Protests are usually a tool used by people who have little formal political power. Thus, they are a form of bargaining that combines solidarity and anger. Protesters derive their visceral power from an implied threat of violence against government actors and/or the community itself.[60] Imagine people marching down a major city street or standing outside a government office building holding signs and chanting slogans, with voices and fists raised, or people "sitting in" to draw attention to unjust conditions.

Protests come in two forms. **Instrumental protests** are designed to achieve some tangible result or response from government for the people demanding action. Examples of instrumental protests include people protesting against police misconduct or the lack of jobs, lack of fair housing, or discrimination.[61] **Expressive protests**, as the label suggests, express a viewpoint on an issue, a condition, or simply anger at government actions or officials. Although they may be related to local issues, these kinds of protests are often about national or international issues for which the city merely serves as the site for protest activity. Examples of expressive protests include the civil rights and Vietnam War protests of the 1960s and 1970s, World Trade Organization protests in Seattle, Occupy Wall Street, the Million Man March, and immigration and women's marches.[62] Both types of protests are designed to broaden the scope of the conflict to empower the movements behind them. While instrumental protests have a specific target, expressive protests are about raising awareness.[63]

Protest is most likely to occur when the perception of local conditions warrants such actions. David Snow, Sarah Soule, and Daniel Cress studied antihomelessness protests in the US during the 1980s and found that the incidence of protests was a function of economic conditions, in particular the economic strain felt by city residents (measured by variables such as the ratio of housing values to personal income, unemployment rate, and the city's poverty level) and the low levels of local resources (measured by personal income and government assistance payments).[64] In other words, high levels of economic strain and low levels of resources to address the issue were central to these protest activities.

In addition to severe conditions, there must be a perception that the official governmental system is ignoring the problem, is ineffectual in dealing with it, or is making it worse. Simply having and sharing attitudes that conditions and issues are not being addressed may not be sufficient inducement to generate protest activity. For example, protest activity among whites opposed to busing was not a function of general attitudes about busing as a policy to promote desegregation in schools. Rather, it was a function of self-interest; residents in neighborhoods directly affected by busing orders were more likely to engage in protest than those not directly affected, even though both groups shared similar *attitudes* about the issues.[65]

Riots or Rebellions?

While protest carries with it an implicit threat of violence, urban riots or rebellions carry with them actual violence to people and/or property. Most definitions of rebellions consider the size and number of groups involved; illegal activity such as assault or property damage; intensity and duration of the rebellion; numbers of arrests, injuries, and death; and spread of the damage (i.e., number of neighborhoods involved).[66]

Scholars have disagreed about whether urban riots are forms of political expression. Early theories on the urban riots of the 1960s suggested that rioters were merely opportunistic lawless youths willing to exploit local political instability for "fun and profit."[67] However, extensive research on the 1965 Watts Riot in Los Angeles indicated that, although younger people were disproportionately involved, their attitudes about what they were doing and why had little to do with fun or profit. So-called new "urban blacks" who had come of age during the Civil Rights struggle were more likely than their elders (most of whom were reared and came of age in the segregated South) to connect their behavior in the riots to larger questions of ideology, representation, and fair treatment by local officials.

Compared to older black residents, younger black residents had a deeper sense of their own political power and how to use it to secure greater equality and better representation, and improve societal outcomes.[68]

In the 1960s, there were hundreds of riots across the US:

> Between 1963 and 1972 America experienced over 750 revolts. Upwards of 525 cities were affected, including nearly every one with a black population over 50,000. The two largest waves came during the summer of 1967 and during Holy Week in 1968 following the assassination of Martin Luther King, Jr. In these two years alone, 125 people were killed, nearly 7,000 were injured, approximately 45,000 arrests were made, and property damage topped $127 million or approximately $900 million in 2017 dollars.[69]

The summer of 1967 was particularly brutal, so much so that President Lyndon B. Johnson ordered the US Army into Newark and Detroit, the locations of the worst rioting, to replace state-level National Guard troops sent in to restore order. Whole sections of black neighborhoods were burned out, looted, and destroyed. Although Detroit and Newark received a great deal of attention, the rioting that summer extended to smaller places like Plainfield (New Jersey), Cambridge (Maryland), and Grand Rapids (Michigan) and to other mid-size cities like Atlanta, Buffalo, Cincinnati, Milwaukee, Minneapolis, and Tampa.[70] Riots or rebellions are usually triggered by an event, such as conflict with local police or—in the 1960s especially—the assassination of civil rights leaders.

Often forgotten in the history of urban revolts is the number of disturbances involving Latinos, which occurred mainly in the 1970s. A 2017 *CityLab* article discussed research on the history of Hispanic uprisings in US cities, including places like Anaheim (California), Passaic (New Jersey), Hartford (Connecticut), Miami, Durham (North Carolina), Chicago, Denver, and Albuquerque. At the heart of these incidents were the same kinds of issues that fueled African Americans the decade before, including police brutality, housing discrimination, racism, and inter-group tension.[71]

Although the 1960s and 1970s stood out for the frequency and intensity of rebellions, major urban riots happened in the mid- to late 19th century and throughout the 20th century.[72] The incidence of large-scale urban violence is usually triggered by some kind of conflict either between racial groups, as in Chicago in 1919, or between racial groups and local police departments, where a minority group is protesting and a mostly white police department is trying to maintain order. The Los Angeles riot in 1992 followed the videotaped police beating of African American motorist Rodney King and the acquittal of the officers involved by a jury that did not include a single African American. The 2014 riots in Ferguson followed a police shooting. The 2015 protest and rioting in Baltimore followed the death of Freddie Gray, a black man who died while in police custody, and subsequent conflict between the black community and police on the day of his funeral. The 2016 rioting in Charlotte (North Carolina) followed the shooting death of Keith Lamont Scott, a 43-year-old black man, by police.[73]

TABLE 9.1	The Ten Deadliest Urban Riots in US History	
City	Dates	Deaths
New York City	July 13–16, 1863	119 or 120
Atlanta	September 22–24, 1906	25–100[a]
Tulsa	May 31–June 1, 1921	300[b]
New York City	July 12, 1870 & 1871	70[c]
Los Angeles	April 29–May 4, 1992	63
Memphis	May 1–3, 1866	48
Detroit	July 23–27, 1967	43
New Orleans	July 30, 1866	44
Detroit	June 20–22, 1943	34
Los Angeles	August 11–16, 1965	34

[a] True figure may never be known.
[b] This is an estimate from the Red Cross; the official state of Oklahoma figure was 39.
[c] This is an approximate figure.

Source: Real Clear History, "10 Deadliest Riots in US History," https://www.realclearhistory.com/articles/2018/05/02/10_deadliest_riots_in_us_history_302.html.

Regardless of the triggering event, the foundation of large-scale urban violence remains tension and hostility between minority communities and local police departments, housing and economic discrimination, and demographic and economic changes that limit opportunities for minorities or that put them into conflict with one another. [74] The National Advisory Commission on Civil Disorders, created by President Johnson to understand why the rioting occurred, concluded that white racism was at the core of the problem that led to the violence.[75] Sadly, in many cities the conditions that often prefigure riots—discrimination, segregation, lack of hope, conflict with police—are still present today.

Table 9.1 summarizes the deadliest rebellions in US history, and figure 9.2 shows the locations of major riots between 1980 and 2014.

Protests and Rebellions: Do They Matter?

Mass protests and rebellions represent an extraordinary form of political participation. Today's social media combined with urban density make mass political action more dynamic and easier to coordinate than ever before. They highlight issues in ways that elections, contacting, lobbying, and campaigns can never dream of, and they make people feel that they have a voice and the power to produce change in their communities.

For these reasons, protests and rebellions, which capture substantial amounts of media and political attention, *are* worth it. No one can deny that protests organized to promote civil rights in the US changed not only the country but the world. The Civil Rights Era laid the foundation for the

Figure 9.2 Urban Rebellions, 1980–2014

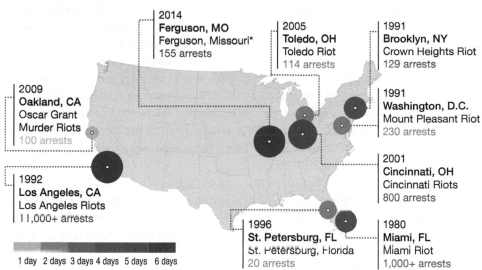

2014	2005	1991
Ferguson, MO	**Toledo, OH**	**Brooklyn, NY**
Ferguson, Missouri*	Toledo Riot	Crown Heights Riot
155 arrests	114 arrests	129 arrests

2009
Oakland, CA
Oscar Grant
Murder Riots
100 arrests

1991
Washington, D.C.
Mount Pleasant Riot
230 arrests

2001
Cincinnati, OH
Cincinnati Riots
800 arrests

1992
Los Angeles, CA
Los Angeles Riots
11,000+ arrests

1996
St. Petersburg, FL
St. Petersburg, Florida
20 arrests

1980
Miami, FL
Miami Riot
1,000+ arrests

1 day 2 days 3 days 4 days 5 days 6 days

Source: Forbes, "A Chart of Three Decades of Racial Unrest across America: The Cities with the Most Devastating Gang Riots," https://www.forbes.com/sites/niallmccarthy/2014/08/22/chart-over-three-decades-of-racial-unrest-across-america-the-cities-with-the-most-devastating-race-riots.

unprecedented expansion of a black and Latino middle class.[76] However, when it comes to producing lasting change, especially for those who live in the direst urban circumstances, the answers are less clear. The title of one of the most important urban politics books on representation, institutions, and policy answers the question of whether they matter: *Protest Is Not Enough*. Its central thesis is that in order for lasting change to occur, communities directly and negatively affected by urban conditions, government policies, and the actions of local agencies need to become fully incorporated into city government by organizing to win political office and to have a seat at the policy-making table.[77] While mass rebellions produce many government reports, new federal programs, and private efforts to address the core conditions that give rise to them, there is often a backlash against rioters that limits the effect of the collective expression of dissatisfaction and the impact of new initiatives that might follow.[78]

VOTING WITH YOUR FEET

Finally, nonvoting participation in urban politics can also take the form of exit, or "voting with your feet." According to Lyons and Lowery, exit is an active and destructive form of participation. Voting with your feet is a political statement that says that you are unhappy with local taxes and services, or perhaps local conditions generally, and are choosing to express that dissatisfaction by leaving.

An individual, family, or business may leave one municipality for another because taxes are too high, or crime is rampant, or local business regulations are too onerous. Indeed, the threat of exit is central to major theories of urban politics. In the mid-1950s, economist Charles Tiebout articulated the view that at the heart of urban politics was a desire on the part of voter-taxpayers to shop for tax-service bundles that fit their preferences, much like people shop for consumer goods.[79] According to this theory, voter-taxpayers would exit a city if the value of taxes paid was greater than the value of services received. The job of city leaders, then, was to maximize the value of services relative to their costs in order to ensure a steady supply of residents. The private decisions of voter-taxpayers throughout a metropolitan area, where exit decisions are least costly, would, in theory, discipline local officials to provide high-quality services at the lowest price.

The question of whether people actually behave this way and to what degree their behavior reflects narrow calculations about relative taxes and services is an open one. Do people have sufficient knowledge about local government taxes and services to be able to link their own behavior—especially on something as difficult as moving—to government policies? And is that the central motivation for leaving? Some say no. Others ask whether that kind of detailed knowledge is necessary to make a move that fits personal preferences.[80] People might be able to align their preferences for government taxes and services through the use of heuristics or cognitive shortcuts that allow them to make rational decisions without detailed knowledge.[81] Still others might rely on the actions of *marginal consumers*, people with detailed knowledge about government taxes and services who through their own behavior establish a market for public goods.[82]

Reasons for moving are numerous. Some move to start a new life or to pursue a better job opportunity. Some move to be closer to family, especially when starting a family of their own. Exiting behavior is real, but the explanation for why it occurs is a matter of debate. The history of "white flight" suggests that racial animus was at the heart of the decisions of many white urbanites to vacate central cities for the suburbs. However, not everyone is equally able to exit, because of racial discrimination in housing markets, job security, the cost of moving, or some combination of all three. Thus, in cities, millions of seemingly private decisions have representational consequences.

The ability to move is a fundamental freedom, so there is little that the government can do to prevent it. What the government can do, however, is create incentives for a different kind of urban development that might limit suburban options. Efforts to slow suburban sprawl by redirecting business investment and residential choices downtown fall into this category. However, these efforts may have negative economic consequences if they reduce the overall supply of housing. Exit behavior has given rise to calls to reform the structure of government in metropolitan areas. The problem to be addressed here is simple, but solutions are not. The tax dollars required to tackle problems of poor housing, poor schools, neighborhood blight, and family dislocation in the inner city are found in the suburbs, beyond the reach of urban officials, who must fend for themselves in the highly competitive world of municipal sorting, with minimal state or federal commitment to solving urban problems. One solution is to build larger governmental systems that merge suburbs with cities, allowing government to capture suburban wealth to address inner city problems. This, though, may stoke the ire of urban minority groups that have gained political power in central cities.[83] There are only about forty consolidated city/county governments in the US and many more in which this form of metropolitan government has been proposed but failed. The lack of popularity of metropolitan or regional governments is, in part at least, a function of politics.[84]

SUMMARY

Although voting is the means by which local residents choose their representatives, not all forms of participation in urban politics are designed with this in mind. In fact, nonvoting forms of participation are meant to influence the direction and behaviors of those already in office and/or those unelected officials who provide essential government services. Contacting local government, engaging the process through political parties and interest groups, campaigning, making campaign contributions, protests and rebellions, and "voting with your feet" are all important forms of participation.

Each of these forms of participation is a means for the will of the people to be expressed in urban politics. As such, they are a critical mechanism of representation at the local level. None of the behaviors described in this chapter are new. Because of technological advances, ways that people individually or collectively can express themselves or engage the process have changed, as have the ways in which government responds. Although anyone or any group can engage in these forms of participation, as with voting, there are socioeconomic patterns in these behaviors. Therefore, who contacts, who contributes, who gets involved with parties or interest groups, who protests, and who exits are essential questions to consider.

Key Terms

citizen contacting (182)
citizen lobbyists (191)
community power structure (186)
defensive contributing (193)
democracy vouchers (195)
electoral coalition (188)
elitism (186)
exit (182)
expressive protests (195)
general referent contact (183)
growth machine (187)
instrumental protest (195)

interest group (185)
loyalty (182)
neglect (182)
particularized contact (183)
pluralism (186)
political efficacy (183)
political party (185)
protest (195)
public matching funds (194)
rebellion (195)
regime theory (188)
voice (182)

Discussion Questions

1. How are nonvoting forms of participation essential to urban democracy?

2. Why is the class bias so prevalent in most forms of political participation not as relevant to citizen contacting?

3. Why, in general, are political parties weak at the city level? Do you think that steps should be taken to strengthen parties in city government?

4. What are the main threats to urban democracy posed by interest groups and campaign donations?

5. Are urban rebellions a form of political expression? Why or why not?

6. What are the economic and policy implications of "voting with your feet?"

Exercises

1. Does your city uses a 311 system to handle citizen contacts? If so, attempt to determine the nature of the contacts, the frequency of them, and where they come from (geographically) within your city. If not, does your city have a centralized complaint unit, or are contacts handled on an agency-by-agency basis?

2. Consult your local governments for information on campaign finance disclosure in local elections.

   a. Choose the city council, mayoral, or school board election and conduct an analysis of the kinds of people and interests that donated to local campaigns in the most recent election. Was there any outside money in the campaign? If so, where did it come from?

   b. Choose the city council, mayoral, or school board election and assess the strength of the campaign finance system according to transparency in campaign finance disclosure, ease of access, efforts to level the financial playing field among candidates, and reduction of the impact and corrupting influence of large contributions.

3. Investigate the types of interest groups in your city or county. Is there a broad range of groups or a fairly narrow set of actors? Then reach out to group leaders and interview them about the nature of their work, their memberships, and the tactics they employ to achieve their objectives.

4. Select a city in your own state or another that had a mass protest and/or riot or rebellion. What were its origins? Consult government sources and news accounts to determine how many people were involved and the nature of the core issues. How did the government respond?

5. Using census data, study the movement of people within your metropolitan area. Which areas are gaining population and which are losing? What patterns can you see that seem related to conditions in particular cities?

PART IV

LOCAL GOVERNMENT POLICIES

10

LOCAL GOVERNMENT POLICY MAKING AND SERVICES

GUIDING QUESTIONS

1. What are the major steps in the policy making process, and who are the major participants influencing decisions at each stage?
2. What are the differences among developmental, redistributive, and allocational policies? What are some examples of each type of policy?
3. To what extent is production of government services similar to or different from companies making and selling products to consumers? What goals do governments often pursue in providing services, and how might they conflict?
4. What are the strengths and weaknesses of the different ways of providing services to a community? Are there best-case and worst-case examples associated with the different ways of providing services?

LOCAL OFFICIALS, candidates, media, and interest groups often try to identify issues that they believe deserve a community's attention. As the case of Nashville demonstrates, however, that does not guarantee change. A major concern going into the 2015 elections was growth and transportation. The new mayor, Megan Barry, was a strong advocate of a light rail system to help ease congestion. In 2017, the legislature and governor overwhelmingly passed a law allowing local governments to adopt a sales tax for transit. The mayor, council, newspapers, and business community backed a 0.5 percent sales tax increase to add twenty-six miles of light rail and twenty-five miles of bus rapid transit by 2032 in Nashville-Davidson County. The referendum was scheduled for May 1, 2018, and early polls suggested that it would pass.

Then the wheels came off the campaign bus. In January, the mayor became embroiled in scandal connected to her affair with the head of her security detail and resigned. One opposition group raised over $1 million, mainly from unknown sources, and several council members came out against the plan. In the end, it failed by a two-to-one margin.[1] In contrast, leaders in growing regions like Denver, Salt Lake City, and Charlotte were able to create rail systems. As the Nashville example suggests, policy making is complicated. This chapter covers the policy process and service provision, another basic activity of local governments.

THE POLICY PROCESS

As chapter 1 explained, *policy* is a government's course of action about a perceived problem. Keep in mind, though, that inaction is also a policy, and policies can seem contradictory. Although scholars have used many approaches for studying policy,[2] many see it as a process involving several stages or steps (see figure 10.1).[3] The process in this very general illustration usually does not look so tidy and seldom has a strict time line. Common actions that do tend to follow a calendar include budget adoption and contract approval.

Problem Identification

The first stage in the policy process is getting a community and its government decision makers to perceive something as a problem that needs to be addressed. **Problem identification** can happen in multiple ways. Sometimes events leave officials with no choice. Obvious examples are natural disasters like floods, wildfires, tornados, or hurricanes. Human acts like mass shootings or terrorist attacks also pressure local officials to act. Crises related to government services also prompt responses, such as the 2007 collapse of an interstate highway bridge in Minneapolis, the contamination of Flint's water supply beginning in 2014, and the hacking that disrupted Atlanta's computer system in 2018.

Interest groups (see chapter 8) are also active in problem identification. They can highlight issues in many ways, including petitions, protests, news

---

Figure 10.1 Model of the Policy Process

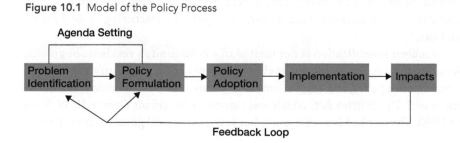

conferences, public comments at city council meetings, and lobbying local officials. Some organizations, like the local chamber of commerce, maintain full-time staffs that conduct research and lobby on behalf of business regarding issues such as tax rates and economic development. Others, such as neighborhood organizations, can organize and take their case to city council over issues such as traffic, crime, and land use. They often get involved in zoning cases with the local planning commission well before a case makes it to the council.[4] In recent years, Black Lives Matter and other groups have pressured local governments in multiple ways to provide for civilian review of police officers and practices.

Officials and candidates also try to identify problems that a local government should address. For example, most mayors deliver an annual "State of the City" address, allowing them to describe current conditions and highlight their priorities for the coming year. One study of these speeches in several dozen large cities during 2010–13 found that city finances and economic development were the most common topics. Social welfare issues were the sixth most common. The researchers found that emphasis on economic development was higher in cities that had higher poverty rates, were more conservative ideologically, and were less segregated. It is worth noting, though, that the study examined years still affected by the Great Recession.[5] As economic conditions improved by the late 2010s, infrastructure also became a major topic in a majority of addresses, but its ranking varied by city size.[6] Even though mayors emphasize similar issues, they might not discuss them in the same way. For instance, one study discovered that male and female mayors framed economic development issues differently, with men using themes emphasizing strength and self-reliance and women tapping those *plus* themes that were labeled nurturing, such as supporting others, concern for others, connectedness, and support for new ideas.[7]

The media, too, can turn something into an issue that policy makers have to address, with both news coverage and editorials. For example, beginning in late 2008, investigative reporting by an Atlanta newspaper into possible cheating on standardized tests in the city's schools led to a state investigation and the retirement of the superintendent. Almost 150 educators resigned or were terminated and thirty-five were indicted; one died, one was acquitted, and the rest either pled guilty along the way or were convicted in April 2015.[8]

As chapter 7 described, citizens in some communities are permitted to use direct democracy to get issues on the ballot for voters to decide. This essentially allows activists to bypass the city council and move to the adoption stage. For example, several dozen cities in recent years voted on initiatives to increase the local minimum wage. Petition drives also led to many communities voting on questions related to marijuana, LGBTQ issues, development and land use, and environmental issues such as banning hydraulic fracturing to drill for oil and gas.[9]

Problem identification is not limited to a community's residents or groups. As chapter 3 suggested, higher-level governments can also identify a local problem, impose a policy, and suggest how to implement it. One example is the Americans with Disabilities Act, which was signed by President George H. W. Bush in 1990. The law had laudable goals, but it required local governments to make major changes with little federal money—a classic unfunded mandate, as discussed in chapter 4. Local governments had to make and pay for major changes to sidewalks, parking areas, ramps to buildings, transit systems, and even the availability of government documents.

Policy Formulation

Once public officials and others recognize that a problem exists, the next step is **policy formulation**, considering alternatives to address the issue. The first two stages—problem identification and policy formulation—are often collectively called **agenda setting**, which one study defines as "a process in which certain public problems are identified, recognized, and defined, and specific solutions or alternatives are generated, considered, and attached to these problems."[10]

One obvious source of alternative remedies for a problem is government agencies. For example, a city council might turn to the public works department for possible remedies for neighborhood flooding. Cities and counties sometimes complement internal advice by hiring outside consultants to help them assess the cost and possible effects of different strategies for addressing problems.

Many professional organizations sponsor research and hold conferences that are important sources of information for addressing local problems. These include the International City/County Management Association (ICMA), the National League of Cities (NLC), and the US Conference of Mayors. Most states have comparable organizations, such as a state municipal league representing cities. These groups also engage in advocacy to promote the interests of local governments. Other organizations are more specialized, frequently sponsoring training and publishing reports on "best practices" in their area of expertise. For example, the Government Finance Officers Association has over 17,000 members and deals with financial management in state and local governments.[11] The American Public Works Association is designed to serve the needs of those involved in infrastructure and public works, including agency accreditation, continuing education credits, and certification programs for various specialists.[12]

Interest groups are usually at the ready with policy suggestions for solving a problem. For example, housing activists pressed Seattle to impose a tax on large employers to fund affordable housing and deal with homelessness. Despite opposition from Amazon and other businesses, the city council unanimously adopted a modified version of the proposal in May 2018; it was expected to raise $47 million over 5 years, considered a moderate amount given high home prices and rents in the area. After threats from Amazon and other companies, including a possible campaign to repeal the ordinance, just one month later the council voted 7–2 to repeal it.[13] In less visible policy areas, national groups can sometimes play key roles in developing policy options, as with environmentally friendly building design.[14]

Alternatives must often take into account what other governments do. Local governments also learn from one another in a process called **policy diffusion**. As leading scholars Shipan and Volden observe, "In its most generic form, policy diffusion is defined as one government's policy choices being influenced by the choices of other governments."[15] Diffusion is usually studied in terms of how a policy spreads among governments once it is launched, as with the proliferation of antismoking ordinances after they caught on initially. Because of variation from place to place, it is not a mere process of imitation, however. It can also be a matter of competition or learning from early adopters.[16]

Alternatives and diffusion can also be constrained by higher-level governments. In 2011, after decades of prohibiting the practice, Georgia's legislature avoided the risk of voting on Sunday alcohol sales statewide by kicking down the decision to city and county voters. Many places were worried about their ability to attract chain restaurants if they banned Sunday sales; others saw them as a way to generate sales tax revenue. In their first chance to vote, 105 of 127 places approved Sunday sales.[17]

In contrast, as chapter 3 indicated, a number of states have prevented their local governments from banning plastic bags, adopting a minimum wage, or using certain revenue sources. The federal government can also limit local policy options. For example, beginning in 2009, issues of police conduct led the US Department of Justice to sue multiple police departments, including Baltimore, Chicago, and Cleveland. Several departments reached agreements to change policies under federal oversight. Research on such agreements suggests that they can have at least modest effects, but use of this strategy was curtailed by the Trump administration. Advocates argue that only this type of outside pressure can change local practices.[18] State governments can also intervene locally in the absence of federal action, as California has done regarding police conduct.[19]

In addition to intervention by higher-level governments, external economic or social conditions can also limit local governments' options for addressing problems. During the years surrounding the 2007–9 Great Recession, local governments faced declining tax and state revenues, along with legal limitations imposed by states, and growing obligations for debt, pensions, and employee health care. They considered multiple options for dealing with these pressures, usually starting with raising revenues other than taxes and finding ways to reduce personnel costs. Responses often extended to service cuts, layoffs, and increased reliance on fees, particularly for utilities, but there are doubts about how permanent many of the changes will be.[20] The flip side of this scenario is a local government being threatened or enticed by location decisions of a major employer such as Amazon (see box 1.2).

Policy Adoption

Given alternatives formulated to "solve" a problem, the next step is **policy adoption**, formal approval of a policy in response to an identified problem—or maybe even deciding to change nothing. Few city councils are as large as those in Chicago (50) or New York (51), and few local legislatures have as many constituents per member as the Los Angeles County Board of Supervisors (five members for a county with more than ten million residents). Some research suggests that there is a tendency for members to push for consensus in smaller bodies.[21] One study of environmental policy making, which requires multiple governments, found participants aiming for coalition building and consensus during the early 2000s along the US Gulf Coast.[22] However, as anyone following local news knows, city councils and county boards are not always harmonious. One study found that council conflict was highest regarding policy decisions that members thought were most important and was more common in cities with higher poverty rates.[23] Other research discovered council conflict related to interpersonal relations but noted that mayoral leadership could enhance a council's effectiveness in reaching decisions.[24] This is not entirely at odds with research on over 150 medium-sized cities, in which conflict was highest and cooperation lowest in councils without a professional manager as well as those for which only the mayor, rather than the council and the mayor, selected the manager.[25] Thus, a professional administrator hired by the mayor and council, as well as mayoral leadership, appear to have a stabilizing effect on council decision making.

Research suggests that the decisions of local legislatures are related to public opinion as well as the aims of interest groups. Residents' trust in local government can provide support for adopting policy changes.[26] Some research has compared communities' ideological characteristics with their policies. One study of spending by California counties in the 1990s found that more liberal counties spent more on social welfare programs, but the relationship also depended on whether the county had a home rule charter. Factors other than ideology had the most influence on spending in less conflictual policy areas such as public safety and infrastructure.[27] A study of twenty-six cities in different regions of the country uncovered a similar impact of ideology on spending patterns.[28] A statistical analysis of more than 13,000 cities between 1987 and 2002 found that more Democratic-leaning cities spent more on redistributive programs, as did richer cities, those with more federal and state support, and cities with term limits on elected officials.[29] Subsequent research also found local policies to be responsive to a community's ideological leanings, regardless of its municipal government structure[30] or its partisan leanings.[31]

Not all research on policy adoption focuses on government spending. One study of hundreds of cities included in a 1997 survey did a statistical analysis of the likelihood of adopting reforms in operations, service delivery, and finances. One of the strongest predictors of changes in service delivery and the use of citizen surveys was how long the city manager had held the position. **Contracting out** (hiring a private company to perform a service, such as paving streets, collecting trash, or mowing grass in parks) was more likely the more affluent the community but less likely when council members were elected by districts and when more of the work force was unionized. With regard to finances, support for fees in place of tax increases was less likely when councils used committees and had a mix of district and at-large members. Support for creating enterprise funds (that usually separate utilities from other operations) was stronger in larger cities, those with more state restrictions on revenue sources, and those with partisan elections; it was weaker with mixed systems of representation. Overall, then, there is no "one size fits all" for predicting policy changes, but they are affected by a mix of political factors, community characteristics, and city manager tenure.[32]

Adopting a policy is not limited to passage of an ordinance by a city council. A new policy could be adopted simply by administrative action, as when a department changes the way it enforces regulations or a transit agency modifies bus routes and schedules. Adoption can also take the form of a court decision. During the 1970s and 1980s, for example, multiple lawsuits in federal courts under the Voting Rights Act led to decisions that forced city councils to change from at-large elections to the use of district representation.[33]

Implementation

Adopting a policy does not mean that something automatically changes. There must also be a plan to carry out or implement the policy. **Implementation** usually involves the government bureaucracy, but policies can also be implemented by other governments, companies, or nonprofit organizations (more on the latter appears later in this chapter). Implementation can be difficult, depending on how radical the policy change is and how entrenched the existing system and procedures are. For example, moving to electronic tolls on New York City subways and buses took years—and a lot of planning—to implement.[34]

Impacts

Implementing a policy has certain goals, but other things can occur as well. **Impacts** are the broad set of effects, both intended and unintended, of a policy. Take, for example, a drug treatment program.[35] There are already impacts when the program is first implemented: hiring staff, acquiring equipment, leasing office space, etc. Once the staff delivers treatment, the effects can extend well beyond the individual client. Success or failure affects a client's family, coworkers, and neighbors. On a larger scale, if the program is effective in a given area, crime could drop, in which case insurance could become cheaper, people and businesses might be more willing to move to the area, and real estate values could increase. Unintended or unanticipated consequences can be positive or negative. A classic example for those in the South was the introduction of kudzu decades ago to impede soil erosion; the vine grew relentlessly and spread over huge swaths of land, seemingly covering everything in its path.

Policy Feedback Loop

The policy process often does not end with implementation and its effects. Residents and others react to impacts and often act to defend the policy, redefine the problem, or modify the solution, creating a **feedback loop**. Governments often set up methods to evaluate policy effectiveness, and the findings provide useful feedback to agencies and elected officials. A simple example is gathering data to evaluate whether constructing "speed humps" in residential areas actually slows traffic and improves safety. Many cities survey residents for their impressions of service quality; over 500 have used the services associated with the National Citizen Survey.[36] Many use special phone or email contacts to provide feedback on service problems. Hundreds of local governments also have auditors who assess the performance of programs, projects, and facilities. In Portland, Oregon, the elected Multnomah County auditor decides what to audit, which included animal services in 2016, homeless services in 2017, major county construction projects in 2018, and dozens of other issues dating back to 1993. Multnomah County also maintains a Good Government Hotline that citizens can use to report suspected fraud and similar problems involving county resources.[37]

Participants can also use political pressure as feedback to reshape the agenda by changing problem identification or the range of alternatives used to address the original issue. Imagine that a city adopts a policy on apartment inspections in response to the perception that many units and buildings are not properly maintained. As the inspections proceed, landlords fight back against the new system, perhaps in hopes of repealing it. Others might push in the other direction to have inspections more often, for example, annually instead of every few years, or to increase landlords' fines for violations. As these debates focusing on safety and health proceed, environmentalists might get involved by trying to redefine the issue and yet the city to require new buildings to have individual water meters for each apartment. They might argue that, rather than the landlord "hiding" water costs for an entire building in tenants' rent, the meters would encourage residents to look at their own bills and conserve water to save money.

TYPES OF POLICIES

Not all policies are the same, of course, even in the same community. Participants and their strategies can also vary significantly. Researchers tend to classify policies in two ways: (1) the policy's goals or effects; (2) the service or substantive area, for example, housing, transportation, elder care, public safety, recreation.

In terms of goals or effects, in his book *City Limits*, Paul Peterson lays out a common division. Peterson analyzes what he calls three "policy arenas": developmental, redistributive, and allocational. *Developmental policies* "enhance the economic position of the city." In Peterson's view, developmental policies are designed to compete with other areas: "They strengthen the local economy, enhance the local tax base, and generate additional resources that can be used for the community's welfare." Peterson's underlying concern is the economic position of a city compared to others. It is worth noting, however, that he wrote before the growth of major tax breaks for large corporations.[38] Strong support for developmental policies comes from business groups as well as from labor unions with members who might benefit from construction jobs.

At the other end of the spectrum are *redistributive policies*, which are designed to "benefit low-income residents." Peterson adds, though, that such policies "at the same time negatively affect the local economy." He asserts that the state and national governments should take the lead on these policies, since the more that local governments engage in redistribution, the more they encourage affluent residents to "vote with their feet" and leave a city. The poor generally lack the resources and organization to influence redistributive policies, especially in competition with antitax and other groups.

The third category covers *allocational policies*, which are "more or less neutral in their economic effects." These include basic services like garbage collection and symbolic issues like honorary street-naming. Public employees are active in this area because of the large number of jobs connected to basic services, which are a large share of local budgets.

Peterson's categories focus on policies' economic effects on a city and ignore others that do not fit neatly into his policy arenas. One such arena is *regulatory policies*. While it has economic effects, regulation is generally aimed at setting standards or influencing behavior, for example, licenses for businesses, health standards for restaurants, noise control, snow removal from sidewalks, and leash laws for dog owners. The general public pays limited attention to regulations, but those affected, such as the taxi drivers affected by taxi driver standards, are quite active in this policy area. A second type of policy that has received more attention starting in the 1990s is usually connected to "culture wars" or "morality politics." Local conflicts have dealt with issues from abortion clinics, prostitution, and needle exchange programs to LGBTQ issues (see chapter 13 for more).[39]

Classifying policies by service, function, or mission is also common. In many communities and professional organizations, this classification scheme follows the agency or department lines that organize workers and budgets. For instance, a city could look separately at police, fire, ambulance services, and emergency preparedness. More broadly, there could be a coordinated effort to provide public safety.

PROVIDING LOCAL SERVICES

Adopting and implementing new policies are regular activities of local governments. Residents and businesses expect their local government to be there when they need police, firefighters, streets, water, libraries, and other services. Yet perhaps nothing besides taxes can generate more public concern than the level and quality of services, particularly when things are not working well. As you might expect, debates over services often involve goals and the "best" ways to reach them.[40]

Analysts usually distinguish between providing and producing services. Providing a service generally refers to making it available. For example, a city with its own fire department would both provide the service and produce it. It might also hire the county sheriff to give it police protection, which means that the city provides the service but the county actually produces it. The city might also elect to *not* provide a service through inaction, as when it does nothing regarding homeless shelters and leaves producing them to congregations or other charities.

Production of Public Services

Urban scholar Bryan Jones approaches service delivery by contrasting production of public services with companies making and selling products.[41] In his model (see figure 10.2), a company might make dishwashers, which are

Figure 10.2 Model of the Public Service Production Process

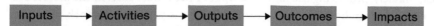

Source: Bryan D. Jones, "Assessing the Products of Government," in Richard C. Rich, ed., *Analyzing Urban Service Distributions* (Lexington: Lexington Books, 1982), 161.

distributed through retailers. *Inputs* are the raw materials and other components in the dishwasher, *activities* represent the actual process of manufacturing them, and *outputs* are the dishwashers. The process is guided by pricing at each stage. The company's goal is to produce dishwashers at a profit, not to promote cleanliness in American kitchens. The consumer's goal is to buy a good and reliable dishwasher.

Government-provided services are different, Jones argues, with outcomes and impacts added to the other three categories. Examples of specific *outcomes* include reading levels of third graders, a desired level of recycling, or ending clients' drug dependency. These outcomes are produced by outputs, including the time devoted to teaching, collecting recycling, and caseworkers' sessions with addicted clients respectively. Achieving these outcomes can also have broader *impacts*. One example is the drug treatment program described above. Similarly, collecting more material for recycling could reduce the volume of waste going to the landfill, extending its useful life, and might generate revenue through the sale of recyclable materials. These outcomes and impacts often exist even if the government provides a service without producing it.

Determining whether outcomes or impacts are successful is challenging. The first issue is measurement or monitoring of a program, as with fire or police response times. Is low response time sufficient to determine public safety? If not, what other indicators should be considered? The second dilemma is determining what level demonstrates success. With reading, for example, what percentage of third graders reading at grade level should be considered satisfactory for a school district: 75, 85, or 100 percent? If a student is not reading at a minimum level, what actions can be taken to raise proficiency?

Keep in mind that the model of service production in figure 10.2 is not the same as the policy process mapped out in figure 10.1. In fact, figure 10.2 essentially lays out the implementation stage of the policy process after decisions are made about which services to provide and how to do so. Such decisions, including formulation of goals, are not always easy.

Goals in Providing Public Services

In their highly regarded book on urban management, Robert England, John Pelissero, and David Morgan examine the various—and sometimes competing—aims that can guide provision of services: efficiency, effectiveness, equity, and responsiveness.[42] For both elected officials and government managers, deciding which of these goals to emphasize can be difficult, as well as hazardous politically.

Efficiency might sound simple. People often think of it as "best bang for the buck," namely, producing the highest output at the lowest cost. In the private sector, efficiency can be measured by profit, dividends per share of stock, or similar measures. For government, inputs and workloads are usually easy to measure. This is easier for physical outputs, for example, the cost of treating each gallon of wastewater to a specific standard of cleanliness. Things get more complicated for other services, however. It is more difficult to measure procedural efficiency, for example, the time it takes to get a driver's license or building permit, response times for police or fire departments, or error rates in processing property tax payments.

Effectiveness can be even more difficult to assess. People think of effectiveness in terms of outcomes (see figure 10.2), that is, something "working" or a program "reaching its goals," often without reference to costs. Combining efficiency and effectiveness yields measures of productivity, for example, number of miles of street paved per crew hour worked. Professional organizations and researchers have entered this discussion by promoting **benchmarking**, the comparison of local performance against a national standard. Benchmarking based on a sample of similar cities or results of national surveys can allow local governments to improve operations, hold managers accountable, manage contracts better, and engage in better planning and budgeting.[43]

Responsiveness—meeting residents' demands—is also difficult to conceptualize and measure. At times responsiveness can be determined when local officials adopt policies at the request of citizen requests or mobilization.[44] Another means of assessment is monitoring of citizen contacts with local government. Kansas City and Chicago are among the many cities using 311 calls (as opposed to 911 emergencies) and online submission systems for residents to report and follow up on service problems.[45] Contacting a central source rather than individual departments is easier for residents, who do not have to guess which department does what. Plus, the 311 center can provide independent data on problem resolution timeliness and success that can be used for evaluating departments and their managers.

As already discussed, local governments also use surveys to assess citizen satisfaction with services. Surveys can be done by phone or online.[46] One survey dilemma is reliance on residents' ability to recall use of services. The random sample of residents responding to a yearly survey might not remember when or how much they used different services, whether the local government is actually producing the service, or any special circumstances (e.g., weather conditions) that might have affected the service. Some research suggests that satisfaction levels vary with the personal characteristics of survey respondents. However, other results indicate that satisfaction varies by city area. Still, surveys can provide useful information to local government managers about agencies' performance as well as about problems that might be concentrated in certain locations or among certain populations. Surveys are usually used to evaluate services in conjunction with other data, such as complaints made online or by phone.[47]

Equity can be especially fraught with conflict—how do you determine what is "fair"? One standard might be treating every neighborhood equally. Having the same level of patrols might not seem fair if some neighborhoods have more crimes against persons or property than others. Another approach aims for comparable outcomes in terms of quality of life. Beginning in the 1970s, for instance, Savannah, Georgia (a city dating to Colonial America), used indicators such as crime, street conditions, water and sewer adequacy, dog control, and fire incidence to identify areas in greater need of services and concentrated efforts there. This was especially helpful in the city's poor black neighborhoods.[48] In contrast, judging public libraries based on circulation of books can favor more affluent areas; libraries in poorer areas might be open fewer hours and often focus more on providing services like internet access to job-seekers and others without computer access at home than on checking out books.[49]

ALTERNATIVE SERVICE METHODS

Although the idea was not new, beginning in the 1980s and 1990s, there was a concerted effort to consider alternatives to government-produced services. An early apostle of **privatization** was E. S. Savas, who promoted this process of turning over services to the private sector to produce and sell. Other advocates included conservative and free-market think tanks like the Manhattan Institute and the Cato Institute. They were joined by advocates of "reinventing government" such as David Osborne and Ted Gaebler, who pushed government to see residents and taxpayers as "customers."[50] The debates focused on which organizations could best produce services, with an emphasis on efficiency.

Savas examines ten ways to produce services; Osborne and Gaebler listed three dozen, although many overlap. In 2007, the International City/County Management Association (ICMA) surveyed more than 6,000 cities and counties about their service delivery and received 1,599 responses (26.2%). Half reported studying the feasibility of private service delivery during the previous 5 years, with 87 percent indicating that it was part of an internal cost reduction effort and half identifying external fiscal pressures as a factor. Over one-third reported obstacles to private service delivery, mainly opposition from government employees and the lack of private contractors.[51]

Table 10.1 displays the results of ICMA's 2007 survey. Respondents were given eight options for service delivery; the three major ones are presented in the table. "Government" in the table represents the response "Your employees only." The five omitted survey categories were "Your employees in part," another government or authority, franchises/concessions, subsidies, and volunteers. The only cases in which any of the omitted options were the dominant response were related to other governments: social welfare programs (where counties have an

TABLE 10.1	Delivery Method for Selected Local Services (Percent), 2007		
Service	Government	For-Profit Firm	Nonprofit
Payroll (1,228)	89.0	7.1	0.2
Personnel (898)	88.5	5.8	0.7
Crime Prevention/Patrol (1,206)	88.0	0.5	0.2
Traffic Control/Parking Enforcement (1,028)	83.5	4.0	0.5
Public Relations/Public Information (1,116)	83.2	8.2	1.3
Inspection/Code Enforcement (938)	81.6	7.7	0.1
Data Processing (1,090)	74.6	10.7	0.6
Snow Plowing/Sanding (917)	74.2	9.6	0.3
Operating/Maintaining Recreation Facilities (1,130)	72.7	7.0	3.7
Water Distribution (908)	72.5	5.7	1.7
Fire Prevention/Suppression (1,044)	71.6	0.8	2.5
Building Security (958)	70.1	18.8	0.7
Vehicle Towing and Storage (422)	12.3	65.4	5.5
Commercial Solid Waste Collection (699)	22.2	56.2	1.7
Operating Day Care Facilities (320)	13.8	53.8	32.8
Legal Services (1,042)	31.0	51.9	2.7
Operating/Managing Electric Utilities (387)	27.6	47.8	4.9
Solid Waste Disposal (851)	25.9	42.7	1.8
Operating/Managing Hospitals (253)	2.8	39.5	37.5
Cultural and Arts Programs (567)	26.6	6.9	35.3
Museums (433)	23.8	3.9	38.3
Operating Homeless Shelters (288)	2.8	4.5	56.3

Note: The figure in parentheses is the number of governments that answered the question.

Source: ICMA, "Profile of Local Government Service Delivery Choices, 2007," 2009, https://icma.org/sites/default/files/107037_asd2007_2008web.pdf.

active role) and several transit programs (where an independent county or state authority could be the lead agency).

Many of the services in the top twelve rows, which represent government employees usually doing the work, are internal (e.g., payroll and personnel). Others relate to safety and public works. In the middle (shaded) panel, the private sector dominates. In many of these cases, firms could be selling their services to others, not just governments (e.g., vehicle towing, daycare). Outside legal services are common with governments that have a limited number of in-house attorneys and hire expertise as needed, for example, when the contract for a cable television franchise is up for renewal. Finally, the bottom three rows show the presence of nonprofits, which have major roles in cultural programs and social services. The remainder of the chapter describes alternative service methods and examines their strengths and weaknesses.

Government Production of Services

With traditional government production of services, taxes (and revenue from higher-level governments) are used to pay for a service delivered by public employees. Libraries, police, fire protection, parks, water, and public school systems are common examples. One strength of government service is public access, generally without regard to residents' income, as with public libraries or parks. Government service also allows more direct control by elected officials, although patronage and other political conflicts can emerge. Unlike private firms interested in profit, government production could promote a broader set of impacts, as with the drug treatment example affecting clients' families and neighborhoods, possibly reducing crime. Similarly, a system of trails or parks would provide access to the public, but it can also stimulate nearby construction of businesses or residences. One difficulty is gauging service demand: How much or how little is enough? How and when should it be delivered? Such decisions seem easier with consumer goods that are easily differentiated in the for profit sector, such as restaurant meals or event tickets, than with government services.[52]

Government Vending

Savas calls another type of service *government vending*, but defines it too narrowly, as when a government charges a concert promoter for extra police protection. It is better to think of **government vending** as government delivering services for which it charges a fee. Such fees do not have to cover the full cost of the service. Osborne and Gaebler cite three conditions under which fees work well: "when the service is primarily a 'private good,' benefiting the individuals who use it; when those who don't pay for it can be excluded from enjoying its benefits; and when fees can be collected efficiently."[53] Common examples include water, toll bridges/roads (see box 10.1), and bus services—the more you use them, the more you pay. Fees are enacted according to the **user-benefit principle**, which suggests that those who use something should pay for it rather than spreading the cost among all taxpayers.

Charging for government services can have other purposes as well. Fees can ration the service or avoid overcrowding, as when using a ferry boat requires tickets for fixed times rather than making it free to all comers. Charges can also be structured to achieve other ends. Water rates can be subsidized to help low-income residents. City-owned electric utilities can offer lower rates for times of the day with low demand, such as evening hours. This can help extend the life of generating plants, which normally must be built to meet demand at peak times.

Fees can be used for other purposes as well. For example, some local governments have used high charges for utilities like water and electricity to keep property taxes low and have attempted to get revenue from usually tax-exempt property like colleges and state office buildings (see chapter 11). Fees have negative effects as well. They can become a barrier, as when charging for participation or equipment in youth sports prevents poor children from participating.

Self-Service and the Market

At the other extreme from government-produced services, Savas describes self-service and the market. Self-service provides complete control by the ultimate consumer, for example, home schooling or producing your own food, fuel, or clothing.[54] A major problem here is expertise, as you can imagine with self-medicating. Savas tends to ignore government's role in guaranteeing health and safety for someone engaging in self-service. He also plays down the interaction between individuals and government, as when he describes an individual taking trash to the local disposal site as if the government had no role in regulating or operating the facility.

Markets rely on transactions between buyers and sellers, a system that works well when there are competing producers and informed consumers. Competition can lead to lower prices, better product differentiation, and more choice. A stark contrast would be grocery stores versus food distribution run completely by government, or individual home ownership as opposed to government-run housing. Other examples include private golf courses and swim clubs as sources of recreation, and trash collection by a for-profit firm.[55]

An obvious limit to reliance on the market is the extent to which price or other factors exclude some residents. An example would be a community where the only way to play tennis or golf is purchase of a membership at a private club. Public libraries, with their printed resources, computers, and staff fill a major gap in the market for poor residents and can prove valuable in educating adults and building a sense of community.[56] In most market relationships, government regulation is important for consumers to be safe, make informed decisions, and be guaranteed access. Imagine the market without restaurant inspections and smoking bans, information labels on products, and protections against discrimination.

With both markets and self-service, there also can be problems with **externalities**, actions affecting a party not involved in a transaction or activity. An example of a negative externality is a property owner being harmed by air pollution, noise, or water runoff from a neighbor. Zoning, other types of government regulation, and the courts can serve as means to prevent or counteract these effects. An example of a positive externality would be the rising value of a family's home when neighbors improve their property.

A relatively new wrinkle in markets is the rise of the so-called sharing economy. This broad term almost immediately brings to mind Uber, Lyft, and Airbnb. It also includes a wide range of person-to-person services usually facilitated online. These include household chores, pet sitting, vehicle sharing, and much more. Local governments often get dragged into conflicts because of pushback from traditional firms like hotels and taxi companies. Residents see selling their services as a new form of income. Consumer groups have raised concerns about the lack of regulation. Neighborhood groups also complain about residents renting space to strangers, in their view creating a quasi-motel when none would be allowed under existing zoning.[57] San Francisco entered the lodging fray by regulating and taxing short-term rentals.[58]

BOX 10.1

Toll Roads

Illinois Tollway, with Separate Lanes for Electronic and Cash Payment

Orange County, California and many of its cities have had a system of local toll roads for more than 20 years. A major goal of the tolls has been to pay off construction debt. Like many other tollway and turnpike systems around the country, technology has brought about major changes. Most have moved to transponders, license plate imaging, and cell phone apps to pay tolls to keep traffic moving and reduce the need for toll booths. Most agencies create incentives to get drivers not to use cash. Orange County drivers who load money from a credit card for use with a transponder get charged $1.00 less per toll compared to other payment methods. The transponder is also good throughout California.[a] Violations? If you want to use cash, you can pay at the system's service center in Irvine or, for an extra $1.99, pay at participating 7-Eleven convenience stores.

Illinois creates an even larger incentive to get auto drivers to use transponders. Electronic tolling is half the price of cash. Plus, the transponder is good in all states using the E-Z Pass.[b]

Massachusetts toll roads, tunnels, and bridges went completely electronic in October 2016. The program includes discounts for using a transponder rather than paying based on license plate information.[c]

[a] The Toll Roads of Orange County, "Ways to Pay Your Toll," https://thetollroads.com/help/paying-tolls.

[b] Illinois Tollway, "Tolling Information Overview," https://www.illinoistollway.com/tolling-information#TRI.

[c] EZDrive MA, "MassDOT's All Electronic Tolling Program," https://www.ezdrivema.com/AboutEZDriveMA.

In the end, the general issue is how local governments will respond to these changes in service delivery in the private market.

Contracting with Other Governments or Private Companies

Sometimes governments contract with one another for services in an **intergovernmental agreement** or with private companies. For example, a smaller jurisdiction might buy fire protection from a larger adjacent one. This saves direct costs of equipment and personnel, but it means losing control over hiring, training, and other aspects of service delivery, including the visible presence of resident firefighters in the smaller community. All of this requires that the purchasing government sign a carefully written contract. The classic example of this relationship was the so-called Lakewood Plan in which suburbs near Los Angeles incorporated to set up their own municipal government and then contracted with

BOX 10.2

Has the Parking Meter Expired for Chicago?

Parking Kiosk in Chicago

The city administration relied heavily on a consultant during closed-door negotiations and a fast-tracked deal. The council was provided only with a summary and had only three days to consider the proposal (approved 40–5). There was no independent financial analysis. Ratings agencies subsequently lowered the city's debt rating and gave solid ratings to bonds issued by the firm, which had 2015 revenues totaling $121.7 million.

Chicago gets nothing during these leases and must even pay for free parking for drivers with disabilities and for putting meters out of service for street repair or festivals. If meters are removed, the city must come up with replacements.

The contract ignored the fact that street parking is real estate that can be used for multiple purposes and made it difficult to create lanes for bikes or bus rapid transit (BRT) and to remove parking spaces to improve sight lines and pedestrian safety. Worse still, Chicago spent the money almost immediately to pay off existing debts, adding little to the city's operating budget.

To help with budget problems, in 2008 Chicago leased its 36,000-space metered parking system for 75 years to a private firm for $1.15 billion and angered many by approving rate increases. This followed a 99-year lease on the I-90 connection to the Indiana Tollway for $1.83 billion in 2004 and a 99-year lease of four parking garages near Millennium Park for $563 million in 2006.

Source: Stephanie Farmer, "Cities as Risk Managers: The Impact of Chicago's Parking Meter P3 on Municipal Governance and Transportation Planning," *Environment and Planning A: Economy and Space* 46:9 (September 2014: 2160–2174; Aaron M. Renn, "The Lessons of Long-Term Privatizations: Why Chicago Got It Wrong and Indiana Got It Right," Manhattan Institute, July 2016, https://www.manhattan-institute.org/sites/default/files/R-AR-0716.pdf; Mick Dumke and Chris Fusco, "Parking Meters, Garages Took in $156 Million—But City Won't See a Cent," *Chicago Sun-Times*, May 23, 2016, http://chicago.suntimes.com/news/parking-meters-garages-took-in-156m-but-city-wont-see-a-cent.

Los Angeles County for services.[59] At the other extreme are Weston, Florida (suburban Fort Lauderdale), and Sandy Springs, Georgia (suburban Atlanta), which contract out all of their services to multiple providers.[60]

Contracts with private firms sometimes yield savings on equipment and personnel. Private firms such as engineering firms, lawyers, landscapers, and paving contractors also have expertise that they sell to other consumers. Contracting is more than accepting the lowest bid for a job, however.[61] For the local government to make comparisons and have negotiating power, it is critical that multiple firms compete for a government contract, which could be a problem in rural communities. In addition, direct government production appears to be more prevalent when there is greater citizen interest in government services, but contracting is more common in communities with a political climate favoring less government.[62] Collaboration can be viewed as a range of opportunities to work with other governments, for-profit firms, or nonprofits. However, no matter which options are considered, they all require vigilance and the need to look beyond costs to the long-term effects.[63]

Following the push to privatize in the 1990s, there is some evidence that local governments moved toward a mixed model with both government and private production of services subject to assessment by benchmarking.[64] The use of collaborative service delivery grew during the 2000s, but the need for transparency, benchmarking, and careful analysis were critical.[65] As Warner and Hefetz note, "Private firms are interested in profit, efficiency, and control. The public sector is interested in efficiency, but it is also expected to provide fail-safe delivery and ensure a higher level of public accountability and involvement."[66] One study of sixty-four services in nearly 15,000 cities and counties found that nearly 70 percent terminated at least one service between 1992 and 1997, primarily those that were being contracted out. These decisions could have been based on grant funding, the lack of the same service in neighboring communities, and/or assumption of a service by another government (e.g., county or special district).[67] Local governments have increasingly engaged in public-private partnerships in which they lease an asset to a private firm to manage and use as a revenue source. One danger with any contracting is adopting short-term goals (see box 10.2). Other concerns are the government's cost of contract oversight—which is not free—and the extent to which contractors have an information advantage in negotiations.[68]

Franchises, Grants, and Vouchers

Other alternatives mixing government and market processes include franchises, grants, and vouchers. A **franchise** is a license to sell a product to the public under government regulation. Electric utilities, cable television, and cab companies are examples. Some are monopolies; without competition, consumers might be subjected to problems with quality and service. However, government regulation can affect prices and other service characteristics, for example, mandatory training for cabbies. A recent challenge to franchises is the aforementioned sharing economy. Operations like Uber and Lyft and lodging options like Airbnb[69] require little investment since "operators" are essentially making their vehicles and homes available, as opposed to a business opening a new hotel.

Grants are financial support by government that subsidizes service providers, which normally have to apply and meet certain criteria.[70] For example, a city government might award a grant to a symphony orchestra to provide free concerts at reduced prices for senior citizens or at parks during the summer. A grant could also be used to support a clinic or day care center with reduced prices for low-income residents. Such support taps the expertise of these organizations and the dedication of their employees and volunteers while allowing them the flexibility to promote their mission without being part of the local government bureaucracy. On the other hand, the use of grants means that government picks winners and losers for subsidies.

Vouchers are entitlements that recipients can redeem for services.[71] Well-known examples include food stamps, college financial aid, private school vouchers, and Medicare. Rather than giving recipients money (e.g., larger Social Security payments) in hopes that it would be used to keep them healthy, seniors and people with disabilities must draw on funding from Medicare. Similarly, restrictions apply to food stamps in terms of what recipients can purchase. Some local governments and nonprofits use vouchers for housing and food for the homeless, even encouraging the public to use this option rather than handing out cash to panhandlers. Vouchers work best when choices among competitors are available. In contrast, it is difficult for food stamp recipients living in "food deserts" lacking a major grocery store to exercise choice.

One major policy change involving vouchers deals with housing. Beginning in the 1930s, the federal government supported local housing authorities in building and renting apartments to low-income tenants. Over time, many high-rise projects became areas of concentrated poverty in poor neighborhoods, including the now-demolished Pruitt-Igoe in St. Louis and Cabrini-Green in Chicago. One response was to give qualified applicants vouchers to help pay rent to private landlords. However, some research suggests that many residents relocated to the suburbs from high-poverty areas that were relatively poor, which might not lead to a noticeable reduction of poverty in the areas they left.[72]

Voluntary Associations

A voluntary association is something of a hybrid service provider that could include a neighborhood organization maintaining a playground, a congregation delivering meals or visiting shut-ins, groups providing tutoring to students or developing literacy among adults, or a youth sports league. Savas tends to treat nonprofits like companies offering services to consumers.[73] This ignores the extent to which entities like congregations or service groups deliver commitment, dedication, and disregard for the time involved. Established organizations set up volunteer groups to complement their work, such as museums and historical societies with trained docents who serve as guides or arts organizations that use volunteer ushers.

Task sharing between government employees and volunteers to enhance services received more attention beginning in the 1980s. There are concerns, however, about nonprofit organizations taking on roles traditionally associated with government without the political participation and accountability involved in government policy making.[74]

SUMMARY

Perhaps the two most common activities of local governments are considering policy alternatives and providing services. The policy process does not have a fixed timeline, but it generally goes through several stages, with various participants and their strategies at each stage. The first two stages, problem identification and policy formulation, are collectively called agenda setting because they put an issue and alternatives for addressing it before public officials. Following the third stage, policy adoption, is implementation by government or organizations selected by government. Implementation often prompts feedback to keep or modify the policy.

Local policy makers increasingly consider alternatives to taxes and services produced by government employees. In some cases, government charges users fees for services such as water or toll roads. In others, governments contract with another government, private companies, or nonprofits to produce a service. Many local governments award franchises in competition to sell services, as with taxis or cable companies. Grants are used to subsidize services, such as arts programs, while vouchers are like coupons that citizens can redeem for services. Finally, residents sometimes produce things like food for themselves and can buy goods in the marketplace, such as joining a swim club. Each of these options has advantages and disadvantages, including costs, availability, and public access.

Key Terms

benchmarking *(214)*
contracting out *(209)*
externalities *(218)*
feedback loop *(210)*
franchise *(221)*
government vending *(217)*
grants *(221)*
impacts *(210)*
implementation *(210)*

intergovernmental
  agreement *(219)*
policy adoption *(208)*
policy diffusion *(207)*
policy formulation *(207)*
privatization *(215)*
problem identification *(205)*
user-benefit principle *(217)*
vouchers *(222)*

Discussion Questions

1. When you think of the policy process in your university city or your hometown, what agency or group has the most influence and why?

2. What are the differences in the issues and types of political participants involved in developmental,

redistributive, and allocational policies? Describe some examples of each type of policy in your community.

3. Are there some local services that you would always want government to produce? Why or why not?

4. Given the patterns and alternatives identified in table 10.1, what are the strengths and weaknesses of the different service methods?

5. In what ways can voluntary associations and nonprofit organizations best contribute services in a community? Provide examples for each answer.

Exercises

1. Identify a policy change adopted by your city council or county board. Based on media accounts, interviews, or other sources, explain why the policy that was adopted was selected over other alternatives.

2. What services does your city or county charge for? Describe the rates for some of these services. Are the revenues kept in a separate fund?

3. To what extent does your city or county contract with nonprofits for services? For a few of these, describe how much they receive and how they are evaluated for the services they provide.

Practice and Review Online
https://textbooks.rowman.com/understanding-urban-politics

11

LOCAL GOVERNMENT FINANCES

GUIDING QUESTIONS

1. How do local governments raise and spend money?
2. What are the strengths and weaknesses of the various revenue sources on which local governments rely?
3. What are the major limitations from the state and other external sources that local governments face in doing their budgets?
4. What challenges do local officials face as they develop and adopt the budget?

GIVEN ITS RAPID GROWTH and rising cost of living, some public officials and advocacy groups in Seattle looked for ways to promote affordable housing and deal with a large homeless population. In May 2018, the city council voted unanimously to restore a tax that had been repealed during the Great Recession. The tax, expected to raise $47 million annually, applied to employers with more than $20 million in taxable gross revenue at a rate of 26 cents per hour worked per employee, capped at $275 annually per employee. Backlash included major employers raising $350,000 for an initiative campaign to repeal the tax, Amazon pausing construction of an office building, and other threats. Less than a month later, the city council voted 7–2 to repeal the tax.[1] This example highlights a perennial question in local government budgeting, namely, what priorities to set and how to fund them.

Local governments try to do many things. A major challenge is deciding the services and programs to be funded, along with how to come up with the money to pay for these efforts. In other words, what should we do and how do we pay for it? As indicated in chapter 4, local government financial decisions are often controlled by the state. In addition, residents and businesses often weigh in on how money is to be spent and what they (and others) will have to pay in taxes and fees for water, trash pickup, and similar services. Much of this discussion plays out in the annual process of adopting a local government's budget, which can be highly politicized.

LOCAL GOVERNMENT SPENDING

Local governments divide their spending several ways. As chapter 1 indicated, budgets cover a *fiscal year*. These twelve-month periods are usually not the same as a calendar year. Sometimes this is designed to match a state fiscal year, which is most commonly either July 1 through the following June 30, or October 1 to the following September 30 (the latter matches the federal fiscal year). Most state legislatures convene in January, review a budget submitted by the governor shortly thereafter, and adopt it in the spring. This allows time to put all of the items in a budget into place. This timeline can be especially helpful for school districts, which need to have their financial picture in place before students show up in August or September.

The simplest way that local governments distinguish their finances is to divide them into operating and capital items. **Operating budgets** cover the expenses and revenues of running the government on an annual basis, such as supplies and personnel. Budgets generally break down this spending by department as well as by function (e.g., streets, fuel, health care). Local governments generally also develop **capital budgets**, which cover expenses and revenues for long-term, durable assets such as buildings, roads, bridges, and certain types of equipment. These expenses are often paid for by borrowing, with costs spread out over multiple years. Budgets usually include special funds for specific services with their own revenue and expenses; a common example is water and sewer services, which are intended to be self-sustaining.

Figure 11.1 covers the $1.5 billion budget in fiscal year 2017 for the city of Minneapolis, which at that time had a population of around 415,000. The pie chart covers all spending. However, two-thirds of the revenue the city collects is restricted to certain uses and is placed in specific accounts. For example, as the city's "Budget in Brief" reminds readers, "the City may not raise water bills to pay for police services."[2] The remaining funds are placed in what most local governments call a **general fund**—money that is not assigned to a specific fund and that can be spent for a broad range of purposes as decided by the elected governing body. With the discretion the city council had over the general fund, for example, Minneapolis spent almost one-third on police.

The overview in chapter 1 lumped together all local governments in order to compare them to the states and the federal government. However, combining the

Figure 11.1 City of Minneapolis Spending, Fiscal Year 2017

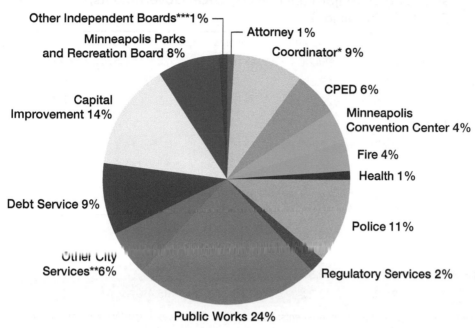

Source: "2017 City of Minneapolis Budget in Brief," 3, http://www.ci.minneapolis.mn.us/www/groups/public/@finance/documents/webcontent/wcmsp-192479.pdf.

finances of all local governments masks key differences among them. Table 11.1 compares spending for each type of local government as reported in the Census of Governments, which is conducted every 5 years.[3] Because the 2017 data were not available when this book was published, they will be posted to the book's website later in 2020. Note that the nation's 16,000 townships are largely rural and suburban governments in the Midwest and Northeast. In the South and West, however, counties generally provide services in areas outside municipalities.

Several features stand out. Counties have higher personnel costs and spend a large share of their budgets on social services. This makes sense given that counties have historically done much of the administrative work of states: courts, jails, official records for things like births and property, and much more. Counties also handle welfare programs, child protection, and similar social services. Municipal spending reflects cities' urban condition, with more than 28 percent of spending going to furnishing water, sewer services, solid waste disposal, and even electricity and natural gas. Special districts are big spenders on capital projects, which constitute 20 percent of their total. These include districts set up to run large facilities like airports, seaports, transit systems, and hospitals, as well as utilities that provide water and sewer services for multiple communities. Finally, school districts stand out for high personnel costs, which reflects the large numbers of teachers, aides, administrators, coaches, and other employees.

The flip side of spending is raising the money to pay for services and programs. There is no universal revenue system for local governments in the United States. The only commonality is that cities, counties, townships, school districts,

TABLE 11.1	Spending on Major Functions by Local Governments, Fiscal 2012 ($billion)				
	Counties	Municipalities	Townships	Special Districts	School Districts
Total Spending:	$384.87	$542.8	$50.96	$208.27	$499.58
Capital Outlay	9.2%	15.6%	11.8%	19.7%	9.2%
Salaries & Wages	32.4%	27.4%	34.1%	20.9%	52.1%
Spending by Function:					
Education	13.8%	9.2%	25.0%	1.8%	96.0%
Social Services & Income Maintenance	38.1%	9.4%	2.1%	21.8%	0
Highways	5.0%	5.6%	11.3%	2.1%	0
Public Safety	14.9%	16.2%	14.0%	3.3%	0
Housing & Community Development	1.0%	3.4%	0.7%	10.0%	0
Sewage & Solid Waste	4.2%	10.5%	8.9%	8.2%	0
Utilities	2.5%	18.2%	4.7%	35.4%	0

Source: US Census Bureau, *2012 Census of Governments: State and Local Finances,* https://www.census.gov//govs/local/historical_data_2012.html.

and special districts are at the mercy of states in terms of how they can fund their budgets, and almost every state requires local governments to have a balanced budget.

LOCAL GOVERNMENT REVENUE SOURCES

Local governments rely heavily on **intergovernmental revenue**, money provided to them by the state or federal government. These funds come from multiple sources and are based on a wide range of criteria (see chapter 4). Local budgets also include **own-source revenues**, funds raised by local government under state regulation. The primary own-source revenues are taxes, fees and charges, and borrowing.

A fundamental step in generating local taxes is defining the **tax base**, items of value subject to taxation. For example, states can allow local governments to levy local property taxes on certain types of real estate but exempt other types (e.g., colleges, houses of worship, nonprofit organizations). States can also identify the goods and services subject to sales taxes while exempting others (e.g., groceries, prescription drugs). Determining the value of the tax base and setting tax rates are other elements affecting the revenue available. Borrowing and a wide range of fees are also important, but the states have substantial control over them as well. Figure 11.2 displays local governments' reliance on different revenue sources since 2004.

Figure 11.2 Major Local Government Revenue Sources, Fiscal Years 2004–2017

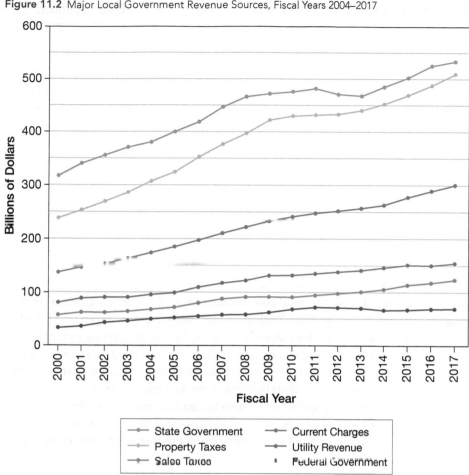

Source: US Census Bureau, "State and Local Government Finance," annual series, https://www.census.gov/programs-surveys/gov-finances/data/datasets.html.

Figure 11.2 captures local governments' heavy reliance on state aid and property taxes as well as the limited role of the federal government. In fiscal 2017, for example, local government revenues totaled $1.9 trillion, with $533 billion in state aid (27.5%) and $509 billion from property taxes (26%). A second notable trend is that state aid and property tax revenue flatten out following the Great Recession, with state aid actually dropping in 2016. In contrast, there is a steady growth in local revenue from charges and fees. The rest of this section examines how revenue varies among the different types of local governments.

Intergovernmental Revenue

Perhaps the "800-pound gorilla in the room" for local governments is the money that they get from the federal and state governments, usually with strings attached. Given the small amount of money coming from the federal government, table 11.2 shows only state aid. Data for 2017 will be available online as soon as the US Census Bureau publishes them.

TABLE 11.2	State Aid to Local Governments: 2002, 2007, 2012 ($billion)			
		2002	2007	2012
Counties	Total State Aid	$86.76	$104.84	$111.36
	% of Total Revenue	33.4%	28.4%	29.1%
Municipalities	Total State Aid	$62.54	$72.63	$77.77
	% of Total Revenue	18.5%	14.3%	14.8%
Townships	Total State Aid	$6.65	$8.10	$8.12
	% of Total Revenue	18.8%	17.5%	16.0%
Special Districts	Total State Aid	$8.59	$11.76	$12.62
	% of Total Revenue	7.0%	6.8%	6.1%
School Districts	Total State Aid	$191.14	$219.37	$260.99
	% of Total Revenue	54.5%	52.8%	52.8%

Source: US Census Bureau, *Census of Governments*, 2002, 2007, 2012.

As the data indicate, local governments enjoyed noticeable increases in state aid between 2002 and 2007. With the Great Recession that began in 2007, state aid was much more modest. Overall, state aid did not increase as a share of local revenue for any type of government. These patterns varied by state, of course, but the bottom line is that local governments turned increasingly to their own revenue sources to bolster their budgets as the economy worsened. This situation was made even worse by declining home values and foreclosures that cost homeowners their houses because they were unable to keep up with their mortgage payments and property taxes. Local governments also had to reduce their budgets as state aid declined.

Property Taxes

As table 11.1 and figure 11.2 indicated, local governments rely heavily on the **property tax**, a tax levied on the value of real or personal property. **Real property** is land and its attachments, such as buildings. Determining the value of real property is tricky. For example, a farm might seem not to be of much value, but it could be quite valuable if it was in a growing area and could be easily developed into homes or office buildings. **Personal property** consists of movable assets, which can be divided into (1) tangible (physical) items such as vehicles, personal possessions, and business inventory and (2) intangible items such as stocks and bonds. During the 1800s, personal property such as livestock, machinery, and expensive furniture was a sign of wealth and was taxed in many jurisdictions.[4] Personal property taxes are less common today, although almost half the states allow a local property tax on the value of vehicles, which is in addition to a state tax.[5]

Administering the property tax comes with four major challenges: deciding what to tax, setting the tax rate, determining the value of property, and administering and enforcing the tax. *Deciding what to tax* is generally set by state law. Because of intergovernmental tax immunity, governments do not tax one another, which means that a state's capital city does not tax the capitol or state office buildings. Local governments also own real estate such as schools and parks that is exempt, as are public rights-of-way such as streets and rivers. Charitable, educational, and religious institutions are also exempt from property taxes. In 2011–12, large cities such as Baltimore, Boston, Columbus, Denver, Fort Worth, Houston, New York, Philadelphia, and Washington, DC each reported that more than 25 percent of the assessed value of their real estate was tax exempt.[6] Citizens often complain that these tax-exempt landowners benefit from services such as police and fire protection but do not pay their "fair share" of the property taxes that fund these services.

Exempting large swaths of real estate from property taxes can be especially significant and controversial in college towns. For example, the University of Michigan pays no property taxes on its land and buildings, which were valued at $5.1 billion in fiscal 2012, while the property tax base for the rest of Ann Arbor was just under $4.7 billion. This disparity generated controversy as the university reduced the tax base further by buying more private property, including $12.8 million in 2014 for seventeen acres that had paid more than $182,000 in annual property taxes and would thereafter pay nothing.[7]

In some cases, tax-exempt universities have given local governments **payment in lieu of taxes (PILOT)**. These are funds paid to help offset the loss in property taxes due to tax-exempt ownership or use of real estate. Such payments are in addition to fees such as water and sewer charges billed to all consumers whether they are residents, businesses, or nonprofits. For example, Ivy-League Brown University paid more than $5.1 million in PILOTs to Providence, Rhode Island, during fiscal 2014 in addition to fees for services.[8] An alternative approach is for tax-exempt organizations to provide services to offset property taxes that might have been paid on their real estate, as with a nonprofit hospital setting up a free clinic for low-income residents.[9]

Some cities have been more aggressive regarding tax-exempt properties. For example, Austin has had a city-run electric utility since 1895, with half of its customers now outside the city. The city council approves rates for Austin Energy, which in recent years has transferred about $100 million to the city's general fund. Large energy users, including Samsung, had their discounts ended in 2015 and were joined by others in challenging proposed rates in 2016, focusing in part on the city's above-average price for electricity. Controversy has also surrounded Austin's history of charging residential customers less than it costs to provide electricity while doing just the opposite for nonresidential customers. Also lurking in the background was a threat that the challengers would lobby the Texas legislature to intervene. Environmental groups entered the litigation in part to get the city to drop the use of coal to generate electricity and joined the final settlement.[10]

Using utilities to supplement or substitute for property taxes is not unusual. One study of South Carolina cities back in the 1980s found that those with electric utilities transferred to their general fund an average of 70 percent of revenues raised from property taxes and other local sources. Cities with water and sewer funds controlled by their city councils behaved similarly, but to a much lesser extent. The study's author concludes that this dynamic allows elected officials to avoid tax increases while creating a fiscal illusion in which citizens are getting more services than they pay for with their taxes.[11]

In addition to complete exemption for certain types of property, states allow local governments to provide partial exemptions to certain property owners. The most common is a **homestead exemption**, which reduces the assessed value of a property by a certain amount before taxing the remaining value, usually for a homeowner's primary residence or for certain classes of people such as seniors, disabled veterans, or those below a certain income level. Homestead exemptions vary substantially, even within a state. For example, in addition to a modest exemption from school taxes by the state of Georgia for some who are aged 62 or older, residents of the part of Atlanta in Fulton County are eligible for other exemptions, including one to freeze a household's assessed value for owners aged 65 or older with an adjusted gross income of $39,000 or less.[12] In neighboring DeKalb County, residents aged 70 or older in 2017 with household adjusted gross incomes of $84,115 or less could be exempted from school property taxes altogether.[13] In Louisiana, where residences are assessed at only 10 percent of market value, the state exempts the first $7,500 of assessed value. The state also allows a freeze on a primary residence's assessed value if a homeowner is 65 or older and had a 2016 household adjusted gross income less than $71,491 (this figure is adjusted annually).[14] In California, the state constitution exempts the first $7,000 in value for owner-occupied homes. This is just a pittance given 21st century home prices in California.[15]

Determining the tax rate is the second key factor in administering local property taxes. The tax rate is usually expressed as a **millage**: the property tax rate calculated as the dollar amount of tax per thousand dollars of assessed valuation. Thus, a city millage of 6.112 applied to a property assessed at $120,348 would be $735.56. Few issues are as controversial locally as setting the tax rate. The process normally occurs during budgeting once spending figures are set, but non-property tax revenues are calculated to offset spending as much as possible. The property tax millage is then set to cover remaining spending to the extent permitted by state law.

Local millage rates, as this suggests, are controlled by state statute. For example, in Michigan, state law limits the increase in millage rates by establishing a cap on the amount of revenue a local government can raise compared to the previous year. If applying the same millage from one year to the next raises the amount of revenue over the cap, the millage must be reduced. Almost every state controls the amount of revenue raised from property taxes by local governments.

Rates are also complicated somewhat by an **assessment ratio**, the percentage of fair market value applied to assessed property value for tax purposes. These are usually set by states, with a bias toward low ratios for owner-occupied homes. In 2017, for example, Arizona had nine classes of property, each of which had a different ratio; the major residential classes had an assessment ratio of 10 percent of market value.[16]

Determining the value of property is the third task for local governments. This has never been easy, going as far back as the 1800s, when elected officials generally exercised this authority but had to face voters to keep their jobs. It also became increasingly difficult to determine the value of intangible property. The 20th century witnessed moves to eliminate property taxes on intangibles, institute an income tax, and create a class of professional assessors to determine the value of real property.[17]

Assessors are expected to determine a property's fair market value, usually annually. For homes, this is determined in part by neighborhood conditions, including recent sale prices. Assessors also consider any improvements to a property, for example, adding a room or in-ground swimming pool. Communities, under state law, have a process for appealing an assessment. In St. Louis, for instance, property owners can initially contest their assessment in an informal hearing with an assessor, but they can appeal after that to the Board of Equalization.[18] In Wisconsin, which has seven classes of property, property owners can appeal their assessment to a local board of review.[19] In most states, property owners can appeal decisions of a local tax tribunal to a state tribunal or a civil court.

Administering and enforcing the property tax is the final element in using this revenue source. Administration normally involves mailing a tax bill including a deadline for payment. In many cases, property taxes are included in mortgage payments, and the bank or other lender holding the mortgage pays the property taxes. In the end, the assessed value, exemptions, assessment ratio, and millage will yield a tax bill for property owners and a stream of revenue for local governments. Box 11.1 analyzes two property tax bills.

A major problem occurs when property owners fail to pay their tax bill. This can result in a **property lien**, a legal claim against the property to secure payment of debt. In such cases, it would be back taxes, usually plus interest and other expenses; liens can also be granted to mortgage companies or other creditors. Although the process varies somewhat by state, the local taxing authority would go to court to foreclose the property because of the overdue taxes. If the owner does not pay the amount of the lien, in most cases the property is sold at a public auction in which bidders must pay off the lien (most auctions today are conducted online).

In Denver, property tax bills are mailed each January. Payment for the full amount is owed on April 30; if done in two installments, the first payment is due on April 30 and the second on June 15. Those who do not pay are assessed 1 percent per month, and the Treasury Division sends numerous delinquency notices. The taxes, interest, and other charges are included in a tax lien, which would then be auctioned off, usually in November. Under Colorado law, if the lien has not been paid off in 3 years, the lien holder can apply to get the deed to the property, thus dispossessing the delinquent taxpayer.[20]

Table 11.3 tracks changes in local property taxes from 2002 to 2012; 2017 data will be posted to the book's website as soon as it is available from the US Census Bureau. A couple of features stand out. First, and consistent with figure 11.2, property tax revenues increased less in 2007–12 than they did in 2002–7. Most of this is due to the drop in housing values during the Great Recession. Second, except for townships, local governments relied on property taxes as a greater share of revenue at the end of the 10 years than at the start. A good deal of speculation would be required, though, to explain the local decision making that led to that result.

BOX 11.1

Authors' Property Tax Bills

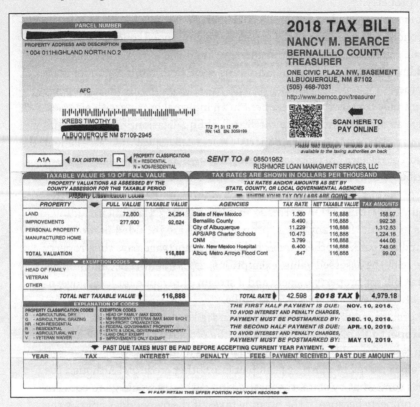

Property Tax Bill for Timothy Krebs

This box applies millage rates to the taxable value of homes (not the same as market value) using the authors' property. Timothy Krebs's 2017 tax bill distinguishes the value of the land from the improvements (the latter is mainly the house). It also does the arithmetic for Tim by multiplying the various rates times the taxable value. Listed agencies should be self-explanatory except for

Sales Taxes

Many local governments also administer a sales tax. Here, too, states generally set the rules. Sales taxes generally are of two types: ad valorem and excise. **Ad valorem sales taxes** are literally what the Latin term suggests: they apply a percentage tax to the total value of items in a purchase. **Excise taxes**, on the other hand, are applied per unit of a specific item sold. This could be per ticket, per gallon of gasoline, per pack of cigarettes, or a similar levy.

Forty-five states collected a statewide ad valorem sales tax as of 2017 and thirty-eight allowed local sales taxes. The only states with no sales tax whatsoever were Delaware, Montana, New Hampshire, and Oregon. Rates varied

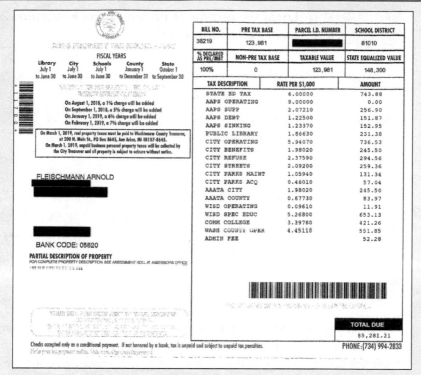

BILL NO.	PRE TAX BASE	PARCEL I.D. NUMBER	SCHOOL DISTRICT
38219	123,981	███████	81010
% DECLARED AS PRE/MBT	NON-PRE TAX BASE	TAXABLE VALUE	STATE EQUALIZED VALUE
100%	0	123,981	148,300

TAX DESCRIPTION	RATE PER $1,000	AMOUNT
STATE ED TAX	6.00000	743.88
AAPS OPERATING	9.00000	0.00
AAPS SUPP	2.07210	256.90
AAPS DEBT	1.22500	151.87
AAPS SINKING	1.23370	152.95
PUBLIC LIBRARY	1.86630	231.38
CITY OPERATING	5.94070	736.53
CITY BENEFITS	1.98020	245.50
CITY REFUSE	2.37590	294.56
CITY STREETS	2.09200	259.36
CITY PARKS MAINT	1.05940	131.34
CITY PARKS ACQ	0.46010	57.04
AAATA CITY	1.98020	245.50
AAATA COUNTY	0.67730	83.97
WISD OPERATING	0.09610	11.91
WISD SPEC EDUC	5.26800	653.13
COMM COLLEGE	3.39780	421.26
WASH COUNTY OPER	4.45110	551.85
ADMIN FEE		52.28

TOTAL DUE
$5,281.21

PHONE:(734) 994-2833

Property Tax Bill for Arnold Fleischmann

the acronym CNM, which is Central New Mexico Community College. Arnold Fleischmann's bill includes different rates for different purposes, some of which require voter approval, and plenty of acronyms without explanations: AAPS (Ann Arbor Public Schools), AATA (Ann Arbor Area Transportation Authority), WISD (Washtenaw Independent School District, which is countywide, mainly for special education), COMM COLLEGE (the local community college district), and WASH COUNTY OPER (Washtenaw County operating—as compared to capital budget items, as described above). The amount due is calculated by multiplying each rate by the taxable value in the top right of the bill. The summer bill is designed mainly to get tax money to schools before the start of the fall semester. Another bill in December for about $800 is mainly for county services. Notice that both authors pay property taxes to their local community colleges but none to the universities where they work, which rely on other sources of revenue.

substantially, with the combined state-local sales tax averaging over 8 percent in Alabama, Arizona, Arkansas, California, Illinois, Kansas, Louisiana, New York, Oklahoma, Tennessee, Texas, and Washington.[21]

As with property taxes, what consumers pay and governments collect is affected by the composition of the tax base in addition to the tax rate. Only fourteen states wholly or partially apply the ad valorem sales tax to groceries. All but six exempt gasoline from the sales tax, but every state levies an excise tax per gallon sold.[22] Minnesota, New Jersey, Pennsylvania, and Vermont exempt clothing from state and local sales taxes; Massachusetts, New York, and Rhode Island partially exempt clothing (below a certain dollar amount).[23]

TABLE 11.3	Local Government Property Tax Revenue: 2002, 2007, 2012 ($billion)			
		2002	2007	2012
Counties	Property Tax Revenue	$62.11	$89.52	$103.79
	% of Total Revenue	23.9%	24.3%	27.2%
Municipalities	Property Tax Revenue	$58.33	$85.38	$102.12
	% of Total Revenue	17.3%	16.8%	19.5%
Townships	Property Tax Revenue	$20.56	$24.29	$28.88
	% of Total Revenue	58.0%	52.4%	57.0%
Special Districts	Property Tax Revenue	$10.25	$15.01	$18.61
	% of Total Revenue	8.3%	8.6%	9.0%
School Districts	Property Tax Revenue	$119.97	$162.09	$179.69
	% of Total Revenue	34.2%	34.3%	36.3%

Source: US Census Bureau, *Census of Governments,* 2002, 2007, 2012.

Local governments are often allowed to levy excise taxes on restaurant meals, rental cars, hotel rooms, and similar items. In Denver and Washington, a 4-percent tax on meals is charged in addition to the general sales tax; the add-on is 3 percent in Minneapolis and 5.5 percent in Virginia Beach. These taxes are often promoted as ways to raise revenue from tourists and out-of-town business travelers.[24] Overall, municipalities earn about 10 percent of their revenue from a variety of sales taxes, while counties garner almost 8 percent.

Fees and Charges

Local governments frequently raise revenue by charging fees for various services. Many of these are consistent with the *user-benefit principle* (see chapter 10). Common examples are tolls for bridges or roadways, parking meters (and fines), bills for utility services such as water, transit fares, tuition, admission to museums and zoos, and charges for recreation such as public golf courses.

Local governments vary in their reliance on fees and charges (see table 11.4). Special districts seem like fee-generating machines, since they rely on those sources for a majority of their revenue. Many of them were established to run hospitals, airports, and sewer and water systems—services where individual users are readily identified and can be charged—and most do not have property taxing authority. Municipalities consistently draw over one-fourth of their funds from fees, much of it from water, sewerage, solid waste, electricity, and hospitals.

One challenge for local governments is deciding what the fee will be at any given point in time. State law may limit local discretion and require that fees only cover the cost of providing a service. Over time, of course, costs will change, requiring updates in fee levels and action by a governing board at budget time. Many states limit the ability of local governments to use fees and charges as a basis for generating general fund revenue.

TABLE 11.4	Local Government Revenue from Fees and Charges: 2002, 2007, 2012 ($billion)			
		2002	2007	2012
Counties	Revenue from Fees & Charges	$50.39	$67.86	$78.95
	% of Total Revenue	19.4%	18.4%	20.7%
Municipalities	Revenue from Fees & Charges	$107.15	$142.46	$170.59
	% of Total Revenue	31.7%	28.0%	32.5%
Townships	Revenue from Fees & Charges	$4.81	$6.19	$7.01
	% of Total Revenue	13.6%	13.3%	13.0%
Special Districts	Revenue from Fees & Charges	$66.90	$91.58	$113.92
	% of Total Revenue	54.3%	52.7%	55.4%
School Districts	Revenue from Fees & Charges	$14.13	$19.46	$19.96
	% of Total Revenue	4.0%	4.1%	4.0%

Note: Includes Census Bureau "Current Charges" category plus utility revenue.
Source: US Census Bureau, *Census of Governments*, 2002, 2007, 2012.

Fees and charges are also used to try to influence behavior. For example, cities can charge higher water rates if users consume above a certain number of gallons per month. They might also require individual units in an apartment building to have their own meters rather than masking the cost of water in everyone's rent when a single meter for the landlord covers the whole building. Both measures are designed to encourage water conservation. Similarly, a city might collect recyclable materials for "free" while charging for trash based on how much a property sets out for collection. A possible downside, though, is the encouragement to cheat by placing garbage in recycling bins. Some communities even charge "impact fees" to developers for the infrastructure and wider costs that their projects impose on the community.[25]

Borrowing

Local governments regularly borrow money, just like other levels of government, businesses, and individuals. Some of this is short-term debt, which is borrowed for less than a year to cover expenses until funds become available from sources such as state aid. In keeping with balanced budget requirements, short-term debt must be closed at the end of a fiscal year. Local governments also borrow money for longer periods (usually up to 30 years) to finance major projects such as buildings, facilities, equipment, bridges, and roads.

Long-term borrowing is usually done with **bonds**, financial instruments sold by local governments with a promise to pay back the principal (amount borrowed) plus a guaranteed interest rate to purchasers. The money that the government raises from selling the bonds is then used for the specified purpose. There are two major types of bonds sold by local governments. **General obligation (GO) bonds** pledge tax revenues to pay off the bonds. These are often called "full faith and credit" bonds because local governments are essentially promising to raise taxes if necessary to pay off the debt. In contrast, **revenue bonds** pledge a stream of revenue to pay off the bonds. For example, revenue bonds for an airport could be paid off with landing fees, airline gate rentals, parking revenue, rents from merchants in the terminal, and similar sources. Revenue bonds are considered somewhat more risky than GO bonds and, as a result, pay a slightly higher interest rate.

Selling bonds depends on investors' willingness to buy them. One of the long-standing benefits of state and local government bonds, usually labeled municipal bonds, is their tax status. The interest earned by investors on bonds sold by corporations is taxable income. Municipal bonds, on the other hand, are not taxed by the federal government or by the state where the bonds are issued. This "double-tax-free" status means that local governments can pay lower interest on debt than corporate borrowers.

Interest rates are linked to ratings that presumably capture the riskiness of the bonds. Three companies are the major sources of ratings: Moody's, Standard & Poor's (S&P), and Fitch. The highest rating from each is AAA (Aaa for Moody's), referred to as triple-A. The ratings move down from there, and once they fall below B, there are increasing risks that the bond seller could default, especially with ratings beginning with C.[26] The bottom line is that the lower the rating, the higher the interest rate that a local government will have to pay investors. For example, a 10-year bond rated single-A in spring 2017, which is considered a good investment, averaged a 3 percent yield, which was one-half percent more than a slightly less risky triple-A.[27] Governments can buy bond insurance to protect against default.

The ratings firms often change ratings as conditions change. For example, income tax cuts in Kansas during 2012 and 2013 were followed by major budget problems, and S&P lowered the state's credit rating twice so that by late 2016 its AA-minus rating was still considered investment grade but made it the fourth-worst state. Similarly, budgetary problems for the state of Illinois and the city of Chicago led Moody's to lower the rating of Chicago Public Schools bonds in late 2016 to a very high level of risk often called "junk" status.[28]

Local government debt is substantial and an important part of portfolios for many investors and retirement funds. In fiscal 2007, local governments had $1.5 trillion in debt outstanding, 98 percent of it long term. By 2012, debt had grown another $300 billion to $1.8 trillion, with local government paying off slightly less that year than they issued in new bonds. The rating firms do not always assign comparable ratings to the same bonds. They also have many critics, especially for the high ratings they assigned to bonds linked to risky mortgages that went into foreclosure during the first decade of the 21st century.[29]

Other Revenue Sources

There are several less common ways that local governments raise funds. Local governments in fourteen states levy an **income tax**, which applies a tax at a certain percentage to the income of a person or business. This is sometimes the same for all taxpayers (*flat rate tax*) or increases with rising income levels (**progressive tax**). The use of an income tax ranges from a single city in a state (Birmingham, Alabama) to all counties in Indiana and Maryland, more than 560 cities and villages in Ohio, and over 600 school districts in Iowa. Major cities with income taxes include Baltimore, Cincinnati, Cleveland, Columbus, Detroit, Kansas City (Missouri), Louisville, New York, Philadelphia, Pittsburgh, and St. Louis.[30] During fiscal 2012, cities raised $25 million from individual and corporate income taxes, about 3 percent of total revenues.

Local governments also use **special assessments**, levies on property owners to help pay for improvements in their area, for example, sidewalks, sewers, or streetlights. Cities and counties raised almost $5 million from this source in 2012. Consistent with the user-benefit principle, such assessments assume that quality of life, safety, or property values will improve for the landowners. It is not an ad valorem property tax. For example, a sidewalk assessment could be a flat charge per foot that a parcel fronts on a street, so a lot that is 120 feet wide would be charged double the assessment of a sixty-foot lot. Local governments sometimes create a district in which a special assessment is imposed, and state laws often require consent by property owners.

Strengths and Weaknesses of Various Revenue Sources

One benefit of taxes on real property is that owners cannot hide land and buildings. Local governments do often have trouble keeping track of improvements, however. Property taxes are also a fairly stable source of income for local governments and are not as responsive to changes in the economy as income or sales taxes. One of the down sides is the extent to which neighborhood changes and economic conditions can affect property values no matter what an owner does. For instance, an economic downturn could reduce a home's value, but its assessment and the owner's monthly mortgage payments might not decline. An opposite problem would be a homeowner on a fixed income living in an area where values—and the accompanying property taxes—are rising.

Controversies can also surround property tax abatements given to developers of major projects, including how much certain financing deals by a local government prevent others from getting the full value of new development taxes or shift the tax burden to others. For example, residents complained about lost revenue for local schools and other services from tax breaks given to new facilities for Detroit's professional hockey and basketball teams. Similarly, school officials in suburban Atlanta opposed tax abatements granted by local economic development agencies that would cost them millions of dollars over several decades; to make up for the losses, the school districts would have to raise tax rates, which hits homeowners especially hard.[31]

Sales and income taxes can fluctuate significantly as the economy speeds up or slows down. Supporters of sales taxes argue that consumers can exercise some control over how much they pay by managing their spending. Some also see the sales tax as an **exportable tax**, one that can be applied to nonresidents who shop or attend events within the local government. A major criticism is that sales taxes, even when groceries are exempted, are a **regressive tax**; that is, they constitute a higher percentage of income for poorer people, who spend most of their income on consumption (the basis of the tax). The affluent pay a lower share of their income on sales taxes because they save more and spend more on services, which are usually not subject to sales taxes. They would be hit harder by a tax for which the rate rises with income, but few local governments levy such *progressive income taxes* on residents.

There are several issues associated with fees and charges aside from the user-benefit principle. One is the extent to which they can be used to influence behavior. For example, merchants have been known to get cities to limit the length of time a driver can park at a meter in order to turn over spaces more frequently. Similarly, rates for items like water and electricity can be structured to promote conservation, for example, higher rates at peak usage times. There are concerns, however, over the costs of necessary services such as water and sanitation for low-income residents.

Still another issue with fees and charges is the lack of clarity for residents as to the basis for setting the fee or charge. Fees are intended to cover not only the current operating costs of providing a service, but future capital investment needed for replacement or expansion of facilities or equipment. This is not always clear or well-explained by local government officials, leading to complaints by residents.

LOCAL GOVERNMENT BUDGETING

Local governments are not completely free to do as they please in preparing and adopting their budgets. Much of what they can—and cannot—do is imposed by the state. For example, in most states local governments are required to provide some services—police and fire protection are common requirements for cities—while some states deny them authority, such as the ability to impose sales taxes. Most common across all states is a balanced budget requirement, namely, a legal standard that a budget's planned spending cannot exceed revenue estimates. This does not mean, however, that the government is debt-free. Rather, budgets include spending for principal and interest payments on money that the government has borrowed, usually through the sale of bonds. In some ways, this is similar to a family building its regular mortgage payments into a household budget. As you learned earlier in the chapter, local governments generally distinguish between their capital and operating budgets, unlike the federal government.

Preparing the budget is generally an executive task. It can be more complicated for county governments, however, because there is not always an elected executive or hired manager, and county governing boards have limited control over independently elected department heads, such as sheriffs. In these cases, independently elected officials prepare the budget for their departments, requiring the governing body to reconcile these competing requests for resources into a single coherent budget. No matter who prepares a local government's budget, it is a difficult task with many challenges.

Budget approval by a city council or other governing body normally requires one or more public hearings on specified dates. Various interest groups lobby during review of a proposed budget, and government agencies often promote their goals in hearings and even privately. Governing bodies have latitude in amending a proposed budget, although this becomes difficult once a proposed balanced budget has been presented for consideration. Changes in one place in the budget, or in revenues or expenses, often require corresponding changes elsewhere in the budget. Most governing bodies allow chief executives to modify budgets within certain parameters when conditions change. Following the end of a fiscal year, states generally require local governments to be audited with an outside evaluation of financial statements and records to make sure that they comply with relevant laws and accounting standards.

Tax and Expenditure Limitations (TELs)

One constant dilemma for local budgeters is the set of constraints states or local voters have placed on their ability to raise and spend money. Tax and Expenditure Limitations (TELs) related to property taxes include restrictions on tax rates, limits on increases in property assessments, limits on the total amount of revenue that can be raised with property taxes, and increases in general revenue or expenditures. The use of TELs has increased dramatically since 1970, and twenty-seven states used more than one of these limits by 2015; eight states used three of them. Some states combine TELs with limits on alternative revenue sources.[32]

The pathbreaking TEL was California's Proposition 13 (Prop 13) in 1978. Voters overwhelmingly ratified this constitutional amendment following a major initiative campaign and years of rising taxes paid on the value of their homes, which escalated during a period of high inflation. Prop 13 rolled back property values to their 1975 levels and limited increases in assessments to 2 percent annually; plus, the tax on the property could not exceed 1 percent of its value. The only major change in assessments for real property occurs when it is sold, and that value becomes the new base year for imposing the limits on increases. Prop 13 produced major changes in government services and how they were funded. Critics increasingly focused on the benefit Prop 13 provided for wealthy homeowners. An initiative drive succeeded in 2018 in putting a measure on the ballot in November 2020 to leave the limits in place for residential property while removing them for businesses.[33] Prop 13's legacy is clear, however: It spawned a "Tax Revolt" that has spread across the country.[34]

Mandates

Over and above TELs, local officials complain regularly about mandates (see chapter 4). Local officials are especially vocal about requirements that come without financial support (see chapter 4). For example, there is no grant money dedicated to paying local governments to comply with the federal Americans with Disabilities Act, though the cost of bringing facilities into compliance can be significant. Similarly, most cities bear the costs of training police officers, firefighters, building inspectors, city clerks, and other professionals to meet state standards. Nevertheless, the costs of mandates must be built into local government budgets.

"Rainy Day," Enterprise, and Other Restricted Funds

State and local governments normally try to build up **rainy day funds** or *reserve funds*: money set aside and available during difficult economic times or emergencies when regular sources of funds might not be sufficient. Think of this as "insurance" against adversity. Reserve funds are also an important factor when rating agencies assess a local government's ability to pay off bonds.

Many cities and counties also set up **enterprise funds**, which are like special districts. Rather than including a service with all others in the general fund, revenues and expenses for a specific service such as water or sewers are sequestered and restricted to its operations. As the term implies, enterprise funds are used primarily for business-type operations, and fees or charges are set to offset costs. This also is designed to prevent governing boards from moving excess revenue from the enterprise fund to the general fund, which would use the gains to offset revenues that might be collected from general property taxes or other sources. A strong enterprise fund also helps earn favorable ratings when selling bonds for related capital improvements. Further complicating matters, local officials can set up other restricted funds to segregate certain services in the local budget; these often require voter approval.

Politics and Local Government Budgets

Decisions on taxes and fees are often difficult for elected officials. In many cases, the policies they prefer are subject to voter approval. For example, local governments in California are allowed to add their own sales taxes on top of the state's 7.25 percent. A simple majority is required if the money is to go into the general fund. However, a two-thirds vote is required if the funds are to go to a dedicated purpose or fund. During 2016, there were ninety-nine local sales tax referenda in California, sixty-four of them to increase the general sales tax by 0.25, 0.5, 0.75, or 1 percent. The proposals also varied in duration from a few as short as 4 or 5 years to nineteen permanent ones. These measures were all on the ballot during the June primary or the November general election; on such long ballots voters tend to skip items below major offices. In the end, voters approved fifty-three of the sixty-four proposed general sales tax hikes and rejected ten. Voters in Stanton rejected a proposal to repeal their 1-percent sales tax. Other specific proposals, which required higher approval levels, did not fare well: Fourteen passed, but twenty failed.[35]

In Georgia, voters in counties can approve a permanent 1-percent general sales tax. The state also permits voters in counties or school districts to approve 1-percent special-purpose local option sales taxes (SPLOST). These proposals must include specific projects and total amount to be raised. The tax expires in 5 years or when the specified amount is collected—whichever occurs first.[36] As the California and Georgia cases suggest, officials face political challenges in identifying the need for more revenue, connecting it to service or facility improvements, and selling the package to voters. They do benefit, however, from the public's more favorable view of sales taxes compared to property taxes.[37]

Similar political dynamics surround property taxes. The starting point here is how unpopular they are. National surveys have varied in their question wording, but since the early 1970s, 24 to 45 percent of respondents have identified the local property tax as the least fair of all taxes in the US. It regularly rivals or exceeds the federal income tax as the most disliked tax, including Gallup polls in the early 2000s, when property taxes easily outranked the federal income tax by 15–22 points. In a March 2015 Fox News poll, roughly a quarter of respondents chose the property tax and another quarter chose the federal income tax as the least fair.[38]

Several factors can generate hostility to property taxes. Administratively, people often question assessment practices and results. In addition, unless the taxes are included in mortgage payments, property owners must usually pay it in a lump sum annually, which makes it more visible than incremental sales tax payments. Last is the lack of connection between property taxes and income, and, for that matter, between property tax payments and the specific services provided. All of these can work against support when voters must approve a millage.

Still, one study found that voters will support higher taxes in communities that are more educated, less affluent, and with lower shares of nonwhite residents. Support can also be stronger for more specific proposals.[39] While there is some concern about elderly voters' hostility to tax increases, not all seniors are the same. In fact, long-term residents might see local taxes more favorably than recent arrivals.[40]

Selling local government bonds also involves politics. One political element is choosing the projects to be covered by the bond issue. For bonds requiring voter approval, this means convincing the public that there is some connection between the debt and the quality of public services to be supported. The second political element involves the interest rate paid to bond investors, which often means lobbying the three ratings agencies.

Fees raise issues of access and equity. Poorer households might find sports program charges too expensive for their children to participate. They also might have difficulty paying for basic services such as water. In Detroit, for instance, controversy has surrounded the ability of the poor to pay water bills and the city's cutoff of service due to unpaid bills, some accumulated by previous property owners.[41] Critics often question the basic fairness of communities using traffic violations as a way to raise money, while others question the equity of giving discounted water, sewer, or electric rates as "incentives" for large companies to locate or expand in a community. On the flip side are those who advocate using fees as a way to get money from organizations like universities, churches, and hospitals that are exempt from property taxes.[42]

Recent Financial Crises

The Great Recession lasted officially from December 2007 to June 2009. Its effects on the global economy persisted far longer, and its impact was especially hard on local governments. As the economy worsened, local government revenues, including state aid, dropped dramatically in some cases. Earnings for traditional pension funds worsened, health care costs rose for public employees, and many governments took on more debt. Officials eliminated tens of thousands of jobs in local government, while remaining employees often faced freezes or cuts in wages and benefits. Services like libraries and parks faced funding cuts; some cities even turned off streetlights. Other coping strategies included efforts to find new revenue sources, enhance reliance on increased utility fees, and draw from reserves.

Some see these financial, employment, and service constraints as a "new normal" for local governments already facing public hostility to higher taxes. This could mean more services delivered through privatization or intergovernmental agreements, greater use of fees, and changes to pensions and benefits.[43] One concern was defined-benefit pensions, which promised retirees a specific monthly paycheck but required investment strategies to deliver it.[44] This posed major

BOX 11.2

The 2013 Detroit Bankruptcy

Entrance to the Detroit Institute of Arts

On July 18, 2013, Detroit filed the largest municipal bankruptcy in US history. Population dropped from 1.8 million in 1950 to 714,000 in 2010. The major riot in 1967 accelerated white flight. Deindustrialization weakened the economy. Forty percent of residents were below the poverty level. State aid to the city had dropped significantly. Services, including public safety, declined while the property tax base shrank and debt soared. The major union-run pension fund distributed $1 billion in earnings to retired and active workers as a "13th check" in years with strong earnings rather than reinvesting the money.

financial problems for many local governments, including cities as large as Dallas and Houston staring at the possibility of bankruptcy due to pension obligations.[45] An alternative was a defined-contribution plan, whereby the local government promised to pay a certain amount per pay period into an employee's retirement account, with the employee responsible for managing the account. Other observers, however, have doubts about local governments adopting major changes.[46]

A second significant concern for many local governments related to financing is promised health care benefits to current and retired employees. Most local governments have covered health care costs from current operating budgets rather than setting aside funds on an annual basis as they do for pension benefits. As revenues declined dramatically following the Great Recession, it became more and more difficult to support the health care benefits promised to employees, especially as more employees retired or were laid off.

The "legacy" of unfunded health care costs and pensions contributed to decisions by local officials to consider bankruptcy. Not every state allows local governments to declare bankruptcy, but between 2010 and late 2017 there were sixty-one local government bankruptcy filings. Most were special districts such as water utilities and hospital authorities. Only nine were general-purpose local governments (cities or counties), but they included places as large as Stockton and San Bernardino, California, and Jefferson County, Alabama, which has more than 650,000 residents and the state's largest city (Birmingham). Some states intervened to prevent local governments from collapsing financially, including New Jersey's 2016 takeover of Atlantic City and Michigan's imposition of emergency managers to run cities the state considered distressed.[47] Perhaps the most visible of these financial disasters was Detroit's filing under Chapter 9 of federal bankruptcy law (see box 11.2).

By 2013, the city had $18–20 billion in debt and unfunded pension liabilities. In March, the governor appointed an emergency manager, who could supersede the elected mayor and city council. Public focus shifted to the possible sale of holdings at the Detroit Institute of Arts (DIA). Negotiations with creditors went nowhere, and the city filed for bankruptcy.

The court-appointed mediator prompted exchanges among foundations that pledged over $300 million by January 2014. The judge pressured major banks. The DIA pledged to raise $100 million and become a separate nonprofit. The legislature appropriated $195 million. The city gave up its water and sewer departments to a new regional water authority. Retirees agreed to a 4.5 percent cut in pensions, with no annual increases, and health benefit cuts of 90 percent. City unions made concessions.

The deal-making slashed more than $7 billion in liabilities, but the city still faced two large bond insurers. One settled for 13 cents on the dollar, toll rights for the tunnel between Detroit and Canada, and valuable real estate. The other got a similar payout and rights to develop Joe Louis Arena, set to be demolished. On December 7, 2014, the judge approved the bankruptcy, which has breathed life into Detroit's rebirth.

Source: Nathan Bomey and John Gallagher, "How Detroit Went Broke," *Detroit Free Press*, September 15, 2013, 1A; Nathan Bomey, John Gallagher, and Mark Stryker, "How Detroit Was Reborn: The Inside Story of Detroit's Historic Bankruptcy," *Detroit Free Press*, November 9, 2014, 1A; Nathan Bomey, *Detroit Resurrected: To Bankruptcy and Back* (New York: W. W. Norton, 2016).

Local officials face competing demands for government to be efficient, fair, and responsive. Many of these decisions play out in the annual budgeting process. Officials face major limitations under their state's constitution and laws. They also face competing demands from voters: Some seek improved services while others push for lower taxes. Department heads advocate for increased spending for their units without considering the total revenue picture, leaving it to the governing board to reconcile and accommodate the competing pressures. These pressures were especially keen during and after the Great Recession that began in the mid-2000s, which reduced local government revenues for many years. The concern moving forward is how to adapt as the economic recovery of the 2010s continues—or if it falters.

SUMMARY

Local government spending is significant—$1.9 trillion in 2017—and is devoted to a wide range of services different from those provided by states and the federal government. Local government revenues primarily come from property taxes, sales taxes, fees charged for services, borrowing, and state and federal aid. Each of these revenue sources is affected by multiple factors and has major strengths and weaknesses. In addition, states have adopted restrictions that limit local officials' discretion in raising and spending money, even as they impose service mandates or requirements on local units.

Financial pressures on local governments got worse during the Great Recession that began in 2007. Its major effects included several government bankruptcies. Cities, counties, school systems, and special districts face ever-changing revenue flows and must look constantly for ways to provide services more effectively and efficiently.

Key Terms

ad valorem sales taxes (234)
assessment ratio (232)
bonds (238)
capital budgets (226)
enterprise funds (242)
excise taxes (234)
exportable tax (240)
general fund (226)
general obligation (GO) bonds (238)
homestead exemption (232)
income tax (239)
intergovernmental revenue (228)
millage (232)

operating budgets (226)
own-source revenues (228)
payment in lieu of taxes (PILOT) (231)
personal property (230)
progressive tax (239)
property lien (233)
property tax (230)
rainy day funds (242)
real property (230)
regressive tax (240)
revenue bonds (238)
special assessments (239)
tax base (228)

Discussion Questions

1. What are the strengths and weaknesses of local government property taxes?

2. What are the benefits and problems of user fees? Why are they used, and what services are best or worst suited to this method of funding?

3. In what ways do states limit the ability of local governments to raise and spend money?

4. What are the challenges facing local governing boards as they seek to balance their budgets?

Exercises

1. Find your current city or county budget online. Describe its major revenue sources. How have they changed over the past 5 or 10 years?

2. What are the major expenses in your city or county budget? How have they changed in the past 5 or 10 years?

3. What services does your city or county finance through user fees or charges? Describe the rates for some of these services. Are the revenues included in the general fund or are they kept separate in some way?

4. Find a table that provides a state or national comparison of local government revenues and expenditures and see how your local government compares with others. The Census of Governments, which is published every 5 years, might be helpful for this purpose.

Practice and Review Online
https://textbooks.rowman.com/understanding-urban-politics

12

BUILDING THE CITY: ECONOMIC DEVELOPMENT, LAND USE, AND HOUSING POLICIES

GUIDING QUESTIONS

1. How do local government policies and other factors influence economic development in a community?
2. In what ways do local governments control land and affect its use?
3. How do national and local policies influence the availability of housing?
4. What options exist for the challenges facing communities as they develop in the future?

AMAZON WAS NOT the only high-stakes corporate location decision in recent years (see box 1.2). Several states competed to land a facility from Foxconn, a Taiwanese manufacturing firm that promised $10 billion in investment and 13,000 jobs in LCD TV production. Wisconsin won the bidding, and in a June 2018 groundbreaking at the construction site, President Trump was joined by Governor Scott Walker and then-House Speaker Paul Ryan (it was his district) and repeated claims about reviving US manufacturing. However, Wisconsin and some of its local governments were on the hook for $3 billion in incentives (some estimates were as high as $4.5 billion), and the most optimistic predictions did not see the state breaking even on the deal until 2042. There were also legal and environmental concessions. Plus, the company kept shifting its description of the site's purposes, scope, and job estimates. At the end of 2018, Foxconn had hired 178 full-time employees, missing a first-year target of 1,040 that would have given it the year's tax credits. Finally, initial wage and benefit levels turned out to be well below expectations.[1]

As this example suggests, governments are generally expected to improve communities by promoting economic development and good jobs, regulating land use, furnishing basic infrastructure, and assuring high-quality, affordable housing. Implementing policies to address these aims is not easy given the limited powers of local governments.

ECONOMIC DEVELOPMENT POLICIES

Local governments and organizations have long pushed growth in communities, including what chapter 2 called *boosterism*. Economic development efforts have varied, however, in their underlying assumptions, organization, and strategies. Common are financial incentives, changes in land use, workforce development, and regulatory relief. Nevertheless, local leaders must still contend with external political and economic forces over which they have little control.

Theories and Strategies

Local policy makers often do not distinguish between growth and development.[2] Growth is generally measured in overall gains and losses: number of jobs, new businesses, value of products produced, size of the tax base, etc. These are straightforward *quantitative* measures that can be stated in absolute numbers or percentage changes. However, analysts increasingly treat development in *qualitative* terms: skill or educational levels of the workforce, wage levels, benefit packages associated with jobs, and similar indicators. Growth and development are different, but not mutually exclusive, ways to view progress. The analogy might be monitoring a child's growth in terms of height but also measuring development in terms of skills such as reading, mathematics, musical ability, or physical dexterity.

A distinction has also evolved between supply-side and demand-side strategies for economic development. Supply-side policies are those that try to establish a location's comparative advantage by reducing a company's costs of producing there versus other places. This would include the traditional costs of land, labor, and capital. Demand-side policies, on the other hand, aim to stimulate demand for an area's products, essentially bringing money into a community by "exporting" goods and services produced there.[3] There have been other ways to classify these general approaches as well.[4] Broad strategies such as downtown development, international business investment, or promoting the health care industry are usually broken down into several specific tactics to implement the strategy's goals that are like "tools" in the kit for promoting the local economy.

Supply-side policies have a long history, including governments giving land in the 1800s to companies developing canals, railroads, and telegraph lines. This approach took off beginning in the 1930s, when states and communities in the South subsidized manufacturing.[5] The financial incentives that state and local governments offer to business have grown substantially since then. Demand-side policies expanded, beginning in the 1980s, and include everything from advertising and marketing to product development, support to business incubators, mentoring programs, and office or production space.

There is some concern that communities will follow the fad of the moment, be it festival marketplaces, trolley lines, a new stadium, or other projects. Some places and analysts promote specific sectors thought to offer good jobs and stability even during economic downturns, for example, education and health care ("eds and meds"). Certain theories have also attracted followings. Richard Florida of the University of Toronto, for instance, has argued that communities should aim to attract the "creative class" that works in knowledge-intensive industries. These are people in technology, the arts, education, and similar fields. To do this, Florida argues, local leaders need to provide an environment characterized by the three T's: talent, technology, and tolerance—a combination built around a range of amenities. In many ways, this is consistent with an argument by economist Ann Markusen that cities should think in terms of attracting certain occupations, not just certain industries.[6]

In another approach, Michael Porter of the Harvard Business School contends that places should emphasize clusters of related firms. He sometimes uses the example of the wine industry, in which several different activities support growers and vineyards. There are wineries, of course, but others connected to producing and selling the wine include bottles, barrels, labels, corks and caps, advertising, marketing, and tourism. The basic premise is that having these related firms concentrated in an area means not having to "import" their products or services from elsewhere.[7]

As economic development policies have expanded, many see an "arms race" in which states and communities try to outgun one another with incentives to lure new investment. A more critical view sees these efforts as a "race to the bottom" to see which place can give away the most to attract companies.

Promotion: The Selling of Place

As chapters 2 and 3 demonstrated, American communities have engaged in boosterism almost since the founding of the country. In modern times, this is often the responsibility of local organizations funded by business groups and governments. Their basic aims are to secure investment in a city or get people to visit it. Both can be thought of as exporting—getting outsiders to spend money for something produced in the city.

Perhaps the most basic type of promotion is advertising. This is more than the type of flashy television and social media ads selling Las Vegas. Most areas have a convention and visitors bureau (CVB), often supported by local taxes on things like stays in hotel rooms. Beyond general ads, these organizations often advertise in travel and in-flight airline magazines, publications catering to certain demographic groups, and people with certain interests (e.g., food magazines). Many areas also promote their features or products with special events, ranging from the St. Paul Winter Carnival in late January and early February to the Castroville Artichoke Festival every June, major auto races, and cultural events like the Boston Symphony's summer home at Tanglewood in western Massachusetts. Even more local is the Atlanta CVB's staff devoted to staging reunions—down to logos, banners, and t-shirts.[8] These efforts also extend to social media and are all designed to pour money into the local economy.

Beyond strategies to lure tourists, CVBs also try to attract conventions. Some are so large (upwards of 100,000 attendees) that only a few places (Las Vegas, Atlanta, or Chicago) have facilities and hotel rooms to handle them. Other sites draw gatherings of around 50,000.[9] Smaller places try to attract regional or statewide gatherings. In this "arms race," cities try to keep up with one another, continually expand facilities with little net gain in crowds or revenues, without much public involvement in decisions, but under continuous pressure by local business boosters and growing involvement by state governments.[10]

Cities often participate in trade missions to other countries, which are organized by the US Department of Commerce, other federal agencies, state governments, and even regional efforts by groups of cities. Their purpose is twofold: to promote US exports abroad and to encourage investment in the United States. For instance, in 2017, the mayors of Dallas and Fort Worth led a trade mission to Canada. In 2018, they led a delegation to London, Paris, and Brussels. Both missions were designed to encourage tourism and investment in the region, where companies from these countries already had an important presence.[11]

Organizing to Promote Economic Development

With growing competition, many communities have developed formal plans for economic development. Others do things on an ad hoc basis. Some even followed a "build it and they will come" approach by setting aside land or buildings for an industrial park. A survey by the International City/County Management Association (ICMA) in 2014 found that just 57 percent of the more than 1,000 responding local governments actually had a formal plan for economic development.[12]

Communities vary in how they assign responsibility and deploy resources to deal with economic development. Indeed, the number of participants at each stage of the policy process identified in chapter 11 can be quite numerous. Like it or not, local government has a role. In the 2014 ICMA survey, two-thirds of respondents reported that local government has the primary responsibility for economic development. Another 20 percent said that a nonprofit economic development corporation has primary responsibility.

TABLE 12.1	Ten Most Common Participants in Formulating Local Economic Development Strategies	
Participant		**% Communities Reporting Participation**
City Government		86
Chamber of Commerce		57
County Government		55
Economic Development Corporation		40
Regional Organization		38
State Government		37
Public-Private Partnership		33
Private Business		32
Citizen Advisory Board		26
College or University		25

Note: Number of respondents=1,195.

Source: International City/County Management Association, "Economic Development 2014 Survey Results," 2.

The cast of characters involved in developing strategies can be rather broad, so conflict can arise both between and within organizations. While city governments were overwhelmingly the lead players in the 2014 ICMA survey, the next most common was the local chamber of commerce (see table 12.1). Also prominent were county governments, economic development corporations, and regional organizations. Organizations like nonprofits showed up less than 10 percent of the time.

Some local governments create a separate department to deal with economic development, but these units seldom operate in isolation. In smaller jurisdictions, a city manager or mayor can have this responsibility. Chambers of commerce are often key players, but they are an interest group representing local businesses. In many ways, a local chamber is a coalition of companies (and some nonprofits) of different sizes and from different sectors that often compete with one another or have conflicting goals. Chambers provide services to their members, engage in community service, host events, and often conduct advertising campaigns for the area. Broad membership can put a chamber in the position of advocating only for policies that have wide appeal, such as low property taxes or better infrastructure.

Economic development corporations and public-private partnerships are interesting hybrids in terms of their public role. An **economic development corporation (EDC)** is a relatively independent nonprofit organization established by a local government with authority and resources to enhance the local economy. EDCs often have authority to use public and private funds for projects and operation of facilities. In many places, they also play a role in business financing through loans and tax breaks. In addition, EDCs often conduct research and provide small businesses with support services such as marketing, technical assistance, and low-cost space. EDCs also operate "under the radar" compared to the media coverage and public participation devoted to city councils and traditional government bureaucracies.[13]

Similar to an EDC, a public authority devoted to economic development is set up as a special district by a city or county just like the special-purpose governments set up to run a hospital or transit system (see chapter 4). Quite common are authorities set up to promote downtown or other zones within the community, industrial development, or revitalization of **brownfields** (abandoned, idle, or underused industrial and commercial properties where expansion or redevelopment is complicated by real or perceived environmental contamination).[14]

Communities also use a range of **public-private partnerships (3Ps)**, contracts between government and a private entity to finance, build, or manage projects usually involving a mix of public and private resources. In many communities, for instance, a 3P promotes conventions and tourism, often with a subsidy from local government in the form of taxes on hotel stays, rental cars, or event tickets.

Given the different ways of organizing to promote economic development, what tactics do communities use? Table 12.2 provides an overview of some strategies other than business incentives. The data are from a 2014 ICMA survey with responses from about 1,200 cities and counties out of over 5,200 polled. For one question, respondents indicated whether their "level of use" of thirty-two "economic development tools" was high, medium, low, or not at all. The tools were grouped into the four general strategies listed in the table.

The largest share of high use is for education and amenities (35%) followed by the 3Ps, infrastructure, tourism, and efforts to attract new businesses. Not included are things that almost no place uses, such as assistance to support child care, microenterprise programs, and community development loan funds.

Tax Breaks and Other Financial Support

Among the most common tactics that local governments use to promote growth is reducing businesses' tax and financing costs. Tax breaks take many forms and, as critics point out, are subsidies to the companies that benefit. Perhaps the most basic is a **tax abatement**, the reduction or elimination of a company's property taxes for a specified period of time. These normally require approval by a city council or county board. For example, the Polk County (Florida) Board of Commissioners granted a 100-percent property tax abatement for 10 years if Amazon located one of its fulfillment centers there. The incentive cost the county $4.5 million in tax revenue. Another eleven abatements in Polk County as of 2018 were for as few as 3 years, generally reduced property taxes by 25 or 50 percent, and totaled another $4.5 million in tax reductions.[15] Some states also permit local governments to rebate property taxes to companies.

TABLE 12.2	Local Use of Selected Economic Development Tools, 2014			
	Percentage of Cities Using Tool			
	High	Medium	Low	Not at All
Small Business				
Matching grants to improve property	12	25	24	39
Small business development center	11	28	26	34
Revolving loan fund	8	18	24	39
Business Retention and Expansion Tools				
Main Street program	18	21	21	40
Surveys of local business	15	36	34	16
Business clusters/industrial districts	12	30	28	30
Business improvement districts	11	24	24	41
Business Attraction				
Government rep calls on prospective companies	26	33	26	15
Promotional and advertising activities	20	33	33	14
Community Development				
Investments in education, recreation, arts/ culture	35	38	19	9
Tourism promotion	29	31	23	17
Public/private partnerships	25	36	26	13
High-quality infrastructure	24	38	24	14

Note: Number of respondents varied by question from 1,158 to 1,176.

Source: International City/County Management Association, "Economic Development 2014 Survey Results," 5–6.

In addition to incentives linked to property taxes, some states exempt companies from sales taxes under certain circumstances, often so that firms do not pay the taxes when buying materials used to build or expand facilities. Exemptions have also been applied to utility taxes such as those for electric or gas bills. Under certain conditions, South Carolina exempts sales taxes on recycling equipment, as well as companies' purchase of machinery, materials used in manufacturing, electricity and other fuels used in manufacturing, packaging equipment, pollution control equipment, and other activities.[16]

Also common is **tax increment financing (TIF)**, which has been around since the early 1950s and is often used by entities like downtown development authorities. TIF is an agreement between a local government and a company to freeze a property's assessed value in exchange for development of the land, with the tax on any increase in the property's value due to the development (the increment) used to pay for improvements such as infrastructure. Once the improvements are paid for, the freeze is eliminated and the developed property is taxed at its new, higher value. In some cases, the developer of the land pays first, with the local governments using the incremental tax revenue to reimburse the costs.[17] In 2000, the city of Milwaukee created a tax improvement district to support construction of a Hilton hotel, which included a major parking deck and other improvements paid for initially by the developer. As of 2017, the incremental value of the property was $21 million. The city created another district in 2004 to support building the Harley-Davidson Museum, which has added $17 million to the tax base, about $10 million less than was projected before the Great Recession.[18]

Local governments will sometimes make loans to companies. In other cases, communities make outright grants, although they can include conditions. For example, when Toyota looked to consolidate its operations away from its existing headquarters in California, with its high cost of living, it chose the Dallas suburb of Plano. As part of its package, the city offered $6.75 million in grants related to the $350 million headquarters, but it required Toyota to meet certain deadlines for construction and employment.[19]

Since the 1980s, a number of states and the federal government have adopted policies that give a range of incentives to firms investing in specific areas, usually parts of cities characterized by their lack of businesses or jobs. Sometimes called *enterprise zones*, the most recent iteration was labeled *opportunity zones* in Congress's 2017 overhaul of federal tax law. The US Treasury approved about 8,700 of the proposed zones (using census tracts) submitted by states. Investors could defer taxes on capital gains invested in zones and even eliminate part of their tax depending on the length of time they maintain their investment in the zone.[20] Some case studies report success with these ventures.[21] Others have reached contrary conclusions, and skeptics question the value of these programs, including whether investment would have occurred anyway or was just a matter of choosing one part of the city over another.[22]

Land, Improvements, Training, and Regulatory Relief

In some cases, local governments or states give companies land or make physical improvements to an area. When Volvo decided to locate its first US plant in South Carolina, in what critic Good Jobs First labels one of its "Megadeals," the state and Berkeley County provided funds to buy the land for the plant. The state was expected to spend $120 million for road improvements and other infrastructure.[23] Similarly, the state and local subsidies for the joint Mazda-Toyota investment in Alabama even included a railroad spur line.[24]

Support for employee training usually comes from state governments, but that is often part of a larger package of incentives for large firms that also includes local government resources. Marriott opened a large hotel in the nation's capital in May 2014, with 40 percent of the $520 million cost subsidized by the DC government. Part of the agreement required hiring DC residents. Two thousand people applied for a $2 million training program run through Goodwill Industries, with 719 trained and referred to Marriott. Eventually 28 percent of the hotel's 650 hourly workers came from the program, and three-quarters had stayed after 1 year.[25] In 2017, Missouri was reported to have provided $9 million in training reimbursement to the Cerner Corporation, a major medical IT firm headquartered in the state, while Arkansas provided almost $1 million in training reimbursement to heavy equipment manufacturer Caterpillar.[26]

Governments will also loosen regulations at times to promote investment. As already indicated, Wisconsin modified standards regarding air pollution and wetlands, and the city of Racine requested permission to divert up to seven million gallons of water per day from Lake Michigan, both as part of a deal with Foxconn. Objections came from some local residents, environmental groups, and nearby Illinois governments sharing a flood plain with the site.[27]

External Forces

Even with the best strategies, there are many factors in economic development that local leaders cannot control—or in many cases, even hope to influence. Most obvious is the inability to affect the ups and downs in the national economy. One example is Elkhart, Indiana, where 80 percent of the recreational vehicles in the US are made. Drops in orders for RVs are often thought to signal problems in the national economy, but they also serve as a warning for northern Indiana, as happened following President Trump's imposition of tariffs on steel and aluminum.[28] One study found that local governments increased their reliance on financial incentives after the onset of the Great Recession, although governments increasingly turned to accountability measures in dealing with companies. In addition, communities devoted more attention to amenities, training, and other factors that would make them more attractive to employees.[29]

Moreover, areas can fall behind when the structure of the economy changes. Alan Ehrenhalt is among those who have noted that "legacy cities" thrived in the industrial economy, but as the economy changed, they lost decent-paying jobs to automation and foreign competition, and often companies and corporate headquarters also left town. However, some places have rebounded thanks to actions by major corporate employers.[30] An even more difficult legacy to modify is an area's physical features. This goes beyond the obvious like topography and bodies of water to include buildings, infrastructure, and routes for vehicles and trains. All of these can become obsolete or inadequate for changing conditions. An obvious historical case is replacement of water power with steam and electricity in the 1800s.

The local labor force is another legacy that is difficult to change. Education levels and skills are not immutable, but they can take a generation to modify. Some areas might be so dependent on one industry—timber, oil and gas, mining, or tourism, for example—that a downturn in that sector depresses the local economy much more than in areas with a more diverse economic base. Moreover, sectors such as agriculture and tourism can move up and down with the seasons—and the weather. Plus, strategies that work in larger places might not be as effective in smaller communities, which might need to invest more heavily to enhance residents' basic technical skills.[31]

As chapter 4 suggested, state governments can also have a major influence on local economic development efforts, including basic actions like investment in highways, ports, and other infrastructure. States also control the types of incentives local governments can use, ranging from the ability to set up development authorities to tax abatements to rules for issuing various types of bonds to the use of tax credits for historic preservation. One rationale for state supervision is to prevent local governments from entering a bidding war over a company that is investing in the state anyway.

Economic Development Policy, Performance, and Accountability

In the end, local governments make wide use of business incentives, although some are harder to implement in smaller cities and counties. As figure 12.1 demonstrates, 80–90 percent of cities provide some level of zoning/permit assistance or infrastructure improvements. At the other extreme, almost no local governments make high use of utility rate reductions, subsidized

Figure 12.1 Use of Business Incentives, 2014

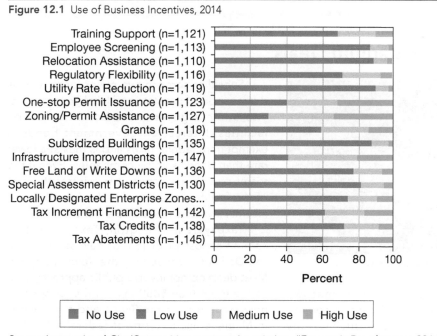

Source: International City/County Management Association, "Economic Development 2014 Survey Results," 7.

buildings, relocation assistance, or employee screening. Still, over 75 percent utilize one-stop permit issuance; more than 70 percent use grants to promote development; 60 percent make some use of tax abatements, tax increment financing, and regulatory flexibility; and over half employ tax credits. Note that the figure covers only local efforts, to which states often add more incentives.

As state and local governments have gotten more aggressive about promoting economic development, critics have highlighted several concerns (see box 12.1). One is how policies are adopted and implemented, particularly transparency and responsiveness to the public. Because many deals involve state or local economic development corporations, public-private partnerships, and authorities, there is not the same level of public notice and participation involved with city councils making policy and budget decisions.[32] A move toward greater transparency occurred in 2015, however, when the national board regulating government accounting required state and local governments to document in their annual financial reports the amount of revenue lost through tax incentives granted by it or another government.[33]

Second is effectiveness: Does any of this stuff work, and if not, why do we keep doing it? As cities upped the ante for economic development beginning in the 1980s, several studies suggested that many would try anything, with the most disadvantaged cities becoming the most active players.[34] Many observers called this the "flypaper effect"—keep throwing things out there in the hope that something will stick. There is even some evidence that cities

BOX 12.1

Taxpayers and Stadium Deals

The New Yankee Stadium in the Bronx

Americans take pride in their hometown professional sports teams. Politicians recognize this, and team owners have successfully pressured officials for large public subsidies for facilities.

Subsidies come in two major forms. One is direct support from state and local governments. The other is government bonds for sports facilities. Interest on government bonds is exempt from federal taxes and is thus at a lower rate than bonds sold by companies. Even if the teams pay off the bonds, it subsidizes the cost of the facilities and benefits the (usually high-income) investors who buy the bonds.

Taxpayers in Arlington, Texas, voted to commit almost $1 billion for new stadiums for the Dallas Cowboys and the Texas Rangers. Most deals do not involve public approval, such as the more than $850 million that supported new stadiums for the Twins and the Vikings in Minneapolis. In terms of federal subsidies, tax-exempt bonds subsidized the new Yankee Stadium about $431 million, while holders of the became more aggressive when their economies soured during the Great Recession.[35] A narrow focus on taxes and regulation can ignore other factors important in business decisions, such as talent, growth of the labor force, operating costs, crime, public services, and amenities.[36] Some suggest that outside the major growth hubs on both coasts, mid-size cities that make major public investments and are part of regional efforts can do better at attracting investment.[37] Some still advocate subsidizing manufacturing because it generates higher wages than jobs in the service sector and can be a source of product innovation.[38]

The third criticism focuses on who benefits from these policies and whether companies making promises deliver what they claim. For example, residents in some communities have increasingly questioned tax breaks for developers building high-end condominium and apartment projects in downtown areas.[39] Political pressure has prompted a number of cities to adopt accountability measures, including performance agreements, cost-benefit analyses before awarding incentives, metrics to assess effectiveness, and **clawback provisions** (agreements requiring companies to pay back government financial support if they fail to meet promised employment or other goals). Adopting these limitations is more likely in cities that have some experience with incentives and have the bureaucratic capacity to do the analysis.[40]

The issue of "who benefits" resonated throughout 2018. Congress's 2017 massive overhaul of the federal tax code, which created tax breaks for opportunity zones, eventually included over 8,700 census tracts. Skeptics wondered

bonds benefitted by another $61 billion. The new leader in subsidies is the NFL Raiders, who are leaving Oakland for Las Vegas to play in a stadium with $750 million in government subsidies. The list of subsidies even includes cities scrambling to attract or retain minor-league baseball. Several teams own their facilities, including the Los Angeles Dodgers, the San Francisco Giants, the New England Patriots, the Golden State Warriors, and the Los Angeles (formerly St. Louis, Los Angeles, and Cleveland) Rams. The major exception to sports ownership is the Green Bay Packers, which is a publicly owned nonprofit corporation with over 360,000 shareholders. Depending on contracts, local governments might still be on the hook for stadium expenses or could lose potential revenues such as sales taxes or parking.[a] Still, taxpayers may be souring on the idea of public financing for sports teams.[b]

See Jason Rossi, "The 15 Cities Where Your Tax Dollars Paid for Billion-Dollar Stadiums,"

CheatSheet, April 30, 2018, https://www.cheatsheet.com/culture/taxpayer-money-billion-dollar-stadiums.html/; Ted Gayer, Austin J. Drukker, and Alexander K. Gold, "Tax-Exempt Municipal Bonds and the Financing of Professional Sports Stadiums," Brookings Institution Economic Studies, September 2016, https://www.brookings.edu/wp-content/uploads/2016/09/gayerdrukkergold_stadiumsubsidies_090816.pdf. Several studies years ago warned about the problems of cities chasing minor league baseball, for example, Arthur T. Johnson, "Professional Baseball at the Minor League Level: Considerations for Cities Large and Small," *State and Local Government Review* 22:2 (Spring 1990): 90–96.

[a] Liz Farmer, "Even When Teams Pay, Stadiums Still Aren't Free for Cities," *Governing* (Finance), August 22, 2018, http://www.governing.com/topics/finance/gov-sports-stadium-columbus-soccer-mls-austin.html.

[b] Liz Farmer, "Stadium Fatigue," *Governing*, May 2018, 46–50.

whether loose regulations would end up subsidizing development that would have occurred anyway and were designed more to eliminate investors' capital gains taxes than to improve poor sections of cities. Indeed, up to 30 percent of a qualifying investment did not have to be in one of the zones, and many college towns qualified based on students' presumed poverty.[41]

Louder still was the chorus criticizing Amazon's search for its second headquarters, described in box 1.2. Announcing its decision in November 2018, the company split the $5-billion, 50,000-job HQ2 between New York City and suburban Washington, DC (a combined $2 billion in incentives for Amazon, three-fourths by New York), plus an operations center with 5,000 jobs in Nashville. Despite the image of Amazon spreading its footprint beyond high-cost coastal areas, it spurned over 200 metropolitan areas between Seattle and the East Coast. One critic described the search "spectacle" as "shameful" and argued that Congress should ban such subsidies.[42] Even before the original list was cut to twenty finalists, many thought that the cities submitting bids had been scammed into giveaways to one of America's richest companies. Amazon got reams of information about urban areas for free and forced bidders to reveal the benefits (usually kept secret) that they might throw at the company, which was useful to Amazon in future negotiations.[43] Others thought that "losing" Amazon might be a blessing, allowing cities to plan better for the future and not get caught up in such a sweepstakes again.[44] Perhaps another black eye for Amazon was its decision to abandon the New York location a few months later after complaints by some public officials and unions, along with protests by community activists.[45]

LAND USE

Perhaps the greatest power of local governments is their control over land. This takes several forms: ownership, zoning, and several types of regulations. Many observers forget how much land local governments own: buildings, roadways, bridges and other infrastructure, foreclosed property, easements of various types—plus parks and other open spaces. All of this property can be used in efforts to promote economic development, efficient transportation, flood control, wildlife habitat, neighborhood amenities, and more.

Zoning

Influence over land in a community usually revolves around zoning, which the US Supreme Court upheld as constitutional in 1926.[46] The basic tools of zoning are an ordinance and a map covering every parcel of land.[47] The ordinance classifies each parcel in terms of its permitted uses, usually with four general categories ranging from the most to the least restrictive: agriculture or open space, residential, commercial, and industrial. Property owners are allowed to have a more restrictive use in a less restrictive area, but not the reverse. For example, a person could operate a blueberry farm in property classified as industrial, but could not operate an iron smelter on land zoned for agriculture. Each type of use is normally divided further. In residential zones, for instance, single-family homes would be a more restrictive category than duplexes, which would be more restrictive than apartment buildings. Zones can be more complicated, for example, different categories for single-family homes based on minimum lot sizes.

Those wanting to change the classification of a specific property go through a process to "rezone" it. This usually involves a formal application (with a fee), a review by the planning staff (sometimes with a formal recommendation), followed by a public meeting and a vote by an appointed planning commission to recommend a certain decision by the city council, and a vote by the council on whether to amend the zoning ordinance by reclassifying the property. Both the planning commission and city council meetings can be contentious with plenty of speakers for or against a proposal. Indeed, public meetings on zoning are often the poster child for NIMBYism (see chapter 3). Public involvement can be much lower, though, in areas that are not very extensively built up, in which case developers can have outsize influence.[48]

The final decision on rezoning a property is often not a simple yes/no vote. Cities will often put conditions on land they rezone. For example, a developer wanting to build an apartment complex might have to limit its height, screen the building from its neighbors with certain types of landscaping, or add a turn lane into the property. Council decisions are not always the last word, since developers will sometimes sue to get the land use that they want. The litigation in some states asserts that denying the rezoning is like government "taking" the property through eminent domain as they would to build a highway. Under the 5th Amendment to the US Constitution, the government would have to pay the applicant *just compensation* for denying the developer the highest and best use of the land, that is, the greatest return on the investment. State constitutions often have similar guarantees.

Local governments often have other ordinances that "overlay" additional regulations on an existing zoning map. A common one is to zone an area as a historic district, which adds additional restrictions, such as types of building materials, paint colors, and even landscaping. Many cities also limit signs and noise in certain zones.

There are also cases in which a property owner might want a modest exception to zoning restrictions. An example would be building a garage nine feet from the property line in a single-family area rather than the required minimum of ten feet. These adjustments, called *variances*, are often handled more simply than rezoning because the basic use of the property would not change.

The goals of zoning's early advocates included separating residential from industrial areas, with many local ordinances placing primacy on protecting single-family homes.[49] As chapter 2 indicates, zoning has long been criticized for promoting racial segregation, but it also separates residents by income through requirements such as large house and lot sizes. Some communities even prohibit apartments. Activists have also turned to zoning to limit the availability of alcohol, tobacco, firearms, and fast food; restrict the placement of facilities such as group homes; and prohibit hydraulic fracturing for oil and gas.[50] Local governments have also wrestled with how to adapt zoning to technological changes such as solar energy and economic innovations such as Airbnb, which is very different from traditional hotels.[51] Some cities have changed their zoning ordinances to address the rising cost of housing, including Minneapolis eliminating single-family zoning citywide, a decision that affected a majority of land in the city.[52]

Conflicts also arise over *sprawl*, which has multiple meanings and images. Opponents treat sprawl as unregulated dispersion of development over the rural landscape. It is often attacked for negative effects on the environment and inefficient use of public services because construction seems to "leapfrog" all over rather than extending from existing built-up areas. Others see sprawl as an escape from high-density urban living and an opportunity for Americans to find more space than in central cities and older suburbs. They do not necessarily see cities and suburbs as an either/or view of urban development and sometimes see the other side as hostile to or belittling suburbia.[53] Economists often see the ability of cities to spread out as a way to provide more affordable housing with new construction on raw land. Some even see dispersion as part of the "natural" growth of urban areas.

Infrastructure

Infrastructure—streets, bridges, sidewalks, water, sewers, telecommunications, major buildings, dams, airports, harbors—is not a very "hot" topic until something fails. How these systems are developed is integral to land use and the physical layout of a community. Infrastructure involves costly undertakings by local governments, although they are not the only ones involved. The federal government has played a role in infrastructure since the 1800s, when it supported the development of canals, railroads, and harbors. These efforts grew with financial aid for major roadways and state cooperation in the adoption of the numbered US highways in the 1920s. The biggest federal push was the Interstate Highway System established in 1956.

In 2017, state and local governments accounted for 59 percent of the $174 billion in capital spending on infrastructure and 90 percent of the $266 billion in spending for operations and maintenance. This is a lot of money, but state and local capital spending for transportation and water infrastructure, adjusted for inflation, has been virtually flat since the early 2000s after increasing steadily since the 1980s. Spending for operation and maintenance has grown, but capital expenditures have dropped to the level of the early 1990s.[54] All of this has occurred as local and state officials, along with professional organizations, have decried the condition of the nation's infrastructure (see box 12.2).

Following the Minneapolis tragedy, a majority of states approved fuel tax increases to fund road and bridge improvements. Still, the American Society of Civil Engineers (ASCE) found that over 9 percent of the nation's bridges were structurally deficient in 2016, including more than 20 percent of bridges in Iowa and Rhode Island. In 2017, a national organization representing transportation builders estimated that over 55,000 bridges needed to be repaired or replaced.[55]

BOX 12.2

America's Fragile Infrastructure

Interstate-35W Bridge Collapse, Minneapolis, 2007

On August 1, 2007, an Interstate Highway bridge in Minneapolis carrying four lanes of traffic collapsed during the afternoon rush hour, killing thirteen and injuring 145. The bridge had been classified as deficient in several ways due to deterioration, but the National Transportation Safety Board concluded that a design flaw was the cause. A contributing factor was the stockpiling on the bridge of equipment and material to be used for repair work. The bridge was rebuilt in fourteen months, and the Minnesota Department of Transportation did major inspections of bridges of similar construction. The collapse also prompted national soul-searching about the status of the country's infrastructure.

Source: David Schaper, "10 Years after Bridge Collapse, America Is Still Crumbling," *National Public Radio*, August 1, 2017, https://www.npr.org/2017/08/01/540669701/10-years-after-bridge-collapse-america-is-still-crumbling.

ASCE issues an infrastructure report card every 4 years, and the results for 2017 were not pretty. In evaluating sixteen categories, ACSE gave the US a D+. None of the categories got an F, but transit got a D-. The highest grade was a B for railways, which are mainly investments by the private sector. Ports, bridges, and solid waste services rated a C+. The remainder earned a D+ or D, including drinking water, roads, schools, and hazardous waste.[56]

In its 2018 analysis of mayors' annual "State of the City" speeches, the National League of Cities reported economic development and infrastructure as mayors' most important issues. In terms of infrastructure, 53 percent of mayoral speeches emphasized roads, streets, and signage; 31 percent emphasized water, sewers, and waste. Less than 30 percent mentioned transit, pedestrian issues, and funding.[57] Thus, the bottom line seems to be that a long list of projects need significant attention, but the resources to address them are insufficient.

HOUSING

As chapter 2 demonstrates, the federal government began assuming a major role in housing during the 1930s. The focus was twofold: supporting affordable rental units and bolstering home ownership. Local governments also have a significant impact on the supply, quality, and affordability of housing, not just through zoning but via building codes and other regulations, location of facilities, transportation, and amenities like parks and open spaces.

Federal Housing Programs

Federal subsidies and local policies can have a huge impact on renters. Many older cities established a housing authority in the 1930s, but most suburbs have not. Local housing authorities normally own and manage apartment buildings. Since the 1980s, state and local agencies have increasingly issued federally financed vouchers that households can use for rentals with private landlords. In addition, some federal programs are designated for certain groups, such as the elderly and people with disabilities. Landlords have been found to refuse potential tenants using vouchers, although building managers in low-income areas see voucher holders as more dependable tenants. Cities and counties in at least sixteen states, including Denver, along with fifteen state governments, have responded by making it illegal to reject a tenant based on source of payment or use of other public assistance (e.g., vouchers, Social Security, or veterans benefits).[58]

The US Department of Housing and Urban Development (HUD) sets income limits to qualify for housing assistance based on median family income, which varies by family size, and fair market rents calculated within each metropolitan area and for each nonmetropolitan county. For instance, for Louisville in 2016, low income for a family of four was $53,600 (defined as 80 percent of the metropolitan area median of $67,000), very low income (50% of the median) was $33,500, and extremely low income was $24,300. In contrast, the median income for a family of four in Boston was $98,100, which meant that the comparable eligible incomes were $73,050 for low income, $49,050 for very low income, and $29,450 for extremely low income. The other part of the equation is fair market rent. In 2016, a two-bedroom unit cost $817 per month in Louisville but $1,567 in Boston.[59] Tenants generally pay 30 percent of their income on rent, minus certain exclusions, with the federal government paying the remainder. Those who experience major increases in income or violate certain policies may no longer be eligible for assistance.

What does all of this mean in practice? The major rental assistance programs supported almost 10 million people in 2016, with 54 percent of households headed by an elderly person (aged 62 or older) or a disabled person younger than 62. Two-thirds of assisted households fell into the very-low-income category, but three-fourths of eligible renters in the low-income category received no support, reflecting the long waiting lists in most of the country.

The other major federal program is the Low-Income Housing Tax Credit (LIHTC), which provides tax credits for buildings rented to eligible low-income tenants. Detailed research on Charlotte and Cleveland suggests that adding LIHTC developments is associated with higher turnover among neighborhood homeowners, especially in higher-income areas. This raises issues about the impact of assisted housing on neighborhood stability.[60] Other research suggests that when Democratic governors have influence over the state agencies selecting locations for LIHTC housing, there is a slight bias in favor of areas voting for the governor's party.[61] More generally, one study covering 1977 to 2008 found that poverty rates increased when neighborhoods gained assisted housing of various types. Losing assisted housing units slowed, but did not reverse, poverty rate increases. Gaining a few units had little effect on a neighborhood's poverty level. It is worth noting that the study did not analyze other impacts of assisted housing.[62]

Housing remains dominated by the private real estate market. The Congressional Budget Office reported that the $50 billion the federal government spent on rental assistance in 2014 was far less than the $130 billion in tax breaks benefiting homeowners.[63] Various federal agencies also affect housing in several ways. The Federal Reserve, for instance, shapes interest rates, which affect investors, developers, and households. The Fed was also instrumental in stabilizing markets during and after the Great Recession by buying government and private debt. Quasi-public organizations that sell, buy, and insure mortgages also have a substantial impact on the housing market.[64] Critics argue that increasingly weak federal regulation had helped stimulate high-risk mortgage lending as early as the 1990s, with 17 percent of subprime mortgages in foreclosure by 2008, with disastrous effects on minority borrowers and neighborhoods, adjacent homeowners, and the tax base of local governments.[65] **Foreclosure** is the process by which a lender or local government moves to reclaim a property because the homeowners have fallen behind on their mortgage payments, property taxes, or both.

The federal government also regulates lending practices. The Community Reinvestment Act (CRA), which was passed in 1977 to assure that banks were making credit available throughout the areas that they served, was designed to combat any remaining redlining (denying or limiting financial services to certain neighborhoods based on racial or ethnic composition without regard for residents' qualifications or creditworthiness; see chapter 2). Requirements include public reporting of loan activity by census tract. A leading housing policy researcher sees both positive effects and a need for improvement of the CRA.[66]

Local Housing Policies

Beyond federal policies are local actions, most notably regulation and support services. In addition to zoning, regulation includes subdivision standards, building codes, use of permits, and inspections. Standards for developing subdivisions usually include how land will be divided into lots, how streets and other infrastructure are laid out, and how topography, vegetation, and runoff are managed.[67] Building codes can vary for different types of structures, but all generally cover materials for foundations, plumbing, roofing, electrical work, mechanical systems, and the like. Over time, they have come to include energy efficiency standards, fire and carbon monoxide warning devices, use of renewable resources, earthquake protection, and mitigation of lead and other health threats. National organizations can also influence local codes, such as the US Green Building Council's rating system for certifying projects for energy efficiency, resource conservation, and sustainability.[68]

Like other policies, the final stage with building requirements is implementation. Most local governments have agencies that review plans and drawings, issue permits, and inspect work once it is completed. Replacing a roof or furnace would be pretty routine, while getting approval to put an addition onto a house would be a bit more time-consuming given the range of work and contractors involved. In the case of new construction, an occupancy permit is required before people or businesses move in. All of these steps are designed in part to promote safety and protect buyers and renters. The real test, though, is enforcement. If a city does not carefully monitor construction or require licensed workers, and especially if it does not impose sanctions on violators, many projects will be completed informally outside the system.

One often-overlooked participant in housing regulation is the local legal system, particularly the role of the courts in landlord-tenant relations. Recently, wages have not kept pace with rents in many cities, which has challenged low-income workers, retirees, and people with disabilities to keep up with rent payments. Research using legal records nationwide found that over 2 percent of all renters in 2016 received a court-ordered eviction, and more than twice that number received notices that did not end in a court judgment. These actions are more common in the Southeast and areas with high concentrations of African Americans, but they are not confined to large cities. In some places, 7–10 percent of renters have faced a court-ordered eviction.[69]

Landlords are more advantaged in some Southeast and Midwest states and use the courts not just for evictions but to force tenants to pay overdue rent. A report covering the five core counties in Metropolitan Atlanta found that one-third of the one million eviction notices during 2000–2016 were filings against the same tenant at the same address. One company has its managers file eviction notices whenever rent is not paid by the tenth of the month. Most landlords have attorneys for court proceedings, while most tenants do not. Worse for poor renters are the court costs and late payment fees. Moreover, a court judgment can show up on background checks and credit records, making it hard for someone who has been evicted to get another rental.[70] During the Great Recession, the courts, along with local officials such as county treasurers and tax assessors, were also major players in millions of foreclosures.

Some local governments attempt to protect low-income homeowners, particularly seniors, from losing their homes because they are unable to pay their property taxes. This is often done using a homestead exemption that exempts part of the value of an owner-occupied home from property taxes. In Atlanta, for instance, if at least one person on the deed to the home is aged 65 or older with taxable household income under $40,000, the value of the house subject to city property taxes is reduced by $40,000. Seniors also qualify for other homestead exemptions for county and school property taxes, which must be approved by voters.[71] In Louisiana, the state grants a homestead exemption of $7,500 for all owner-occupied homes, plus a freeze in assessed value for those aged 65 or older below a certain income level.[72] Some recent research suggests that state property tax limitations might not protect homeowners in gentrifying neighborhoods, but they are no more likely to move than in other areas. The real movers from gentrifying areas are renters.[73] Nevertheless, foreclosures tend to depress the value of neighboring homes.[74]

Many local governments responded to foreclosure problems by establishing **land banks**, "governmental entities or nonprofit corporations that are focused on the conversion of vacant, abandoned, and tax delinquent properties into productive use."[75] There are over 170 land banks in the US, mainly east of the Mississippi River. Most have an inventory of properties obtained in tax foreclosures. Their strategies include renovating and selling houses, demolishing severely damaged buildings, and selling vacant lots to neighboring homeowners. Some places also have *community land trusts* (CLTs), nonprofits designed to hold properties as affordable housing options. These organizations can complement one another, especially in neighborhoods with both foreclosed properties and growth pressures. For instance, this was the situation in Houston following Hurricane Harvey in 2017.[76]

Another dimension of housing problems is homelessness, which is visible to many Americans on sidewalks, street corners, and freeway ramps. Local governments and nonprofits play a substantial role in providing support services to homeless people, others who lack traditional housing, or those who need short-term assistance. The homeless population in the US was estimated in 2017 to be over 550,000, about one-third of whom did not use shelters or transitional housing.[77] Those paying more than 50 percent of their income for rent are most likely to end up homeless. The numbers do not include those who have doubled up with family and friends—an estimated 4.6 million people in 2016. Local services for homeless people include shelter, food, clothing, and other essentials. Shelters also operate for victims of abuse and domestic violence. Yet many communities treat homelessness as a crime, with arrests for things like sleeping in public, camping, or panhandling.[78]

CRITICAL ISSUES IN THE SHAPING OF URBAN AMERICA

Communities face a range of challenges regarding how they develop economically and physically, with a host of proposed remedies. Promoting economic development requires careful assessment of the community's physical and human resources. A danger for local leaders is selecting strategies to support local businesses and to compete with other places for new investment, especially by large companies. There is often the temptation to invest in physical assets rather than training. One critic summed this up in an essay called "The Uselessness of Economic Development Incentives"—and that was well before the deals with Foxconn and Amazon's HQ2.[79]

A recurring issue with housing is affordability and quality. In places such as California and New York City, housing is terribly expensive. In some rapidly growing areas, there are debates over the meaning and effects of sprawl. In places like San Francisco, housing advocates have promoted more high-rise development, and some have tried unsuccessfully to enact rent controls. Others have promoted zoning changes or incremental strategies like adding accessory apartments to existing structures.[80] In declining or slowly growing areas, the issue is often maintenance of the housing stock, sometimes in the face of abandonment.

Professors Edward Glaeser and Joseph Gyourko have argued for major changes in housing policy to improve supply and affordability. Their basic criticism is that federal policies "have focused on supporting housing demand through tax breaks and cheaper credit, while allowing housing supply to get ever more restricted in many areas of the country." They fault local governments' NIMBYism and argue that the "proper role of the federal governments is to lean against the local tendency to block new projects."[81] This not-uncommon view is captured in figure 12.2.

Figure 12.2 Goals and Critiques of Major Housing Policies

Policy Type	Goals	Critiques
Taxes *Property Taxes* *Impact Fees* *Capital Gains Exclusion*	Raise revenues for public services	Rewards homeowners over renters Distort families' investment decisions
Subsidies *Mortgage Interest Deduction* *Housing Choice Vouchers* *LIHTC*	Encourage homeownership Supplement housing budget for poor families	Larger subsidies for wealthy homeowners than low-income renters
Regulations *Land Use* *Consumer Protection* *Rent Control*	Mitigate negative impacts of new housing on neighbors Provide clear information for housing transactions Protect tenants from rapid rent increases	Block housing supply from growing to meet demand Creates barrriers for apartments relative to single-family homes May increase costs and reduce access to mortgages Reduces housing supply Discourages maintaining safe, healthy housing

Source: Jenny Schuetz, "Under US Housing Policies, Homeowners Mostly Win, while Renters Mostly Lose," *Brookings Metropolitan Policy Update*, July 19, 2018, https://www.brookings.edu/research/under-us-housing-policies-homeowners-mostly-win-while-renters-mostly-lose.

Glaeser and Gyourko argue that housing markets are quite diverse, with at least three general types: limited demand in areas with low prices and little new construction (older cities in the North), moderate prices and abundant new construction (the Sunbelt), and high prices and rare new construction (much of the Northeast and the West Coast). Their agenda includes the following:

- remove local housing authorities from the allocation of vouchers, which would be portable across the entire country;
- eliminate the subsidized production program (LIHTC) because its benefits accrue primarily to landlords rather than renters;
- cap the amount of mortgage interest that homeowners can deduct on their taxes, which they argue benefits high-income buyers in expensive markets.

The tax savings would be rebated to local governments that show sustained increases in housing construction.[02]

Economic development and housing often involve political battles over land use. In growing areas, there often include sprawl, congestion, and the capacity of transportation systems and other infrastructure. For older industrial cities, along with many small towns, population and job losses, along with abandonment, pose multiple problems.

SUMMARY

Local governments have significant impacts on the space they govern because of the land and structures they own, as well as the ways that they regulate private property. Within this context, local officials try to promote the local economy, often in partnership with the private sector. Their efforts include marketing, land and infrastructure, financial incentives like tax breaks and loans, and relief from regulations. Competition among communities is often intense, and critics focus on the large amounts of these incentives, their effectiveness, and companies' lack of accountability.

Local governments also influence development through the infrastructure they provide and their regulatory policies. Infrastructure needs are great, but spending on projects has not kept pace. Property is regulated primarily through zoning, but governments also use building codes, permits, and inspections to influence quality. Housing is also affected by federal policies to assist low-income renters and subsidize home ownership.

Key Terms

brownfields *(253)*

clawback provisions *(259)*

economic development corporation (EDC) *(252)*

foreclosure *(265)*

land banks *(267)*

public-private partnerships (3Ps) *(253)*

tax abatement *(253)*

tax increment financing (TIF) *(254)*

Discussion Questions

1. What strategies could your college town or the city where you grew up pursue to improve the local economy?

2. How controversial are land use and infrastructure in your college town or hometown? What causes division over issues? What can be done to resolve the major controversies?

3. Describe the condition and cost of off-campus housing near your college and university. To what extent does local government regulate landlords effectively?

4. How do you see your college town developing over the next 10 to 20 years? How well is local government planning for this development?

Exercises

1. Use the website Good Jobs First (https://www.goodjobsfirst.org) to develop a list of the financial support of companies in your area. Be sure to identify the firms along with the types and dollar amounts of government financial assistance. Use media and other sources to explain the decisions that were made to aid these companies.

2. Identify two or three land-use issues in your community that have generated controversy during the past few years. What were the disputes? Who were the major participants, and what were their goals and strategies? Explain how the issues were resolved.

Practice and Review Online
https://textbooks.rowman.com/understanding-urban-politics

13

POLICIES TO PROMOTE QUALITY OF LIFE

GUIDING QUESTIONS

1. What issues have local governments had to face in promoting safety for their residents?
2. What strategies have local governments adopted to promote a clean environment for their community? What constraints do they face in these efforts?
3. How can local governments promote amenities that attract and retain residents?
4. What types of controversies have local governments had to address regarding community values? What factors influence these policy decisions?

WHEN PRESIDENT TRUMP announced in June 2017 that the United States would withdraw from the 2015 Paris climate agreement, some of the strongest negative reactions came from over 400 American mayors, led by Eric Garcetti of Los Angeles. Many mayors saw themselves on the front lines in dealing with climate change and signed a pledge to meet the goals of the agreement by reducing greenhouse gas emissions, turning to renewable energy sources, using electric vehicles, and adopting similar policies. Salt Lake City worried that climate change could ruin its winter recreational tourism, coastal areas worried about rising sea levels, and all areas worried about public health. The "Climate Mayors" organization also opposed Trump administration efforts to roll back regulations promoting clean power.[1]

As this account suggests, local governments—and residents, businesses, and a wide array of organizations—are all active in trying to maintain a high quality of life in communities. These efforts take many forms, but most basically they involve creating a locale that is a safe, healthy, and enjoyable place to live and work. That does not mean there is no political conflict over such matters. Far from it.

PUBLIC SAFETY

"Safety" has become an increasingly elusive goal for both residents and local officials. Decades ago, it might have boiled down simply to crime statistics. Today, it extends to concerns such as terrorism, mass shootings, the conduct of police and prosecutors, and hate crimes.

Crime Trends

The FBI has been gathering data for several decades based on reports from local agencies (over 18,500 in 2018), plus estimates for missing data. **Crime rate** is expressed as the number of crimes per 100,000 residents. While 100 murders in a year might seem low for Chicago, it would be positively frightening in suburban Schaumburg. Using this ratio to express the crime rate allows one to compare the intensity of crime over time and among different places. Figure 13.1 is based on the FBI's "Uniform Crime Reports." The figure demonstrates the decline since 2000 in violent crimes (homicide, rape, robbery, and aggravated assault), with an uptick in 2014 before leveling off.

Figure 13.1 Violent Crimes per 100,000 Population, 2000–2018

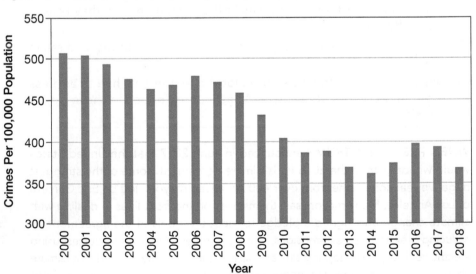

Note: Violent crimes include homicide, rape, robbery, and aggravated assault.

Source: Figure created from data available from the Federal Bureau of Investigation, "Uniform Crime Reporting (UCR) Program," https://www.fbi.gov/services/cjis/ucr.

Figure 13.2 Property Crimes per 100,000 Population, 2000–2018

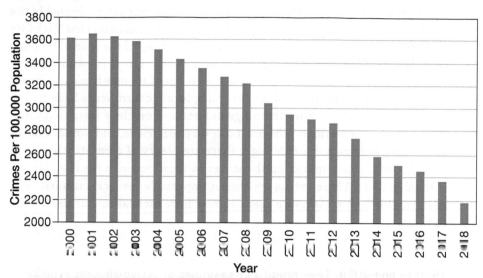

Note: Property crimes include arson, burglary, larceny theft, and motor vehicle theft.

Source: Figure created from data available from the Federal Bureau of Investigation, "Uniform Crime Reporting (UCR) Program," https://www.fbi.gov/services/cjis/ucr.

The trend line was not identical for all types of violence. Homicides ranged between 5.4 and 5.8 per 100,000 from 2000 to 2007 before beginning a long decline to 4.4 in 2014 before jumping back to 5.4 in 2016 and then dropping to 5.3 in 2017 and 5.0 in 2018. Aggravated assault, which includes a weapon or results in a serious injury without one, mirrored the general trend for violent crimes. Robbery declined consistently. Rape followed the general decline until 2013 and then turned upward. The FBI reports two measures: The revised measure has rapes in 2018 as 42.6 per 100,000 compared to its long-standing definition of 30.9 per 100,000.[2]

Property crimes (arson, burglary, larceny theft, and motor vehicle theft) followed a similar pattern (see figure 13.2). Keep in mind that major property crimes are more likely to be reported because of reimbursement from insurance. Burglary experienced a steep decline after 2011. Motor vehicle theft, in contrast, dropped significantly from 2005 to 2011 and then leveled off. Larceny includes crimes such as purse snatching, shoplifting, and theft from a coin-operated machine. Larceny also declined, although it leveled off during 2006–8—the middle of the Great Recession.

These patterns suggest that American communities have become safer during the 21st century, which some observers argue is a key factor in the revival of central cities.[3] Still, crimes vary by type and by city. Despite the significant drop in crime, surveys indicate that many Americans believe that crime has gotten worse.[4] Perhaps this is based on watching their local news, where critics suggest that newscasts follow the policy "If it bleeds, it leads," often with images of crime scenes.

New Threats

The 21st century has also brought new concerns about safety. Probably the most jarring moments were the September 11, 2001 attacks on New York City and Washington, DC. Despite the April 1995 bombing of the federal building in Oklahoma City, terrorism was not a major part of local law enforcement around the country. As you might expect, New York City now has a significant Counterterrorism Bureau.[5] More generally, local governments have had to prepare not just for major bombings but attacks on their water supplies, threats to transit systems, vehicle attacks on pedestrians, and similar events. Plus, terrorists are not just foreign; there are plenty of domestic threats as well, including multiple mass shootings in locations all over the country (see table 13.1). These events are almost impossible for local authorities to predict, although most police agencies now have tactical squads to respond to them.

Perhaps most riveting have been school shootings. The *New York Times* examined a database of more than 1,000 cases of gunfire at schools from 1970 to mid-2019. They found 111 examples of active-shooter attacks on schools, with 202 killed and another 454 injured. Most of the shooters were white boys or young white men, many of whom were current or former students at the schools.[6]

Official Conduct

Perhaps at no time since the civil rights movement and the Vietnam War have the public and the media focused so much on the behavior of police and prosecutors. While there were several notable police killings of civilians during the 1990s and early 2000s, several events in 2012–15 prompted public outcries. The first did not involve a police officer, but a Neighborhood Watch captain in Sanford, Florida, in February 2012. He reported a suspicious person in his gated community and disregarded a dispatcher's advice not to leave his vehicle or engage the person. Shortly thereafter, George Zimmerman shot and killed an unarmed teenager, Trayvon Martin. A flurry of activity followed, and Zimmerman was charged with second-degree murder and acquitted in July 2013.[7] The activist group Black Lives Matter formed following the verdict.

Things became even more heated after that:

- In July 2014, Eric Garner died after being tackled by New York officers and held in a hold, to which he responded, "I can't breathe." The city settled a claim by the victim's family. A grand jury did not indict the officer, who eventually faced an internal inquest in May 2019 that eventually resulted in his termination.[8] This killing generated protests in several cities.
- In August 2014, the police fatally shot teenager Michael Brown in Ferguson, Missouri. Demonstrations followed, the officer was not indicted, and protests escalated. The US Department of Justice issued a highly critical report in

Publ. Safety | **275**

TABLE 13.1	Major US Mass Shootings since 2000		
Date	City	Site	Killed
March 25, 2005	Red Lake, MN	high school	9
April 16, 2007	Blacksburg, VA	Virginia Tech University	32
December 5, 2007	Omaha, NE	shopping mall	8
March 10, 2009	Kinston, AL	home	10
March 29, 2009	Carthage, NC	nursing home	8
April 3, 2009	Binghamton, NY	immigrant community center	13
November 5, 2009	Fort Hood, TX	army base	13
January 19, 2010	Appomattox, VA	home	8
August 3, 2010	Manchester, CT	workplace	8
October 12, 2011	Seal Beach, CA	business	8
July 20, 2012	Aurora, CO	movie theater	12
December 14, 2012	Newtown, CT	Sandy Hook Elementary School	27
September 16, 2013	Washington, DC	Washington Navy Yard	12
June 17, 2015	Charleston, SC	African American church	9
October 1, 2015	Roseburg, OR	community college	9
December 2, 2015	San Bernadino, CA	worker gathering place	14
June 12, 2016	Orlando, FL	Pulse nightclub	49
October 1, 2017	Las Vegas, NV	concertgoers	58
November 5, 2017	Sutherland Springs, TX	church	25
February 14, 2018	Parkland City, FL	Marjory Stoneman Douglas High School	17
May 18, 2018	Santa Fe, TX	high school	10
October 27, 2018	Pittsburgh, PA	Tree of Life Synagogue	11
November 7, 2018	Thousand Oaks, CA	restaurant and bar	12
May 31, 2019	Virginia Beach, VA	local government offices	12
August 3, 2019	El Paso, TX	Walmart store	22

Source: "Mass Shootings in the US: Fast Facts," *CNN*, August 18, 2019, https://www.cnn.com/2019/08/19/us/mass-shootings-fast-facts/index.html.

March 2015, and protests with some vandalism occurred on the anniversary of Brown's killing.[9]

- In October 2014, a Chicago police officer shot teenager Laquan McDonald, who was armed with a knife, sixteen times. Controversy surrounded release of a police dashcam video, and several officers faced charges. Others were eventually exonerated, but the officer who shot McDonald was convicted of second-degree murder and sentenced to 6 years and nine months in prison.

- In November 2014, 12-year-old Tamir Rice was shot to death by police in Cleveland. No indictments were issued, and the officer who killed Rice was fired for other reasons; he got hired for another job, but quickly withdrew in the face of strong opposition.[10]
- In April 2015, a North Charleston, South Carolina, police officer fatally shot Walter Scott. Cell phone video showed the officer shooting Scott in the back. The officer was charged with first-degree murder, but a jury could not reach a verdict. Federal prosecutors charged the officer with using excessive force; he reached a plea deal that dropped all state charges and resulted in a 20-year federal prison sentence.
- Later in April 2015, Freddie Gray died following confinement in a Baltimore prisoner transport van. Violence ensued, but by July 2016, none of the officers involved was convicted.

Similar widely publicized shootings followed, including Philandro Castile in Minnesota in 2016 and others.[11]

The cases just described represent some of the shootings that generated the greatest criticism and protest, particularly with officers not being charged or convicted. Protests were especially likely to occur in places where there was a history of police killings of black people.[12] In a few cases, people ambushed police, including 2016 attacks that killed five officers in Dallas and three in Baton Rouge.[13] The FBI reported that fifty-five officers were killed on duty in 2018, plus several hundred injured.[14] With about 1,000 civilians killed annually, a study by several health researchers found that rates of fatal police shootings of civilians were higher in states with higher levels of household gun ownership.[15] They suggested that states with more private gun ownership may have "higher rates of potentially adversarial police-civilian interactions."[16]

A major newspaper, the *Washington Post*, created a database of police killings of civilians starting in 2015. In 2018, the *Post* counted 992 civilians shot and killed by police, 452 of them white, 229 black, 164 Hispanic, and the rest other or unknown. The most common age category killed was between 30 and 44 (38%), followed by those aged 18–29 (29%). Of those killed, 56 percent were reported to have had a gun, 18 percent had a knife, 5 percent were listed as unarmed, and the remainder were unknown or had another weapon.[17]

There were responses to police actions other than protests. In some cases, local governments adopted policies to establish or strengthen civilian review boards to oversee the police. One report in 2017 found about 200 boards among the nation's roughly 18,000 police departments, mainly in large cities.[18] Structure and procedures vary significantly. For example, the Los Angeles system adopted in 2017 allowed the accused officer to decide whether to face a three-member civilian panel or a panel with one civilian and two high-ranking officers. In New York, the internal inquiry makes a recommendation to the police commissioner, who has the final say on discipline. Some raise concerns about limitations on the background of civilian review board members, the limited resources and information they are provided, and the extent to which reviews by other officers adhere to a chief's disciplinary recommendations, including termination. Another concern is transparency, with the majority of states limiting or prohibiting access to officers' disciplinary records.[19]

Another response has been external, as local governments signed consent decrees with federal or state authorities. There are several actions that the US Department of Justice (DOJ) can take when it appears that a police department has a pattern of civil rights violations. If lesser efforts yield little change, the DOJ can sue, as it did with Ferguson. A resulting consent decree functions like a contract overseen by a federal court without a "guilty" plea by the local government. One study of consent decrees during 1990–2013 in twenty-three jurisdictions suggests that DOJ intervention could reduce individuals' civil rights filings against local departments by as much as 43 percent. The authors add, however, that it is unclear how widespread and long-term these impacts are.[20] Major investigations produced federal consent decrees in Baltimore, Chicago, and Seattle. The Trump administration cut back on such actions, but California's attorney general intervened to force a consent decree with San Francisco.[21] In comparing his city to Baltimore, Rahm Emanuel, then mayor of Chicago, argued that including rank-and-file officers and citizens in the process made reform efforts more effective at reducing both crime and public complaints.[22]

Wrongful convictions have become another controversy. Probably the most visible effort here is the Innocence Project, which has used DNA and other evidence to exonerate those falsely convicted and imprisoned.[23] More than thirty jurisdictions have recognized this problem and have begun to review felony convictions to make sure that proper procedures were followed. The most notable is Brooklyn, where the district attorney's office quashed twenty-five convictions between 2014 and 2019 because of actions by police and prosecutors.[24]

Critics have also faulted law enforcement for the handling of sexual assault cases. Much of this ire focuses on large backlogs in testing sexual assault evidence (*rape kits*), which victims can allow to be used to gather DNA evidence. The backlog can occur when police do not submit kits to labs, or labs do not complete tests. At a cost of about $1,000, testing kits, comparing databases, and other work can lead to identification and prosecution of attackers. Most states do not require kits to be tested, however.

In 2015, *USA Today* identified 70,000 rape kits nationally that had been logged as evidence without ever being tested. Dallas had about 4,000, Phoenix had accumulated almost 1,800 since 2000, and 10,000 were discovered in Detroit in 2008. This situation, which can cause tension between police and prosecutors, is not just a problem in big cities, however.[25] Several organizations have also entered the fray. RAINN (Rape, Abuse & Incest National Network), which has for more than two decades worked on sexual assault, including hotline services, has joined those pressing for full and complete testing of kits.[26] End the Backlog, a project of the Joyful Heart Foundation, highlights the lack of priority by police departments, bias against victims, poor training in handling assault cases, and inadequate policies regarding labs.[27] Pressure from such groups and exposure in the media have led to renewed efforts at testing. End the Backlog argues that such efforts are especially critical in convicting serial rapists.[28]

This discussion suggests the difficult environment of local law enforcement, where officers are expected to protect the public but—like most professions—might work with some "bad apples" or face a problematic organizational culture. Law enforcement agencies are better educated and trained than a generation ago. They are also more diverse, although many police departments have trouble mirroring population changes in their communities.[29]

Hate Crimes

Police and prosecutors have also been pressed to deal with **hate crime**, a "committed criminal offense which is motivated, in whole or in part, by the offender's bias(es) against a race, religion, disability, sexual orientation, ethnicity, gender, or gender identity."[30] Most cases are prosecuted under state laws, which vary, but most include enhanced penalties. Congress required the collection of hate crime statistics in 1990. Federal agencies must report data; submission to the FBI by other law enforcement agencies (including colleges and universities) is voluntary.[31] Note that a hate crime and hate speech are not the same thing. Speech is protected by the First Amendment, but hate crimes are bias-motivated acts, for example, attacking someone based on ethnicity or religion as opposed to getting into a bar fight with another customer.[32] The FBI data cover both single and multiple motives for attacks, although the latter are generally under 1 percent of the total. Data also cover the numbers of incidents, offenses (a single incident could involve several criminal offenses), victims, offenders, and other details.

Hate crimes take many forms. Of the 8,437 offenses in 2017, for example, 5,084 were against individuals. Another 3,115 were crimes against property, 75 percent of them vandalism or destruction of property of individuals, businesses, government, or religious organizations. Of the forty-two arson cases, thirty-one were directed at property of individuals.[33] Venues also varied. Of the 4,131 incidents based on race, ethnicity, or ancestry, 27 percent occurred in residences; 19 percent were in public spaces like streets, sidewalks, or alleys; 7 percent occurred in parking lots or garages; and 10 percent were at schools or colleges. Most of the incidents based on religion occurred in residences (23%), although 15 percent occurred at places of worship.[34] The data do not identify all offenders' races or ethnicities. Among the 8,126 single-bias incidents during 2017, white-against-black incidents were 15 percent while black-against-white were 5 percent. Of the 314 anti-Islamic incidents, 44 percent of offenders were white. In the 131

Figure 13.3 Hate Crime Incidents, 2007–2018

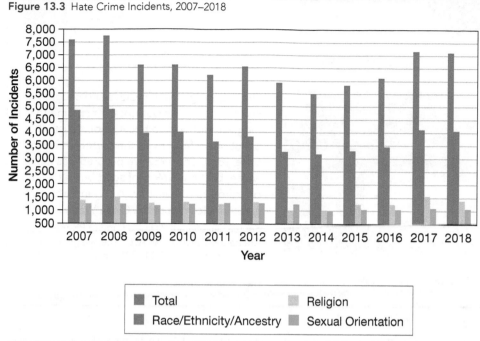

Note: Race/ethnicity/ancestry was identified as a major category in 2015; data for prior years in the figure combine the former categories of race and ethnicity. The number of law enforcement agencies reporting ranged from 13,241 to 16,149. Data for 2013 include the late submissions from four states included in a supplement to the annual report.

Source: Federal Bureau of Investigation, "Hate Crime Statistics," annual reports available at https://www.fbi.gov/services/cjis/ucr/publications#Hate-Crime%20Statistics.

incidents based on gender identity, white and black people each comprised about 32 percent of the offenders.[35]

Figure 13.3 tracks total hate crime incidents from 2007 to 2018, along with single-bias incidents for the three largest categories: race/ethnicity/ancestry, religion, and sexual orientation. Among the other major categories, disability and gender combined total fewer than 125 incidents annually. Gender identity was not included until 2013 and reached a little over 100 cases beginning in 2015. Of the race/ethnicity/ancestry incidents, 47–57 percent targeted African Americans during 2007–17; antiwhite attacks were 13–21 percent. Of the religious incidents in the figure, 50–72 percent were anti-Jewish. The incidents based on sexual orientation are roughly equal in number to those for religion (1,000–1,600 annually).

ENVIRONMENTAL POLICIES

American cities during the industrial era faced a range of threats to people's health and safety, perhaps best depicted by smog looming over many skylines (such as Pittsburgh's) and waste dumped into rivers, lakes, and streams. In some

BOX 13.1

Urban America and Environmental Problems

The Cuyahoga River Burning in Cleveland, 1952

The Cuyahoga River in Cleveland caught fire in June 1969. This was not the first time that the river had burned because of industrial pollution. In fact, it was the thirteenth episode since 1868. The 1952 fire pictured was much worse, but the 1969 conflagration was a fitting backdrop for the first Earth Day in April 1970 and the adoption of the Clean Water Act.

Source: Julie Grant, "How a Burning River Helped Create the Clean Water Act," The Allegheny Front (radio program), April 21, 2017, https://www.allegh-enyfront.org/how-a-burning-river-helped-create-the-clean-water-act.

cases, pollutants even proved combustible (see box 13.1). This is not to mention the impact of invasive species, such as the mussels and Asian carp threatening the Great Lakes.[36]

During the 1960s and 1970s, Congress passed several laws to deal with contamination of air, water, and land; President Nixon created the Environmental Protection Agency (EPA) in 1970 to enforce national standards. States were major partners in implementing and enforcing standards. For local governments, this meant changes in their water and sewer systems, proactive steps in protecting sensitive areas, monitoring of air quality, and other steps.

Protecting Air, Water, and Land

The EPA works with states to monitor compliance with standards for air, water, brownfields, and a range of toxic substances.[37] Governments in urban areas deal in part with **point-source pollution**, an identifiable location such as a sewage treatment plant or factory. Older cities, in particular, have combined sewer systems, which "are designed to collect rainwater runoff, domestic sewage, and industrial wastewater in the same pipe," usually taking all of it to a sewage treatment plant to be treated and then discharged to a body of water. The EPA adds that with heavy rain or melting snow, combined sewer systems can exceed their treatment capacity and can "contain untreated or partially treated human and industrial waste, toxic materials, and debris as well as stormwater." The EPA has identified nearly 860 cities with such combined sewer systems.[38] Discharges from these systems can pose major health threats. There are options for mitigating these, including stormwater diversion strategies, but most cities try to avoid the cost of building separate sanitary and storm sewers.[39] In addition, some areas, including new suburban developments, rely on individual septic tanks, which come with their own challenges.[40]

BOX 13.2

The Flint Water Crisis

Resident Showing Tainted Water to Officials

Flint, the birthplace of General Motors, has been on a path of population and economic decline since the 1950s. Michigan governors responded to its fiscal troubles by appointing a series of emergency financial managers beginning in 2002, all with the goal of reducing the cost of city government. One strategy was to get a cheaper source of water rather than buying it from the city of Detroit, which had its own emergency manager. Flint's new supply of water from Lake Huron would not be available for several years, but Detroit responded in 2014 by cancelling Flint's contract. Flint then turned to the Flint River as a source. Based on assurances from the state, the city did not prepare its water works to guard against corrosion in pipes. What followed was foul water, state reassurances and delay, and the emergency manager's

refusal to reconnect to Detroit. Experts detected heightened levels of lead in the city's water. A task force appointed by the governor issued a damning report in late 2015, and Flint reconnected to Detroit water. There was also a series of resignations and firings at the federal EPA and the Michigan Department of Environmental Quality, along with criminal and civil litigation. In part with $100 million from the EPA, Flint is still trying to identify and replace its many lead water lines with copper. Yet it might be far from alone in combatting threats to local water supplies in the US. This broader problem is one reason two medical professionals, one of whom published a study of blood lead levels in Flint youths, argued against using the word "poisoned" to describe Flint children.

Source: Paul Rozycki, "Flint's Water Crisis: A Case Study in Historical Context, Decline, Responses to Challenges, and State-Local Government Relations," in John S. Klemanski and David Dulio, eds., *Michigan Government, Politics, and Policy* (Ann Arbor: University of Michigan Press, 2017), 343–63; Benjamin J. Pauli, *Flint Fights Back: Environmental Justice and Democracy in the Flint Water Crisis* (Cambridge, MA: MIT Press, 2019). Also see EPA, "Flint Drinking Water Response," https://www.epa.gov/flint; Kristi Pullen Fedinick, Mae Wu, and Erik D. Olson, "Threats on Tap: Widespread Violations Highlight Need for Investment in Water Infrastructure and Protections," National Resources Defense Council, report, May 2, 2017, https://www.nrdc.org/resources/threats-tap-widespread-violations-water-infrastructure; Hernan Gomez and Kim Dietrich, "Flint Kids Were Not 'Poisoned,'" *New York Times*, July 23, 2018, A19.

More difficult are **nonpoint pollution sources**, diffuse locations that produce runoff into streams, including croplands, feed lots, roads and parking lots, suburban development, forestry and mining, and boating.[41] The obvious dilemma is that both point and nonpoint sources affect intake and treatment of water downstream, as well as activities such as fishing. For example, algae growth in Lake Erie during August 2014 forced Toledo, Ohio, to ban use of tap water for the city's 500,000 customers.[42] This is different from the water crisis in Flint, Michigan (see box 13.2).

Implementing the 1970 Clean Air Act has been a federal-state partnership. However, some states have allowed a role for cities and counties. California has established special districts to deal with air quality, and some regions rely on partnerships among governments, nonprofits, and business. Dealing with air pollution in gas or particle form must address both stationary sources such as power plants or landfills and mobile sources such as vehicles. At a minimum, local governments must meet requirements for their buildings, vehicle fleets, landfills, and open burning. One study has found that the presence of an air quality office in a region's largest city has a positive effect on air quality.[43] This was not due to the regulations imposed; instead, "local governments have employed the carrot and the sermon to encourage alternative behaviors across target populations and sectors through cooperation and collaboration."[44] In addition, organizations such as the International City/County Management Association (ICMA) and National League of Cities (NLC) provide resources such as reports, suggestions for best practices, and blogs to help their members deal with air quality and other environmental issues.[45]

Damage to land has gone on for generations. Perhaps the worst legacies are brownfields (see chapter 12), abandoned, idle, or underused industrial and commercial properties where expansion or redevelopment is complicated by real or perceived environmental contamination. The Environmental Protection Agency estimates that there are over 450,000 brownfields in the US.[46] In 1980, Congress enacted the so-called **Superfund law**, which established a tax on the chemical and petroleum industries to clean up the nation's toxic waste sites. Many of these locations had been abandoned, so it was often difficult to assign liability for the hazards. The first strategy is to negotiate with responsible parties, but litigation is an alternative.[47] Many local governments have also been pressured to address *environmental justice*, the tendency of flood-prone zones, landfills, noxious industries, and other health-threatening sites to be concentrated in neighborhoods inhabited by the poor and communities of color.[48]

Sustainability

Beyond the efforts to promote air and water quality, since the late 1980s there has been growing pressure to advance *sustainability*, a broad concept that focuses on policies to balance what planners have called the three Es: environment, economy, and equity. How these elements are balanced is a continuing source of conflict. Historically, planners have long been involved in debates about shaping the urban environment.[49] Often added to the mix is an effort to make conditions better for subsequent generations.[50] As Portney explains, "The basic premise of sustainability is that Earth's resources cannot be used, depleted, and damaged indefinitely."[51]

Implementation of strategies for sustainability has taken multiple forms. Americans probably associate it most with their local recycling programs. In 2015, 25.8 percent of the 262 million tons of municipal solid waste was recycled, and another 8.9 percent was composted. Another 13 percent was combusted with energy recovery, but that left 52.5 percent (137 million tons) going to landfills. This was a major improvement from the recycling rates of the late 1980s, when about two-thirds of recyclables were paper and cardboard. Still, Americans throw out an average of almost 4.5 pounds of waste per person daily.[52]

Communities have made it easier to recycle, with many using **single-stream recycling**, which allows consumers to place materials in a single container rather than sorting them (usually into paper and nonpaper waste) for collection. This leaves the local government or a private contractor to sort materials. Two trends have made recycling more difficult in recent years: users' behavior and the recycling market. Easier recycling seems to have made people less careful about what they discard for recycling, particularly nonacceptable items like plastic bags or contaminated plastic and paper products (such as the ubiquitous greasy pizza box). This prompted China, the largest buyer of materials from the US, to impose tough standards and reduce its purchases. Recyclable materials already compete in the market with "new" products created from raw materials, and China's action drove down the price of many recycled materials. Given these reduced prices, trash companies began raising recycling fees to local governments. Faced with much higher costs, some communities dropped recycling altogether and sent materials to landfill sites or incinerators, which have their own problems.[53]

In addition to waste management, sustainability efforts have extended to water, sanitation, transportation, renewable energy sources such as wind and solar, land use, and buildings.[54] Cities have modified their zoning codes to encourage higher density, increase transportation alternatives and protection of ecosystems, and improve stormwater management, tree canopies, and local food production.[55] Many cities, though, still do not have strong policies in place to prevent construction in flood-prone areas, not to mention allowing rebuilding after flooding. Instead, the focus has been on clean-up after the fact.[56]

National organizations have also created metrics to assess sustainability efforts. One of the more visible is LEED (Leadership in Energy and Environmental Design) certification, established by the US Green Building Council (USGBC), which was founded in 1993. LEED uses a points system to designate building design and construction, interior design and construction, building operations and maintenance, neighborhood development, homes, and cities and communities as certified, silver, gold, or platinum.[57] USGBC also has a system for certifying professionals.[58] Finally, individual leaders and organizations like the US Conference of Mayors have opposed the Trump administration's withdrawal from the 2015 Paris Climate Accord and have taken local actions to deal with climate change.[59]

URBAN AMENITIES

Beyond health and safety, quality of life also includes *amenities*, features that make a place enjoyable—architecture, natural and scenic areas, parks, museums, libraries, performing arts venues, convenient services, night life, and much more.

These things do not just happen but result from innumerable decisions by governments, businesses, individuals, and groups.

Sites and Sights

American cities in the 1800s were often crowded, chaotic, polluted, and unsightly. Public officials reacted to these conditions with efforts to acquire public spaces for events, relaxation, recreation, and socializing. New York City began developing Central Park in the decade before the Civil War under Frederick Law Olmsted, considered the father of landscape architecture, who also designed major projects in New York, Chicago, Buffalo, Boston, Detroit, Atlanta, Louisville, and elsewhere during the late 1800s.[60] Olmsted teamed up with architect Daniel Burnham to design the 1893 World's Fair in Chicago; along with Charles McKim, they developed the plan for the National Mall in Washington, DC. Burnham also developed the master plan for Chicago, perhaps the landmark project during the rise of "The City Beautiful Movement" in the 1890s. Such initiatives were instrumental in adding large public spaces along Lake Michigan in Chicago and Milwaukee, Golden Gate Park and the Civic Center in San Francisco, and major public buildings and botanical gardens throughout the country. Aside from aesthetics, local elites saw public space as a remedy for many of the social ills of urban life.

Efforts to carve out public sites have continued, with everything ranging from establishing dog parks, skate parks, and neighborhood pocket parks to replacing freeway routes in Milwaukee, San Francisco, Portland, and Seattle. It has included repurposing space as well, such as converting former railroad lines to trails and waterfront industrial land to walkways. Perhaps the most unusual of these is New York City's High Line (see box 13.3).

Beyond efforts to create sites that make urban living more attractive, cities have taken steps to enhance their visual appeal. This can be as simple as landscaping and public art, but it is also associated with the rise of historic preservation. Early efforts included a commission established in 1925 to help preserve historic structures in New Orleans' French Quarter and a 1930 ordinance in Charleston, South Carolina, to regulate the city's historic buildings. In 1949, the National Trust for Historic Preservation formed as a nonprofit that "protects significant places representing our diverse cultural experience by taking direct action and inspiring broad public support." This mission extends not only to endangered buildings but also to landscapes and communities.[61]

Perhaps best captured by Jane Jacobs' activism in New York City and her 1961 book, *The Death and Life of Great American Cities*, a backlash developed against the destruction of neighborhoods for freeways and urban renewal.[62] The push for historic preservation was fueled further by the uproar when New York City allowed the demolition of Pennsylvania Station, which was opened to train passengers in 1910, to build Madison Square Garden. These and similar actions led Congress to enact tax credits for investing in the rehabilitation and reuse of historic buildings, the establishment of state tax breaks and

BOX 13.3

Innovative Ways to Create Public Spaces

Originally designed as rail connections to the second level of warehouses and factories on the west side of Manhattan, the High Line was largely abandoned or destroyed by the 1980s. By the 2000s, an effort began to convert the space into a park. Today, it extends almost a mile and a half, is maintained by a nonprofit and the city, and includes plants and trees. No dogs or bikes are allowed, and it attracts thousands of visitors daily.

Source: The High Line, "History," https://www.the highline.org/history.

New York City's High Line

historic preservation offices, and adoption of local historic preservation ordinances throughout the country. One 2016 estimate puts the benefits at 1,299 completed projects generating $7.16 billion in rehabilitation work and over 108,000 jobs.[63]

History is not without controversy, however. Residents often battle with local historic commissions over which properties should receive a historic designation, changes to historic structures such as an addition to a house, or the appropriateness of building materials or paint colors. More recent conflicts have focused on memorials, especially Confederate monuments constructed during the codification of legal segregation during the early 1900s. Some cities have removed monuments, including four large ones in New Orleans, but several southern legislatures have moved to prohibit such local actions.[64]

Arts and Entertainment

People moving to any metropolitan or micropolitan area would expect to find movie theaters, performing arts programs in schools and colleges, live music of several genres, museums, good restaurants, sporting events, perhaps wineries and microbreweries, and more. The private sector provides many of these opportunities, but government and nonprofits often play a role as well. The government's role usually involves providing facilities and subsidies, and most arts organizations are set up as nonprofits.

The League of American Orchestras reported in 2014 that there were over 1,200 orchestras distributed across all fifty states, contributing $1.8 billion to the US economy and drawing audiences totaling almost twenty-five million people. The cautionary tale, though, was that two-thirds of the orchestras operated on budgets under $300,000, saw single-ticket sales surpass subscription sales, and provided more free concerts while ticket prices fell.[65] Many areas have regional theater companies using professional actors, community theaters relying upon amateurs, local opera or ballet companies, summer theater, and music festivals. These organizations are typically set up as nonprofits, but they often use public facilities.

Smaller urban areas are often home to sports franchises. Minor league baseball includes over 150 teams, most independently owned but connected to a Major League club. There are similar leagues for basketball and hockey. As with the arts, these teams generally utilize publicly owned facilities. Together, these arts and sports organizations enhance the quality of life by providing a wide range of entertainment options for urban areas large and small.

MORALITY POLITICS: BATTLING OVER COMMUNITY VALUES

Research on urban politics often focuses on participants' economic motivations or goals. Morality politics is different. We often think of **morality politics** in terms of modern-day "culture wars." Elaine Sharp describes morality politics as political conflict grounded in moral concerns that is extraordinarily passionate and strident, is broad-based rather than organized by neighborhoods, and often involves nonconventional forms of participation.[66] Similarly, Kenneth Meier describes morality politics as "one segment of society attempt[ing] by government fiat to impose their values on the rest of society."[67] Assumed in both of these characterizations is the effort to control people's conduct.

These controversies are nothing new. It might not have been labeled "quality of life" in the 1800s, but local activists and officials made great effort to promote what they considered appropriate behavior and establishments. These early conflicts dealt with things like alcohol and obscenity, but similar battles continue today over things like drugs and abortion clinics. On the flip side, since at least the 1960s, many communities have proposed or adopted policies seeking to protect marginalized groups: open-housing ordinances, protections for LGBTQ residents, needle-exchange programs, and similar policies.

The Long History of Policies to Regulate All Things Sexual

Local conflicts over morality date to the 1800s. The most pervasive policies prohibited prostitution and obscenity. Commercial sex might seem easy to define and prohibit; however, prostitution is legal in eight rural counties in

Nevada.[68] The Bureau of Justice Statistics reported almost 48,000 arrests in 2014 for prostitution and commercialized vice; 66 percent of those arrested were women.[69]

Defining what is obscene has proven more difficult, as the US Supreme Court demonstrated in multiple cases beginning in the 1950s. Justice Potter Stewart was left to conclude famously, "I know it when I see it."[70] The court eventually came up with more specific standards, and various federal and state laws regulate certain practices. Still, it has fallen to local officials to police what a community might deem obscene. Early efforts targeted books and other printed material because of their sexual content. Censors later restricted films and a range of "adult entertainment" establishments.

Decency advocates convinced Congress to ban interstate distribution of "lewd" or "indecent" books in the 1870s, which included a book on using contraception. Controversies have often occurred over availability of items in public libraries and public schools for reasons ranging from offensive language and religious objections to inclusion of homosexuality. The American Library Association publicizes these efforts each fall during "Banned Books Week." The most commonly challenged book during 2000–2009? The *Harry Potter* series, with Mark Twain's *Huckleberry Finn* at #14 and Harper Lee's *To Kill a Mockingbird* at #21.[71]

Outright prohibition of things considered obscene has been difficult given courts' application of the 1st Amendment's free speech guarantee as it relates to adults. For example, the Georgia Supreme Court overturned local ordinances that prohibited nude dancing in clubs, holding that such expression was protected under the US and state constitutions. The legislature responded by asking voters to approve a constitutional amendment in 1994 that allowed local governments to prohibit the sale of alcohol at such establishments. After the amendment passed overwhelmingly, cities tried to drive nude clubs out of business by prohibiting alcohol sales, which the court subsequently ruled were not constitutionally protected.[72]

Similarly, the US Supreme Court overturned Indianapolis's feminist-inspired ordinance banning pornography as sex discrimination. Local governments have had more leeway, however, in using zoning to regulate adult entertainment and places serving alcohol. Such ordinances often limit business hours and locations, such as proximity to schools, churches, or residential areas.[73]

Battles over Alcohol, Gambling, and Drugs

Most Americans probably assume that battles over alcohol ended when the 21st Amendment to the US Constitution ended Prohibition in 1933. What it actually did was return regulation of alcohol to the states and their local governments, where there was already a long history of conflict. After the Civil War, the Women's Christian Temperance Union campaigned against alcohol, as did the Prohibition Party, which had limited electoral success. They were joined in 1893 by the Anti-Saloon League, which saw the evils of saloons extending beyond drinking to gambling and prostitution. These battles generally pitted middle-class, white Protestants and their churches against working-class, immigrant, and Catholic residents in cities, where political machines often had connections to saloons and brewers.[74] With the repeal of Prohibition, eight states opted to remain dry, mainly southern and border states with a strong fundamentalist Protestant presence. Another fifteen states created agencies for the sale of alcohol, while the remaining twenty-five adopted a licensing system for alcohol sales. Both systems for selling liquor generated revenues for state governments. Initially, thirty-eight states allowed local governments the option of becoming dry.[75]

States still retain control over alcohol policies. Nevada has the most liberal policies; aside from drinking age, alcohol is virtually unregulated. In other states, local governments often regulate licensing for bars and retail outlets, identify hours of operation for bars and for retail sales of alcohol, and monitor whether establishments sell to those who are underage. Local governments also use zoning to limit the locations of places selling alcohol, which is supported by many public health experts.[76]

In addition to their crusades against alcohol, 19th-century activists also targeted gambling. Local police departments often had "vice squads" targeting gaming, which was often run by organized crime groups. Today, however, government is in the gambling business—big time. State lotteries started in the Northeast during the 1960s and 1970s to help shore up finances. By 2013, forty-four states had adopted them, including those in the Bible Belt, with modest impacts on state budgets.[77]

Drugs were largely unregulated until the late 1800s. Aimed mainly at Chinese immigrants, local ordinances in California and then a state law in 1881 banned the smoking of opium. Local ordinances and state laws in areas with large Hispanic or black populations outlawed the use of marijuana by 1930. Federal regulation of narcotics began in 1914, was followed by the Marijuana Tax Act of 1937, and created tougher penalties for drug use and distribution beginning in the 1960s. Many states joined these efforts during the antidrug campaigns of the 1980s and 1990s.[78] As with other morality campaigns, local governments had to share the burden of enforcement and prosecution.

In his 1994 book, political scientist Kenneth Meier reminds us that, despite their limited success, "drug wars are good politics."[79] That could have changed during the two decades since his claim, however. By 2015, four western states had adopted initiatives legalizing the sale and possession of marijuana, and more than a dozen had decriminalized possession. More states have made the drug legal since then, with pressure within others to follow suit. Using marijuana remains illegal under federal law.

Colorado, the first state to legalize it, allowed local governments to decide whether or not to have recreational marijuana establishments. Cities and counties tended to follow their residents' prevailing values, which were somewhat evident in election results in the statewide vote. The majority of places chose to ban sales. Local adopters generally had experience with medical marijuana, and it usually took multiple departments to plan and implement the change, including zoning, licensing, and law enforcement.[80] In 2018, the state collected over $266 million in taxes, licenses, and fees for marijuana, much of which goes to school construction and programs.[81] Colorado taxes marijuana sales at 15 percent and returns 10 percent of the total to the jurisdictions where it is sold. Local governments can add their own sales taxes on top of that. One study estimated that local governments would take in $80 million in 2018 with special marijuana taxes, but some also levied a regular sales tax. The revenue was important in smaller communities, as were jobs related to cultivation, distribution, and sales. Cities and counties used the money for homeless services, college scholarships, and other programs.[82]

Abortion and Other Protests

Many observers think of abortion politics as being fought at the national and state levels. That ignores the extent to which services are delivered in specific locations. Abortion opponents often target individual clinics, while others seek to protect them, their employees and volunteers, and their clients. All of this can put local governments in the political hot seat. These conditions can be worsened if national groups join the fray, as when Operation Rescue targeted Denver in 1989. That experience exposed the dilemmas of managing the competing interests of clinic access versus the ability to protest, with police, prosecutors, and elected officials developing strategies over time so that normalcy was more or less in place by the mid-1990s.[83] Local officials must still contend with abortion protests, as well as those related to police conduct, immigration, white nationalism, and other volatile issues.

Protection for Marginalized Groups

On what many see as the liberal side of the policy agenda, communities have sought to display support of diversity and a welcoming environment with ordinances prohibiting discrimination based on multiple personal characteristics, including race, ethnicity, gender, religion, age, sexual orientation, and gender identity. Many have also adopted policies to aid groups like immigrants and those dealing with addiction.

State and local nondiscrimination laws have long covered race, ethnicity, gender, and religion, but their passage was not always easy, especially regarding housing. Subsequent calls to protect members of the LGBTQ community have been at least as controversial. Efforts began in college towns, starting in 1972 with East Lansing (home of Michigan State University). LGBTQ protection encountered a backlash from religious conservatives, who gained national visibility when celebrity Anita Bryant led a successful campaign to repeal a 1978 protective ordinance in Dade County (Miami), Florida. Nonetheless, nondiscrimination measures were increasingly adopted in the 1980s and 1990s. However, they varied in the extent to which they covered employment, housing, or other activities.[84] Some states tried to undercut local ordinances by prohibiting them, but the US Supreme Court overturned one such measure because it prevented only one group—gay men and lesbians—from being granted protection.[85] Over time, many cities and counties (at least 225 by early 2018) had ordinances that included gender identity, although this, too, generated backlash, most visibly in state preemption of a measure adopted by Charlotte, North Carolina, in 2014.[86]

The most recent local efforts to protect marginalized groups have attempted to blunt deportation of immigrants. Several hundred local governments fall under the label of "sanctuary city." This has generally taken the form of refusal to cooperate with agents of US Immigration and Customs Enforcement (ICE), but Los Angeles, San Francisco, and Chicago are among the cities that have established legal aid funds for immigrants facing deportation. The Trump administration has attempted to outlaw such practices or withhold federal funds from so-called sanctuary cities.[87] These efforts have been opposed by organizations such as the National League of Cities and the US Conference of Mayors.[88] At the other extreme was the Maricopa County (Phoenix, Arizona) sheriff, Joe Arpaio, who built a reputation targeting illegal immigrants until defeated at election in 2016. Ironically, Arpaio was subject to prosecution for violating a federal court order to stop his targeting practices until he was pardoned by President Trump.[89]

SUMMARY

Many local government policies can affect residents' quality of life. Most have benefited from a significant drop in major crimes during the past two decades, although they have increasingly contended with terrorism threats and mass shootings. More recently, many have had to confront problems with police and prosecutors, including fatal shootings of civilians, wrongful convictions, inadequate pursuit of sexual assault cases, and lack of protection from hate crimes.

Many local governments have sought to protect the local environment with policies regarding clean air and water, use of renewable energy sources, recycling, and building construction. They have also created a wide variety of public spaces, tried to maintain historic locations, and supported entertainment and the arts as key amenities. Finally, the pursuit of a higher quality of life has occasionally involved efforts to determine and promote a community's values, including a range of issues from alcohol and tobacco, abortion, prostitution, drugs, and gambling to immigration.

Key Terms

crime rate (272)
hate crime (278)
morality politics (286)
nonpoint pollution sources (281)

point-source pollution (280)
single-stream recycling (283)
Superfund law (282)

Discussion Questions

1. How safe is your college town or hometown? How well does local law enforcement interact with residents, and how does that vary among groups or locations?

2. What kinds of actions does your city or college/university take to promote environmental quality? How successful are they? Are there other things that they should be doing? If so, how feasible or publicly acceptable are they?

3. How vibrant is your area in terms of cultural, artistic, recreational, and entertainment options? Are there any major gaps in these opportunities? If so, how would you fill them?

4. Are there issues in your city or on your campus that pit groups with significantly opposing values against each other? What is the basis for these disagreements, and how have they been—or how can they be—resolved?

Exercises

1. This exercise covers several alternatives for analyzing public safety. Your instructor will probably add more detail. Start by reviewing the FBI's overview of the data it provides: https://www.fbi.gov/services/cjis/ucr.

   a. Use the Crime Data Explorer to examine changes in the rates of major crimes in your state and then for one or more jurisdictions assigned by your instructor, who could also have you cover certain periods of time and ask you to compare local rates to state or national trends. All of these designations are controlled with the tabs at the left of the page. Below the graphs are icons that allow you to download the data to spreadsheets.

   b. Review figure 13.3 and the FBI's description and FAQ on hate crimes. From "Resources" at the bottom of the page, use the annual reports link. For the most recent year, follow the links for "Hate Crimes by Jurisdiction." Tables 11 and 13 will allow you to see the number and types of hate crimes in specific states and places. Your instructor could have you cover a specific place (called "agency" in the data), record the totals, and then analyze local media coverage of these crimes. Another alternative would be to compare hate crimes in different years. That will require you to examine different annual reports and probably build your own spreadsheet before examining how much different types of hate crimes have changed over time.

2. Based on its website or other sources, determine the extent to which your city, county, or college/university has goals regarding sustainability or climate change. Examine the extent to which these goals can be measured, the extent to which they are being met, and how performance could be improved. For example, your city

might have goals for renewable energy sources (e.g., use of electric vehicles or reliance on solar power) or recycling (participation levels, tons of waste kept out of landfill, etc.)

3. Determine how many municipalities in your county have historic preservation ordinances. Select one community and review its ordinance. Identify how many historic districts or structures the city has classified. Review media accounts and minutes from the historic commission to describe the kinds of problems with and controversies over preservation that the community faces. How valuable do you think preservation is to the community?

4. Develop a profile of the arts in your community, primarily by identifying venues/organizations, their budgets, and ticket sales. How do they raise money? Identify broader effects on the community from the work of these organizations.

Practice and Review Online
https://textbooks.rowman.com/understanding-urban-politics

Glossary

A

administration A main component of local governance that refers to the execution of policy; ideally it should be handled by administrators

ad valorem sales tax A percentage tax applied to the total value of items in a purchase

agenda setting The act of establishing the policy priorities of the city

annexation The process of a city adding unincorporated territory to its city limits

assessment ratio The percentage of fair market value applied to the assessed value of a property for tax purposes

at-large elections Elections in which candidates for city council run city-wide rather than in particular districts

at-large representation system System of representation in which each legislator represents the jurisdiction as a whole

B

benchmarking Comparison of local performance against a national standard

block grants Federal funds for a range of activities that are usually awarded based on formulas; they give local officials more discretion and less federal oversight than categorical grants

bonds Financial instruments sold by local governments that promise to pay back the principal (amount borrowed) plus a guaranteed interest rate to purchasers

boosterism Enthusiastic promotion of a place to stimulate its growth and economic development

brownfields Abandoned, idle, or underused industrial and commercial properties where expansion or redevelopment is complicated by real or perceived environmental contamination

C

campaign Organized effort to persuade and mobilize voters to support or oppose a candidate or cause

campaign message The issues and themes that candidates create and run on to persuade voters to support them

candidate-centered elections Elections in which candidates, rather than parties or groups, take the initiative to run, build, and fund their campaigns

candidate emergence The process that moves people to declare candidacy

capital budgets Expenses and revenues for long-term, durable assets such as buildings, roads, bridges, and certain types of equipment

categorical grants Federal funds that must be used for specific purposes, usually with a required application and often along with local matching funds; the federal agency administering the grant has significant discretion in imposing standards on the "winners" selected to receive the funds

citizen contacting Actions by people to inform and therefore prompt government to do something

citizen lobbyists Regular people in a community who identify issues,

develop political goals, and lobby local government

city charter A "constitution" that lays out the structure of city government; assigns authority among various officials and bodies; details procedures such as elections, lawmaking, and charter revision; and specifies certain rights and protections

city council Local legislature at the municipal or city level

Civil Rights Act of 1964 Federal legislation that outlawed racial segregation in public places, including businesses, and banned employment discrimination based on race, national origin, religion, or sex

civil service A system of hiring and promotion based on certain qualifications, which usually include level of education and examination scores

class bias Degree to which electoral participation is skewed in the direction of particular economic groups

clawback provisions Agreements requiring companies to pay back government financial support if they fail to meet promised employment or other goals

collective action Efforts taken by a group in pursuit of a common objective

collective bargaining A term used to describe how labor and management negotiate union contracts

Combined Statistical Areas (CSAs) Two or more adjacent metropolitan and micropolitan statistical areas that have substantial employment interchange

commission-administrator County form of government in which elected commissioners serve as the legislature but appoint a chief executive to manage and administer the county on a day-to-day basis

commission-elected executive County form of government in which elected commissioners serve as the legislature but the chief executive is elected on a countywide basis to lead the executive branch

community power structure Web of elites that dominate local decision-making and policy

consolidation The process of merging a city with another city or its overlapping county

constituency service Practice of responding to constituent demands to solve particular problems, often involving a local bureaucracy

contextual effects Features of the environment that affect individual political actors, for example, demographics, city size, electoral competition, and campaigns

contracting out A decision by a local government to hire a private company to perform a service, such as paving streets, collecting trash, or mowing grass in parks

contrast advertising Campaign advertising that contains both positive information about the sponsor of an ad and negative information about an opponent

Core Based Statistical Area (CBSA) Counties or equivalent entities associated with at least one core urbanized cluster with a population of at least 10,000, plus any adjacent counties with a high degree of social and economic integration with the core as measured through commuting ties with counties associated with the core

council-manager system A form of local government in which voters elect a city council, which in turn hires a professional manager to run city operations on a day-to-day basis

county board Local legislature at the county level

county commission County form of government in which elected commissioners perform both legislative and executive functions

creative class A socioeconomic class composed of people whose work involves creating meaningful new forms, typically well educated and including engineers, scientists, designers, entertainers and artists, researchers, editors, knowledge-intensive workers in finance and business, and similar professionals

crime rate The number of crimes per 100,000 residents in a given location

D

defensive contributing Tendency of committed followers to rally to their favored candidate by donating more money in the face of negative information

de jure segregation Racial segregation enacted by law and enforced by government

democracy vouchers A campaign finance reform program in which residents get a set amount of money from taxes to support candidates of their choice

democratic accountability Ability of the citizenry to hold the government accountable for its performance

deracialized campaign A campaign waged by minority candidates that deemphasizes issues that might be viewed through a racial lens

descriptive representation The extent to which those who serve in the institutions of government look like, in demographic, political, and ideological terms, the people they are supposed to represent

direct democracy Form of democracy in which citizens become directly involved in the process of self-government through activities such as elections, especially on policy questions

discretion The freedom street-level bureaucrats have to execute their jobs when directives from appointed and elected officials are unclear

E

earned media Media coverage gained through campaign activities

economic development corporation (EDC) A relatively independent nonprofit organization established by a local government with authority and resources to enhance the local economy

edge cities Outlying office, retail, and logistics clusters that challenged the role of the traditional downtown

electoral coalition The economic, racial/ethnic, and/or neighborhood-based alliance of groups that prevail behind the successful candidate or set of candidates in an election

electoral majority A number of votes in an election equal to 50 percent plus one vote

electoral mandate The message sent by the results of an election that guides the agenda of the winning candidate

elitism An interest group theory arguing that economic and social elites are the primary decision-makers in a polity

eminent domain Government seizure of private property for a public purpose in exchange for compensation to the property owner

enterprise funds Revenues and expenses for a specific service, such as water or sewers, that are sequestered and restricted to its operations rather than being included in the wide range of services supported by a general fund

excise tax Tax applied per unit of a specific item sold

exit A response to dissatisfaction where a person exits a city for a different one; often referred to as "voting with your feet"

exportable tax A tax, such as a sales tax, that can be applied to nonresidents

expressive protests Protests that express a viewpoint on an issue or a condition, or simply anger at government actions or officials

externalities Actions affecting a party that is not involved in a transaction or activity

exurbs Areas at the fringes of metropolitan areas characterized by low density, high growth, and significant numbers of workers commuting to jobs in adjoining urbanized areas

F

feedback loop The last stage in the policy process in which residents and others react to impacts and often act to influence the agenda by defending the policy or trying to redefine the problem or modify the solution

fiscal year The twelve-month period covered by a budget, which is named after the calendar year in which it ends

foreclosure The process by which a lender or local government moves to reclaim a property because the homeowners have fallen behind on their mortgage payments, property taxes, or both

formal powers The legal authority given to elected officials to act in their official capacities

franchise A license to sell a product to the public under government regulation

free riding A situation in which a member of group fails to contribute to the group effort but nevertheless derives a benefit because someone else steps up to do the work

frontrunner A candidate who is leading in the polls

G

general fund Revenue that is not assigned to a specific fund and that can be spent for a broad range of purposes as decided by the elected governing body

general obligation (GO) bonds Debt instruments that pledge tax revenues to pay off the debt

general-purpose governments Local governments that perform a range of public services, normally counties, municipalities, and (in some states) towns

general-purpose local governments Local governments that provide a range of services within their territories, which may include counties, municipalities, and townships

general referent contact Nonvoting form of participation where a resident contacts city government to express an opinion or alert the city to a matter of general concern

get-out-the-vote (GOTV) Efforts made by candidates and campaigns to mobilize voters to participate in and support them in their effort to win an election

globalization The increasing interaction and integration of people, companies, and governments around the world

governing coalition Coalition of groups and political leaders that effectively govern a community toward a set of policy goals

government bureaucracy The departments of local government instituted to deliver services and enforce law for a population

government vending Government producing a service for which it charges a fee, such as a toll bridge or water and sewer service

grants Financial support by government that subsidizes service providers, who normally have to apply and meet certain criteria

grants-in-aid Funds made available to local governments for specified purposes and under guidelines set by the higher-level government

Great Migration The movement of millions of southerners to the North and West (primarily black people relocating to cities) between World War I and the 1960s

group-centered elections Elections in which local party machine and nonpartisan slating groups are the dominant actors

growth machine The constellation of interests in finance, real estate, banking, development, and media that promote a growth agenda

H

hate crime A committed criminal offense which is motivated, in whole or in part, by the offender's bias(es) against a race, religion, disability, sexual orientation, ethnicity, gender, or gender identity

heuristic A cognitive shortcut used in decision-making

home rule Grant of authority to cities that permits them to do anything not prohibited by the state, usually including the ability to amend their charters

homestead exemption Policy that reduces the assessed value of a property by a certain amount before taxing the remaining value, usually for a homeowner's primary residence or for certain classes of people such as seniors, disabled veterans, or those below a certain income level

homestead exemption A legal provision that exempts part of the value of an owner-occupied home from property taxes

I

impacts The broad set of effects of a policy, both intended and unintended

implementation The stage in the policy process in which government agencies or other organizations carry out a policy that has been adopted

income tax Applies a tax at a certain percentage to the income of a person or business

incorporated place Formal designation of a municipality; municipal corporation

incorporation The process of creating a new municipal government under requirements set out in state law

incumbency advantage Electoral advantage that currently serving officials (incumbents) have over their challengers

informal powers Conditions in the environment that enhance a political leader's power

information costs Time and effort required to gather information on candidates and policy proposals

initiative A process that permits citizens to sign petitions to put a question before voters to accept or reject

institution An organization that manages potential conflicts between political rivals, helps them find mutually acceptable solutions, and makes and enforces the society's collective agreements

instrumental protest Protest designed to achieve some tangible result or response from government for the people demanding action

insurgent campaign A campaign designed to mobilize minority group members and other liberals, particularly whites, by stressing progressive themes on social issues like economic justice, discrimination, and civil rights

interest group Group of like-minded individuals who band together to influence the policy agenda

intergovernmental agreement A contract between local governments about sharing or hiring a service, as when governments agree to split costs for a 911 call center or a small city hires the county sheriff for law enforcement

intergovernmental revenue Money provided to local governments by the state or federal governments

Interstate Highway System A network of multi-lane roads authorized by Congress in 1956 to connect the nation's urban centers that permitted high speeds without traditional intersections

L

land banks Governmental entities or nonprofit corporations that are focused on the conversion of vacant, abandoned, and tax-delinquent properties into productive use

localism Motivation for city council service rooted in the desire to help people or a political party

logrolling Common legislative practice of trading votes in return for support

loyalty A response to dissatisfaction that suggests a more optimistic view, including voting in local elections, speaking positively about the city, or attending community functions

M

management A main component of local governance that relates to organizational matters, such as overseeing the personnel needs of city government; ideally it should be handled by administrators

mandate A requirement imposed on one government by a higher-level government

mandates Orders by a higher-level government to a lower-level government to meet a certain standard or follow a specific procedure

mayoral leadership styles Styles of leadership that often reflect the time in which the mayor is governing. Examples include city boss, entrepreneur, crusader, broker, manager, and facilitative leader

merit system A system of hiring employees based on merit rather than on politics

Metropolitan Statistical Areas (MSAs) Core Based Statistical Areas with a core urbanized area of at least 50,000 people

Micropolitan Statistical Areas Core Based Statistical Areas with a core urban cluster of between 10,000 and 50,000 people

millage Property tax rate calculated as the dollar amount of tax per thousand dollars of valuation

Millennials A generation born sometime between 1980 and 1995

mission A main component of local governance in which a statement of broad policy goals is identified; ideally it should be established by elected officials and supported by relevant policies

mixed-representation system System of city council representation in which some councilors represent districts or wards and some councilors represent the city at large

morality politics Political conflict grounded in moral concerns that is extraordinarily passionate and strident, is broad-based rather than organized by neighborhoods, and often involves nonconventional forms of participation

N

negative advertising Campaign advertising that targets an opponent and contains only negative information (aka attack speech)

neglect A response to dissatisfaction that includes behaviors such as not voting and feelings of distrust towards those in power and hopelessness regarding the future of the city

NIMBYism (Not In My Backyard) Neighbors organizing to fight the introduction of unwanted land uses or residents in their area

nonpartisan elections Elections in which ballots do not identify candidates with political parties, including only the names of people running for each office

nonpartisan general election Preliminary contest in which all candidates for an office compete against each other without reference to party affiliation

nonpoint pollution sources Diffuse locations that produce runoff into streams, including croplands, feed lots, roads and parking lots, suburban development, forestry and mining, and boating

O

off-cycle election Election that is held in a year when state and/or national elections are *not* held

open seat race An election for an office that does not have an incumbent on the ballot

operating budgets Expenses and revenues of running the government on an annual basis, such as supplies and personnel

own-source revenues Funds raised by local government under state regulation, primarily taxes, fees and charges, and borrowing

P

paid media Media exposure for a candidate that is purchased (e.g., television ads, direct mail, billboard and newspaper ads, yard signs, digital advertising that targets voters)

parity ratio Ratio between particular groups in society and their representation in local legislatures

particularism Motivation for city council service rooted in desire to advance a cause or issue

particularized contact When a person contacts government to express a concern that is specific to their individual needs

partisan ballots Election ballot that lists the party affiliation of the candidates running for office

patronage A system of hiring local employees that is based on the political support provided by a job-seeker

payment in lieu of taxes (PILOT) Funds paid to local governments to help offset the loss in property taxes due to tax-exempt ownership or use of real estate

personal property Movable assets such as vehicles, stock, or household possessions

pluralism An interest group theory positing that multiple groups in a polity compete with one another to protect and advance their interests in the political process

point-source pollution Pollution from an identifiable location such as a sewage treatment plant or factory

policy A government's course of action about a perceived problem

policy adoption The stage in the policy process in which officials give formal approval of a policy in response to an identified problem

policy diffusion Influence of the choices of other governments on a government's policy choices; usually studied in terms of how a policy spreads among governments once it is launched

policy entrepreneur Candidate or officeholder who is devoted full time to advancing non-incremental solutions to local policy issues; often found in suburban communities as antigrowth advocates

policy formulation The stage in the policy process in which participants propose and officials examine alternatives for addressing a problem

political ambition How candidates think about their future in politics. Types include static and progressive

political efficacy The belief that a person's participation is intrinsically valuable and that it matters

political incorporation The degree to which minorities and interests typically excluded from the process of governing are made a part of it

political machine A local political party organization structured hierarchically and geographically to trade votes for favors in order to control local government

political party A group of like-minded individuals who share a common viewpoint of government and who organize to win elections and control the policy agenda

politico Motivation for city council service for the sheer enjoyment of politics and government

politics The struggle for who gets what, when, and how

popular referendum A type of referendum requiring a public vote on policy changes adopted by elected officials prior to implementation

positive advertising Campaign advertising that contains only positive information about the sponsor of an ad

preemption Laws or administrative rules that remove or restrict the authority of lower-level governments over certain policies

principal-agent problem A way of thinking about the relationship between one who has power (the "principal") and one who is expected to carry out the will of the one who has power (the "agent")

privatization Turning over services to the private sector to produce and sell

problem identification The first stage in the policy process, which involves getting a community and its government decision-makers to think that something is a problem that needs to be addressed

progressive ambition When an officeholder desires to hold a higher office and will behave strategically in the present to achieve the higher office in the future

progressive tax A tax with a rate that rises with taxpayers' income

property lien A legal claim against the property to secure payment of some obligation or debt

property tax A tax levied on the value of real or personal property

protest A type of political participation in which a mass of people, acting collectively, makes demands on the political system

public approval The share of the public that approves of the job a mayor is doing

public-private partnerships (3Ps) Contracts between government and a private entity to finance, build, or manage projects

public matching funds Campaign finance reform program in which taxpayer dollars are used to "match" donations received by candidates from individuals and groups

push and pull factors Conditions that force ("push") households to pack up and move away or attract ("pull") people to move to a particular place

Q

quality challenger Candidate with high levels of political/civic/occupational/educational experience who competes against an incumbent

quid pro quo Latin for "this for that"

R

rainy day funds Money set aside and available during difficult economic times or emergencies when regular sources of funds might not be sufficient

ranked choice voting/instant-runoff voting system A system in which voters rank candidates according to their preferences; if no one wins a majority on the first ballot, the second-choice votes of the last-place candidates get reallocated among the others until a winner is decided

real property Land and its attachments, such as buildings

rebellion A form of collective action designed to express dissatisfaction that involves illegal activity, such as violence to people and property; often referred to as riots

recall Form of direct democracy in which the citizenry removes an elected official before his or her term of office has expired

redlining The practice of denying or limiting financial services to certain neighborhoods based on racial or ethnic composition without regard for residents' qualifications or creditworthiness

referendum Form of direct democracy in which elected officials place a policy proposal directly on the ballot for public consideration

regime theory A theory of urban politics that places governing coalitions at the heart of city decision-making and power; examples include corporate, caretaker, and progressive regimes

regressive tax A tax that constitutes a higher percentage of income for poorer people than those who are more affluent

representation In a broad sense, speaking or acting for others

representative bureaucracy The degree to which local bureaucracies look like, in demographic terms, the populations they are designed to serve

restrictive covenant A clause in a deed to a property designed to keep "undesirables" out of a neighborhood by forbidding property owners from selling to certain groups, most notably black people, Asians, Mexicans, and Jews

revenue bonds Debt instruments that pledge a specific stream of revenue to pay off the debt, as with consumer payments for water or parking and airline landing fees

revenue sharing Federal funds distributed based on formulas that give local governments almost unlimited discretion in spending the money

runoff election An election between the top two finishers in a nonpartisan primary when no candidate wins an outright majority

S

self-regarding Motivation for city council service rooted in the desire to advance self-interest

short cutting A coping method used by government employees to handle repeated and difficult situations; may lead to bias

single-member districts System of city council representation in which each councilor represents a specific territory or subset of the city's overall population; also called *ward system*

single-stream recycling Method that allows consumers to place materials in a single container rather than sorting them (usually into paper and nonpaper waste) for collection

socioeconomic status (SES) Combination of education and income levels that divide society by economic class

special assessments Levies on property owners to help pay for improvements in their area that are designed to benefit those specific properties

special-purpose governments Local governments normally established to provide a single service, usually with their own governing board and revenue sources; these include public school districts and

authorities for services such as airports, hospitals, and water

special-purpose governments Local governments that generally provide a single service, as with public school districts or special districts established to run hospitals, parks, airports, or water and sewer systems

staggered terms Method of organizing the terms of city councilors so that the entire council is not up for re-election at the same time

static ambition When an officeholder desires to hold onto the office she or he currently occupies

street-level bureaucrats Local government employees who deliver services directly to the people, with whom they have frequent interactions

substantive representation The extent to which the processes and decisions of government are in actuality representative of the different perspectives in the community

suburbanization A huge wave of residential and commercial development outside the nation's large cities following the end of World War II

Sunbelt The region extending across the southern tier of the United States from Florida to California that includes Georgia, North Carolina, South Carolina, Tennessee, Alabama, Mississippi, Arkansas, Louisiana, Texas, Oklahoma, New Mexico, Arizona, Southern California, and Las Vegas

Superfund law legislation adopted by Congress in 1982 that established a tax on the chemical and petroleum industries to clean up the nation's toxic waste sites

T

tax abatement A reduction or elimination of a company's property taxes for a specified period of time

tax base Items of value subject to taxation, such as goods and services covered by a sales tax or the kinds of land or buildings subject to property taxes

tax increment financing (TIF) An agreement between a local government and a company to freeze a property's assessed value in exchange for development of the land, with the tax on any increase in the property's value due to the development (the increment) used to pay for improvements such as infrastructure

U

urban area Defined by the US Census Bureau as an incorporated place with at least 2,500 residents

urban hierarchy A ranking of urban centers based on their central role in the economy and ability to withstand economic downturns

urban reform movement An effort by middle-class and business leaders to undermine the power of political machines through changes in election procedures and the structure of local government

urban renewal A government program that combined federal money and local actions, including the taking of private property through eminent domain, to clear "blight" for redevelopment

user-benefit principle Guideline suggesting that those who use something more should pay for it rather than spreading the cost among all taxpayers

V

voice A response to dissatisfaction where a person attempts to change the status quo by speaking out to improve conditions, joining a protest or demonstration, contacting local officials, or being involved in an interest group or party with the goal of changing or influencing policy

volunteerism Motivation for city council service as a form of civic duty not unlike service in a civic organization; service is characterized by a lack of political ambition

voter turnout Number of ballots cast in an election divided by the number of city residents older than 18 years of age

Voting Rights Act of 1965 Law that made voting procedures in the South subject to review by the federal government

vouchers Entitlements that recipients can redeem for services, as with food stamps, Medicare, and federal financial aid

W

white flight The movement of white residents from central cities to separate suburban communities

Z

zoning A set of regulations by local government controlling the types of uses and structures that are permitted on a specific piece of property

Notes

1: STUDYING URBAN POLITICS

1. US Census Bureau, "Following the Frontier Line, 1790 to 1890," September 6, 2012, https://www.census.gov/dataviz/visualizations/001/.
2. See Joseph J. Ellis, *American Dialogue: The Founders and Us* (New York: Alfred A. Knopf, 2018), 22–23, 30–41.
3. Frederick J. Turner, "The Significance of the Frontier in American History," 1893, American Historical Association Historical Archives, https://www.historians.org/about-aha-and-membership/aha-history-and-archives/historical-archives/the-significance-of-the-frontier-in-american-history.
4. Kenneth T. Jackson, *Crabgrass Frontier: The Suburbanization of the United States* (New York: Oxford University Press, 1985).
5. The US Census Bureau provides brief explanations of its changing definitions in "2010 Census Urban Area FAQs," https://www.census.gov/geo/reference/ua/uafaq.html. The bureau provides more detail in its "Geographic Areas Reference Manual," particularly chapters 12 and 13, https://www.census.gov/geo/reference/garm.html. The coverage in this section is based on these sources.
6. US Census Bureau, *Abstract of the Thirteenth Census: 1910*, 59.
7. US Census Bureau, "Geographic Terms and Concepts: Core Based Statistical Areas and Related Statistical Areas," https://www.census.gov/geo/reference/gtc/gtc_cbsa.html.
8. US Census Bureau, July 2015, "Delineation Files: Core Based Statistical Areas (CBSAs), Metropolitan Divisions, and Combined Statistical Areas (CSAs)," https://www.census.gov/geographies/reference-files/time-series/demo/metro-micro/delineation-files.html.
9. See Merriam-Webster's definition of urbanization at https://www.merriam-webster.com/dictionary/urbanization.
10. Merriam-Webster, https://www.merriam-webster.com/dictionary/urban.
11. Merriam-Webster, http://www.dictionary.com/browse/urban.
12. This definition appears in a more extended analysis in *The Encyclopedia Britannica*, https://www.britannica.com/topic/urbanization.
13. For a brief overview of the development of urban America prior to the Civil War, see Howard P. Chudacoff, Judith E. Smith, and Peter C. Baldwin, *The Evolution of American Urban Society* (Boston: Pearson, 2015), 1–21, 38–45, 63–68.
14. See Tertius Chandler and Gerald Fox, *3000 Years of Urban Growth* (New York: Academic Press, 1974), 303–21. For more extended discussion, see Paul Bairoch, *Cities and Economic Development: From the Dawn of History to the Present* (Chicago: University of Chicago Press, 1988); Paul M. Hogenberg and Lynn Hollen Lees, *The Making of Urban Europe, 1000–1950* (Cambridge, MA: Harvard University Press, 1985).
15. Chudacoff et al., *The Evolution of American Urban Society*, 1–10.
16. J. Eric Oliver, *Local Elections and the Politics of Small-Scale Democracy* (Princeton: Princeton University Press, 2012), 22–34.
17. The survey included additional questions, including about the three branches of the federal government. Gallup's general question about trust of the national government is not used here because it is worded differently, has different response categories, was taken at different times of year from surveys including state and local government, and is not available after 2010. See Gallup, "Trust in Government: Gallup Historical Trends," http://news.gallup.com/poll/5392/trust-government.aspx.
18. For comparisons among locations, see Avalara, https://www.taxrates.com.
19. Colorado Department of Education, "A Report on Colorado School District Organization," October 2002, http://www.cosfp.org/HomeFiles/ServicesConsolidation/CDE-2002-SchoolDistrictOrganizationReport.pdf; Tim Weldon, "The Promises and Perils of School District Consolidation," Council of State Governments, January 27, 2012, http://knowledgecenter.csg.org/kc/content/promises-and-perils-school-district-consolidation.
20. Katherine Barrett and Richard Greene, "Why Schools Resist Consolidating," *Governing*, October 2014, http://www.governing.com/columns/smart-mgmt/gov-school-consolidation-wars.html.
21. On the formation of local governments, particularly special districts, see Nancy Burns, *The Formation of American Local Governments: Private Values in Public Institutions* (New York: Oxford University Press, 1994).
22. The federal government's fiscal year is October 1–September 30, so fiscal 2018 runs from October 2017 through September 2018. Every state except Alabama, Michigan, New York, and Texas has a July 1–June 30 fiscal year. About 37 percent of local governments follow that calendar, but the largest share (40%) have budgets that follow the January–December calendar year. US Census Bureau, *Government Finance and Employment: Classification Manual*, October 2006, table 3.1, https://www2.census.gov/govs/pubs/classification/2006_classification_manual.pdf.
23. Richard C. Wade, *The Urban Frontier: The Rise of Western Cities, 1790–1830* (Cambridge, MA: Harvard University Press, 1959); Howard P. Chudacoff, Judith E. Smith, and Peter C. Baldwin, *The Evolution of American Urban*

History (New York: Routledge, 2015), especially chapters 2–4; Peter K. Eisinger, *The Rise of the Entrepreneurial State: State and Local Economic Development Policy in the United States* (Madison: University of Wisconsin Press, 1989).

24. Chris Isidore and Julia Horowitz, "Foxconn Got a Really Good Deal from Wisconsin. And It's Getting Better," *CNN*, December 28, 2017, http://money.cnn.com/2017/12/28/news/companies/foxconn-wisconsin-incentive-package/index.html; Greg Leroy, "Foxconn's $3 Billion Tax-Break Deal Is a Loss for Smart Jobs Policies," *Good Jobs First*, July 29, 2017, https://www.goodjobsfirst.org/news/foxconns-3-billion-tax-break-deal-loss-smart-jobs-policies.

25. For Arizona, see Arizona Department of Public Safety, "Arizona Law Enforcement Academy (ALEA)," https://www.azdps.gov/organization/ASD/alea; for Georgia, see Georgia Public Safety Training Center, https://www.gpstc.org/about-gpstc/training-divisions; for Indiana, see Indiana Law Enforcement Academy, https://www.in.gov/ilea.

26. Kevin Flowers, "Judge Urges More Talks in EMTA Charter Dispute," *Erie Times-News*, October 8, 2016, http://www.goerie.com/news/20161007/judge-urges-more-talks-in-emta-charter-dispute.

27. Jordan Graham, "Great Park Developer, City of Irvine Sue Orange County over Large Retail, Condo Development," *Orange County Register*, December 21, 2017, https://www.ocregister.com/2017/12/21/great-park-developer-city-of-irvine-sue-orange-county-over-large-retail-condo-development.

28. Emily Badger, "Blue Cities Want to Make Their Own Rules. Red State Won't Let Them," *New York Times*, July 6, 2017, https://www.nytimes.com/2017/07/06/upshot/blue-cities-want-to-make-their-own-rules-red-states-wont-let-them.html.

29. *South Dakota v. Dole*, 483 US 203 (1987).

30. Harold Lasswell, *Politics: Who Gets What, When and How* (New York: Whittlesey House, 1936).

31. Samuel Kernell, Gary C. Jacobson, Thad Kousser, and Lynn Vavreck, *The Logic of American Politics*, 8th edition (Thousand Oaks: Sage, 2018), 3.

32. From Theodore J. Lowi, Benjamin Ginsberg, Kenneth Shepsle, and Stephen Ansolabehere, *American Government: Power and Purpose*, brief 13th edition (New York: W. W. Norton and Co.), 10.

33. Hanna Pitkin, *The Concept of Representation* (Berkeley: University of California Press, 1967).

34. Samuel Kernell, Gary C. Jacobson, Thad Kousser, and Lynn Vavreck, *The Logic of American Politics*, 8th edition (Thousand Oaks: Sage, 2016), 682.

35. Melissa J. Marschall, Anirudh V. S. Ruhil, and Paru R. Shah, "The New Racial Calculus: Electoral Institutions and Black Representation in Local Legislatures," *American Journal of Political Science* 54 (2010): 107–24.

36. Sarah F. Anzia, *Timing and Turnout: How Off-Cycle Elections Favor Organized Groups* (Chicago: University of Chicago Press, 2014).

37. Chris Tausanovitch and Christopher Warshaw, "Representation in Municipal Government," *American Political Science Review* 108:3 (2014): 605–41.

2: THE DEVELOPMENT OF URBAN AMERICA THROUGH WORLD WAR II

1. James R. Barrett, *The Irish Way: Becoming American in the Multiethnic City* (New York: Penguin Books, 2012), 195–97.

2. For a brief overview of this period, see Howard P. Chudacoff, Judith E. Smith, and Peter C. Baldwin, *The Evolution of American Urban Society*, 8th edition (Boston: Pearson, 2015), chapter 2.

3. Sam Bass Warner, Jr., *The Private City: Philadelphia in Three Periods of Growth* (Philadelphia: University of Pennsylvania Press, 1968), x.

4. Warner, *The Private City*, chapters 6 and 7.

5. Chudacoff et al., *The Evolution of American Urban Society*, 35–38.

6. US Census Bureau, *Historical Statistics of the United States, Colonial Times to 1970* (Washington, DC: US Bureau of the Census, 1975), Part 1, chapter C, https://www2.census.gov/library/publications/1975/compendia/hist_stats_colonial-1970/hist_stats_colonial-1970p1-chC.pdf, Series C-89-119.

7. Sam Bass Warner, Jr., *Streetcar Suburbs: The Process of Growth in Boston, 1870–1900* (New York: Atheneum, 1976 [1962]), 10.

8. Warner, *The Private City*, chapter 7.

9. Amy Bridges, *A City in the Republic: Antebellum New York and the Origins of Machine Politics* (Ithaca: Cornell University Press, 1987), 85–102.

10. See Chudacoff et al., *The Evolution of American Urban Society*, 109–10.

11. US Census Bureau, "Population of the 100 Largest Cities and Other Urban Places in the United States: 1790 to 1990," tables 9, 10, and 11, https://www.census.gov/population/www/documentation/twps0027/twps0027.html.

12. On the role of local governments in developing infrastructure, especially during the 1800s, see Eric H. Monkkonen, *The Local State: Public Money and American Cities* (Stanford: Stanford University Press, 1995).

13. In Milwaukee, these efforts before the Civil War were aimed at German immigrants. See Bayrd Still, *Milwaukee: The History of a City* (Madison: State Historical Society of Wisconsin, 1948), 113–14.

14. US Census Bureau, "Historical Statistics on the Foreign-Born Population of the United States: 1850–2000," tables 1 and 22, https://www.census.gov/population/www/documentation/twps0081/twps0081.html.

15. US Census Bureau, "Historical Statistics on the Foreign-Born Population of the United States: 1850–2000," table 6.

16. See Steven P. Erie, *Rainbow's End: Irish-Americans and the Dilemmas of Urban Machine Politics, 1840–1985* (Berkeley: University of California Press, 1988), 91–111.

17. Chudacoff et al., *The Evolution of American Urban Society*, 106–8.

18. See Andrew Gyory, *Closing the Gate: Race, Politics, and the Chinese Exclusion Act* (Chapel Hill: University of North Carolina Press, 1998).

19. For a detailed account of these campaigns, beginning in the late 1800s, see Daniel Okrent, *The Guarded Gate: Bigotry, Eugenics, and the Law That Kept Two Generations of Jews, Italians, and Other European Immigrants out of America* (New York: Scribner, 2019).

20. Warner, *The Private City*, chapter 4.

21. Alfred D. Chandler, Jr., *The Visible Hand: The Managerial Revolution in American Business* (Cambridge, MA: Harvard University Press, 1977).

22. Bridges, *A City in the Republic*, 103–10; Warner, *The Private City*, 72–74; Still, *Milwaukee*, 288–91.

23. On strikes and other activity in Milwaukee, see Still, *Milwaukee*, 284–97.

24. See Paul Avrich, *The Haymarket Tragedy* (Princeton: Princeton University Press, 1984).

25. Adna Ferrin Weber, *The Growth of Cities in the Nineteenth Century: A Study in Statistics* (Ithaca: Cornell University Press, 1965 [1899]), 155.

26. Weber, *The Growth of Cities*, 218–22.

27. Warner, *Streetcar Suburbs*, chapters 2–4. Also see Jon C. Teaford, *City and Suburb: The Political Fragmentation of Metropolitan America, 1850–1970* (Baltimore: Johns Hopkins University Press, 1979), 20–22.

28. See Chudacoff et al., *The Evolution of American Urban Society*, 83–92.

29. Teaford, *City and Suburb*, 18–20.

30. Joseph Horowitz, *Classical Music in America: A History of Its Rise and Fall* (New York: W. W. Norton, 2005), especially Book 1; R. Allen Lott, *From Paris to Peoria: How European Virtuosos Brought Classical Music to the American Heartland* (New York: Oxford University Press, 2003); Susan Stamberg, "How Andrew Carnegie Turned His Fortune into a Library Legacy," *National Public Radio*, August 1, 2013, https://www.npr.org/2013/08/01/207272849/how-andrew-carnegie-turned-his-fortune-into-a-library-legacy; Ann Satterthwaite, *Local Glories: Opera Houses on Main Street, Where Art and Community Meet* (New York: Oxford University Press, 2016). Information on the history of other cultural institutions is available on their websites.

31. *Village of Euclid v. Ambler Realty*, 272 US 365 (1926). On zoning and planning more generally, see Emily Talen, "Zoning and Diversity in Historical Perspective," *Journal of Planning History* 11:4 (November 2012): 330–47; Teaford, *City and Suburb*, 40–42.

32. Jon C. Teaford, *The Twentieth-Century American City: Problem, Promise, and Reality* (Baltimore: Johns Hopkins University Press, 1986), 23–30.

33. For a synopsis of this tragedy, see the History Channel, "Triangle Shirtwaist Factory Fire," December 2, 2009 (updated September 13, 2019), https://www.history.com/topics/triangle-shirtwaist-fire.

34. A classic work of that period, originally published in 1938, is Louis Wirth, "Urbanism as a Way of Life," in *Classic Essays on the Culture of Cities*, ed. Richard Sennett (Englewood Cliffs: Prentice-Hall, 1969), 143–64.

35. Robert E. Park and Ernest W. Burgess, *The City*, introduction by Morris Janowitz (Chicago: University of Chicago Press, 1967 [1925]), 47–62.

36. For a brief overview of suburbanization during the 1920s, see Teaford, *The Twentieth-Century American City*, 62–71.

37. See Louis Wirth, *The Ghetto* (Chicago: University of Chicago Press, 1928).

38. For a brief critique, see Chudacoff et al., *The Evolution of American Urban Society*, 87–89.

39. Thomas W. Hanchett, *Sorting Out the New South City: Race, Class, and Urban Development in Charlotte, 1875–1975* (Chapel Hill: University of North Carolina Press, 1998).

40. Brentin Mock, "Louisville Confronts Its Redlining Past and Present," *CityLab*, February 21, 2017, https://www.citylab.com/housing/2017/02/louisville-confronts-its-redlining-past-and-present/517125/. Also see Louisville/Jefferson County Information Consortium (LOJIC), "Redlining Louisville: Racial Capitalism and Real Estate," https://lojic.maps.arcgis.com/apps/MapSeries/index.html?appid=e4d29907953c4094a17cb9ea8f8f89de.

41. Ronald H. Bayor, *Race and the Shaping of Twentieth-Century Atlanta* (Chapel Hill: University of North Carolina Press, 1996), chapter 3; Kevin M. Kruse, *White Flight: Atlanta and the Making of Modern Conservatism* (Princeton: Princeton University Press, 2005), 41–42.

42. *Shelley v. Kraemer*, 334 US 1 (1948). This case between two homeowners involved a decades-old restrictive covenant in St. Louis; it was combined with a similar case from Detroit.

43. Richard C. Wade, *The Urban Frontier: Pioneer Life in Early Pittsburgh, Cincinnati, Lexington, Louisville, and St. Louis* (Chicago: University of Chicago Press, 1959).

44. William Cronon, *Nature's Metropolis: Chicago and the Great West* (New York: W. W. Norton, 1991), chapter 2.

45. On Chicago's links with its hinterlands, see Cronon, *Nature's Metropolis*, Part II; on finance, see chapters 6 and 7; on the 1893 fair, see chapter 8. For a slightly different take on the fair, including its politics and the actions of a serial murderer, see Erik Larson, *The Devil in the White City: Murder, Magic, and Madness at the Fair That Changed America* (New York: Random House, 2003).

46. Bridges, *A City in the Republic*.

47. On Chicago, see a critical journalist's account in Mike Royko, *Boss: Richard J. Daley of Chicago* (New York: E. P. Dutton, 1971). For a more detailed analysis, see Adam Cohen and Elizabeth Taylor, *American Pharaoh: Richard J. Daley, His Battle for Chicago and the Nation* (New York: Little, Brown, 2000).

48. William L. Riordon, *Plunkett of Tammany Hall*, with an introduction by Arthur Mann (New York: E. P. Dutton, 1963), 3–4. Plunkett's comments were first published in 1905.

49. Barrett, *The Irish Way*; Erie, *Rainbow's End*.

50. Peri E. Arnold, "What Bonded Immigrants to Urban Machines? The Case of Jacob Avrey and Chicago's 24th Ward," *Journal of Policy History* 25:4 (October 2013): 463–88.

51. Tomasz Inglot and John P. Pelissero, "Ethnic Power in a Machine City: Chicago's Poles at Rainbow's End," *Urban Affairs Quarterly* 28:4 (June 1993): 526–43.

52. Bruce M. Stave, ed., *Socialism and the Cities* (Port Washington: Kennikat Press, 1975).

53. Teaford, *The Twentieth-Century American City*, 31–32. See the synopsis in Harvard University Library Open Collection Program, "Immigration to the United States,

1789–1930: Settlement House Movement," http://ocp.hul.harvard.edu/immigration/settlement.html.

54. Lincoln Steffens, *The Shame of the Cities*, with an introduction by Louis Joughin (New York: Hill and Wang, 1957 [1904]).

55. For an excellent description and account of efforts in these cities and their effects on local policies, see Amy Bridges, *Morning Glories: Municipal Reform in the Southwest* (Princeton: Princeton University Press, 1997).

56. Teaford, *The Twentieth-Century American City*, 34–37. For a broader view of efforts at political change from the 1890s through the New Deal, see Richard Hofstadter, *The Age of Reform: From Bryan to F. D. R.* (New York: Vintage Books, 1955).

57. Sam Bass Warner, Jr., *Streetcar Suburbs: The Process of Growth in Boston, 1870–1900*, 2nd edition (Cambridge, MA: Harvard University Press, 1978).

58. Stewart E. Tolnay and E. M. Beck, *A Festival of Violence: An Analysis of Southern Lynchings, 1882–1930* (Urbana: University of Illinois Press, 1992), especially 29–39, 93–98. Their data covers the five Deep South states of Alabama, Georgia, Louisiana, Mississippi, and South Carolina, along with the Border South states of Arkansas, Florida, Kentucky, North Carolina, and Tennessee; they do not include Texas in the analysis.

59. See James W. Loewen, *Sundown Towns: A Hidden Dimension of American Racism* (New York: Touchstone, 2005); Patrick Phillips, *Blood at the Root: A Racial Cleansing in America* (New York: W. W. Norton, 2016).

60. Robin D. G. Taylor, "'We Are Not What We Seem': Rethinking Black Working-Class Opposition in the Jim Crow South," *Journal of American History* 80:1 (June 1993): 75–112.

61. David F. Krugler, *1919, The Year of Racial Violence: How African Americans Fought Back* (New York: Cambridge University Press, 2015).

62. James N. Gregory, *The Southern Diaspora: How the Great Migrations of Black and White Southerners Transformed America* (Chapel Hill: University of North Carolina Press, 2005), 12–16.

63. Gregory, *The Southern Diaspora*, 15–16.

64. Gregory, *The Southern Diaspora*, 16–19.

65. Gregory, *The Southern Diaspora*, 47–49, 113–95.

66. Thomas J. Sugrue, *The Origins of the Urban Crisis: Race and Inequality in Postwar Detroit*, 2nd edition (Princeton: Princeton University Press, 2005), 28–31.

67. For an analysis of the problems and responses during 1930–45, see Teaford, *The Twentieth-Century American City*, 74–96.

68. See Kristi Andersen, *The Creation of a Democratic Majority, 1928–1936* (Chicago: University of Chicago Press, 1979).

69. For a brief discussion, see Chudacoff et al., *The Evolution of American Urban Society*, 178–79.

70. Richard Rothstein, *The Color of Law: A Forgotten History of How Our Government Segregated America* (New York: Liveright Publishing, 2017), 17–27; Chudacoff et al., *The Evolution of American Urban Society*, 180–81.

71. For a history of the federal programs that reshaped the housing industry during the 1930s, see David M. P. Freund, *Colored Property: State Policy and White Racial Politics in Suburban America* (Chicago: University of Chicago Press, 2007), chapter 3. For an overview of federal involvement in the private housing market from the late 1800s through the Great Recession, see Dan Immergluck, *Foreclosed: High-Risk Lending, Deregulation, and the Undermining of America's Mortgage Market* (Ithaca: Cornell University Press, 2009), chapter 1.

72. See Chudacoff et al., *The Evolution of American Urban Society*, 179–80; Rothstein, *The Color of Law*, 63–64.

73. Sugrue, *The Origins of the Urban Crisis*, 63–66.

74. Judge Glock, "How the Federal Housing Administration Tried to Save America's Cities," *Journal of Policy History* 28:2 (April 2016): 290–317.

75. Glock, "Federal Housing Administration," 304–8.

76. Freund, *Colored Property*, 186.

77. Chudacoff et al., *The Evolution of American Urban Society*, 180–81; Rothstein, *The Color of Law*, 63–73, 83–91.

78. Chudacoff et al., *The Evolution of American Urban Society*, 198–99; Rothstein, *The Color of Law*, 51–52.

79. Freund, *Colored Property*, 208–13.

80. *Korematsu v. United States*, 323 US 214 (1944), https://www.oyez.org/cases/1940-1955/323us214.

81. Carl Abbott, *The New Urban America: Growth and Politics in Sunbelt Cities*, revised edition (Chapel Hill: University of North Carolina Press, 1987), especially chapter 4; Ann Markusen, Peter Hall, Scott Campbell, and Sabina Deitrick, *The Rise of the Gunbelt: The Military Remapping of Industrial America* (New York: Oxford University Press, 1991).

3: URBAN DEVELOPMENT AFTER WORLD WAR II

1. Richard Rothstein, *The Color of Law: A Forgotten History of How Our Government Segregated America* (New York: Liveright Publishing, 2017), 139–43.

2. US Census Bureau, *Census of Population: 1950, vol. 1, Number of Inhabitants*, table 27; *Statistical Abstract of the United States: 1963*, table 10.

3. Teaford, *The Twentieth-Century American City*, 98–106.

4. For one take on Robert Moses, New York's most notable promoter of infrastructure for half a century, see Robert Caro, *The Power Broker: Robert Moses and the Fall of New York* (New York: Alfred A. Knopf, 1974). Moses's most notable antagonist was Jane Jacobs, who lays out her case in *The Death and Life of Great American Cities* (New York: Random House, 1961).

5. Mark H. Rose, "Reframing American Highway Politics, 1956–1995," *Journal of Planning History* 2:3 (August 2003): 212–36.

6. Raymond A. Mohl, "The Expressway Teardown Movement in American Cities: Rethinking Postwar Highway Policy in the Post-interstate Era," *Journal of Planning History* 11:1 (February 2012): 89–103.

7. There are multiple examples. On Levittown, PA, suburban Chicago, Los Angeles, and Louisville, see Rothstein, *The Color of Law*, chapter 9; on Detroit, see Thomas J. Sugrue, *The Origins of the Urban Crisis: Race and Inequality in Postwar Detroit*, 2nd edition (Princeton: Princeton University Press, 2005), chapters 7 and 8; on Atlanta, see Kevin M. Kruse, *White Flight: Atlanta and the Making of Modern Conservatism* (Princeton: Princeton University Press, 2005).

8. David M. P. Freund, *Colored Property: State Policy and White Racial Politics in Suburban America* (Chicago: University of Chicago Press, 2007), 213.

9. For an overview, see Robert M. Fogelsong, *Downtown: Its Rise and Fall, 1880–1950* (New Haven: Yale University Press, 2001), especially chapter 7. On urban renewal in Detroit, see Sugrue, *The Origins of the Urban Crisis*, 48–51. On Atlanta, see Clarence N. Stone, *Economic Growth and Neighborhood Discontent: System Bias in the Urban Renewal Program of Atlanta* (Chapel Hill: University of North Carolina Press, 1976). On the South and West more generally, see Carl Abbott, *The New Urban America: Growth and Politics in Sunbelt Cities*, revised edition (Chapel Hill: University of North Carolina Press, 1987), chapter 6.

10. Robert B. Fairbanks, "The Texas Exception: San Antonio and Urban Renewal, 1949–1965," *Journal of Planning History* 1:2 (May 2002): 181–96.

11. Arnold R. Hirsch, *Making the Second Ghetto: Race and Housing in Chicago, 1940–1960* (New York: Cambridge University Press, 1983). On this process in Miami, see Raymond A. Mohl, "Making the Second Ghetto in Metropolitan Miami," in *The New African American Urban History*, eds. Kenneth W. Goings and Raymond A. Mohl (Thousand Oaks: Sage, 1996), 266–98.

12. On suburbanization in the Sunbelt, see Abbott, *The New Urban America*, chapters 7 and 8.

13. *Heart of Atlanta Motel v. United States*, 379 US 241 (1964).

14. Chandler Davidson and Bernard Grofman, eds., *Quiet Revolution in the South: The Impact of the Voting Rights Act, 1965–1990* (Princeton: Princeton University Press, 1994). In addition to chapters on individual states, chapter 10 examines municipal elections in the South, and chapter 12 covers changes in voter registration. Also see Peggy Heilig and Robert J. Mundt, *Your Voice at City Hall: The Politics, Procedures and Policies of District Representation* (Albany: State University of New York Press, 1985).

15. *Shelby County v. Holder*, 570 US (2013), https://www.oyez.org/cases/2012/12-96; Vann R. Newkirk II, "How *Shelby County v. Holder* Broke America," *The Atlantic*, July 10, 2018, https://www.theatlantic.com/politics/archive/2018/07/how-shelby-county-broke-america/564707.

16. J. David Greenstone and Paul E. Peterson, *Race and Authority in Urban Politics: Community Participation and the War on Poverty* (Chicago: University of Chicago Press, 1976).

17. Aaron Cavin, "A Right to Housing in the Suburbs: *James v. Valtierra* and the Campaign against Economic Discrimination," *Journal of Urban History*, OnlineFirst, June 10, 2017, http://journals.sagepub.com.ezproxy.emich.edu/doi/10.1177/0096144217712928.

18. Barbara S. Gamble, "Putting Civil Rights to a Popular Vote," *American Journal of Political Science* 41:1 (January 1997): 245–69, especially 255–57.

19. Joe R. Feagin and Harlan Hahn, *Ghetto Revolts: The Politics of Violence in American Cities* (New York: Macmillan, 1973), 101–24. On Detroit, see Sugrue, *The Origins of the Urban Crisis*, 259–64. For a history of the advisory commission, see Steven M. Gillon, *Separate and Unequal: The Kerner Commission and the Unraveling of American Liberalism* (New York: Basic Books, 2018).

20. For interesting case studies, see David R. Colburn and Jeffrey S. Adler, eds., *African-American Mayors: Race, Politics, and the American City* (Urbana: University of Illinois Press, 2001).

21. Teaford, *The Twentieth-Century American City*, chapter 6; Stuart Meck and Rebecca Retzlaff, "President Jimmy Carter's Urban Policy: A Reconstruction and an Appraisal," *Journal of Planning History* 11:3 (August 2012): 242–80; Roger Biles, *The Fate of Cities: Urban America and the Federal Government, 1945–2000* (Lawrence: University Press of Kansas, 2011).

22. Some include all eleven states of the Confederacy, which would mean adding Virginia; others stick with state boundaries and include all of California and Nevada. We will generally follow the definition used by Richard M. Bernard and Bradley R. Rice, eds., *Sunbelt Cities: Politics and Growth Since World War II* (Austin: University of Texas Press, 1983), especially the Introduction (1–30). Abbott, in *The New Urban America* (1–25), takes a different view by emphasizing the fastest-growing states connected to the modern economy of services, energy, and retirement/tourism. That "Economic Sunbelt" excludes Alabama, Arkansas, Mississippi, and Tennessee, but it includes all of California and Nevada, plus the fast-growing western states of Colorado, Utah, Oregon, Washington, and Hawaii. For an interesting review essay on the notion of the Sunbelt, see Rachel M. Guberman, "Is There a Sunbelt After All? And Should We Care?" *Journal of Urban History* 41:6 (November 2015): 1166–74.

23. Peter K. Eisinger, *The Rise of the Entrepreneurial State: State and Local Economic Development Policy in the United States* (Madison: University of Wisconsin Press, 1988); David C. Perry and Alfred J. Watkins, eds., *The Rise of the Sunbelt Cities* (Beverly Hills: Sage, 1977); Abbott, *The New Urban America*, chapter 1.

24. Major League Baseball, "Team Histories," http://mlb.mlb.com/mlb/history/mlb_history_teams.jsp. Some teams moved twice: The Braves went from Boston to Milwaukee before settling in Atlanta, and the Athletics migrated from Philadelphia to Kansas City and then Oakland. Two variants of the American League Washington Senators were created and subsequently moved: One became the Minnesota Twins in 1961; the other became the Texas

Rangers in 1972. Washington, DC was finally rewarded with a National League team, the Nationals, in 2005, when the Expos moved to DC after more than 30 years in Montreal.

25. National Basketball Association, "Franchise History," https://stats.nba.com/history.

26. Pro Football Hall of Fame, "National Football League Franchise Histories," http://www.profootballhof.com/football-history/national-footbal-league-franchise-histories; Jill Disis and Dylan Byers, "NFL Approves Raiders' Move to Las Vegas," *CNN Money*, March 27, 2017, https://money.cnn.com/2017/03/27/news/nfl-raiders-las-vegas-move/index.html.

27. See Robert S. Erickson, Gerald C. Wright, and John P. McIver, "Public Opinion in the States: A Quarter Century of Change and Stability," in *Public Opinion in State Politics*, ed. Jeffrey E. Cohen (Stanford: Stanford University Press, 2006), 229–53.

28. US National Archives and Records Administration, US Electoral College, "Historical Election Results," https://www.archives.gov/federal-register/electoral-college/historical.html.

29. Jennifer Hochschild, "Race and Cities: New Circumstances Imply New Ideas," *Perspectives on Politics* 10:3 (September 2012): 647–58.

30. For a good history of the early years of gay and lesbian history, see John D'Emilio, *Sexual Politics, Sexual Communities: The Making of a Homosexual Minority in the United States, 1940–1970*, 2nd edition (Chicago: University of Chicago Press, 1998). There is also a growing number of histories of individual cities.

31. On the gay rights movement in Atlanta, see Arnold Fleischmann and Jason Hardman, "Hitting Below the Bible Belt: The Development of the Gay Rights Movement in Atlanta," *Journal of Urban Affairs* 26:4 (October 2004): 407–26.

32. Amin Ghaziani, *There Goes the Gayborhood?* (Princeton: Princeton University Press, 2014).

33. William H. Frey, *Diversity Explosion: How New Racial Demographics Are Remaking America*, revised edition (Washington, DC: Brookings Institution Press, 2018), 3–10, 43–63; on Somali adaptation to urban America, see Stefanie Chambers, *Somalis in the Twin Cities and Columbus: Immigrant Incorporation in New Destinations* (Philadelphia: Temple University Press, 2017).

34. On Hispanics, see Frey, *Diversity Explosion*, 53–55, 65–85.

35. This section draws from Frey, *Diversity Explosion*, chapter 5.

36. Frey, *Diversity Explosion*, 107. He covers this change in a chapter titled "The Great Migration of Blacks, in Reverse."

37. Frey, *Diversity Explosion*, chapter 6.

38. Joel Garreau, *Edge City: Life on the New Frontier* (New York: Anchor Books, 1991).

39. Robert E. Lang and Jennifer B. LeFurgy, *Boomburbs: The Rise of America's Accidental Cities* (Washington, DC: Brookings Institution Press, 2007).

40. Alan Berube, Audrey Singer, Jill H. Wilson, and William H. Frey, "Finding Exurbia: America's Fast-Growing Communities at the Metropolitan Fringe" (Washington,

DC: Brookings Metropolitan Policy Program, October 2006), https://www.brookings.edu/wp-content/uploads/2016/06/20061017_exurbia.pdf.

41. Bill Bishop with Robert G. Cushing, *The Big Sort: Why Clustering of Like-Minded America Is Tearing Us Apart* (Boston: Houghton Mifflin, 2008).

42. See the critique in Samuel J. Abrams and Morris P. Fiorina, "'The Big Sort' That Wasn't: A Skeptical Reexamination," *PS: Political Science & Politics* 45:2 (April 2012): 203–10.

43. US Department of Commerce, Bureau of Economic Analysis, "Gross-Domestic-Product-(GDP)-By-Industry Data (Gross Output, 1947–2015)," https://bea.gov/industry/gdpbyind_data.htm.

44. Jesus Leal Trujillo and Joseph Parilla, "Redefining Global Cities: The Seven Types of Global Metro Economies" (Washington, DC: Brookings Institution, Global Cities Initiative, 2016), https://www.brookings.edu/wp-content/uploads/2016/09/metro_20160928_gcitypes.pdf; Richard Florida, "What To Do about the Rise of Mega-Regions," *CityLab*, June 12, 2018, https://www.citylab.com/equity/2018/06/urbanism-shouldnt-be-a-story-of-winners-and-losers/562583. Also see Edward Glaeser, *Triumph of the City* (New York: Penguin, 2011).

45. Gretchen Morgenson and Joshua Rosner, *Reckless Endangerment: How Outsized Ambition, Greed, and Corruption Led to Economic Armageddon* (New York: Times Books, 2011).

46. For a good analysis of the failings of the mortgage market, see Dan Immergluck, *Foreclosed: High-Risk Lending, Deregulation, and the Undermining of America's Mortgage Market* (Ithaca: Cornell University Press, 2009).

47. William R. Emmons, "The End Is in Sight for the US Foreclosure Crisis," Federal Reserve Bank of St. Louis, December 2016, https://www.stlouisfed.org/publications/housing-market-perspectives/issue-3-dec-2016/the-end-is-in-sight-for-the-us-foreclosure-crisis.

48. Frey, *Diversity Explosion*, 3–5.

49. Hochschild, "Race and Cities."

50. The remainder of the "top ten" MSAs are Buffalo, St. Louis, Cincinnati, Philadelphia, and Los Angeles. See Frey, *Diversity Explosion*, 168–77.

51. Elizabeth Kneebone and Alan Berube, *Confronting Suburban Poverty in America* (Washington, DC: Brookings Institution Press, 2013); Jessica L. Semega, Kayla R. Fontenot, and Melissa A. Kolar, "Income and Poverty in the United States: 2016," US Census Bureau, "Current Population Reports," September 2017, https://www.census.gov/content/dam/Census/library/publications/2017/demo/P60-259.pdf.

52. Tanvi Misra, "How Chicago's Aldermen Help Keep It Segregated," *CityLab*, August 2, 2018, https://www.citylab.com/equity/2018/08/how-chicagos-aldermen-help-keep-it-segregated/564983; Jon Murray, "Denver Council Orders New Protections for Renters Using Vouchers or Unconventional Sources of Income," *Denver Post*, August 6, 2018, https://www.denverpost.com/2018/08/06/denver-council-source-of-income-discrimination-section-8.

53. See Frey, *Diversity Explosion*, chapter 7, "White Population Shifts: A Zero-Sum Game." Also see Tom Jacobs, "'White Flight' Persists in America's Suburbs," *CityLab*, March 7, 2018, https://www.citylab.com/equity/2018/03/the-white-flight-from-americas-suburbs/555047.

54. Frey captures these patterns in *Diversity Explosion*, chapter 3, including a series of dramatic maps.

55. Frey, *Diversity Explosion*, chapter 11.

56. Alan Ehrenhalt, *The Great Inversion and the Future of the American City* (New York: Alfred A. Knopf, 2012).

57. This kind of project has caught on in suburban Atlanta, among other areas: see Tyler Estep, "Developers Bet Big on Urbanist County Projects," *Atlanta Journal-Constitution*, August 11, 2018, B1.

58. Richard Florida, *Cities and the Creative Class* (New York: Routledge, 2005), 34.

59. Florida, *Cities and the Creative Class*, 37.

60. Richard Florida, *The New Urban Crisis: How Our Cities Are Increasing Inequality, Deepening Segregation, and Failing the Middle Class—and What We Can Do about It* (New York: Basic Books, 2017).

61. William H. Frey, "US Growth Rate Hits New Low as Migration to the Sunbelt Continues" (Washington, DC: Brookings Institution, *The Avenue* blog, December 23, 2016), https://www.brookings.edu/blog/the-avenue/2016/12/23/u-s-growth-rate-hits-new-low-as-migration-to-the-sun-belt-continues.

62. Kriston Capps, "For Renters, the Housing Crisis Never Ended," *CityLab*, June 16, 2017, https://www.citylab.com/equity/2017/06/harvard-joint-center-for-housing-studies-2017-state-of-the-nation-housing-report/530535.

63. Melissa Hellman, "Seattle City Council Plans to Repeal Head Tax," *Seattle Weekly*, June 12, 2018, http://www.seattleweekly.com/news/seattle-city-council-plans-to-repeal-head-tax.

64. Ronald Brownstein, "The Rust Belt Needs Legal Immigration," *CityLab*, September 18, 2017, https://www.citylab.com/equity/2017/09/the-rust-belt-needs-legal-immigration/540177; Richard Florida, "Returning to the Rust Belt," *CityLab*, August 31, 2017, https://www.citylab.com/life/2017/08/returning-to-the-rust-belt/538572.

65. Sarah Holder, "What Did Cities Actually Offer Amazon?" *CityLab*, May 29, 2018, https://www.citylab.com/life/2018/05/what-did-cities-actually-offer-amazon/559220; Timothy Weaver, "The Problem with Opportunity Zones," *CityLab*, May 16, 2018, https://www.citylab.com/equity/2018/05/the-problem-with-opportunity-zones/560510; Sarah Holder, "The Real Cost of Luring Big Companies to Town," *CityLab*, March 29, 2018, https://www.citylab.com/life/2018/03/when-it-comes-to-econ-development-no-free-lunch/556616; Mike Maciag, "Big Business Tax Beaks May Worsen Inequality," *Governing*, May 2018, http://www.governing.com/topics/finance/gov-tax-breaks-cities-affluent.html.

66. See the Brookings Institution series page on Charlottesville and its aftermath: https://www.brookings.edu/topic/charlottesville-one-year-later.

4: DEALING WITH OTHER GOVERNMENTS AT THE NATIONAL, STATE, AND LOCAL LEVELS

1. Celeste Bott, "Why the Minimum Wage in St. Louis Is Going … Down," *Governing*, July 7, 2017, http://www.governing.com/topics/mgmt/tns-st-louis-minimum-wage.html.

2. National League of Cities, "City Rights in an Era of Preemption: A State-by-State Analysis, 2018 Update," April 2018, https://www.nlc.org/sites/default/files/2017-03/NLC-SML%20Preemption%20Report%202017-pages.pdf.

3. Emily Parker, "50-State Review: Constitutional Obligations for Public Education," Education Commission of the States, 2016, https://www.ecs.org/wp-content/uploads/2016-Constitutional-obligations-for-public-education-1.pdf.

4. Jesse J. Richardson, Jr., "Dillon's Rule Is from Mars, Home Rule Is from Venus: Local Government Autonomy and the Rules of Statutory Construction," *Publius: The Journal of Federalism* 41:1 (Fall 2001): 662–85.

5. For a brief overview, see US Census Bureau, "Government Organization Summary Report: 2012," September 26, 2013, https://www2.census.gov/govs/cog/g12_org.pdf.

6. Kathryn T. Rice, Leora S. Waldner, and Russell M. Smith, "Why New Cities Form: An Examination into Municipal Incorporation in the United States, 1950–2010," *Journal of Planning Literature* 29:2 (May 2014): 141–42.

7. US Census Bureau, "Boundary and Annexation Survey (BAS) New Incorporations, Mergers, Consolidations, and Disincorporations," https://www.census.gov/geographies/reference-files/time-series/geo/bas/new-annex.html.

8. Nancy Burns, *The Formation of American Local Governments: Private Values in Public Institutions* (New York: Oxford University Press, 1994).

9. For a good summary of this research, see Rice et al., "Why New Cities Form," especially 142–47.

10. Rice et al., "Why New Cities Form," 147–50.

11. Augustin Leon-Moreta, "Municipal Incorporation in the United States," *Urban Studies* 52:16 (2015): 3160–80.

12. Russell M. Smith, Leora Waldner, and Craig J. Richardson, "New Cities of Color: Socioeconomic Differentiation between Majority-Minority New Cities and White New Cities," *State and Local Government Review* 48:3 (September 2016): 155–64.

13. Robert M. Howard, Arnold Fleischmann, and Richard N. Engstrom, *Politics in Georgia*, 3rd edition (Athens: University of Georgia Press, 2017), 249–53; Michan Andrew Connor, "Metropolitan Secession and the Space of Color-Blind Racism in Atlanta," *Journal of Urban Affairs* 37:4 (October 2015): 436–61; Sam Rosen, "Atlanta's Controversial Cityhood Movement," *The Atlantic*, April 26, 2017, https://www.theatlantic.com/business/archive/2017/04/the-border-battles-of-atlanta/523884; Brentin Mock, "How to Start Your Own City," *CityLab*,

March 26, 2018, https://www.citylab.com/equity/2018/03/how-to-start-your-own-city/556286.

14. H. George Frederickson, Curtis Wood, and Brett Logan, "How American City Governments Have Changed: The Evolution of the Model City Charter," *National Civic Review* 90:1 (Spring 2001): 3–18.

15. Alexandra W. Lough, "Hazen S. Pingree and the Detroit Model of Urban Reform," *American Journal of Economics and Sociology* 75:1 (January 2016): 58–85; Robert A. Burnham, "Reform, Politics, and Race in Cincinnati: Proportional Representation and the City Charter Committee, 1925–1959," *Journal of Urban History* 23:2 (January 1997): 131–63; Clarence Lang, "Civil Rights versus 'Civic Progress': The St. Louis NAACP and the City Charter Fight, 1956–1957," *Journal of Urban History* 34:4 (May 2008): 609–38; Amy Bridges, *Morning Glories: Municipal Reform in the Southwest* (Princeton: Princeton University Press, 1997).

16. For an overview, see the symposium, "Home Rule Be Damned: Exploring Policy Conflicts between the Statehouse and City Hall," *PS: Political Science & Politics* 51:1 (January 2018): 26–37.

17. Municipal Research and Services Center, "City and Town Classification," http://mrsc.org/getdoc/9ffdd05f-965a-4737-b421-ac4f8749b721/City-and-Town-Classification-Overview.aspx; Deborah A. Dyson, "Classification of Cities," Information Brief, Minnesota House of Representatives, October 2016, http://www.house.leg.state.mn.us/hrd/pubs/cityclass.pdf.

18. Katherine Barrett and Richard Greens, "Closing the Books," *Governing*, June 2018, 60–61.

19. These calculations are from individual entries in Ballotpedia's list in "Local Ballot Measures, California," https://ballotpedia.org/Local_ballot_measures,_California. For more on the interests involved in such campaigns, see Brian E. Adams, "Citizens, Interests Groups, and Local Ballot Initiatives," *Politics & Policy* 40 (February 2012): 43–68.

20. Mark Funkhouser, "Cities, Counties and the Urge to Merge," *Governing*, October 2012, http://www.governing.com/columns/public-money/col-cities-counties-consolidation.html. For more on consolidation politics, see Jered B. Carr and Richard C. Feiock, eds., *City-County Consolidation and Its Alternatives: Reshaping the Local Government Landscape* (Armonk: M. E. Sharpe, 2004); Suzanne M. Leland and Kurt Thurmaier, eds., *Case Studies of City-County Consolidation: Reshaping the Local Government Landscape* (Armonk: M. E. Sharpe, 2004); Arnold Fleischmann, "Regionalism and City-County Consolidation in Small Metro Areas," *State and Local Government Review* 32:3 (Fall 2000): 213–26.

21. William Blomquist and Roger Parks, "Fiscal, Service, and Political Impacts of Indianapolis-Marion County's Unigov," *Publius* 25:4 (Autumn 1995): 37–54; Shaina Cavazos, "Racial Bias and the Crumbling of a City," *The Atlantic*, August 17, 2016, https://www.theatlantic.com/education/archive/2016/08/indianapolis-school-districts/496145. Calls for further consolidation have been common in the *Indianapolis Business Journal*, e.g.,

Ted Boehm, "It's Time to Talk about Expanding Unigov," November 14, 2011, 4B.

22. Neal Peirce, "Kellogg Ultimatum Demands Government Merger," *Dallas Times-Herald*, October 31, 1982, M-3; Haya El Nasser, "Battle Creek Snap-Crackle-Pops Back to Life," *USA Today*, January 3, 1997, 9A; Rick Haglund, "Battle Creek Merger Kept Kellogg Popping," *MLive*, September 6, 2012, http://www.mlive.com/business/index.ssf/2012/09/battle_creek_merger_kept_kello.html.

23. James J. Lopach and Lauren S. McKinsey, "Local Government Reform by Referendum: Lessons from Montana's Voter Review Experience," *State and Local Government Review* 11:1 (January 1979): 35–39.

24. Suzanne M. Leland and Kurt Thurmaier, eds., *City-County Consolidation: Promises Made, Promises Kept?* (Washington, DC: Georgetown University Press, 2010). Also see Charles D. Taylor, Dagney Faulk, and Pamela Schaal, "Where Are the Cost Savings in City-County Consolidation?" *Urban Affairs Review* 39:2 (March 2017): 185–204; Ruth H. DeHoog, David Lowery, and William E. Lyons, "Citizen Satisfaction with Local Governance: A Test of Individual, Jurisdictional, and City-Specific Explanations," *Journal of Politics* 52:3 (August 1990): 807–28.

25. Michael Gaffney and Justin Marlowe, "Fiscal Implications of City-City Consolidations," *State and Local Government Review* 46:3 (September 2014): 197–204.

26. Paul Studenski, *The Government of Metropolitan Areas in the United States* (New York: National Municipal League, 1930), 173–87.

27. Raphael J. Sonenshein and Tom Hogen-Esch, "Bringing the (State) Government Back in: Home Rule and the Politics of Secession in Los Angeles and New York City," *Urban Affairs Review* 41:4 (March 2006): 467–91.

28. Maureen Downey, "Judge Allows Alabama School System's Wish," *Atlanta Journal-Constitution*, May 8, 2017, B1.

29. Brentin Mock, "The Deal That Might Break Georgia into Pieces," *CityLab*, May 17, 2018, https://www.citylab.com/equity/2018/05/the-deal-that-may-have-just-broken-georgia/560528.

30. Jess Bidgood, "In Maine, Local Control Is Luxury Fewer Towns Can Afford" *New York Times*, January 16, 2017, A17.

31. Raymond L. Chambers, "Municipal Services," *New Georgia Encyclopedia*, June 8, 2017, https://www.georgiaencyclopedia.org/articles/government-politics/municipal-services.

32. County Commissioners Association of Pennsylvania, "Pennsylvania Counties Are," https://www.pacounties.org/GR/Documents/CountiesAreFactSheet.pdf.

33. Radley Balko, "It's Time to Abolish the Coroner" (editorial), *Washington Post*, December 12, 2017, https://www.washingtonpost.com/news/the-watch/wp/2017/12/12/its-time-to-abolish-the-coroner. Also see National Research Council, Committee on Identifying the Needs of the Forensic Sciences Community, "Strengthening Forensic Science in the United States: A Path Forward" (US Department of Justice Award 2006-DN-BX-0001,

August 2009), especially chapter 9, https://www.ncjrs.gov/pdffiles1/nij/grants/228091.pdf.

34. On South Carolina, see Municipal Association of South Carolina, "Municipal Clerks and Treasurers Institute Curriculum," http://www.masc.sc/Pages/programs/knowledge/training/MCTI-curriculum.aspx; on California see City Clerks Association of California, "Technical Training for Clerks (TTC)," https://www.californiacityclerks.org/technical-training-for-clerks-ttc-.

35. Arizona Judicial Branch, "Limited Jurisdiction Courts," https://www.azcourts.gov/guidetoazcourts/Limited-Jurisdiction-Courts.

36. Arizona Judicial Branch, "Arizona Code of Judicial Administration," http://www.azcourts.gov/Portals/0/admcode/pdfcurrentcode/1-302_Tech_Amendment_11-25-2015.pdf.

37. The Center for Popular Democracy, "State Takeovers of Low Performing Schools: A Record of Academic Failure, Financial Mismanagement and Student Harm," February 2016, https://populardemocracy.org/sites/default/files/National%20Takeover%20Ed%20Report.pdf.

38. South Carolina Department of Education, "Active Student Headcounts," https://ed.sc.gov/data/other/student-counts/active-student-headcounts; Wisconsin Department of Public Instruction, "WISEdash (FOR DISTRICTS): Enrollment Dashboards," https://dpi.wi.gov/wisedash/districts/about-data/enrollment.

39. Matt Burress, "County State-Aid Highway System," House Research, Minnesota House of Representatives, October 2017, http://www.house.leg.state.mn.us/hrd/pubs/ss/sscsah.pdf.

40. US Census Bureau, "Summary of Public Elementary-Secondary School System Finances by State: Fiscal Year 2016," https://www.census.gov/data/tables/2016/econ/school-finances/secondary-education-finance.html.

41. Emily Badger, "Red States and Blue Cities: A Partisan Battle Intensifies," New York Times, July 6, 2017, A1; Lori Rivetstone-Newell, "The Rise of State Preemption Laws in Response to Local Policy Innovation," Publius: The Journal of Federalism 47:3 (Summer 2017): 403–25.

42. Bryan Lyman, "Monuments Get Legal Protection from Removal in Alabama," Governing, May 26, 2017, http://www.governing.com/topics/politics/tns-alabama-confederate.html.

43. Tony Pugh, "As Confederate Monuments Come Down in Cities, Some Southern States Still Resist," Governing, August 17, 2017, https://www.governing.com/topics/politics/tns-confederate-monuments-states.html.

44. Jason Hanna, Madison Park, and Eliott C. McLaughlin, "North Carolina Repeals 'Bathroom Bill'," CNN News, March 30, 2107, https://www.cnn.com/2017/03/30/politics/north-carolina-hb2-agreement/index.html; Ann Blythe, "As Transgender Rights Case Goes Back to Court, NC Second-Grader Questions Bathroom Restrictions," Raleigh News & Observer, June 24, 2018, http://www.newsobserver.com/news/politics-government/state-politics/article213755849.html.

45. Mandy McLaren, "State Takeover of JCPS: What the Audit Says and the District Has Done,"

Louisville Courier-Journal, May 7, 2018, https://www.courier-journal.com/story/news/education/2018/05/07/kentucky-jcps-takeover-audit-findings/569640002.

46. Emily Richmond, "What Would Happen If the State Took Over Your School District?" The Atlantic, April 1, 2013, https://www.theatlantic.com/national/archive/2013/04/what-would-happen-if-the-state-took-over-your-school-district/274527; Alan Greenblatt, "The Problem with School Takeovers," Governing, June 2018, 12; Carmel Martin, Scott Sargard, and Samantha Batel, "Making the Grade: A 50-State Analysis of School Accountability Systems" (Washington, DC: Center for American Progress, May 2016), https://www.education.nh.gov/essa/documents/accountability-analysis.pdf.

47. Pew Charitable Trusts, "State Strategies to Detect Local Fiscal Distress" (Washington, DC: Pew Trusts, September 2016), http://www.pewtrusts.org/~/media/assets/2016/09/detecting_local_distress_report.pdf; Ashley E. Nickels, "Approaches to Municipal Takeover: Home Rule Erosion and State Intervention in Michigan and New Jersey," State and Local Government Review 48:3 (September 2016): 194–207; Patrick McGeehan and John Taggart, "Atlantic City Bets Big, and Hopes Visitors Will Follow," New York Times, June 26, 2018, A1.

48. Greg Bluestein, "Hartsfield-Jackson: Opponents Promise to Fight More State Control of Airport," Atlanta Journal-Constitution, January 31, 2018, A1.

49. Shelby County v. Holder, 570 US (2013), https://www.oyez.org/cases/2012/12-96.

50. South Dakota v. Dole, 483 US 203 (1987), https://www.oyez.org/cases/1986/86-260; The History Channel, "Nixon Signs National Speed Limit into Law," https://www.history.com/this-day-in-history/nixon-signs-national-speed-limit-into-law.

51. Matthew L. Wald, "US Presses States for Strict Seat Belt Laws," New York Times, March 5, 2004, https://www.nytimes.com/2004/03/05/us/us-presses-states-for-strict-seat-belt-laws.html.

52. For a discussion of these and similar efforts, see Rachel A. Harmon, "Evaluating and Improving Structural Reform in Police Departments," Criminology & Public Policy 16:2 (May 2017): 617–27.

53. For a list of recent actions, see US Environmental Protection Agency, "Civil Cases and Settlements," https://cfpub.epa.gov/enforcement/cases.

54. See the history of federal grants in Robert Jay Dilger, "Federal Grants to State and Local Governments: An Historical Perspective on Contemporary Issues," R40638 (Washington, DC: Congressional Research Service, May 7, 2018), https://fas.org/sgp/crs/misc/R40638.pdf.

55. See Dilger, "Federal Grants," 23–26, and Michael J. Rich, "Community Development Block Grants at 40: Time for a Makeover," Housing Policy Debate 24:1 (2014): 46–90.

56. Brett Theodos, Christina Pierhoples Stacy, and Helen Ho, "Taking Stock of the Community Development Block Grant," Urban Institute, Metropolitan Housing and Communities Policy Center, April 2017, 2–5, https://www.urban.org/sites/default/files/publication/89551/cdbg_brief.pdf; Rich, "Community Development Block

Grants at 40," 54–65; Laura Bliss, "What the '$1.5 Trillion Infrastructure Plan' Really Pays For," *CityLab*, February 12, 2018, https://www.citylab.com/transportation/2018/02/what-the-15-trillion-infrastructure-plan-really-pays-for/553058; Bob Bryan, "Trump is Punting on One of His Biggest Goals for the Year," *Business Insider*, May 10, 2018, http://www.businessinsider.com/trump-gop-infrastructure-bill-dead-2018-5.

57. Theodos et al., "Taking Stock," 5–6.

58. See Rich, "Community Development Block Grants at 40," 65–83.

59. For more on the Center, see State and Local Legal Center, http://www.statelocallc.org.

60. Alan Greenblatt, "'Sanctuary Cities' Just the Start of Mayors' Opposition to Trump," *Governing*, January 27, 2017, http://www.governing.com/topics/urban/gov-trump-sanctuary-cities-mayors.html; Kate Irby, "DOJ Threatens 23 Sanctuary Jurisdictions with Subpoenas," *Governing*, January 24, 2018, http://www.governing.com/topics/public-justice-safety/tns-sanctuary-subpoenas-justice-department.html; Carolyn Berndt, "Five Things City Leaders Should Know about the Paris Withdrawal," National League of Cities, June 5, 2017, https://www.nlc.org/article/five-things-city-leaders-should-know-about-the-paris-withdrawal.

61. Matt W. Loftis and Jaclyn J. Kettler, "Lobbying from inside the System: Why Local Governments Pay for Representation in the US Congress," *Political Research Quarterly* 68:1 (March 2014): 193–206.

62. For an analysis of officials' views on changes in local government authority, see Ann O'M. Bowman and Richard C. Kearney, "Are US Cities Losing Power and Authority? Perceptions of Local Government Actors," *Urban Affairs Review* 48:4 (July 2012): 528–46.

63. On the two organizations, see https://www.pacounties.org/Pages/default.aspx and Pennsylvania Municipal League, https://www.pml.org. Data on lobbying expenses are available by searching the Pennsylvania Department of State Lobbying Directory: https://www.palobbyingservices.pa.gov/Public/wfSearch.aspx#bottom.

64. National School Boards Association, https://www.nsba.org/services/state-association-services.

65. Special District Association of Colorado, https://www.sdaco.org.

66. David Barboza, "Chicago, Offering Big Incentives, Will Be Boeing's New Home," *New York Times*, May 11, 2011, https://www.nytimes.com/2001/05/11/business/chicago-offering-big-incentives-will-be-boeing-s-new-home.html; Kevin McCoy and Kaja Whitehouse, "GE Relocating Headquarters to Boston," *USA Today*, January 13, 2016, https://www.usatoday.com/story/money/2016/01/13/report-ge-relocating-headquarters-boston/78734268.

67. International City/County Management Association (ICMA) and Center for Sharing Public Health Services of the Kansas Health Institute, "Sharing Administrative Services across Jurisdictions," April 2017, https://icma.org/sites/default/files/Sharing%20Administrative%20Services%20across%20Jurisdictions%20Full%20Report-1.pdf.

68. Cheryl Hilvert and David Swindell, "Collaborative Service Delivery: What Every Local Government Manager Should Know," *State and Local Government Review* 45:4 (December 2013): 240–54.

69. National Association of Regional Councils, "History," http://narc.org/about-narc/about-the-association/history.

70. US Department of Transportation, Federal Transit Administration, "Metropolitan Transportation Plan (MTP)," https://www.transit.dot.gov/regulations-and-guidance/transportation-planning/metropolitan-transportation-plan-mtp.

71. Duluth-Superior Metropolitan Interstate Council, https://dsmic.org; Mid-America Regional Council, http://www.marc.org/transportation.

72. For more detail on this process, see Local Government Center, Montana State University, "Voter Review," http://www.msulocalgov.org/technicalassistance/voterreview.html.

73. Michael B. Brown and James V. Burgess, Jr., "Service Delivery Strategy," in Georgia Municipal Association, *Handbook for Georgia Mayors and Council Members* February 22, 2018 update, https://www.gmanet.com/Advice-Knowledge/Handbook-for-Georgia-Mayors-and-Councilmembers/Part-Three-management-of-municipal-government/Service-Delivery-Strategy.aspx.

74. Thomas H. Reed, "What Government Should a Region Have?" *National Municipal Review* 15:2 (February 1926): 92–99; Thomas H. Reed, "The Metropolitan Problem: 1941," *National Municipal Review* 30:7 (July 1941): 400–408, 460.

75. Among the strongest advocates for expanding central cities is former Albuquerque mayor David Rusk, who lays out his case in *Cities without Suburbs: A Census 2010 Perspective*, 4th edition (Washington, DC: Woodrow Wilson Center Press, 2013).

76. For a summary and analysis of this "public choice" perspective, see Michael Howell-Moroney, "The Tiebout Hypothesis 50 Years Later: Lessons and Lingering Challenges for Metropolitan Governance in the 21st Century," *Public Administration Review* 68:1 (January/February 2008): 97–109. A series of articles using survey data compared residents in a consolidated metropolitan area to those in a fragmented area; see W. E. Lyons and David Lowery, "Governmental Fragmentation Versus Consolidation: Five Public-Choice Myths about How to Create Informed, Involved, and Happy Citizens," *Public Administration Review* 49:6 (November/December 1989): 533–43.

77. See, for example, Gary J. Miller, *Cities by Contract: The Politics of Municipal Incorporation* (Cambridge, MA: MIT Press, 1981); David Lowery, "A Transactions Costs Model of Metropolitan Governance: Allocation Versus Redistribution in Urban America," *Journal of Public Administration Research and Theory* 10:1 (January 2000): 49–78.

78. On Portland, see Metro, "What Is Metro?" https://www.oregonmetro.gov/regional-leadership/what-metro; on the Metropolitan Council in the Minneapolis-St. Paul area, see Metropolitan Council, https://metrocouncil.org.

79. For example, Wisconsin passed a law in 1995 creating a five-county special district to levy a 0.1 percent sales

tax to build and maintain Miller Park, the baseball stadium for the Milwaukee Brewers: Southeast Wisconsin Professional Baseball Park District, "Miller Park Sales Tax: Frequently Asked Questions," 2017, http://www.millerparkdistrict.com/images/PDFs/MillerPark_SalesTaxFAQs_2017.pdf.

80. Paul S. Lewis, "An Old Debate Confronts New Realities: Large Suburbs and Economic Development in the Metropolis," in *Metropolitan Governance: Conflict, Competition, and Cooperation*, ed. Richard C. Feiock (Washington, DC: Georgetown University Press, 2004), 95–123.

81. California Association of Local Agency Formation Commissions, "A Citizen's Guide to LAFCOs," https://calafco.org/resources/introduction-lafco/citizens-guide-lafcos; League of Minnesota Cities, "Handbook for Minnesota Cities," November 2017, chapter 2, https://www.lmc.org/media/document/1/changeofboundariesstatusandname pdf?inline=true.

5. LOCAL LEGISLATURES

1. Maddy Hayden, "Council Passes Tax Hike on 'Difficult' Vote," *Albuquerque Journal*, March 5, 2018, https://www.abqjournal.com/1141748/council-votes-for-three-eighths-tax-increase.html, accessed June 15, 2019.

2. Craig Burnett, "Parties as an Organizational Force on Nonpartisan City Councils," *Party Politics* (article first published online: October 27, 2017); Richard Florida, "Are Local Politics as Polarized as National? Depends on the Issue," *CityLab*, April 24, 2019, https://www.citylab.com/life/2019/04/polarization-cities-education-labor-public-opinion-taxes/587746, accessed June 17, 2019.

3. Alonzo L. Hamby, "Harry S. Truman: Life Before the Presidency," https://millercenter.org/president/truman/life-before-the-presidency, accessed September 1, 2018.

4. Richard E. Cohen, James A. Barnes, Charlie Cook, and Michael Barone, *2016 Almanac of American Politics* (Bethesda: Columbia Books, 2017).

5. Victor S. DeSantis, "County Government: A Century of Change," in *Forms of Local Government: A Handbook on City, County and Regional Options*, ed. Roger L. Kemp (Jefferson: McFarland & Company, 1999), 245–54. Technically speaking, there is a fourth form of government: commission-manager. To simplify matters the chapter sticks to the designation of three forms, given the closeness of the commission-manager and commission-administrator forms.

6. Robert M. Howard, Arnold Fleischmann, and Richard N. Engstrom, *Politics in Georgia,* 3rd edition (Athens: University of Georgia Press, 2017), 259–60.

7. ICMA, *County Form of Government 2014 Survey Results* (Washington, DC: International City/County Management Association, 2015), 1. The survey distinguishes between a council (commission)-administrator form, and a council (commission)-manager form. The 64 percent figure combines the responses between these two. In the survey, 37 percent reported that they used the council (commission)-administrator form and 27 percent reported that they

used the council (commission)-manager form. The key difference between the two is that the executive's powers are broader in the latter than in the former.

8. ICMA, *County Form of Government 2014 Survey Results* (Washington, DC: International City/County Management Association, 2015), 7. The number reported does not add up to 100 percent, but it is unclear from the survey why that is so. It could be that 1 percent of survey respondents failed to include an answer to this question.

9. ICMA, *County Form of Government 2014 Survey Results*.

10. ICMA, *County Form of Government 2014 Survey Results*, 8.

11. ICMA, *County Form of Government 2014 Survey Results*, 5.

12. J. Edwin Benton, "County Service Delivery: Does Government Structure Matter?" *Public Administration Review* 62:4 (July–August 2002): 471–79; Victor S. DeSantis and Tari Renner, "The Impact of Political Structures on Public Policies in American Counties," *Public Administration Review* 54:3 (May–June 1994): 291–95; Vincent L. Marando and Mavis Mann Reeves, "Counties as Local Governments: Research Issues and Questions," *Journal of Urban Affairs* 14:1 (March 1992): 45–53; Mark Schneider and Kee Ok Park, "Metropolitan Counties as Service Delivery Agents: The Still Forgotten Governments," *Public Administration Review* 49:4 (July–August 1989): 345–52.

13. Garrick L. Percival, Martin Johnson, and Max Neiman, "Representation and Local Policy: Relating County-Level Public Opinion to Policy Outputs," *Political Research Quarterly* 62:1 (March 2009): 164–77.

14. US Census Bureau, "Census Bureau Reports there are 89,004 Local Governments in the United States," https://www.census.gov/newsroom/releases/archives/governments/cb12-161.html, accessed January 23, 2017.

15. National League of Cities, "City Councils," http://www.nlc.org/city-councils, accessed June 16, 2017.

16. Peverill Squire, "Measuring Legislative Professionalism: The Squire Index Revisited," *State Politics and Policy Quarterly* 7:2 (June 2007): 211–27; David Mayhew, *Congress: The Electoral Connection*, 2nd edition (New Haven: Yale University Press, 2004).

17. James H. Svara, *Official Leadership in the City: Patterns of Conflict and Cooperation* (New York: Oxford University Press, 1990).

18. Svara, *Official Leadership in the City*, 165.

19. ICMA, *2011 Municipal Form of Government Survey Summary*, 1.

20. ICMA, *2011 Municipal Form of Government Survey Summary*.

21. National League of Cities, January 2, 2015, https://www.nlc.org/city-councils, accessed May 25, 2019.

22. National League of Cities, https://www.nlc.org/city-councils.

23. Brian E. Adams, *Citizen Lobbyists: Local Efforts to Influence Public Policy* (Philadelphia: Temple University Press, 2007).

24. Kenneth Prewitt, *The Recruitment of Political Leaders: A Study of Citizen-Politicians* (New York: Bobbs-Merrill Company, 1970).

25. National Conference of State Legislatures, "2016 Survey: State Legislative Compensation, Session per Diem and

Mileage," http://www.ncsl.org/Portals/1/Documents/legismgt/2016_Leg_Comp_Session_Per%20Diem_Mileage.pdf, accessed June 5, 2017.

26. Samuel Kernell, Gary C. Jacobson, Thad Kousser, and Lynn Vavreck, *The Logic of American Politics*, 8th edition (Washington, DC: CQ Press, 2018). See chapter 1 for a discussion of common collective action problems.

27. For the information about newspaper coverage, see Pew Research Center, "Media Coverage of City Governments: A Study of 175 Cities and Communities," http://www.journalism.org/2010/07/29/media-coverage-city-governments. For declines in newspaper coverage, see Pew Research Center, "Newspapers Fact Sheet," http://www.journalism.org/fact-sheet/newspapers, accessed June 14, 2017.

28. Hannah Fenichel Pitken, *The Concept of Representation* (Berkeley: University of California Press, 1967).

29. Seth Masket, "Non-white Representation on America's City Councils," *Washington Post*, https://www.washingtonpost.com/news/monkey-cage/wp/2014/08/21/non-white-representation-on-americas-city-councils, accessed October 21, 2018.

30. Susan Welch and Timothy Bledsoe, *Urban Reform and Its Consequences: A Study in Representation* (Chicago: University of Chicago Press, 1988).

31. ICMA, *2011 Municipal Form of Government Survey Summary*, 9.

32. Craig M. Burnett and Vladimir Kogan, "Local Logrolling? Assessing the Impact of Legislative Districting in Los Angeles," *Urban Affairs Review* 50:5 (September 2014): 648–71, 650–51.

33. Rufus Browning, Dale Rogers Marshall, and David H. Tabb, eds., *Racial Politics in American Cities*, 3rd edition (New York: Pearson, 2003).

34. Browning et al., *Racial Politics in American Cities*.

35. Richard L. Engstrom and Michael D. McDonald, "The Election of Blacks to City Councils: Clarifying the Impact of Electoral Arrangements on the Seats/Population Relationship," *American Political Science Review* 75:2 (June 1981): 344–54; Richard L. Engstrom and Michael D. McDonald, "The Underrepresentation of Blacks on City Councils: Comparing the Structural and Socioeconomic Explanations for South/Non-South Differences," *The Journal of Politics* 44:4 (November 1982): 1088–99; Jessica Trounstine and Melody E. Valdini, "The Context Matters: The Effects of Single-Member versus At-Large Districts on City Council Diversity," *American Journal of Political Science* 52:3 (July 2008): 554–69; Susan Welch, "The Impact of At-Large Elections on the Representation of Blacks and Hispanics," *The Journal of Politics* 52:4 (November 1990): 1050–76; Jeffrey S. Zax, "Election Methods and Black and Hispanic City Council Membership," *Social Science Quarterly* 71:2 (June 1990): 338–55.

36. *Rogers v. Lodge*, 458 US 613 (1982).

37. *Thornburg v. Gingles* S. Ct. 2752 (1986). For a broader discussion, see Sid Hemsley, "At-Large Electoral Systems and Voting Rights," 1991, Tennessee Research and Creative Exchange (TRACE), MTAS Publications: Technical Bulletins, http://trace.tennessee.edu/utk_mtastech/332, accessed January 29, 2017.

38. Tim R. Sass, "The Determinants of Hispanic Representation in Municipal Government," *Southern Economic Journal* 66:3 (January 2000): 609–30.

39. James W. Button, Kenneth D. Wald, and Barbara A. Rienzo, "The Election of Openly Gay Public Officials in American Communities," *Urban Affairs Review* 35:2 (November 1999): 188–209.

40. Susan Welch and Timothy Bledsoe, *Urban Reform and Its Consequences* (Chicago: University of Chicago Press, 1988), 51; see also Tim R. Sass and Stephen L. Mehay, "The Voting Rights Act, District Elections, and the Success of Black Candidates in Municipal Elections," *Journal of Law and Economics* 38:2 (October 1995): 367–92.

41. Melissa J. Marschall, Anirudh V. S. Ruhil, and Paru R. Shah, "The New Racial Calculus: Electoral Institutions and Black Representation in Local Legislatures," *American Journal of Political Science* 54:1 (January 2010): 107–24.

42. ICMA, *2011 Municipal Form of Government Survey Summary*, 9.

43. Charles S. Bullock III and Susan A. MacManus, "Municipal Electoral Structure and the Election of Councilwomen," *The Journal of Politics* 53:1 (February 1991): 75–89.

44. Trounstine and Valdini, "The Context Matters."

45. Adrienne R. Smith, Beth Reingold, and Michael Leo Owens, "The Political Determinants of Women's Descriptive Representation in Cities," *Political Research Quarterly* 65:2 (June 2012): 315–29.

46. Bullock III and MacManus, "Municipal Electoral Structure and the Election of Councilwomen."

47. Bullock III and MacManus, "Municipal Electoral Structure and the Election of Councilwomen"; Trounstine and Valdini, "The Context Matters."

48. Browning et al., *Racial Politics in American Cities*; Engstrom and McDonald, "The Election of Blacks to City Councils"; Engstrom and McDonald, "The Underrepresentation of Blacks on City Councils"; Trounstine and Valdini, "The Context Matters."

49. Welch and Bledsoe, *Urban Reform and Its Consequences*, 42.

50. Willis D. Hawley, *Nonpartisan Elections and the Case for Party Politics* (New York: Wiley, 1973); Eugene Lee, *The Politics of Nonpartisanship* (Berkeley: University of California Press, 1960), 56–57.

51. Welch and Bledsoe, *Urban Reform and Its Consequences*, 51.

52. Brian F. Schaffner, Matthew J. Streb, and Gerald C. Wright, "A New Look at the Republican Advantage in Nonpartisan Elections," *Political Research Quarterly* 60:2 (June 2007): 240–49.

53. Trounstine and Valdini, "The Context Matters"; Smith, Reingold, and Owens. "The Political Determinants of Women's Descriptive Representation in Cities."

54. Timothy Bledsoe, *Careers in City Politics: The Case for Urban Democracy* (Pittsburgh: University of Pittsburgh Press, 1993), 54; Prewitt, *The Recruitment of Political Leaders*.

55. Bledsoe, *Careers in City Politics*, 56.

56. Bledsoe, *Careers in City Politics*, 58–59.

57. Pitken, *The Concept of Representation*.

58. Welch and Bledsoe, *Urban Reform and Its Consequences*.

59. Peggy Heilig and Robert J. Mundt, *Your Voice at City Hall* (Albany: State University of New York Press, 1984), 96; Welch and Bledsoe, *Urban Reform and Its Consequences*, 73–75.

60. James C. Clingermayer and Richard C. Feiock, "Constituencies, Campaign Support and Council Member Intervention in City Development Policy," *Social Science Quarterly* 74:1 (March 1993): 199–215; James C. Clingermayer and Richard C. Feiock, "Campaigns, Careerism, and Constituencies: Contacting Council Members about Economic Development Policy," *American Politics Quarterly* 22:4 (October 1994): 453–68; James C. Clingermayer and Richard C. Feiock, "Council Views toward Targeting of Development Policy Benefits," *The Journal of Politics* 57:2 (May 1995): 508–20.

61. Clingermayer and Feiock, "Campaigns, Careerism, and Constituencies," 463.

62. Clingermayer and Feiock, "Constituencies, Campaign Support and Council Member Intervention in City Development Policy."

63. Brinck Kerr and Kenneth R. Mladenka, "Does Politics Matter? A Time-Series Analysis of Minority Employment Patterns," *American Journal of Political Science* 38:4 (November 1994): 918–43.

64. Brinck Kerr, Will Miller, and Margaret Reid, "Determinants of Female Employment Patterns in US Cities: A Time-Series Analysis," *Urban Affairs Review* 33:4 (March 1998): 559–78.

65. ICMA, *2011 Municipal Form of Government Survey Summary*, 7.

66. ICMA, *2011 Municipal Form of Government Survey Summary* (Washington, DC: International City/County Management Association, 2012), 11.

67. Brian E. Adams, *Citizen Lobbyists: Local Efforts to Influence Public Policy* (Philadelphia: Temple University Press, 2006), 31.

68. ICMA, *2011 Municipal Form of Government Survey Summary*, 12.

69. John P. Pelissero and Timothy B. Krebs, "City Council Legislative Committees and Policy-Making in Large United States Cities," *American Journal of Political Science* 41:2 (April 1997): 499–518.

70. Bertram Johnson, "Collective Action, City Council Committees, and State Aid to Cities," *Urban Affairs Review* 42:4 (March 2007): 457–78.

71. Edward C. Banfield and James Q. Wilson, *City Politics* (Cambridge, MA: Harvard University Press, 1963).

72. Mayhew, *Congress: The Electoral Connection*.

73. Clingermayer and Feiock, "Council Views toward Targeting of Development Policy Benefits."

74. Burnett and Kogan, "Local Logrolling?"

75. Yue Zhang, "Boundaries of Power: Politics of Urban Preservation in Two Chicago Neighborhoods," *Urban Affairs Review* 47:4 (July 2011): 511–40; see also Dick Simpson, *Rogues, Rebels, and Rubber Stamps: The Politics of the Chicago City Council from 1863 to the Present* (Boulder: Westview Press, 2001).

76. Svara, *Official Leadership in the City*.

77. Timothy B. Krebs and John P. Pelissero, "What Influences City Council Adoption and Support for Reinventing Government? Environmental or Institutional Factors?" *Public Administration Review* 70:2 (February 2010): 258–67.

78. Kimberly L. Nelson and Karl Nollenberger, "Conflict and Cooperation in Municipalities: Do Variations in Form of Government Have an Effect?" *Urban Affairs Review* 47:5 (September 2011): 696–720.

79. Welch and Bledsoe, *Urban Reform and Its Consequences*; Heilig and Mundt, *Your Voice at City Hall*, 128; Krebs and Pelissero, "What Influences City Council Adoption and Support for Reinventing Government?"; but see Nelson and Nollenberger, "Conflict and Cooperation in Municipalities."

80. Welch and Bledsoe, *Urban Reform and Its Consequences*; see also Heilig and Mundt, *Your Voice at City Hall*, 128.

81. For examples of this relationship in the city of Chicago, see Simpson, *Rogues, Rebels, and Rubber Stamps*.

82. Svara, *Official Leadership in the City*.

83. Susan A. MacManus, "Seniors in City Hall: Causes and Consequences of the Graying of City Councils," *Social Science Quarterly* 79:3 (August 1998): 620–33.

84. Rory Allan Austin, "Seats That May Not Matter: Testing for Racial Polarization in US City Councils," *Legislative Studies Quarterly* 27:3 (August 2002): 481–508.

85. Browning et al., *Racial Politics in American Cities*.

86. Zoltan Hajnal and Jessica Trounstine, "Where Turnout Matters: The Consequences of Uneven Turnout in City Politics," *The Journal of Politics* 67:2 (May 2005): 515–35; see also Zoltan L. Hajnal and Jessica Trounstine, "Who or What Governs? The Effects of Economics, Politics, Institutions, and Needs on Local Spending," *American Politics Research* 38:6 (November 2010): 1130–63.

87. Zoltan L. Hajnal, *Changing White Attitudes towards Black Political Leadership* (Cambridge, UK: Cambridge University Press, 2007); Melissa J. Marschall and Anirudh V. S. Ruhil, "Substantive Symbols: The Attitudinal Dimension of Black Political Incorporation in Local Government," *American Journal of Political Science* 51:5 (January 2007): 17–33.

88. Katherine Levine Einstein and Vladimir Kogan, "Pushing the City Limits: Policy Responsiveness in Municipal Government," *Urban Affairs Review* 52:1 (January 2016): 3–32.

89. Christine Kelleher Palus, "Responsiveness in American Local Governments," *State & Local Government Review* 42:2 (August 2010): 133–50; Chris Tausanovitch and Christopher Warshaw, "Representation in Municipal Government," *American Political Science Review* 108:3 (August 2014): 605–41.

90. National League of Cities, "Forms of Municipal Government," http://www.nlc.org/forms-of-municipal-government, accessed June 14, 2017.

6: MAYORS AND EXECUTIVES

1. Molly Cohen, "A Lawyer's Playbook to Fight State Preemption," *CityLab*, July 19, 2017, https://www.citylab.com/equity/2017/07/a-lawyers-playbook-to-fight-state-preemption/533862, accessed August 4, 2018.

2. Eric B. Herzik, "The President, Governors and Mayors: A Framework for Comparative Analysis," *Presidential Studies Quarterly*, 15:2 (Spring, 1985): 353–71.

3. Melvin G. Holli, *The American Mayor: The Best and the Worst Big-City Leaders* (University Park, PA: Pennsylvania State University Press, 1999).

4. Mancur Olson, *The Logic of Collective Action: Public Goods and the Theory of Groups* (Cambridge, MA: Harvard University Press, 1965).

5. Douglas Yates, "The Mayor's Eight-Ring Circus: The Shape of Urban in Its Evolving Policy Arenas," in *Urban Policymaking*, ed. Dale Rogers Marshall (Beverly Hills: Sage, 1979), 41–69, 41.

6. Scott C. James, "The Evolution of the Presidency: Between the Promise and the Fear," in *The Executive Branch*, eds. Joel D. Aberbach and Mark A. Peterson (Oxford: Oxford University Press, 2005), 25–26; Richard Neustadt, *Presidential Power and the Modern Presidents: From Roosevelt to Reagan* (New York: Free Press, 1991); Samuel Kernell, *Going Public: New Strategies of Presidential Leadership* (Washington, DC: CQ Press, 2007).

7. H. George Frederickson and Gary Alan Johnson, "The Adapted American City: A Study of Institutional Dynamics," *Urban Affairs Review* 36:6 (July 2001): 872–84.

8. Frederickson and Johnson, "The Adapted American City."

9. Kenneth K. Wong and Francis X. Shen, *Mayoral Governance and Student Achievement: How Mayor-Led Districts Are Improving School and Student Performance* (Washington, DC: Center for American Progress, March 2013), https://files.eric.ed.gov/fulltext/ED561083.pdf, accessed August 4, 2018.

10. Wong and Shen, *Mayoral Governance and Student Achievement*; Jeffrey R. Henig and Wilbur C. Rich, eds., *Mayors in the Middle: Politics, Race, and Mayoral Control of Urban Schools* (Princeton: Princeton University Press, 2004), 262.

11. Neustadt, *Presidential Power and the Modern Presidents*.

12. Jeffrey L. Pressman, "The Preconditions of Mayoral Leadership," *American Political Science Review* 66:2 (June 1972): 511–24. See also James H. Svara, "Mayoral Leadership in Council Manager Cities: Preconditions Versus Preconceptions," *The Journal of Politics* 49:1 (February 1987): 207–27.

13. Barbara Ferman, *Governing the Ungovernable City: Political Skill, Leadership, and the Modern Mayor* (Philadelphia: Temple University Press, 1985); Barbara Ferman, *Challenging the Growth Machine: Neighborhood Politics in Chicago and Pittsburgh* (Lawrence: Kansas University Press, 1996).

14. Raphael Sonenshein, *Politics in Black and White: Race and Power in Los Angeles*.

15. Richard M. Flanagan, *Mayors and the Challenge of Urban Leadership* (Lanham: University Press of America, 2004); Dennis Judd, "Strong Leadership," *Urban Studies* 37:5–6 (May 2000): 951–61, 957.

16. Douglas Yates, "The Mayor's Eight-Ring Circus," 44–45.

17. *Rutan v. Republican Party*, 497 US 62 (1990); *Elrod v. Burns*, 427 US 347 (1976).

18. Douglas Yates, *The Ungovernable City: The Politics of Urban Problems and Policy Making* (Cambridge, MA: MIT Press, 1979), 49–50; Robert A. Dahl, *Who Governs? Democracy and Power in an American City* (New Haven: Yale University Press, 1961), chapter 17; Douglas Rae, *City: Urbanism and Its End* (New Haven: Yale University Press, 2003), chapter 10.

19. For the broker style, also see Floyd Hunter, *Community Power Structure* (Chapel Hill: University of North Carolina Press, 1953) and Edward C. Banfield, *Political Influence* (New York: Free Press, 1961).

20. But see Wen H. Kuo, "Mayoral Infuence in Urban Policy Making," *The American Journal of Sociology* 79:3 (November 1973): 620–38. Kuo argued that the broker style was largely inaccurate. By contrast, his research showed that mayors were aggressive in initiating city policies and programs, and therefore much more powerful in their policy-making role.

21. Peter Eisinger, "City Politics in an Era of Federal Devolution," *Urban Affairs Review* 33:3 (January 1998): 308–25. For the Philadelphia example, see Buzz Bissinger, *A Prayer for the City* (New York: Vintage, 1997).

22. David Osborne and Ted Gaebler, *Reinventing Government* (New York: Addison Wesley Publishing, 1992).

23. Judd, "Strong Leadership."

24. Svara, "Mayoral Leadership in Council Manager Cities."

25. Cohen, "A Lawyer's Playbook to Fight State Preemption."

26. Rufus P. Browning, Dale Rogers Marshall, and David H. Tabb, eds., *Racial Politics in American Cities*, 3rd edition (New York: Pearson, 2003).

27. Marion Orr and Domingo Morell, *Latino Mayors: Political Change in the Postindustrial City* (Philadelphia: Temple University Press, 2018), chapter 1.

28. Steven P. Erie, *Rainbow's End: Irish-Americans and the Dilemmas of Urban Machine Politics, 1840–1985* (Berkley: University of California Press, 1988).

29. Orr and Morel, *Latino Mayors*.

30. Carlos E. Cuellar, "Patterns of Representation: A Descriptive Analysis of Latino-Mayor Cities in the United States," in *Latino Mayors: Political Change in the Postindustrial City*, eds. Marion Orr and Domingo Morel (Philadelphia: Temple University Press, 2018), 37.

31. Browning et al., *Racial Politics in American Cities*.

32. Browning et al., *Racial Politics in American Cities*.

33. Daniel J. Hopkins and Katherine T. McCabe, "After It's Too Late: Estimating the Policy Impacts of Black Mayoralties in US Cities," *American Politics Research* 40:4 (July 2012): 665–700; John P. Pelissero, David B. Holian, and Laura A. Tomaka, "Does Political Incorporation Matter? The Impact of Minority Mayors over Time," *Urban Affairs Review* 36:1 (September 2000): 84–92.

34. Mirya Holman, *Women in Politics in the American City* (Philadelphia: Temple University Press, 2014).

35. For a list of female mayors in the US's 100 largest cities, see Rutgers, Center for American Women and Politics, "Women in Elective Office 2018," http://www.cawp.

rutgers.edu/women-elective-office-2018#mayors, accessed August 4, 2018.

36. Grace Hall Saltzstein, "Female Mayors and Women in Municipal Jobs," *American Journal of Political Science* 30:1 (January 1986): 130–46; Brinck Kerr, Will Miller, and Margaret Reid, "Determinants of Female Employment Patterns in US Cities: A Time-Series Analysis," *Urban Affairs Review* 33 (March 1998): 559–78.

37. Holman, *Women in Politics in the American City*; Lynne A. Weikart, Greg Chen, Daniel H. Williams, and Haris Hromic, "The Democratic Sex: Gender Differences and the Exercise of Power," *Journal of Women, Politics and Policy* 28:1 (2006): 119–40.

38. Fernando Ferriera and Joseph Gyourko, "Does Gender Matter for Political Leadership? The Case of US Mayors," *Journal of Public Economics* 112 (April 2014): 24–39; Weikart et al., "The Democratic Sex."

39. Ferriera and Gyourko, "Does Gender Matter for Political Leadership?"; Holman, *Women in Politics in the American City*.

40. R. Douglas Arnold and Nicholas L. Carnes, "Holding Mayors Accountable: New York's Executives from Koch to Bloomberg," *American Journal of Political Science* 56:4 (October 2012): 949–63.

41. See also Susan E. Howell, *Race, Performance and Approval of Mayors* (New York: Palgrave Macmillan, 2007).

42. Kernell, *Going Public*.

43. National League of Cities, "State of the Cities 2018," https://www.nlc.org/resource/state-of-the-cities-2018, accessed August 4, 2018.

44. Beau Dure, "Millennials Continue Urbanization Of America, Leaving Small Towns," October 2014, NPR, https://www.npr.org/2014/10/21/357723069/millennials-continue-urbanization-of-america-leaving-small-towns, accessed August 4, 2018.

45. J. Wesley Leckrone, Michael Atherton, Nicole Crossey, Andrea Stickley, and Meghan E. Rubado, "Does Anyone Care about the Poor? The Role of Redistribution in Mayoral Policy Agendas," *State and Local Government Review* 47:4 (December 2015): 240–54.

46. Katherine Levine Einstein and David M. Glick, "Mayors, Partisanship, and Redistribution: Evidence Directly from US Mayors," *Urban Affairs Review* 54:1 (January 2018): 74–106.

47. Alan I. Abramowitz and Kyle L. Saunders, "Is Polarization a Myth?" *The Journal of Politics* 70 (April 2008): 542–55; Morris P. Fiorina, *Culture War: The Myth of a Polarized America* (Boston: Pearson Longman, 2005).

48. Richard Florida, "America's 'Big Sort' Is Only Getting Bigger," *CityLab*, Oct 25, 2016, https://www.citylab.com/equity/2016/10/the-big-sort-revisited/504830, accessed June 25, 2019.

49. Fernando Ferreira and Joseph Gyourko, "Do Political Parties Matter? Evidence from US Cities," *Quarterly Journal of Economics* 124 (February 2009): 349–97; Elisabeth R. Gerber and Daniel Hopkins, "When Mayors Matter: Estimating the Impact of Mayoral Partisanship on City Policy," *American Journal of Political Science* 55 (February 2011): 326–39.

50. Gerber and Hopkins, "When Mayors Matter," 333–34.

51. Justin de Benedictis-Kessner and Christopher Warshaw, "Mayoral Partisanship and Municipal Fiscal Policy," *Journal of Politics* 78 (October 2016): 1124–38.

52. Einstein and Glick, "Mayors, Partisanship, and Redistribution."

53. Einstein and Glick, "Mayors, Partisanship, and Redistribution," 98.

54. John R. Petrocik, "Issue Ownership in Presidential Elections, with a 1980 Case Study," *American Journal of Political Science* 40 (August 1996): 825–50.

55. Clarence N. Stone and Heywood T. Sanders, eds., *The Politics of Urban Development* (Lawrence: University Press of Kansas, 1987).

56. Jered B. Carr, "What Have We Learned about the Performance of Council-Manager Government? A Review and Synthesis of Research," *Public Administration Review* 75:5 (August 2015): 673–89.

57. ICMA, *Municipal Form of Government, 2011*, https://icma.org/documents/icma-survey-research-2011-municipal-form-government-survey-summary, accessed August 4, 2018.

58. Robert E. England, John P. Pelissero, and David R. Morgan, *Managing Urban America*, 7th edition (Washington, DC: CQ Press, 2012), 104–6.

59. England et al., *Managing Urban America*, 104.

60. Leann Beaty and Trenton J. Davis, "Gender Disparity in Professional City Management: Making the Case for Enhancing Leadership Curriculumm," *Journal of Public Affairs Education* 18:4 (2012): 617–32.

61. Richard L. Fox and Robert A. Schuhmann, "Gender and Local Government: A Comparison of Women and Men City Managers," *Public Administration Review* 59:3 (May–June 1999): 231–42.

62. John Nalbandian, "Facilitating Community, Enabling Democracy: New Roles for Local Government Managers," *Public Administration Review* 59:3 (May–June, 1999): 187–97.

63. Douglas J. Watson and Wendy L. Hassett, "Career Paths of City Managers in America's Largest Council-Manager Cities," *Public Administration Review* 64:2 (March 2004): 192–99, 196.

64. Gordon P. Whitaker and Ruth Hoogland DeHoog, "City Managers under Fire: How Conflict Leads to Turnover," *Public Administration Review* 51:2 (March–April 1991): 156–65.

65. Richard C. Feiock, James C. Clingermayer, Christopher Stream, Barbara Coyle McCabe, and Shamina Ahmed, "Political Conflict, Fiscal Stress, and Administrative Turnover in American Cities," *State and Local Government Review* 33:2 (August 2001): 101–8; James B. Kaatz, P. Edward French, and Hazel Prentice-Cooper, "City Council Conflict as a Cause of Psychological Burnout and Voluntary Turnover Among Managers," *State and Local Government Review* 31:3 (September 1999): 162–72.

66. Feiock et al., "Political Conflict, Fiscal Stress, and Administrative Turnover in American Cities."

67. Feiock et al., "Political Conflict, Fiscal Stress, and Administrative Turnover in American Cities."

68. Robert J. Tekniepe and Christopher Stream, "You're Fired! County Manager Turnover in Large American Counties," *American Review of Public Administration* 42:6 (November 1998): 715–29.

69. Watson and Hassett, "Career Paths of City Managers in America's Largest Council-Manager Cities."

70. Greg J. Protasel, "Leadership in Council Manager Cities: The Institutional Implications," in *Ideal and Practice in Council Manager Government,* ed. H. G. Frederickson (Washington, DC: International City and County Manager Association), 114–22.

71. Jennifer M. Connolly, "The Impact of Local Politics on the Principal-Agent Relationship Between Council and Manager in Municipal Government," *Journal of Public Administration Research and Theory* 27:2 (April 2017): 253–68.

72. *Rutan v. Republican Party*, 497 US 62 (1990); *Elrod v. Burns*, 427 US 347 (1976).

73. US Department of Labor, Bureau of Labor Statistics, "Union Members: 2018," press release, January 18, 2019, https://www.bls.gov/news.release/pdf/union2.pdf, accessed May 25, 2019.

74. Olson, *The Logic of Collective Action.*

75. England et al., *Managing Urban America*, 294.

76. England et al., *Managing Urban America*, 293.

77. Supreme Court of the United States blog, "Janus v. American Federation of State, County, and Municipal Employees, Council 31," http://www.scotusblog.com/case-files/cases/janus-v-american-federation-state-county-municipal-employees-council-31, accessed August 4, 2018.

78. Michael Lipsky, *Street-Level Bureaucrats: The Dilemmas of the Individual in Public Services* (New York: Russell Sage Foundation, 1980).

79. Anthony L. Bui, Matthew M. Coates, and Elliot C. Matthay, "Years of Life Lost Due to Encounters with Law Enforcement in the USA, 2015–2016," *Journal of Epidemiology and Community Health* 72 (July 2018): 715–18.

80. Mark D. Bradbury and J. Edward Kellough, "Representative Bureaucracy: Exploring the Potential for Active Representation in Local Government." *Journal of Public Administration Research and Theory* 18 (October 2008): 697–714.

81. Browning et al., *Racial Politics in American Cities*; Kerr and Mladenka, "Does Politics Matter?"; Kerr et al., "Determinants of Female Employment Patterns in US Cities"; Brinck Kerr, Will Miller, William D. Schreckhise, and Margaret Reid, "When Does Politics Matter? A Reexamination of the Determinants of African-American and Latino Municipal Employment Patterns," *Urban Affairs Review* 49:6 (November 2013): 888–912.

82. NYC, "Bill de Blasio, 109th Mayor of New York City," https://www1.nyc.gov/office-of-the-mayor/bio.page, accessed August 4, 2018.

83. City Clerks Association, "What is a City Clerk?" https://ccac.memberclicks.net/what-is-a-city-clerk, accessed August 4, 2018.

84. Sonia R. Carvalho, John Guinn, and Marsha Jones Moutrie, "Stepping into the Evolving Role of the City Attorney: Executive Management Team Member, Crisis Manager, Legal Advisor and Team Builder—What Roles Can or Should You Play?" http://www.cacities.org/getattachment/4c250e84-783c-4a34-9caf-c0152c7e0d92/5-2012Spring-Carvalho-Guinn-Moutrie-Stepping-Into.aspx, accessed August 4, 2018.

85. Run for Office, "City of Chicago Treasurer," https://www.runforoffice.org/elected_offices/22368-city-of-chicago-treasurer, accessed August 4, 2018.

86. ICMA, "ICMA Survey Research: County Form of Government 2014 Survey Results," https://icma.org/documents/icma-survey-research-county-form-government-2014-survey-results, accessed August 4, 2018.

87. Ballotpedia, "Joe Arpaio," https://ballotpedia.org/Joe_Arpaio, accessed June 25, 2019; Will Wright, "Kim Davis, Clerk Who Refused to Sign Marriage Licenses for Gay Couples, Loses to Democrat," *Lexington Herald-Leader*, November 6, 2018, https://www.kentucky.com/news/politics-government/article221121745.html, accessed June 25, 2019.

7: ELECTIONS AND VOTING

1. Zoltan Hajnal and Jessica Trounstine, "Where Turnout Matters: The Consequences of Uneven Turnout in City Politics," *The Journal of Politics* 67:2 (May 2005): 515–35; Kim Q. Hill and Jan E. Leighley, "The Policy Consequences of Class Bias in State Electorates," *American Journal of Political Science* 36:2 (May 1992): 351–65.

2. Neighborhood-based opposition to school busing in the 1970s is an example of the latter type of group. See Donald Philip Green and Jonathan A. Cowden, "Who Protests: Self-Interest and White Opposition to Busing," *The Journal of Politics* 54:2 (May 1992): 471–96. A more current example is groups that have formed to protest against police-officer-involved shootings, ones that often involve minority residents or residents suffering with mental illness.

3. Paul E. Peterson, *City Limits* (Chicago: University of Chicago Press, 1981); Charles M. Tiebout, "A Pure Theory of Local Expenditures," *The Journal of Political Economy* 64:5 (October 1956): 416–24.

4. ICMA, *ICMA 2011 Municipal Form of Government Survey Summary* (Washington, DC: International City/County Management Association, 2012), 8, http://icma.org/en/icma/knowledge_network/documents/kn/Document/303954/ICMA_2011_Municipal_Form_of_Government_Survey_Summary, accessed January 29, 2017.

5. Thresholds for avoiding a runoff vary, but they are typically a simple majority of the vote.

6. Ballotpedia, "Houston, Texas," https://ballotpedia.org/Houston,_Texas, accessed June 1, 2019.

7. For a listing of Houston city councilors by district and at large place, see City of Houston, https://www.houstontx.gov/council, accessed June 1, 2019.

8. In Seattle, the two at-large council members are designated positions 8 and 9, see Seattle City Council, "Meet the Council," https://www.seattle.gov/council/meet-the-council, accessed June 1, 2019. See also Ballotpedia, "Municipal Elections in Seattle, Washington,"

https://ballotpedia.org/Municipal_elections_in_Seattle,_Washington_(2017), accessed June 1, 2019. For Atlanta city council information, see Atlanta City Council, http://citycouncil.atlantaga.gov, accessed June 1, 2019.

9. Patricia Madej, Joseph A. Gambardello, and Jonathan Lai, "Philadelphia Primary Election 2019: Results and Scenes From the Day," *Philadelphia Inquirer*, https://www.inquirer.com/politics/election/philadelphia-philly-election-2019-primary-live-updates-20190521.html, accessed June 1, 2019.

10. Howard Fischer, "US Supreme Court Affirms Tucson's Method of Electing Council Members," May 20, 2017, https://tucson.com/news/local/us-supreme-court-affirms-tucson-s-method-of-electing-council/article_f4db1944-fcc4-51ce-934f-a49106b80bea.html, accessed June 1, 2019.

11. Jason A. McDaniel, "Writing the Rules to Rank the Candidates: Examining the Impact of Instant-Runoff Voting on Racial Group Turnout in San Francisco Mayoral Elections," *Journal of Urban Affairs* 38:3 (November 2016): 387–408.

12. Francis Neely and Corey Cook, "Whose Votes Count? Undervotes, Overvotes, and Ranking in San Francisco's Instant-Runoff Elections," *American Politics Research* 36:4 (July 2008): 530–54.

13. The Progressive Era in the US also produced dramatic electoral changes at the national level, such as the direct election of US Senators via the 17th Amendment to the US Constitution in 1913.

14. See ICMA, *2011 Municipal Form of Government Survey Summary*, 6. The term president or board chair might also be used in place of mayor in some cities or townships.

15. ICMA, *2011 Municipal Form of Government Survey Summary*.

16. It is hard to know exactly how widespread the initiative is at the city level. Data from the Initiative and Referendum Institute indicate that residents in 84 percent of the 1,000 largest US cities have the ability to use this form of direct democracy.

17. For information on both popular referendum and recall see ICMA, *2011 Municipal Form of Government Survey Summary*, 4.

18. Initiative and Referendum Institute, "State-by-State List of Initiative and Referendum Provisions," http://www.iandrinstitute.org/states.cfm, accessed January 22, 2017.

19. ICMA, *2011 Municipal Form of Government Survey Summary*, 4.

20. Alberto Alesina, Reza Baqir, and William Easterly, "Public Goods and Ethnic Divisions," *Quarterly Journal of Economics* 114:4 (November 1999): 1243–84.

21. Jacob S. Rugh and Jessica Trounstine, "The Provision of Local Public Goods in Diverse Communities: Analyzing Municipal Bond Elections," *The Journal of Politics* 73:4 (October 2011): 1038–50.

22. Michael P. McDonald and Samuel Popkin, "The Myth of the Vanishing Voter," *American Political Science Review* 95:4 (December 2001): 963–74.

23. ICMA, *2011 Municipal Form of Government Survey Summary*, 4.

24. Neal Caren, "Big City, Big Turnout? Electoral Participation in American Cities," *Journal of Urban Affairs* 29:1 (2007): 31–46; Thomas M. Holbrook and Aaron C. Weinschenk, "Campaigns, Mobilization, and Turnout in Mayoral Elections," *Political Research Quarterly* 67:1 (March 2014): 42–55. Both articles, using very different samples of cities, show this to be the case.

25. Data gathered from "The American Presidency Project," http://www.presidency.ucsb.edu/data/turnout.php, accessed January 22, 2017.

26. See Kriston Capps, "In the US, Almost No One Votes in Local Elections," *CityLab*, November 1, 2016, https://www.citylab.com/equity/2016/11/in-the-us-almost-no-one-votes-in-local-elections/505766, accessed July 20, 2017.

27. Steven P. Erie, *Rainbow's End: Irish Americans and the Dilemmas of Machine Politics, 1840–1985* (Berkeley: University of California Press, 1988); Jessica Trounstine, *Political Monopolies in American Cities: The Rise and Fall of Bosses and Reformers* (Chicago: University of Chicago Press, 2008).

28. Steven J. Rosenstone and John Mark Hansen, *Mobilization, Participation and Democracy in America* (New York: MacMillan, 1993), Sidney Verba, Kay Lehman Schlozman, and Henry E. Brady, *Voice and Equality: Civic Voluntarism in American Politics* (Cambridge, MA: Harvard University Press, 1995).

29. J. Eric Oliver and Shang E. Ha, "Vote Choice in Suburban Elections," *American Political Science Review* 101:3 (August 2007): 393–408; William A. Fischel, *The Homevoter Hypothesis: How Home Values Influence Local Government Taxation, School Finance, and Land-Use Policies* (Cambridge, MA: Harvard University Press, 2001); Andrew B. Hall and Jesse Yoder, "Does Homeownership Influence Political Behavior? Evidence from Administrative Data," working paper, 2018.

30. Zoltan L. Hajnal and Paul G. Lewis, "Municipal Institutions and Voter Turnout in Local Elections," *Urban Affairs Review* 38:5 (May 2003): 645–68, 657; J. Eric Oliver, "The Effects of Metropolitan Economic Segregation on Local Civic Participation," *American Journal of Political Science* 43:1 (January 1999): 186–212, 195.

31. The national data reflected in the figure are from 1990, but, although old, they are consistent with more recent information gathered by Hajnal and Trounstine on New York, Los Angeles, Chicago, Houston, and Detroit. See Zoltan Hajnal and Jessica Trounstine, "Race and Class Inequality in Local Politics," in *The Politics of Racial and Class Inequalities in the Americas* (Washington, DC: American Political Science Association, 2016).

32. Caren, "Big City, Big Turnout"; Hajnal and Lewis, "Municipal Institutions and Voter Turnout in Local Elections"; Albert K. Karnig and B. Oliver Walter, "Decline in Municipal Voter Turnout," *American Politics Quarterly* 11:4 (October 1983): 491–506; Brian F. Schaffner, Matthew Streb, and Gerald Wright, "Teams without Uniforms: The Nonpartisan Ballot in State and Local Elections," *Political Research Quarterly* 54:1 (March 2001): 7–30; Curtis Wood, "Voter Turnout in City Elections," *Urban Affairs Review* 38:2 (November 2002): 209–31.

33. Karnig and Walter, "Decline in Municipal Voter Turnout"; Neal Caren, "Big City, Big Turnout?"

34. Karnig and Walter, "Decline in Municipal Voter Turnout"; Schaffner et al., "Teams without Uniforms."

35. Sarah F. Anzia, *Timing and Turnout: How Off-Cycle Elections Favor Organized Groups* (Chicago: University of Chicago Press, 2013).

36. Bridges and Kronick, "Writing the Rules to Win the Game: The Middle-Class Regimes of Municipal Reformers," *Urban Affairs Review* 34:5 (May 1991): 691–706.

37. Hajnal and Lewis, "Municipal Institutions and Voter Turnout in Local Elections."

38. Wood, "Voter Turnout in City Elections."

39. Oliver, "The Effects of Metropolitan Economic Segregation on Local Civic Participation."

40. Yvette Alex-Assensoh, "Race, Concentrated Poverty, Social Isolation, and Political Behavior," *Urban Affairs Review* 33:2 (November 1997): 209–27.

41. J. Eric Oliver, "City Size and Civic Involvement in Metropolitan America," *American Political Science Review* 94:2 (June 2000): 361–73.

42. Christine Kelleher and David Lowery, "Political Participation and Metropolitan Institutional Contexts," *Urban Affairs Review* 39:6 (July 2004): 720–57.

43. Trounstine, *Political Monopolies in American Cities*; Melissa Marschall and John Lappie, "Turnout in Local Elections: Is Timing Really Everything?" *Election Law Journal* 17:3 (September 2018): 221–33.

44. Holbrook and Weinschenk, "Campaigns, Mobilization, and Turnout in Mayoral Elections."

45. David Niven, "A Field Experiment on the Negative Effects of Campaign Mail on Voter Turnout in a Municipal Election," *Political Research Quarterly* 59:2 (June 2006): 203–10.

46. Luke J. Keele, Paru R. Shah, Ismail White, and Kristine Kay, "Black Candidates and Black Turnout: A Study of Viability in Louisiana Mayoral Elections," *Journal of Politics* 79:3 (July 2017): 780–91; Matt A. Barreto, Mario Villarreal, and Nathan D. Woods, "Metropolitan Latino Political Behavior: Voter Turnout and Candidate Preference in Los Angeles," *Journal of Urban Affairs* 27:1 (February 2005): 71–91; Paul Kleppner, *Chicago Divided: The Making of a Black Mayor* (DeKalb: Northern Illinois University Press, 1985).

47. Timothy Bledsoe and Susan Welch, "Patterns of Political Party Activity Among US Cities," *Urban Affairs Quarterly* 23:2 (December 1987): 249–69; Erie, *Rainbow's End*; Arnold Fleischmann and Lana Stein, "Campaign Contributions in Local Elections," *Political Research Quarterly* 51:3 (September 1988): 673–89; John P. Pelissero, Timothy B. Krebs, and Shannon Jenkins, "Asian Americans, Political Organizations, and Participation in Chicago Electoral Precincts," *Urban Affairs Review* 35:6 (July 2000): 750–69.

48. Donald P. Green, Alan S. Gerber, and David W. Nickerson, "Getting out the Vote in Local Elections: Results from Six Door-to-Door Canvassing Experiments," *The Journal of Politics* 65:4 (November 2003): 1083–96; David Niven, "The Mobilization Solution? Face-to-Face Contact and Voter Turnout in a Municipal Election," *The Journal of Politics*, 66:3 (August 2004): 868–84.

49. Hajnal and Trounstine, "Where Turnout Matters."

50. Jessica Trounstine, "Turnout and Incumbency in Local Elections," *Urban Affairs Review* 49:2 (March 2013): 167–89.

51. Trounstine, *Political Monopolies in American Cities*.

52. Dan McKay, "Who's Running for Mayor?" *Albuquerque Journal*, 2012, https://www.abqjournal.com/158084/whos-running-for-mayor.html, accessed January 29, 2017.

53. Karen Kaufmann, *The Urban Voter: Group Conflict and Mayoral Voting Behavior in American Cities* (Ann Arbor: University of Michigan Press, 2004).

54. Cheryl Boudreau, Christopher S. Elmendorf, and Scott A. MacKenzie. "Lost in Space? Information Shortcuts, Spatial Voting, and Local Government Representation," *Political Research Quarterly* 68:4 (December 2015): 843–55.

55. Joel Lieske, "The Political Dynamics of Urban Voting Behavior," *American Journal of Political Science* 33:1 (January 1989): 150–74, 169; see also Charles S. Bullock III and Bruce A. Campbell, "Racist or Racial Voting in the 1981 Atlanta Municipal Elections," *Urban Affairs Quarterly* 20:2 (December 1984): 149–64.

56. Zoltan Hajnal and Jessica Trounstine, "What Underlies Urban Politics? Race, Class, Ideology, Partisanship, and the Urban Vote," *Urban Affairs Review* 50:1 (January 2014): 63–99.

57. Thomas M. Carsey, "The Contextual Effects of Race on White Voter Behavior: The 1989 New York City Mayoral Election," *The Journal of Politics* 57:1 (February 1995): 221–28.

58. Boadong Liu and James Vanderleeuw, *Race Rules: Electoral Politics in New Orleans, 1965–2006* (Lanham: Lexington Books, 2007).

59. Karen Kaufmann, *The Urban Voter: Group Conflict and Mayoral Voting Behavior in American Cities* (Ann Arbor: University of Michigan Press, 2004). But see Marisa A. Abrajano, Jonathan Nagler, and R. Michael Alvarez, "A Natural Experiment of Race-Based and Issue Voting: The 2001 City of Los Angeles Elections," *Political Research Quarterly* 58:2 (June 2005): 203–18.

60. Robert M. Stein, Stacy G. Ulbig, and Stephanie Shirley Post, "Voting for Minority Candidates in Multi-Racial/Ethnic Communities," *Urban Affairs Review* 41:2 (October 2005): 157–81.

61. Zoltan L Hajnal, *Changing White Attitudes toward Black Political Leadership* (Cambridge, UK: Cambridge University Press, 2007).

62. Lieske, "The Political Dynamics of Urban Voting Behavior."

63. Thomas M. Holbrook and Aaron C. Weinschenk, "Money, Candidates, and Mayoral Elections," *Electoral Studies* 35 (September 2014): 292–302; Schaffner et al., "Teams without Uniforms."

64. Jessica Trounstine, "Evidence of a Local Incumbency Advantage," *Legislative Studies Quarterly* 36:2 (May 2011): 255–80; Timothy B. Krebs, "The Determinants of Candidates' Vote Share and the Advantages of Incumbency in City Council Elections," *American Journal of Political Science* 42:3 (July 1998): 921–35; Anthony Gierzynski, Paul Kleppner, and James Lewis, "Money or the Machine: Money and Votes in Chicago Aldermanic Elections," *American Politics Research* 26:2 (April 1998): 160–73.

65. Trounstine, "Evidence of a Local Incumbency Advantage."

66. Krebs, "The Determinants of Candidates' Vote Share and the Advantages of Incumbency in City Council Elections"; Timothy B. Krebs, "Political Experience and Fundraising in City Council Elections," *Social Science Quarterly* 82:3 (September 2001): 536–51; Holbrook and Weinschenk, "Money, Candidates, and Mayoral Elections."

67. James C. Clingermayer and Richard C. Feiock, "Council Views toward Targeting of Development Policy Benefits," *The Journal of Politics* 57:2 (May 1995): 508–20.

68. Luis R. Fraga, Kenneth J. Meier, and Robert E. England, "Hispanic Americans and Educational Policy: Limits to Equal Access," *The Journal of Politics*, 48:4 (November 1986): 850–76; Brinck Kerr and Kenneth Mladenka, "Does Politics Matter? A Time-Series Analysis of Minority Employment Patterns," *American Journal of Political Science* 38:4 (November 1994): 918–43; David, L. Leal, Valerie Martinez-Ebers, and Kenneth J. Meier, "The Politics of Latino Elections: The Biases of At-Large Elections," *The Journal of Politics* 66:4 (November 2004): 1224–44; Kenneth J. Meier, Joseph Stewart, and Robert E. England, "The Politics of Bureaucratic Discretion: Education Access as an Urban Service," *American Journal of Political Science* 35:1 (February 1991): 155–77.

69. Grace Hall Saltzstein, "Female Mayors and Women in Municipal Jobs," *American Journal of Political Science* 30:1 (February 1986): 140–64.

70. Donald P. Haider-Markel, Mark R. Joslyn, and Chad J. Kniss, "Minority Group Interests and Political Representation: Gay Elected Officials in the Policy Process," *The Journal of Politics* 62:2 (May 2000): 568–77.

71. Christopher R. Berry and William G. Howell, "Accountability and Local Elections: Rethinking Retrospective Voting," *The Journal of Politics* 69:3 (August 2007): 844–58.

72. Craig M. Burnett and Vladimir Kogan, "The Politics of Potholes: Service Quality and Retrospective Voting in Local Elections," *The Journal of Politics* 79:1 (January 2017): 302–13.

73. Edward L. Lascher, "Constituency Size and Incumbent Safety: A Reexamination," *Political Research Quarterly* 58:2 (June 2005): 269–78.

74. Trounstine, "Turnout and Incumbency in Local Elections."

75. Trounstine, "Turnout and Incumbency in Local Elections."

76. Justin de Benedictis-Kessner, "Off Cycle and out of Office: Election Timing and the Incumbency Advantage," *The Journal of Politics* 80:1 (January 2018): 119–32.

77. How quality challengers affect levels of competition in elections involving incumbents is a major topic in the study of the US Congress. See Gary C. Jacobson and Jamie L. Carson, *The Politics of Congressional Elections*, 9th edition (Lanham: Rowman & Littlefield, 2015). We do not have a precise definition of this at the city level, but it refers generally to prior officeholding, prior civic involvement, occupation, and education.

78. Krebs, "The Determinants of Candidates' Vote Share and the Advantages of Incumbency in City Council Elections"; Lieske, "The Political Dynamics of Urban Voting Behavior."

79. Lieske, "The Political Dynamics of Urban Voting Behavior."

80. Patricia A. Kirkland and Alexander Coppock, "Candidate Choice without Party Labels: New Insights from Conjoint Survey Experiments," *Political Behavior* 40:3 (September 2018): 571–91.

81. Holbrook and Weinschenk, "Money, Candidates, and Mayoral Elections."

82. Brian Adams, "Fundraising Coalitions in Open Seat Mayoral Elections," *Journal of Urban Affairs* 29:5 (December 2007): 481–99; Fleischmann and Stein, "Campaign Contributions in Local Elections"; Krebs, "Political Experience and Fundraising in City Council Elections."

83. Timothy B. Krebs, "The Political and Demographic Predictors of Candidate Emergence in City Council Elections," *Urban Affairs Review* 35:2 (November 1999): 278–99.

84. J. Eric Oliver and Shang E. Ha, "Vote Choice in Suburban Elections," *American Political Science Review* 101:3 (August 2007): 393–408.

85. Oliver and Ha, "Vote Choice in Suburban Elections."

86. ICMA, *2011 Municipal Form of Government Survey Summary.*

87. Lieske, "The Political Dynamics of Urban Voting Behavior"; Krebs, "The Determinants of Candidates' Vote Share and the Advantages of Incumbency in City Council Elections," 929–32; Lana Stein and Arnold Fleischmann, "Newspaper and Business Endorsements in Municipal Elections: A Test of Conventional Wisdom," *Journal of Urban Affairs* 9:4 (December 1987): 325–36.

88. Lieske, "The Political Dynamics of Urban Voting Behavior."

89. Luis Ricardo Fraga, "Domination Through Democratic Means: Nonpartisan Slating Groups in City Electoral Politics," *Urban Affairs Quarterly* 23:4 (June 1988): 528–55.

90. Boudreau et al., "Lost in Space?"

91. Boudreau et al., "Lost in Space?", 851.

8: CANDIDATES AND CAMPAIGNS

1. Timothy B. Krebs and Fraser S. Turner, "Following the Money: The Influence of Campaign Finance Reform in the 2011 Chicago Mayoral Election," *Journal of Urban Affairs* 37:2 (May 2015): 109–21.

2. Jennifer Heerwig and Brian J. McCabe, "High Dollar Donors and Rich Neighborhoods: Representational Distortion in Financing a Municipal Election in Seattle," *Urban Affairs Review*, first published 5 September 2017; Cari Lynn Hennessy, "Money and Influence in the Chicago City Council," *Forum-A Journal of Applied Research in Contemporary Politics* 11:3 (September 2013): 481–97.

3. Hennessy, "Money and Influence in the Chicago City Council."

4. See Gary C. Jacobson and Jamie L. Carson, *Politics of Congressional Elections*, 9th edition (Lanham: Rowman & Littlefield, 2009).

5. Andrea Benjamin and Alexis Miller, "Picking Winners: How Political Organizations Influence Local Elections," *Urban Affairs Review* 55:3 (May 2019): 643–74.

6. Steven P. Erie, *Rainbow's End: Irish-Americans and the Dilemmas of Machine Politics, 1840–1985* (Berkeley: University of California Press, 1988), on the downsides of vote maximizing for machines.

7. Milton Rakove, *Don't Make No Waves, Don't Back No Losers: An Insider's Analysis of the Daley Machine* (Bloomington: Indiana University Press, 1976).

8. Jessica Trounstine, *Political Monopolies in American Cities: The Rise and Fall of Bosses and Reformers* (Chicago: University of Chicago Press, 2008).

9. See Samuel P. Hays, "The Politics of Reform in Municipal Government in the Progressive Era," *The Pacific Northwest Quarterly* 55:4 (October 1964): 157–69; Luis Ricardo Fraga, "Domination through Democratic Means: Nonpartisan Slating Groups in City Electoral Politics," *Urban Affairs Review* 23:4 (June 1988): 528–55; Chandler Davidson and Luis Ricardo Fraga, "Slating Groups as Parties in a 'Nonpartisan' Setting," *The Western Political Quarterly* 41:2 (June 1988): 373–90.

10. Amy Bridges and Richard Kronick, "Writing the Rules to Win the Game: The Middle-Class Regimes of Municipal Reformers"; Trounstine, *Political Monopolies*; Sarah F. Anzia, *Timing and Turnout: How Off-Cycle Elections Favor Organized Groups* (Chicago: University of Chicago Press, 2014).

11. Joel Lieske, "The Political Dynamics of Urban Voting Behavior," *American Journal of Political Science* 33:1 (January 1989): 150–74; Timothy B. Krebs, "Political Experience and Fundraising in City Council Elections," *Social Science Quarterly* 82:3 (September 2001): 536–51; Sarah Reckhow, "The Distinct Patterns of Organized and Elected Representation of Racial and Ethnic Groups," *Urban Affairs Review* 45:2 (November 2009): 188–217; Benjamin and Miller, "Picking Winners."

12. Anthony Downs, *An Economic Theory of Democracy* (New York: Harper, 1957).

13. National Conference of State Legislatures, "State Laws Governing Early Voting," http://www.ncsl.org/research/elections-and-campaigns/early-voting-in-state-elections.aspx, accessed August 11, 2018.

14. Samuel Kernell, Gary C. Jacobson, Thad Kousser, and Lynn Vavreck, *The Logic of American Politics*, 8th edition (Thousand Oaks: Sage, 2018), chapter 11.

15. Osita Nwanevu, "The Right to Run," *Slate*, October 22, 2014, https://slate.com/news-and-politics/2014/10/age-of-candidacy-laws-should-be-abolished-why-18-year-olds-should-be-able-to-run-for-public-office.html, accessed June 2, 2019.

16. ICMA, *2011 Municipal Form of Government Survey Summary* (Washington, DC: International City/County Management Association, 2011), 9.

17. Susan A. MacManus, "Seniors in City Hall: Causes and Consequences of the Graying of City Councils," *Social Science Quarterly* 79:3 (August 1998): 620–33 .

18. "'We Can Do It Better': Meet the Millennials Taking Over City Hall," *Time*, October 12, 2017.

19. MacManus, "Seniors in City Hall," 620–33.

20. Timothy Bledsoe, *Careers in City Politics: The Case for Urban Democracy* (Pittsburgh: University of Pittsburgh Press, 1993); J. Eric Oliver with Shang E. Ha and Zachary Callen, *Local Elections and the Politics of Small Scale Democracy* (Princeton: Princeton University Press, 2012), 99.

21. Melissa Deckman, "Gender Differences in the Decision to Run for School Board," *American Politics Research* 35:4 (July 2007), 548.

22. Bledsoe, Careers in City Politics: The Case for Urban Democracy; Frederick M. Hess and David L. Leal, "School House Politics: Expenditures, Interests, and Competition in School Board Elections," in Besieged: School Boards and the Future of Education Politics, ed. William G. Howell (Washington, DC: Brookings Institution Press, 2005), 250.

23. Kenneth Prewitt, *The Recruitment of Political Leaders: A Study of Citizen-Politicians* (New York: Bobbs-Merrill Company, 1970).

24. Bledsoe, *Careers in City Politics: The Case for Urban Democracy.*

25. Alan Ehrenhalt, *The United States of Ambition: Politicians, Power, and the Pursuit of Office* (New York: Random House, 1992), 42–64.

26. Mark Schneider and Paul Teske with Michael Mintrom, Public Entrepreneurs: Agents for Change in American Government (Princeton: Princeton University Press, 1995).

27. Deckman, "Gender Differences in the Decision to Run for School Board," 551.

28. Ibid.

29. Ibid., 557–558.

30. Melissa Deckman, "School Board Candidates and Gender: Ideology, Party, and Policy Concerns," *Journal of Women, Politics and Policy* 28:1 (October 2006): 87–117.

31. Melissa Deckman, *School Board Battles: The Christian Right in Local Politics* (Washington, DC: Georgetown University Press, 2004), 168.

32. Deckman, *School Board Battles*, 168; Frederick M. Hess and David L. Leal, "School House Politics: Expenditures, Interests, and Competition in School Board Elections," in *Besieged: School Boards and the Future of Education Politics*, ed. William G. Howell (Washington, DC: Brookings Institution Press, 2005).

33. Hess and Leal, "School House Politics," 250.

34. Gordon S. Black, "A Theory of Political Ambition: Career Choices and the Role of Structural Incentives," *American Political Science Review* 66:1 (March 1972): 144–59.

35. Kenneth Prewitt, *The Recruitment of Political Leaders.*

36. Marilyn Gittell, "Metropolitan Mayor: Dead End," *Public Administration Review* 23:1 (March 1963): 20–24; Russell D. Murphy, "Whither The Mayors? A Note on Mayoral Careers," *The Journal of Politics* 42:1 (February 1980): 277–90; Andrew Douglas McNitt, "Tenure in Office of Big City Mayors," *State and Local Government Review* 42:1 (April 2010): 36–47; Harold Wolman, Edward Page, and Martha Reavley, "Mayors and Mayoral Careers," *Urban Affairs Review* 25:3 (March 1990): 500–14; Katherine Levine Einstein, David M. Glick, Maxwell Palmer, and Robert J. Pressel, "Do Mayors Run for

Higher Office? New Evidence on Progressive Ambition," *American Politics Research*, January 2018, https://doi.org/10.1177/1532673X17752322; Eric S. Heberlig, Justin McCoy, Suzanne M. Leland, and David A. Swindell, "Mayors, Accomplishment and Advancement," *Urban Affairs Review* 53:3 (May 2017): 539–58.

37. Gittel, "Metropolitan Mayor: Dead End."
38. Murphy, "Whither The Mayors?"
39. Wolman et al., "Mayors and Mayoral Careers," 511.
40. McNitt, "Tenure in Office of Big City Mayors"; R. Douglas Arnold and Nicholas Carnes, "Holding Mayors Accountable: New York's Executives from Koch to Bloomberg," *American Journal of Political Science* 56:4 (October 2012): 949–63; Heberlig et al., "Mayors, Accomplishment and Advancement."
41. Heberlig et al., "Mayors, Accomplishment and Advancement."
42. Einstein et al., "Do Mayors Run for Higher Office?" 20.
43. Rachel Gordon, "The Mayor's Legacy: Willie Brown/'Da Mayor' Soared during Tenure That Rivals City's Most Notable, But Some Critical Goals Not Met," *San Francisco Chronicle*, January 4, 2004, https://www.sfgate.com/politics/article/the-mayor-s-legacy-willie-brown-Da-Mayor-2832960.php, accessed August 19, 2018.
44. Black, "A Theory of Political Ambition."
45. Timothy B. Krebs, "The Political and Demographic Predictors of Candidate Emergence in City Council Elections," *Urban Affairs Review* 35:2 (October 1999): 279–300.
46. Mark Schneider and Paul Teske, "The Antigrowth Entrepreneur: Challenging the 'Equilibrium' of the Growth Machine," *The Journal of Politics* 55:3 (August 1993): 720–36.
47. Paru Shah, "It Takes a Black Candidate: A Supply-Side Theory of Black Representation," *Political Research Quarterly* 67:2 (June 2014): 266–79.
48. See Kevin B. Smith and Alan Greenblatt, *Governing States and Localities*, 6th edition (Washington, DC: CQ Press, 2018), chapter 7.
49. See Jacobson and Carson, *Politics of Congressional Elections*, 61–69.
50. John Metcalfe, "The Skyrocketing Costs of Running for Mayor of a Major US City," *CityLab*, November 6, 2012, https://www.citylab.com/equity/2012/11/skyrocketing-costs-running-mayor-major-us-city/3814, accessed August 13, 2018.
51. Ester R. Fuchs, E. Scott Adler, and Lincoln A. Mitchell. "Win, Place, Show: Public Opinion Polls and Campaign Contributions in a New York City Election," *Urban Affairs Review* 35:4 (March 2000): 479–501; Timothy B. Krebs and David B. Holian, "Media and Momentum: Strategic Contributing in a Big-City Mayoral Election." *Urban Affairs Review* 40:5 (May 2005): 614–33.
52. Brian E. Adams, "Fundraising Coalitions in Open Seat Mayoral Elections," *Journal of Urban Affairs* 29:5 (December 2007): 481–99; Arnold Fleischmann and Lana Stein, "Campaign Contributions in Local Elections," *Political Research Quarterly* 51:3 (September 1998): 673–89.
53. Fleischmann and Stein, "Campaign Contributions in Local Elections"; Timothy B. Krebs and John P. Pelissero,

"Fund-Raising Coalitions in Mayoral Campaigns," *Urban Affairs Review* 37:1 (September 2001): 67–84.
54. Theodore S. Arrington and Gerald L. Ingalls. "Effects of Campaign Spending on Local Elections: The Charlotte Case," *American Politics Quarterly* 12:1 (January 1984): 117–27; Krebs, "Political Experience and Fundraising in City Council Elections."
55. Norman Luttbeg, "Role of Newspaper Coverage and Political Ads in Local Elections," *Journalism and Mass Communication Quarterly* 65:4 (December 1988): 881–88; Esther Thorson, Scott Swafford, and Eunjin (Anna) Kim, "Newspaper News Exposure Predicts Political Participation," *Newspaper Research Journal* 38:2 (June 2017): 231–44.
56. Andrea Benjamin and Alexis Miller, "Picking Winners: How Political Organizations Influence Local Elections," *Urban Affairs Review*, https://doi.org/10.1177/1078087417732647.
57. Benjamin and Miller, "Picking Winners"; Lana Stein and Arnold Fleischmann, "Newspaper and Business Endorsements in Municipal Elections: A Test of Conventional Wisdom," *Journal of Urban Affairs* 9:4 (December 1987): 325–36; Timothy B. Krebs, "The Determinants of Candidates' Vote Share and the Advantages of Incumbency in City Council Elections," *American Journal of Political Science* 42:3 (July 1998): 921–35; Lieske, "The Political Dynamics of Urban Voting Behavior."
58. Benjamin and Miller, "Picking Winners: How Political Organizations Influence Local Elections."
59. Stergios Skaperdas and Bernard Grofman, "Modeling Negative Campaigning," *American Political Science Review* 89:1 (March 1995): 49–61.
60. Timothy B. Krebs and David B. Holian, "Competitive Positioning, Deracialization, and Attack Speech: A Study of Negative Campaigning in the 2001 Los Angeles Mayoral Election," *American Politics Research* 35:1 (January 2007): 123–49.
61. John Theilmann and Allen Wilhite, "Campaign Tactics and the Decision to Attack," *The Journal of Politics* 60:4 (October 1998): 1050–62.
62. Denise-Marie Ordway and John Wihbey, "Negative Political Ads and Their Effect on Voters: Updated Collection of Research," September 25, 2016, https://journalistsresource.org/studies/politics/ads-public-opinion/negative-political-ads-effects-voters-research-roundup, accessed August 18, 2018.
63. David Niven, "A Field Experiment on the Negative Effects of Campaign Mail on Voter Turnout in a Municipal Election," *Political Research Quarterly* 59:2 (June 2006): 203–10.
64. Niven, "A Field Experiment." Data for individual cities can be located by searching on city name and state.
65. Matt A. Barreto, "Sí Se Puede! Latino Candidates and the Mobilization of Latino Voters," *The American Political Science Review* 101:3 (August 2007): 425–41; Thomas M. Carsey, "The Contextual Effects of Race on White Voter Behavior: The 1989 New York City Mayoral Election," *The Journal of Politics* 57:1 (February 1995): 221–28.

66. Rufus P. Browning, Dale Rogers Marshall, and David H. Tabb, eds., *Racial Politics in American Cities*, 3rd edition (New York: Pearson, 2003).

67. Byran O. Jackson, "The Effect of Racial Group Consciousness on Political Mobilization in American Cities," *Western Political Quarterly* 40:4 (December 1987): 631–46; Byran O. Jackson, Elisabeth R. Gerber, and Bruce E. Cain, "Coalitional Prospects in a Multi-Racial Society: African American Attitudes toward Other Minority Groups," *Political Research Quarterly* 47:2 (June 1994): 277–94; Reuel R. Rogers, *Afro-Caribbean Immigrants and the Politics of Incorporation: Ethnicity, Exception, or Exit* (Cambridge, UK: Cambridge University Press, 2006).

68. James Vanderleeuw, Baodong Liu, and Gregory Marsh, "Applying Black Threat Theory, Urban Regime Theory and Deracialization: The Memphis Mayoral Elections of 1991, 1995 and 1999," *Journal of Urban Affairs* 26:4 (October 2004): 505–19.

69. See John Mollenkopf, "New York: Still the Great Anomaly," chapter 3; Dianne M. Pinderhughes, "Chicago Politics: Political Incorporation and Restoration," chapter 5; and Marion Orr, "The Struggle For Black Empowerment in Baltimore," chapter 9, in Browning et al., eds., *Racial Politics in American Cities*.

70. Melissa J. Marschall and Anirudh V. S. Ruhil, "The Pomp of Power: Black Mayoralties in Urban America," *Social Science Quarterly* 87:4 (December 2006): 828–50.

71. Joseph P. McCormick II and Charles E. Jones, "The Conceptualization of Deracialization," in *Dilemmas of Black Politics: Issues of Leadership and Strategy*, ed. Georgia A. Persons (New York: HarperCollins College Publishers, 1993), 66–84, 77; Sharon D. Austin Wright and Richard T. Middleton IV, "The Limitations of the Deracialization Concept in the 2001 Los Angeles Mayoral Election," *Political Research Quarterly* 57:2 (June 2004): 283–93; Boadong Liu, "Deracialization and Urban Racial Contexts," *Urban Affairs Review* 38:4 (March 2003): 572–91; David Haywood Metz and Katherine Tate, "The Color of Urban Campaigns," in *Classifying By Race*, ed. Paul E. Peterson (Princeton: Princeton University Press, 1995), 262–77; Huey L. Perry, "Deracialization as an Analytical Construct in American Urban Politics," *Urban Affairs Quarterly* 27:2 (December 1991): 181–91; Katherine Underwood, "Ethnicity Is Not Enough: Latino-Led Multiracial Coalitions in Los Angeles," *Urban Affairs Review* 33:1 (September 1997): 3–27.

72. Christian Collet, "Minority Candidates, Alternative Media, and Multi-Ethnic America: Deracialization or Toggling?" *Perspectives on Politics* 6:4 (December 2008): 707–28.

73. Boadong Liu, "Deracialization and Urban Racial Contexts"; Vanderleeuw et al., "Applying Black Threat Theory." A deracialized strategy may apply equally to Latinx candidates: see Eric Gonzales Juenke and Anna Christina Sampaio, "Deracialization and Latino Politics: The Case of the Salazar Brothers in Colorado," *Political Research Quarterly* 63:1 (2010): 43–54; Rodney Hero, "The Election of Hispanics in City Government: An Examination of the Election of Federico Pena as Mayor of Denver," *Western Political Quarterly* 40:1 (March 1987): 93–105; Underwood, "Ethnicity is Not Enough"; Marion Orr and Domingo Morel, *Latino Mayors: Political Change in the Postindustrial City* (Philadelphia: Temple University Press, 2018), chapter 1.

74. Georgia Persons, ed., *Dilemmas of Black Politics* (New York: HarperCollins, 1993), 45.

75. Austin Wright and Middleton IV, "The Limitations of the Deracialization Concept in the 2001 Los Angeles Mayoral Election"; Thomas Longoria, "The Impact of Office on Cross-Racial Voting: Evidence from the 1996 Milwaukee Mayoral Election," *Urban Affairs Review* 34:4 (March 1999): 596–603.

76. Baodong Liu and James M. Vanderleeuw, *Race Rules: Electoral Politics in New Orleans, 1965–2006* (Lanham: Rowman & Littlefield, 2007).

77. Nichole M. Bauer, "Running Local: Gender Stereotyping and Female Candidates in Local Elections," *Urban Affairs Review*, first published online April 2018, https://doi.org/10.1177/1078087418770807.

78. Janet A. Flammang, *Women's Political Voice: How Women are Transforming the Practice and Study of Politics* (Philadelphia: Temple University Press, 1997); Joyce Gelb and Marilyn Gittell, "Seeking Equality: The Role of Activist Women in Cities," in *The Egalitarian City: Issues of Rights, Distribution, Access, and Power*, ed. Janet K. Boles (New York: Praeger, 1986), 93–99.

79. Leonie Huddy and Nadya Terkildsen, "The Consequences of Gender Stereotypes for Women at Different Levels and Types of Offices," *Political Research Quarterly* 46:3 (September 1993): 503–25.

80. Paul Peterson, *City Limits* (Chicago: University of Chicago Press, 1981); Elisabeth R. Gerber and Daniel Hopkins, "When Mayors Matter: Estimating the Impact of Mayoral Partisanship on City Policy," *American Journal of Political Science* 55:2 (April 2011): 326–39.

81. Nichole M. Bauer, "Running Local."

82. Danny Hayes, "Candidate Qualities through a Partisan Lens: A Theory of Trait Ownership," *American Journal of Political Science* 49:4 (October 2005): 908–23.

83. Thomas M. Holbrook and Aaron C. Weinschenk, "Money, Candidates, and Mayoral Elections," *Electoral Studies* 35 (September 2014): 292–302.

84. Thomas M. Holbrook and Aaron C. Weinschenk, "Campaigns, Mobilization, and Turnout in Mayoral Elections," *Political Research Quarterly* 67:1 (March 2014): 42–55.

85. See Jacobson and Carson, *Politics of Congressional Elections*.

86. See Jacobson and Carson, *Politics of Congressional Elections*, 61–69.

87. Aaron C. Weinschenk and Thomas M. Holbrook, "The Determinants of Campaign Spending in Mayoral Elections," *State and Local Government Review* 46:1 (2014): 13–27, 19.

88. Zoltan L. Hajnal, *Changing White Attitudes toward Black Political Leadership* (Cambridge, UK: Cambridge University Press, 2007).

89. Orr and Morel, *Latino Mayors*.

9: NONVOTING FORMS OF PARTICIPATION

1. "Q&A, What Happened in Ferguson?" *New York Times*, August 10, 2015, https://www.nytimes.com/interactive/2014/08/13/us/ferguson-missouri-town-under-siege-after-police-shooting.html, accessed June 13, 2019.

2. William E. Lyons and David Lowery, "The Organization of Political Space and Citizen Responses to Dissatisfaction in Urban Communities: An Integrative Model," *The Journal of Politics*, 48:2 (May 1986): 321–46.

3. Michael W. Hirlinger, "Citizen-Initiated Contacting of Local Government Officials: A Multivariate Explanation," *The Journal of Politics* 54:2 (May 1992): 553–64.

4. The literature on citizen contacting in urban politics is voluminous. Some of the central works include Bryan Jones, Saadia Greenberg, Clifford Kaufman, and Joseph Drew, "Bureaucratic Response to Citizen-Initiated Contacts: Environmental Enforcement in Detroit," *American Political Science Review* 71:1 (March 1977): 148–65; Elaine B. Sharp, "Citizen-Initiated Contacting of Government Officials and Socioeconomic Status: Determining the Relationship and Accounting for It," *American Political Science Review* 76:1 (February 1982): 109–15; Arnold Vedlitz, James A. Dyer, and Roger Durand, "Citizens' Contacts with Local Governments: A Comparative View," *American Journal of Political Science*, 24:1 (February 1980): 50–67; John Clayton Thomas and Julia Melkers, "Explaining Citizen-Initiated Contacts with Municipal Bureaucracies: Lessons from the Atlanta Experience," *Urban Affairs Review* 34:5 (May 1999): 667–90.

5. Rufus P. Browning, Dale Rodgers Marshall, and David H. Tabb, *Protest Is Not Enough: The Struggle for Blacks and Hispanics for Equality in Urban Politics* (Berkeley: University of California Press, 1984).

6. Harold Lasswell, Politics: Who Gets What, When and How (New York: Whittlesey House, 1936).

7. Colin Wood, "What Is 311?" August 4, 2016, http://www.govtech.com/dc/What-is-311.html, accessed June 8, 2019.

8. Sarah Goodyear, "3-1-1: A City Services Revolution," *CityLab*, https://www.citylab.com/city-makers-connections/311, accessed June 8, 2019.

9. Scott L. Minkoff, "NYC 311: A Tract Level Analysis of Citizen-Government Contacting in New York City," *Urban Affairs Review* 52:2 (March 2016): 211–46.

10. Anthony Downs, An Economic Theory of Democracy (New York: Harper and Row, 1957), 25.

11. Susan Welch and Timothy Bledsoe, *Urban Reform and Its Consequences: A Study in Representation* (Chicago: University of Chicago Press, 1988).

12. Timothy Bledsoe and Susan Welch, "Patterns of Political Party Activity among US Cities," *Urban Affairs Review* 23:2 (November 1987): 249–69; see also David Schleicher, "Why Is There No Partisan Competition in City Council Elections? The Role of Election Law," *The Journal of Law and Politics* 23:4 (Fall 2007): 419–73.

13. Fernando Ferreira and Joseph Gyourko, "Do Political Parties Matter? Evidence from US Cities," *The Quarterly Journal of Economics* 124:1 (February 2009): 399–422; Bill Bishop, *The Big Sort: Why the Clustering of Like-Minded America is Tearing Us Apart* (New York: First Mariner Edition, 2008).

14. Karen Kaufmann, *The Urban Voter: Group Conflict and Mayoral Voting Behavior* (Ann Arbor: University of Michigan Press, 2004).

15. Joel Lieske, "The Political Dynamics of Urban Voting Behavior," *American Journal of Political Science* 33:1 (January 1989): 150–74; Paula Christian, "A Year after Infighting Crippled Charter Committee, Party Is Ready to Endorse in City Elections," February 24, 2017, https://www.wcpo.com/news/insider/a-year-after-infighting-crippled-charter-committee-party-is-ready-to-endorse-in-city-elections, accessed June 10, 2019.

16. Steven P. Erie, *Rainbow's End: Irish-Americans and the Dilemmas of Urban Machine Politics, 1840–1985* (Berkeley: University of California Press, 1988).

17. Raymond E. Wolfinger, "Why Political Machines Have Not Withered Away and Other Revisionist Thoughts," *The Journal of Politics* 34:2 (May 1972): 365–98.

18. Frank Scaturro, "How a Political Machine Crushed Conservatism—and Democracy," *National Review*, July 13, 2017, https://www.nationalreview.com/2017/07/nassau-county-gop-corrupt-party-machine-crushes-challengers/, accessed June 10, 2019.

19. Timothy B. Krebs, "Political Experience and Fundraising in City Council Elections," *Social Science Quarterly* 82:3 (September 2001): 536–51, 547; Timothy B. Krebs, "Money and Machine Politics: An Analysis of Corporate and Labor Contributions in Chicago City Council Elections," *Urban Affairs Review* 41:1 (September 2005): 47–64; Dick Simpson, *Rogues, Rebels, and Rubber Stamps: The Politics of the Chicago City Council from 1863 to the Present* (Boulder: Westview Press, 2001).

20. US Constitution, Amendment I.

21. Paul Schumaker, "Group Involvements in City Politics and Pluralist Theory," *Urban Affairs Review* 49:2 (March 2013): 254–81; Christopher A. Cooper, Anthony J. Nownes, and Steven Roberts, "Perceptions of Power: Interest Groups in Local Politics," *State and Local Government Review* 37:3 (December 2005): 206–16; Kenneth K. Wong and Pushpam Jain, "Newspapers as Policy Actors in Urban School Systems: The Chicago Story," *Urban Affairs Review* 35:2 (November 1999): 210–46; Michael Leo Owens, God and Government in the Ghetto: The Politics of Church-State Collaboration in Black America (Chicago: University of Chicago Press, 2007).

22. Examples include groups that formed to block busing in the 1970s: see Donald Philip Green and Jonathan A. Cowden, "Who Protests: Self-Interest and White Opposition to Busing," *The Journal of Politics* 54:2 (May 1992): 471–96. More recent examples include ad hoc coalitions that form to advance antidiscrimination and living wage laws: see Schumaker, "Group Involvements in City Politics and Pluralist Theory," 270.

23. Floyd Hunter, *Community Power Structure: A Study of Decision Makers* (Chapel Hill: University of North Carolina Press, 1953).

24. Robert A. Dahl, *Who Governs? Democracy and Power in an American City* (New Haven: Yale University Press, 1961).

25. Harvey Molotch, "The City as Growth Machine: Toward a Political Economy of Place," *American Sociological Review* 82:2 (September 1976): 309–32.

26. Clarence N. Stone and Heywood T. Sanders, eds., *The Politics of Urban Development* (Lawrence: University of Kansas Press, 1987); Clarence N. Stone, *Regime Politics: Governing Atlanta, 1946–1988* (Lawrence: University of Kansas Press, 1987).

27. Stone, *Regime Politics*; Stephen L. Elkin, *City and Regime in the American Republic* (Chicago: University of Chicago Press, 1987).

28. Stone and Sanders, *The Politics of Urban Development*.

29. Karen Mossberger and Gerry Stoker, "The Evolution of Urban Regime Theory: The Challenge of Conceptualization," *Urban Affairs Review* 36:6 (July 2001): 810–35.

30. David T. Canon and William T. Bianco. American Politics Today, Sixth Essentials Edition (New York: W.W. Norton), chapter 9.

31. Glenn Abney and Thomas P. Lauth, "Interest Group Influence in City Policy-Making: The Views of Administrators," *Western Political Quarterly* 38:1 (March 1985): 148–61.

32. Peter Bachrach and Morton S. Baratz, "Two Faces of Power," *The American Political Science Review* 56:4 (December 1962): 947–52.

33. Zoltan L. Hajnal and Terry Nichols Clark, "The Local Interest-Group System: Who Governs and Why?" *Social Science Quarterly* 79:1 (March 1998): 227–24.

34. See Paul Schumaker, "Group Involvements in City Politics and Pluralist Theory," *Urban Affairs Review* 49:2 (March 2013): 254–81; and Christopher A. Cooper, Anthony J. Nownes, and Steven Roberts, "Perceptions of Power: Interest Groups in Local Politics," *State and Local Government Review* 37:3 (December 2005): 206–16.

35. Elisabeth R. Gerber and Justin H. Phillips, "Development Ballot Measures, Interest Group Endorsements, and the Political Geography of Growth Preferences," *American Journal of Political Science* 47:4 (October 2003): 625–39.

36. Jeffrey M. Berry, Kent E. Portney, Robin Liss, Jessica Simoncelli, and Lisa Berger, *Power and Interest Groups in City Politics* (Cambridge, MA: Rappaport Institute for Greater Boston, Kennedy School of Government, Harvard University, 2006).

37. Berry et al., *Power and Interest Groups in City Politics*, 18–19.

38. Wong and Jain, "Newspapers as Policy Actors in Urban School Systems."

39. Alan Greenblatt, "When No News Isn't Good News: What the Decline of Newspapers Means for Government," *Governing*, April 24, 2019, https://www.governing.com/topics/politics/gov-newspapers-government-studies.html, accessed November 3, 2019.

40. Sarah Reckhow, "The Distinct Patterns of Organized and Elected Representation of Racial and Ethnic Groups," *Urban Affairs Review* 45:2 (November 2009): 188–217.

41. Frederick M. Hess and David L. Leal, "School House Politics: Expenditures, Interests, and Competition in School Board Elections," in *Besieged: School Boards and the Future of Education Politics*, ed. William G. Howell (Washington, DC: Brookings Institution Press, 2005), 249.

42. See also Brian E. Adams, "Fund-Raising Coalitions in School Board Elections," *Education and Urban Society* 40:4 (May 2008): 411–27.

43. Terry M. Moe, "Teacher Unions and School Board Elections," in Howell, *Besieged*, 254–87.

44. Sarah F. Anzia, "Election Timing and the Electoral Influence of Interest Groups," *The Journal of Politics* 73:2 (May 2011): 412–27.

45. Sarah Holder, "Cities Take Aim at the Spiraling Costs of Local Elections," *CityLab*, September 4, 2018, https://www.citylab.com/equity/2018/09/cities-take-aim-at-the-spiraling-costs-of-local-elections/567727, accessed June 12, 2019.

46. Arnold Fleischmann and Lana Stein, "Campaign Contributions in Local Elections," *Political Research Quarterly* 51:2 (September 1998): 673–89; Timothy B. Krebs, "Urban Interests and Campaign Contributions: Evidence from Los Angeles," *Journal of Urban Affairs* 27:2 (June 2005): 165–75.

47. Jennifer Heerwig and Brian McCabe, "High Dollar Donors and Rich Neighborhoods: Representational Distortion in Financing a Municipal Election in Seattle," *Urban Affairs Review*, article first published online: September 5, 2017.

48. Brian E. Adams, "Suburban Money in Central City Elections: The Geographic Distribution of Campaign Contributions," *Urban Affairs Review* 42:2 (November 2006): 267–80.

49. Timothy B. Krebs and John P. Pelissero, "Fund-Raising Coalitions in Mayoral Campaigns," *Urban Affairs Review* 37:1 (September 2001): 67–84; Sean Hogan and Dick Simpson, "Campaign Contributions and Mayoral/Aldermanic Relationships: Building on Krebs and Pelissero," *Urban Affairs Review* 37:1 (September 2001): 85–95; see also Brian Adams, "Fundraising Coalitions in Open Seat Mayoral Elections," *Journal of Urban Affairs* 29:5 (November 2007): 481–99.

50. Ester R. Fuchs, E. Scott Adler, and Lincoln A. Mitchell, "Win, Place, Show: Public Opinion Polls and Campaign Contributions in a New York City Election," *Urban Affairs Review* 35:4 (March 2000): 479–501; Timothy B. Krebs and David B. Holian, "Media and Momentum: Strategic Contributing in a Big-City Mayoral Election," *Urban Affairs Review* 40:5 (May 2005): 614–33.

51. Timothy B. Krebs, "Political Experience and Fundraising in City Council Elections," *Social Science Quarterly* 82:3 (September 2001): 536–51.

52. Fuchs et al., "Win, Place, Show"; Krebs and Holian, "Media and Momentum."

53. Cari Lynn Hennessy, "Money and Influence in the Chicago City Council," *Forum-A Journal of Applied Research in Contemporary Politics* 11:3 (September 2013): 481–97.

54. *Citizens United v. Federal Election Commission*, 558 US 310 (2010).

55. Sarah Reckhow, Jeffrey R. Henig, Rebecca Jacobson, and Jamie Alter Litt, "Outsiders with Deep Pockets: The Nationalization of Local School Board Elections," *Urban Affairs Review* 53:5 (September 2017): 783–811.

56. *Buckley v. Valeo*, 424 US 1 (1976).

57. Holder, "Cities Take Aim at the Spiraling Costs of Local Elections."

58. *Arizona Free Enterprise Club's Freedom Club PAC, et al. v. Bennett, et al.*, 564 US 721 (2011).

59. Brian E. Adams, *Campaign Finance in Local Elections: Buying the Grassroots* (First Forum Press, a division of Lynne-Rienner Publishers, 2010), 164.

60. These insights are drawn from some of the earliest work on this subject in the urban political field, including Peter K.

Eisinger, "The Conditions of Protest Behavior in American Cities," *American Political Science Review* 67:1 (March 1973): 11–28; Michael Lipsky, "Protest as a Political Resource," *American Political Science Review* 62:4 (December 1968): 1144–58; and James Q. Wilson, "The Strategy of Protest: Problems of Negro Civic Action," *The Journal of Conflict Resolution* 5:3 (September 1961): 291–303.

61. Ulf Himmelstrand, "Verbal Attitudes and Behavior: A Paradigm for the Study of Message Transmission and Transformation," *Public Opinion Quarterly* 24:2 (Summer 1960): 224–50; Peter K. Eisinger, "Protest Behavior and the Integration of the Urban Political System," *Journal of Politics* 33:4 (November 1971): 980–1007, 984–85.

62. Nathan Heller, "Is There Any Point to Protesting?" *The New Yorker*, https://www.newyorker.com/magazine/2017/08/21/is-there-any-point-to-protesting, accessed May 21, 2019.

63. E. E. Schattschneider, *The Semi-Sovereign People: A Realist's View of Democracy in America* (New York: Holt, Rinehart and Winston, 1960).

64. Lloyd A. Snow, Sarah A. Soule, and Daniel M. Cress, "Identifying the Precipitants of Homeless Protest Across 17 Cities, 1980–1990," *Social Forces* 83:3 (March 2005): 1183–210.

65. Green and Cowden, "Who Protests."

66. See Peter B. Levy, *The Great Uprising: Race Riots in Urban America during the 1960s* (Cambridge, UK: Cambridge University Press, 2018), 1, footnote 1; David Halle and Kevin Rafter, "Riots in New York and Los Angeles, 1935–2002," in David Halle, ed., *New York and Los Angeles: Politics, Society and Culture: A Comparative View*, as quoted in Janet L. Abu-Lughod, *Race, Space and Riots in Chicago, New York and Los Angeles* (Oxford: Oxford University Press, 2007), 12.

67. Edward C. Banfield, "Rioting for Fun and Profit," in *The Unheavenly City Revisited* (Boston: Little, Brown, 1978). See also Michael Konczal, "Rioting Mainly for Fun and Profit: The Neoconservative Origins of Our Police Problem," http://rooseveltinstitute.org/rioting-mainly-fun-and-profit-neoconservative-origins-our-police-problem, accessed May 20, 2019.

68. David Sears and John B. McConahay, *The Politics of Violence: The New Urban Blacks and the Watts Riot* (Boston: Houghton Mifflin Company, 1973).

69. Levy, *The Great Uprising*, 1.

70. Fred Harris and Alan Curtis, eds., *Healing Our Divided Society: Investing in America Fifty Years After the Kerner Report* (Philadelphia: Temple University Press, 2018), 1–2.

71. Natalie Delgadillo, "The Forgotten History of Latino Riots," *CityLab*, April 11, 2017, https://www.citylab.com/equity/2017/04/the-forgotten-history-of-latino-riots/522570, accessed May 21, 2019. The article includes an interactive map which can be used to get more information on each of the Latinx rebellions discussed in the report, which is based on doctoral dissertation research conducted by Aaron Fountain, Jr., of Indiana University.

72. Abu-Lughod, *Race, Space and Riots in Chicago, New York and Los Angeles*, 12–13.

73. George Joseph, "From Ferguson to Charlotte, Why Police Protests Turn into Riots," *CityLab*, September 22, 2016, https://www.citylab.com/equity/2016/09/from-ferguson-to-charlotte-why-police-protests-turn-into-riots/500981/;, accessed June 14, 2019.

74. Joe R. Feagin and Harlan Hahn, *Ghetto Revolts: The Politics of Violence in American Cities* (New York: Macmillan, 1973), 101–24; Michael Jones Correa, "Riots as Critical Junctures," in *The City in American Political Development*, ed. Richardson Dilworth (New York: Routledge, 2009), 179–99; Abu-Lughod, *Race, Space and Riots in Chicago, New York and Los Angeles*, 59–60, 141–50, 258–59; George Joseph, "From Ferguson to Charlotte, Why Police Protests Turn into Riots."

75. *Report of the National Advisory Commission on Civil Disorders* (Washington, DC: Kerner Commission: US GPO, 1968).

76. Harris and Curtis, eds., *Healing Our Divided Society: Investing in America Fifty Years After the Kerner Report*, 11.

77. Browning et al., *Protest is Not Enough*.

78. Jones Correa, "Riots as Critical Junctures"; Dennis E. Gale, *Understanding Urban Unrest: From Reverend King to Rodney King* (Thousand Oaks: Sage, 1996).

79. Charles M. Tiebout, "A Pure Theory of Local Expenditures," *Journal of Political Economy* 64:5 (October 1956): 416–24.

80. David Lowery and William E. Lyons, "The Impact of Jurisdictional Boundaries: An Individual-Level Test of the Tiebout Model," *Journal of Politics* 51:1 (February 1989): 73–97, 92.

81. Kenneth N. Bickers and Robert M. Stein, "The Microfoundations of the Tiebout Model," *Urban Affairs Review* 34:1 (September 1998): 76–93.

82. Paul Teske, Mark Schneider, Michael Mintrom, and Samuel Best, "Establishing the Micro Foundations of a Macro Theory: Information, Movers, and the Competitive Local Market for Public Goods," *The American Political Science Review* 87:3 (September 1993): 702–13.

83. Peter Dreier, John Mollenkopf, and Todd Swanstrom, *Place Matters: Metropolitics for the Twenty-First Century*, 3rd edition (Lawrence: University Press of Kansas, 2014).

84. Jack Grone, "City, Meet County: St. Louis Weighs Historic Merger," *CityLab*, January 30, 2019, https://www.citylab.com/equity/2019/01/st-louis-missouri-city-county-consolidation-vote-2020/579436, accessed June 13, 2019.

10: LOCAL GOVERNMENT POLICY MAKING AND SERVICES

1. Joey Garrison, "Interactive Map: A Sweeping Loss for Nashville Transit Referendum Everywhere but City's Core," *The Tennessean*, May 3, 2018, https://www.tennessean.com/story/news/2018/05/03/interactive-map-see-how-nashville-tn-transit-vote-lost-election-results/573756002; Joey Garrison, "Analysis: 6 Reasons Why the Nashville Transit Referendum Lost Big," *The Tennessean*, May 3, 2018, https://www.tennessean.com/story/news/2018/05/02/nashville-transit-referendum-6-reasons-why-lost-big/571782002; Nick Stockton, "Why Traffic-Choked Nashville Said 'No Thanks' to Public Transit," *Wired*, May 9, 2018, https://www.wired.com/story/nashville-transit-referendum-vote-plan; Kriston Capps, "Nashville's Transit Plan Just Got Trounced," *CityLab*, May 2,

2018, https://www.citylab.com/transportation/2018/05/what-went-wrong-with-nashvilles-transit-plan/559436.

2. For a good overview of approaches to studying policy, although mainly with a national perspective, see Christopher M. Weible and Paul A. Sabatier, eds., *Theories of the Policy Process* (Boulder: Westview, 2017).

3. For an extended treatment of this approach, see B. Guy Peters, *American Public Policy: Promise and Performance*, 11th edition (Washington, DC: CQ Press, 2018), especially chapters 4–6.

4. For an analysis of zoning cases as development picked up in Metropolitan Atlanta during the mid-1980s, see Arnold Fleischmann, "Politics, Administration, and Local Land-Use Regulation: Examining Zoning as a Policy Process," *Public Administration Review* 49 (July/August 1989): 337–44.

5. J. Wesley Leckrone, Michelle Atherton, Nicole Crossey, Andrea Stickley, and Meghan E. Rubardo, "Does Anyone Care about the Poor? Redistribution in Mayoral Policy Agendas," *State and Local Government Review* 47:4 (December 2015): 240–54.

6. Anita Yadavalli and Christiana K. McFarland, "State of the Cities 2018" (Washington, DC: National League of Cities, May 2018), https://www.nlc.org/sites/default/files/2018-05/NLC%20State%20of%20the%20Cities%202018%20FINAL%20WEB.pdf; Nicole Flatow, "What Mayors Are Talking About," *CityLab*, June 1, 2018, https://www.citylab.com/life/2018/06/what-mayors-are-talking-about/561623.

7. Mirya R. Holman, "Gender, Political Rhetoric, and Moral Metaphors in State of the City Addresses," *Urban Affairs Review* 52:4 (July 2016): 501–30.

8. "A Timeline of How the Atlanta School Cheating Scandal Unfolded," *Atlanta Journal-Constitution*, May 3, 2018, https://www.ajc.com/news/timeline-how-the-atlanta-school-cheating-scandal-unfolded/jn4vTk7GZUQoQRJTVR7UHK. Also see Rhonda Cook, "A Year Later, How Cheating Trial Is Still Epic," *Atlanta Journal-Constitution*, April 2, 2016, A1.

9. For general coverage, as well as descriptions of recent measures in specific places, see the "Local Ballot Measures" tab in *Ballotpedia*, https://ballotpedia.org/Local_Ballot_Measures.

10. Xinsheng Liu, Eric Lindquist, Arnold Vedlitz, and Kenneth Vincent, "Understanding Local Policymaking: Perceptions of Local Agenda Setting and Alternative Policy Selection," *Policy Studies Journal* 38:1 (February 2010): 69–91.

11. More information is available on the Government Finance Officers Association website: http://www.gfoa.org.

12. See the American Public Works Association website for more details: https://www.apwa.net.

13. Gregory Scruggs, "Seattle Unanimously Passes an 'Amazon Tax' to Fund Affordable Housing," *CityLab*, May 15, 2018, https://www.citylab.com/equity/2018/05/seattle-unanimously-passes-its-amazon-tax/560411; David Streitfeld and Claire Ballentine, "Amazon Played Hardball on New Tax. Now Seattle Is Killing the Tax," *New York Times*, June 13, 2018, B1.

14. Chris Koski, "Greening America's Skylines: The Diffusion of Low-Salience Policies," *Policy Studies Journal* 38:1 (February 2010): 93–117.

15. Charles R. Shipan and Craig Volden, "Policy Diffusion: Seven Lessons for Scholars and Practitioners," *Public Administration Review* 72:6 (November/December 2012): 788.

16. For an analysis of the diffusion of local antismoking policies, see Charles R. Shipan and Craig Volden, "The Mechanisms of Policy Diffusion," *American Journal of Political Science* 52:4 (October 2008): 840–57.

17. Robbie Brown, "In Georgia, Some Vote to Stay Dry on Sundays," *New York Times*, November 11, 2011, https://www.nytimes.com/2011/11/12/us/georgia-or-most-of-it-ends-sunday-ban-on-alcohol-sales.html.

18. Zachary A. Powell, Michele Bisaccia Meitl, and John L. Worrall, "Police Consent Decrees and Section 1983 Civil Rights Litigation," *Criminology & Public Policy* 16:2 (May 2017): 575–605; Stephen Rushin, *Federal Intervention in American Police Departments* (New York: Cambridge University Press, 2017); Sheryl Gay Stolberg and Eric Lichtblau, "Sweeping Federal Review Could Affect Consent Decrees Nationwide," *New York Times*, April 3, 2017, https://www.nytimes.com/2017/04/03/us/justice-department-jeff-sessions-baltimore-police.html; "Corrupt Police Need Federal Oversight" (editorial), *New York Times*, February 18, 2018, https://www.nytimes.com/2018/02/18/opinion/baltimore-police-federal-oversight.html.

19. See Anita Chabria and Kate Irby, "California Steps in to Oversee Police Reform after Trump Administration Pulls Out," *Sacramento Bee*, February 6, 2018, http://www.sacbee.com/news/local/article198562044.html.

20. Kimberly L. Nelson, "Municipal Choices during a Recession: Bounded Rationality and Innovation," *State and Local Government Review* 44:special issue (August 2012): 44–63; Lawrence L. Martin, Richard Levey, and Jenna Cawley, "The 'New Normal' for Local Government," *State and Local Government Review* 44:special issue (August 2012): 17–28; David N. Ammons, Karl W. Smith, and Carl W. Stenberg, "The Future of Local Government: Will Current Stresses Bring Major, Permanent Changes?" *State and Local Government Review* 44:special issue (August 2012): 64–75.

21. Fleischmann, "Politics, Administration, and Local Land-Use Regulation."

22. Liu et al., "Understanding Local Policymaking."

23. Brianne Heidbreder, Nathan Grasse, Douglas Ihrke, and Brian D. Cherry, "Determinants of Policy Conflict in Michigan Municipalities," *State and Local Government Review* 43:1 (April 2011): 32–45.

24. Kimberly L. Nelson, Gerald T. Gabris, and Trenton J. Davis, "What Makes Municipal Councils Effective? An Empirical Analysis of How Council Members Perceive Their Group Interactions and Processes," *State and Local Government Review* 43:3 (December 2011): 196–204.

25. Kimberly L. Nelson and Karl Nollenberger, "Conflict and Cooperation in Municipalities: Do Variations in Form of Government Have an Effect?" *Urban Affairs Review* 47:5 (September 2011): 696–720.

26. Christopher A. Cooper, H. Gibbs Knotts, and Kathleen M. Brennan, "The Importance of Trust in Government for Public Administration: The Case of Zoning," *Public Administration Review* 68:3 (May/June 2008): 459–68.

27. Garrick L. Percival, Martin Johnson, and Max Neiman, "Representation and Local Policy: Relating County-Level Public Opinion to Policy Outputs," *Political Research Quarterly* 62:1 (March 2009): 164–77.

28. Christine Kelleher Paulus, "Responsiveness in American Local Governments," *State and Local Government Review* 42:2 (August 2010): 133–50.

29. Zoltan L. Hajnal and Jessica Trounstine, "Who or What Governs? The Effects of Economics, Politics, Institutions, and Needs on Local Spending," *American Politics Research* 38:6 (November 2010): 1130–63.

30. Chris Tausanovitch and Christopher Warshaw, "Representation in Municipal Government," *American Political Science Review* 108:3 (August 2014): 605–41.

31. Katherine Levine Einstein and Vladimir Kogan, "Pushing the City Limits: Policy Responsiveness in Municipal Government," *Urban Affairs Review* 52:1 (January 2016): 3–32.

32. Timothy B. Krebs and John P. Pelissero, "What Influences City Council Adoption and Support for Reinventing Government: Environmental or Institutional Factors?" *Public Administration Review* 70:2 (March/April 2010): 258–67. The analysis included eight statistical models, with the lowest number of cases being 362, one having 466, and the remaining six models having between 548 and 6,675 cities in the model.

33. Chandler Davidson and Bernard Grofman, eds., *Quiet Revolution in the South: The Impact of the Voting Rights Act, 1965–1990* (Princeton: Princeton University Press, 1994), especially chapter 10; Peggy Heilig and Robert J. Mundt, *Your Voice at City Hall: The Politics, Procedures and Policies of District Representation* (Albany: State University of New York Press, 1985).

34. Richard Perez-Pena, "Subway Token, Currency of the City Dies at 50," *New York Times*, March 15, 2003, https://www.nytimes.com/2003/03/15/nyregion/subway-token-currency-of-the-city-dies-at-50.html.

35. This example is borrowed from Brian D. Jones, "Assessing the Products of Government," in *Analyzing Urban-Service Distributions*, ed. Richard C. Rich (Lexington: Lexington Books, 1982), 155–69.

36. The survey and related products are sold by the National Research Center: https://www.n-r-c.com.

37. https://multco.us/auditor. There is also a national organization for local government auditors, who do much more than traditional financial auditing: https://algaonline.org.

38. The definitions are spelled out in Paul E. Peterson, *City Limits* (Chicago: University of Chicago Press, 1981), 41–43.

39. See Elaine B. Sharp, ed., *Culture Wars and Local Politics* (Lawrence: University Press of Kansas, 1999); Elaine B. Sharp, *Morality Politics in American Cities* (Lawrence: University Press of Kansas, 2005).

40. For a good analysis of providing urban services, see Charles K. Coe, *Handbook of Urban Services: A Basic Guide for Local Governments* (Armonk: M. E. Sharpe, 2009).

41. Bryan D. Jones, "Assessing the Products of Government," in *Analyzing Urban Service Distributions*, ed. Richard C. Rich (Lexington: Lexington Books, 1982), 155–69.

42. Robert E. England, John P. Pelissero, and David R. Morgan, *Managing Urban America*, 8th edition (Washington, DC: CQ Press, 2017), chapter 7.

43. David N. Ammons, *Municipal Benchmarks: Assessing Local Performance and Establishing Community Standards* (Thousand Oaks: Sage, 2001), 10–14. Ammons covers performance measurement in greater detail in chapter 2 and applies it to specific services in chapters 3–32.

44. On the dynamics among citizen groups, elected officials, and agencies in St. Louis, including battles over stop signs, see Lana Stein, *Holding Bureaucrats Accountable: Politicians and Professionals in St. Louis* (Tuscaloosa: University of Alabama Press, 1991).

45. For Kansas City, see https://www.kcmo.gov/city-hall/31; for Chicago, see City of Chicago, https://www.cityofchicago.org/city/en/depts/311.html.

46. For a discussion of different survey methods, see Mitchel N. Herian and Alan J. Tomkins, "Citizen Satisfaction Survey Data: A Mode Comparison of the Derive Importance-Performance Approach," *American Review of Public Administration* 44:1 (January 2014): 66–86.

47. Janet M. Kelly and David Swindell, "A Multiple-Indicator Approach to Municipal Service Evaluation: Correlating Performance Measurement and Citizen Satisfaction across Jurisdictions," *Public Administration Review* 52:5 (September/October 2002): 610–21; David Swindell and Janet Kelly, "Performance Measurement versus City Service Satisfaction: Intra-city Variations in Quality," *Social Science Quarterly* 86:3 (September 2005): 704–23.

48. Llewellyn M. Toulmin, "Equity as a Decision Rule in Determining the Distribution of Urban Public Services," *Urban Affairs Quarterly* 23:3 (March 1988): 389–413.

49. John Horrigan, "Libraries at the Crossroads," *Pew Research Center*, September 15, 2015, http://www.pewresearch.org/wp-content/uploads/sites/9/2015/09/2015_09_15_libraries_FINAL.pdf.

50. E. S. Savas, *Privatization: The Key to Better Government* (Chatham: Chatham House, 1987); David Osborne and Ted Gaebler, *Reinventing Government: How the Entrepreneurial Spirit is Transforming the Public Sector* (Reading: Addison-Wesley, 1992).

51. International City/County Management Association, "Profile of Local Government Service Delivery Choices, 2007" (Washington, DC: ICMA, 2009), https://icma.org/sites/default/files/107037_asd2007_2008web.pdf.

52. Savas, *Privatization*, 62–63, 84–87, 95–112. For comparison, see Elliott D. Sclar, *You Don't Always Get What You Pay For: The Economics of Privatization* (Ithaca: Cornell University Press, 2000), chapter 3.

53. Osborne and Gaebler, *Reinventing Government*, 204. Also see Savas, *Privatization*, 248–50.

54. Savas, *Privatization*, 81–87.

55. Savas, *Privatization*, 79, 86–87.

56. David Vinjamuri, "Why Public Libraries Matter: And How They Can Do More," *Forbes*, January 16, 2013, https://www.forbes.com/sites/davidvinjamuri/2013/01/16/why-public-libraries-matter-and-how-they-can-do-more/#2c2a512669be; Marcela Cabello and Stuart M. Butler, "How Public Libraries Help Build Healthy Communities," Brookings Institution, *Up Front* blog, March 30, 2017,

https://www.brookings.edu/blog/up-front/2017/03/30/how-public-libraries-help-build-healthy-communities.

57. J. B. Wogan, "How Will the Sharing Economy Change the Way Cities Function?" *Governing*, October 2013, http://www.governing.com/topics/urban/gov-how-sharing-economy-will-change-cities.html; Brooks Rainwater, "The Sharing Economy Needs to Be Better Partners with Cities," *CityLab*, February 7, 2018, https://www.citylab.com/equity/2018/02/the-sharing-economy-needs-to-be-better-partners-with-cities/552626.

58. Carolyn Said, "Airbnb Loses Thousands of Hosts in SF as Registration Rules Kick In," *San Francisco Chronicle*, January 14, 2018, https://www.sfchronicle.com/business/article/Airbnb-loses-thousands-of-hosts-in-SF-as-12496624.php.

59. Gary J. Miller, *Cities by Contract: The Politics of Municipal Incorporation* (Cambridge, MA: MIT Press, 1981).

60. Jonas Prager, "Contract City Redux: Weston, Florida, as the Ultimate New Public Management Model City," *Public Administration Review* 68:1 (January/February 2008): 167–80; David Segal, "A Georgia Town Takes the People's Business Private," *New York Times*, June 23, 2012, http://www.memphisshelbyinform.com/wp-content/uploads/2014/01/062312_sandy-springs-a-georgia-town-takes.pdf.

61. Phillip J. Cooper, *Governing by Contract: Challenges and Opportunities for Public Managers* (Washington, DC: CQ Press, 2003).

62. Amir Hefetz and Mildred E. Warner, "Contracting or Public Delivery? Importance of Service, Market, and Management Characteristics," *Journal of Public Administration Research and Theory* 22:2 (April 2012): 289–317.

63. Cheryl Hilvert and David Swindell, "Collaborative Service Delivery: What Every Local Government Manager Should Know," *State and Local Government Review* 45:4 (December 2013): 240–54.

64. Mildred E. Warner and Amir Hefetz, "Managing Markets for Public Service: The Role of Mixed Public-Private Delivery of City Services," *Public Administration Review* 68:1 (January/February 2008): 155–66.

65. Warner and Hefetz, "Managing Markets for Public Service"; Hilvert and Swindell, "Collaborative Service Delivery."

66. Werner and Hefetz, "Managing Markets for Public Service," 163.

67. Scott Lamothe and Meeyoung Lamothe, "Service Shedding Local Government: Why Do They Do It?" *Journal of Public Administration Research and Theory* 26:2 (April 2016): 359–74.

68. See Elliott D. Sclar, *You Don't Always Get What You Pay For: The Economics of Privatization* (Ithaca: Cornell University Press, 2000).

69. Bernard Marr, "The Sharing Economy: What It Is, Examples, and How Big Data, Platforms and Algorithms Fuel It," *Forbes*, October 21, 2016, https://www.forbes.com/sites/bernardmarr/2016/10/21/the-sharing-economy-what-it-is-examples-and-how-big-data-platforms-and-algorithms-fuel/#5341d1f07c5a.

70. Savas, *Privatization*, 77–78, 84–85.

71. Savas, *Privatization*, 78–79, 84–85.

72. David P. Varady and Carole C. Walker, "Using Housing Vouchers to Move to the Suburbs: The Alameda County, California, Case," *Urban Affairs Review* 39:2 (November 2003): 143–80; Anne R. Williamson, Marc T. Smith, and Marta Strambi-Kramer, "Housing Choice Vouchers, the Low-Income Housing Tax Credit, and the Federal Poverty Deconcentration Goal," *Urban Affairs Review* 45:1 (September 2009): 119–32; Ann Owens, "Assisted Housing and Neighborhood Poverty Dynamics, 1977 to 2008," *Urban Affairs Review* 52:3 (January 2016): 287–322.

73. Savas, *Privatization*, 80–81.

74. For one expression of this concern, see David Callahan, "The Rising Power of Philanthropy," *New York Times*, June 20, 2017, A25.

11: LOCAL GOVERNMENT FINANCES

1. Alana Samuels, "How Amazon Helped Kill a Seattle Tax on Business," *The Atlantic*, June 13, 2018, https://www.theatlantic.com/technology/archive/2018/06/how-amazon-helped-kill-a-seattle-tax-on-business/562736; James Doubek, "Seattle Repeals Tax on Big Business after Opposition from Amazon, Starbucks," *National Public Radio*, June 13, 2018, https://www.npr.org/2018/06/13/619444956/seattle-repeals-tax-on-big-business-after-opposition-from-amazon-starbucks; Sarah Holder, "The Precipitous Fall of Seattle's 'Amazon Tax'," *CityLab*, June 13, 2018, https://www.citylab.com/equity/2018/06/in-seattle-business-won/562691.

2. City of Minneapolis, "2017 City of Minneapolis Budget in Brief," 3, http://www.ci.minneapolis.mn.us/www/groups/public/@finance/documents/webcontent/wcmsp-192479.pdf.

3. The US Census Bureau conducts the Census of Governments every 5 years in years ending in 2 and 5. Data gathered in other years are from samples and are subject to some error, but they are still quite reliable.

4. For a brief historical overview, see Glenn W. Fisher, "History of Property Taxes in the United States," *EH.net Encyclopedia of Economic and Business History* (maintained by the Economic History Association), https://eh.net/encyclopedia/history-of-property-taxes-in-the-united-states.

5. John S. Kiernan, "2017's Property Taxes by State," *WalletHub*, March 1, 2017, https://wallethub.com/edu/states-with-the-highest-and-lowest-property-taxes/11585; F&I tools, "Car Tax by State," http://www.factorywarrantylist.com/car-tax-by-state.html.

6. "Property Tax Exemption Data for US Cities," *Governing* ("Governing Data"), October 2012, http://www.governing.com/gov-data/finance/tax-exempt-property-values-totals-for-cities.html.

7. Kellie Woodhouse, "University of Michigan Expansion: Buying Land Raises Questions about Tax Base," *Ann Arbor News*, February 10, 2013, http://www.annarbor.com/news/university-of-michigan-land-acquisition-means-less-money-for-the-city-of-ann-arbor; Jeremy Allen, "Edwards Brothers Malloy Move from U-M-Owned South State Street Facility Nearly Complete," *MLive News*, December 8, 2014,

http://www.mlive.com/news/ann-arbor/index.ssf/2014/12/edwards_brothers_malloy_move_f.html.

8. Brown University, "Taxes, Voluntary Payments and Fees," https://www.brown.edu/about/providence/taxes.

9. See Kelly McGiverin-Bohan, Kirsten Gronbjerg, Lauren Dula, and Rachel Miller, "Local Officials' Support for PILOTs/SILOTs: Nonprofit Engagement, Economic Stress, and Politics," *Public Administration Review* 76:6 (November/December 2016): 951–63.

10. See the utility's profiles at https://austinenergy.com/ae/about/company-profile; on rate controversies see Lilly Rockwell, "Coming in 2016: A Debate over New Electricity Rates from Austin Energy," *Austin American-Statesman*, December 21, 2015, https://www.mystatesman.com/news/local/coming-2016-debate-over-new-electricity-rates-from-austin-energy/j5oY41boyq8GU57KXcDNxM; Elizabeth Findell, "Austin Energy Reaches Tentative Deal over Utility Rates," *Austin American-Statesman*, August 15, 2016, https://www.mystatesman.com/news/local/austin-energy-reaches-tentative-deal-over-utility-rates/VOOnWobVprJF12BNOoLoWU; Sierra Club, Lone Star Chapter, "It's Official. Austin City Council Approves New Austin Energy Rates," August 29, 2016, https://www.sierraclub.org/texas/blog/2016/08/it-s-official-austin-city-council-approves-new-austin-energy-rates.

11. Charlie B. Tyer, "Municipal Enterprises and Taxing and Spending Policies: Public Avoidance and Fiscal Illusions," *Public Administration Review* 49:3 (May/June 1989): 249–56.

12. Fulton County Board of Assessors, "Homestead Exemptions," https://www.qpublic.net/ga/fulton/programs.html#xl_city:32of:32atlanta:32school:32:3625:44000:32exemption.

13. DeKalb County Tax Commissioner, "Exemptions," https://www.dekalbcountyga.gov/tax-commissioner/exemptions.

14. Louisiana Tax Commission, "FAQ," http://www.latax.state.la.us/Menu_FAQ/FAQ.aspx#faq7.

15. California State Board of Equalization, "Homeowners' Exemption," http://www.boe.ca.gov/proptaxes/homeowners_exemption.htm.

16. Arizona Department of Revenue, Property Tax Division, "Assessment Procedures Manual, Part 3: Assessment Procedures," January 1, 2017, https://www.azdor.gov/Portals/0/Property/2016Part3Chapter1.pdf.

17. Fisher, "History of Property Taxes in the United States."

18. City of St. Louis Assessor's Office, "Property Assessment Appeals," https://www.stlouis-mo.gov/government/departments/assessor/real-estate/appeal-your-property-assessment.cfm.

19. Wisconsin Department of Revenue, "2017 Property Assessment Appeal Guide for Wisconsin Real Property Owners," https://www.revenue.wi.gov/DOR%20Publications/pb055.pdf.

20. Denver Treasury Division, "Real Estate Tax Lien Sale Information," https://www.denvergov.org/content/denvergov/en/treasury-division/property-taxes/delinquent-taxes-and-tax-lien-sale.html; "City and County of Denver, Colorado: Tax Certificate Process," https://denver.coloradotaxsale.com/index.cfm?folder=showDocument&documentName=taxCertificateProcess.

21. Jared Walczak and Scott Drenkard, "State and Local Sales Taxes in 2017," *Tax Foundation Fiscal Fact*, no. 539, January 2017, https://files.taxfoundation.org/20170131121743/TaxFoundation-FF539.pdf. The Tax Foundation is a nonprofit research and advocacy organization founded in 1937 and based in Washington, DC.

22. Jared Walczak, Scott Drenkard, and Joseph Henchman, *2017 State Business Climate Index* (Washington, DC: Tax Foundation, 2017), 35–42, https://www.dropbox.com/sh/ijecxnhl3egojd9/AAAeL1yZYVDgGlX2W6Mjql6na?dl=0&preview=Full+Study.pdf.

23. Liz Malm and Richard Borean, "How Does Your State Sales Tax See That Blue and Black (or White and Gold) Dress?" Tax Foundation, February 27, 2015, https://taxfoundation.org/how-does-your-state-sales-tax-see-blue-and-black-or-white-and-gold-dress.

24. Joseph Henchman, Alex Raut, and Kevin Duncan, "Meals Taxes in Major US Cities," *Tax Foundation Fiscal Fact*, no. 293, March 1, 2012, https://taxfoundation.org/meals-taxes-major-us-cities-0.

25. Abigail M. York, Kevin Kane, Christopher M. Clark, Lauren E. Gentile, Amber Wutich, and Sharon L. Harlan, "What Determines Public Support for Graduated Development Impact Fees?" *State and Local Government Review* 49:1 (March 2017): 15–26.

26. For more on municipal bonds, see the Municipal Securities Rulemaking Board, http://www.msrb.org/.

27. Carla Fried, "The Muni Market Turns toward Washington," *New York Times*, April 14, 2017, https://www.nytimes.com/2017/04/14/business/mutfund/trump-municipal-bonds.html.

28. "S&P Downgrades Kansas' Rating, Again," *Governing*, July 28, 2016, http://www.governing.com/topics/finance/SP-Drops-Kansas-Credit-Rating.html; Juan Perez, Jr., "Moody's Downgrades Chicago Schools Further into Junk States," *Governing*, September 27, 2016, http://www.governing.com/templates/gov_print_article?id=394934251.

29. Gretchen Morgenson, "Pension Funds, Dancing a Two-Step with Ratings Funds," *New York Times*, June 14, 2014, https://www.nytimes.com/2014/06/15/business/pension-funds-dancing-a-two-step-with-ratings-firms.html; Gretchen Morgenson and Louise Story, "Rating Agency Data Aided Wall Street in Deals," *New York Times*, April 23, 2010, http://www.nytimes.com/2010/04/24/business/24rating.html; Liz Farmer, "Do Credit Ratings Matter Anymore?" *Governing*, January 2015, http://www.governing.com/topics/finance/gov-credit-ratings-still-matter.html.

30. Tonya Moreno, "US Cities That Levy Income Taxes," February 2, 2017, *The Balance*, https://www.thebalance.com/cities-that-levy-income-taxes-3193246. This site is a financial information site that is part of a series of sites and companies associated with IAC: http://iac.com/about/overview.

31. Katrease Stafford, "Detroit Councilwoman Sheffield May Reconsider Her 'Yes' Vote on $34.5M Pistons Arena Deal," *Detroit Free Press*, June 23, 2017, http://www.

freep.com/story/news/local/michigan/detroit/2017/06/23/
detroit-councilwoman-sheffield-may-reconsider-her-
yes-vote-34-5-m-pistons-arena-deal/421389001; Mark
Niesse, "Little-Noticed Metro Atlanta Agencies Give
Big Tax Breaks," *Atlanta Journal-Constitution*, April 1,
2017, http://www.myajc.com/news/local-govt–politics/
little-noticed-metro-atlanta-agencies-give-big-tax-breaks/
YexR3cP7mQzz7kdDXBwG8I.

32. Joshua Sapotichne, Erika Rosebrook, Eric A. Scorsone,
Danielle Kaminski, Mary Doidge, and Traci Taylor, "Be-
yond State Takeovers: Reconsidering the Role of State
Government in Local Fiscal Distress, with Important
Lessons for Michigan and its Embattled Cities" (East
Lansing: Michigan State University Extension White Pa-
per, August 2015), http://msue.anr.msu.edu/resources/
beyond_state_takeovers.

33. Liam Dillon, "Proposition 13 Has Strictly Limited Property
Tax Increases since 1978. Voters Could Get a Chance to
Change That," *Los Angeles Times*, October 17, 2018,
https://www.latimes.com/politics/la-pol-ca-prop-13-
changes-20181017-story.html.

34. Office of the Assessor, Santa Clara County,
"Understanding Proposition 13," https://www.
sccassessor.org/index.php/faq/understanding-
proposition-13; Clyde Haberman, "Retro Report: The
California Ballot Measure That Inspired a Tax Revolt,"
New York Times, October 16, 2016, https://www.
nytimes.com/2016/10/17/us/the-california-ballot-
measure-that-inspired-a-tax-revolt.html; Michael Hiltzik,
"Four Decades Later, California Experts Find That
Proposition 13 Is a Boon to the Rich," *Los Angeles
Times*, September 30, 2016, http://www.latimes.com/
business/hiltzik/la-fi-hiltzik-prop-13–20160929-snap-
story.html; Dan Walters, "California's Proposition 13
Turns 40 This Year. Its Midlife Crisis May Be on the Way,"
Sacramento Bee, February 18, 2018, http://www.sacbee.
com/opinion/california-forum/article200137504.html.

35. "Sales Tax in California," *Ballotpedia*, https://ballotpedia.
org/Sales_tax_in_California.

36. Robert M. Howard, Arnold Fleischmann, and Richard N.
Engstrom, *Politics in Georgia*, 3rd edition (Athens: University of Georgia Press, 2017), 255–56, 269–70.

37. See, for example, Dennis Jacobe, "Which Is the Unfairest
Tax of Them All?" *Gallup News*, April 19, 2005, http://news.
gallup.com/poll/15937/Which-Unfairest-Tax-Them-All.aspx.

38. "Public Opinion on Taxes: 1937 to Today," *AEI Public
Opinion Studies* (Washington, DC: American Enterprise
Institute for Public Policy Research, April 2017), 28–30,
http://www.aei.org/wp-content/uploads/2017/04/
Bowman_Public-Opinion-Study_Taxes_April-2017.pdf.

39. Douglas D. Roscoe, "Yes, Raise My Taxes: Property Tax
Cap Override Elections," *Social Science Quarterly* 95:1
(March 2014): 145–64.

40. Michael B. Berkman and Eric Plutzer, "Gray Peril or Loyal
Support? The Effects of the Elderly on Educational Expenditures," *Social Science Quarterly* 85:5 (December 2004):
1178–92.

41. Joel Kurth, "Detroit Hits Residents on Water Shut-
offs as Businesses Slide," *Detroit News*, April 1,

2016, http://www.detroitnews.com/story/news/local/
detroit-city/2016/03/31/detroit-water-shutoffs/82497496.

42. For an overview of Boston's efforts to get payments in lieu
of taxes (PILOTs) from its universities and other nonprofits,
see Alan Greenblatt, "PILOTs Under Pressure," *Governing*, June 2019, 13.

43. Kimberly L. Nelson, "Municipal Choices during a Recession: Bounded Rationality and Innovation," *State and
Local Government Review* 44:special issue (August 2012):
44–63; Lawrence L. Martin, Richard Levey, and Jenna
Cawley, "The 'New Normal' for Local Government," *State
and Local Government Review* 44:special issue (August
2012): 17–28.

44. On possible resolutions of this problem, see Mary Williams Walsh, "Houston and Dallas Get Relief on Pensions," *New York Times*, June 2, 2017, B1.

45. Mary Williams Walsh, "Houston and Dallas Get Relief on
Pensions," *New York Times*, June 2, 2017, B1.

46. David N. Ammons, Karl W. Smith, and Carl W. Stenberg,
"The Future of Local Government: Will Current Stresses
Bring Major, Permanent Changes?" *State and Local Gov-
ernment Review* 44:special issue (August 2012): 64–75.

47. "Bankrupt Cities, Municipalities and Map," *Governing*,
http://www.governing.com/gov-data/municipal-cities-
counties-bankruptcies-and-defaults.html; Amy S. Rosen-
berg, "New Jersey Assumes Control of Atlantic City's
Government," *Governing*, November 10, 2016, http://
www.governing.com/topics/mgmt/tns-atlantic-city-new-
jersey.html. Also see Ashley E. Nickels, "Approaches to
Municipal Takeover: Home Rule Erosion and State Intervention in Michigan and New Jersey," *State and Local
Government Review* 48:3 (September 2016): 194–207;
David Oliver Kasdan, "Emergency Management 2.0: This
Time, It's Financial," *Urban Affairs Review* 52:5 (September 2016): 864–82; Anna Fountain Clark and Evgenia
Gorina, "Emergency Financial Management in Small
Michigan Cities: Short-Term Fix or Long-Term Sustain-
ability?" *Public Administration Quarterly* 41:3 (Fall 2017):
532–68.

12: BUILDING THE CITY: ECONOMIC DEVELOPMENT, LAND USE, AND HOUSING POLICIES

1. Austin Carr, "Inside Wisconsin's Disastrous $4.5 Billion Deal
with Foxconn," *Bloomberg Businessweek*, February 6, 2019,
https://www.bloomberg.com/news/features/2019-02-06/
inside-wisconsin-s-disastrous-4-5-billion-deal-with-foxconn;
Michael J. Hicks, "Wisconsin Taxpayers Need to Pull the
Plug on This Con of a Foxconn Deal," *MarketWatch*,
November 4, 2018, https://www.marketwatch.com/story/
wisconsin-taxpayers-need-to-pull-the-plug-on-this-con-of-
a-foxconn-deal-2018-11-02; Kif Leswing, "Trump Called
Foxconn's Wisconsin Factory an 'Incredible Investment,' but
Evidence Is Mounting It's a Terrible Deal," *Business Insider*,

November 6, 2018, https://www.businessinsider.com/why-foxconns-wisconsin-factory-is-terrible-deal-2018-11; Robert Channick, "As Foxconn Changes Wisconsin Plans, Job Promises Fall Short," *Chicago Tribune*, February 8, 2019, https://www.chicagotribune.com/business/ct-biz-foxconn-plant-hiring-target-20190205-story.html.

2. For a comparison, see Peter K. Eisinger, *The Rise of the Entrepreneurial State: State and Local Economic Development Policy in the United States* (Madison: University of Wisconsin Press, 1988), 36–41.

3. Eisinger, *The Rise of the Entrepreneurial State*, 76–82, 227–40.

4. Alternatives are analyzed in an extended review essay: Harold Wolman with David Spitzley, "The Politics of Local Economic Development," *Economic Development Quarterly* 10:2 (May 1996): 115–50, especially 122–24.

5. James C. Cobb, *The Selling of the South: The Southern Crusade for Industrial Development, 1936–1980* (Baton Rouge: Louisiana State University Press, 1982), chapter 1.

6. For a summary of Richard Florida's perspective, see his essay, "The Creative Class and Economic Development," *Economic Development Quarterly* 28:3 (August 2014): 196–205. See also Ann Markusen, "Targeting Occupations in Regional and Community Economic Development," *Journal of the American Planning Association* 70:3 (Summer 2004): 253–68; Ann Markusen, Gregory H. Wassall, Douglas DeNatale, and Randy Cohen, "Defining the Creative Economy: Industry and Occupational Approaches," *Economic Development Quarterly* 22:1 (February 2008): 24–45.

7. On clusters, see Michael E. Porter, "Location, Competition, and Economic Development: Local Clusters in a Global Economy," *Economic Development Quarterly* 14:1 (February 2000): 15–34.

8. Atlanta Convention and Visitors Bureau, "Reunions in Atlanta," https://www.atlanta.net/reunions.

9. Trade Show News Network, "2017 Top US Trade Shows," https://www.tsnn.com/toplists-us.

10. For an analysis of this competition, see Heywood T. Sanders, *Convention Center Follies: Politics, Power, and Investment in American Cities* (Philadelphia: University of Pennsylvania Press, 2014).

11. Bill Hethcock, "Fort Worth, Dallas Leading Trade Mission to London, Paris, Brussels," *Dallas Business Journal*, June 14, 2018, https://www.bizjournals.com/dallas/news/2018/06/14/fort-worth-dallas-mayors-leading-trade-mission-to.html.

12. ICMA, *Economic Development 2014 Survey Results*, https://icma.org/sites/default/files/306723_Economic%20Development%202014%20Survey%20Results%20for%20website.pdf.

13. For an overview, see Nancy Green Leigh and Edward J. Blakely, *Planning Local Economic Development: Theory and Practice*, 6th edition (Los Angeles: Sage, 2017), 132–33, 451.

14. Leigh and Blakely, *Planning Local Economic Development*, 402–4, 443–46.

15. Lakeland Economic Development Council, "Tax Abatements," 2018, http://www.lakelandedc.com/site-selection/incentives/tax-abatement; Ryan E. Little, "Polk Commission OK's Tax Abatement for Amazon If Warehouse Built Here," *Lakeland Ledger*, July 9, 2013, http://www.theledger.com/news/20130709/polk-commission-oks-tax-abatement-for-amazon-if-warehouse-built-here.

16. South Carolina Department of Commerce, "Sales and Use Tax Incentives," https://www.sccommerce.com/incentives/south-carolina-sales-use-tax-incentives.

17. Nicholas Greifer, "*An Elected Official's Guide to Tax Increment Financing*" (Chicago: Government Finance Officers Association of the United States and Canada, 2005), https://www.gfoa.org/sites/default/files/EOGTIF.pdf; Richard Dye and David Merriman, "Tax Increment Financing: A Tool for Local Economic Development" (Cambridge, MA: Lincoln Institute of Land Policy, 2006), https://www.lincolninst.edu/publications/articles/tax-increment-financing.

18. City of Milwaukee, Department of City Development, TID Project Summaries (December 31, 2017); "TID 39—Hilton Parking Ramp," https://city.milwaukee.gov/ImageLibrary/Groups/cityDCD/business/TIF/2017-Reports/TID39.pdf; "TID 57—Harley Davidson Museum," https://city.milwaukee.gov/ImageLibrary/Groups/cityDCD/business/TIF/2017-Reports/TID57.pdf.

19. Wendley Hundley, "Plano Approves $6.75 Million in Grants and Other Incentives for Toyota," *Dallas Morning News*, May 12, 2014, https://www.dallasnews.com/news/plano/2014/05/12/plano-approves-675-million-grant-and-other-incentives-for-toyota.

20. Brett Theodos, Steven M. Rosenthal, and Brady Meixell, "The IRS Proposes Generous Rules for Opportunity Zone Investors But What Will They Mean for Communities?" *TaxVox Blog*, Tax Policy Center (Urban Institute and Brookings Institution), https://www.taxpolicycenter.org/taxvox/irs-proposes-generous-rules-opportunity-zone-investors-what-will-they-mean-communities.

21. Sumei Zhang, "Impacts of Enterprise Zone Policy on Industry Growth: New Evidence from the Louisville Program," *Economic Development Quarterly* 29:4 (November 2015): 347–62.

22. David Neumark and Jed Kolko, "Do Enterprise Zones Create Jobs? Evidence from California's Enterprise Program," NBER Working Paper Series, no. 14530 (revised 2010), National Bureau of Economic Research, https://www.nber.org/papers/w14530; C. Lockwood Reynolds and Shawn M. Rohlin, "The Effects of Location-Based Tax Policies on the Distribution of Household Income: Evidence from the Federal Empowerment Zone Program," *Journal of Urban Economics* 88 (July 2015): 1–15; Good Jobs First, "Enterprise Zones," https://www.goodjobsfirst.org/accountable-development/enterprise-zones.

23. Good Jobs First, "Supported by Megadeal, Volvo Choses South Carolina," https://www.goodjobsfirst.org/blog/supported-megadeal-volvo-choses-south-carolina.

24. Jason Margolis, "How Alabama Is Becoming the Auto Capital of the South," *PRI's The World* (Public Radio International), April 3,

2018, https://www.pri.org/stories/2018-04-03/how-alabama-becoming-auto-capital-south.

25. Abha Bhattarai, "Nearly a Year In, Marriott Marquis Says Job Training Program Has Worked," *Washington Post*, March 20, 2015, https://www.washingtonpost.com/business/capitalbusiness/nearly-as-year-in-marriott-marquis-says-job-training-program-has-worked/2015/03/19/7417c056-ccb4-11e4-8c54-ffb5ba6f2f69_story.html?noredirect=on&utm_term=.84cc41c4f289.

26. Good Jobs First, "Subsidy Tracker," with state/local government and training terms for 2017, https://subsidy-tracker.goodjobsfirst.org, accessed 10 October 2018.

27. Scott Gordon, "Foxconn Taps into the Plenitude and Perils of Great Lakes Water," *WisContext*, April 12, 2018, https://www.wiscontext.org/foxconn-taps-plenitude-and-perils-great-lakes-water; Ron Kirchen, "Foxconn to Spend $30M on Technology to Cut Lake Michigan Water Use," *Milwaukee Business Journal*, June 19, 2018, https://www.bizjournals.com/milwaukee/news/2018/06/19/foxconn-to-spend-30m-on-technology-to-cut-lake.html; Frank Abderholden, "Lake County Board Joins Outcry over Foxconn Environmental Impact," *Chicago Tribune—Lake County Sun-News*, June 12, 2018, http://www.chicagotribune.com/suburbs/lake-county-news-sun/news/ct-lns-foxconn-lake-county-board-opposes-st-0613-story.html.

28. Michael Tackett, "Economic Bellweather Is Making a Midwestern City Nervous," *New York Times*, September 12, 2018, B1.

29. Mildred E. Warner and Lingwen Zhang, "Business Incentive Adoption in the Recession," *Economic Development Quarterly* 27:2 (May 2013): 90–101.

30. Alan Ehrenhalt, "The Plight of Legacy Cities," *Governing*, December 2017, 14–15.

31. Janet Kelly, Matt Ruther, Sarah Ehresman, and Bridget Nickerson, "Placemaking as an Economic Development Strategy for Small and Midsized Cities," *Urban Affairs Review* 53:3 (May 2017): 435–62. See also Neil Irwin, "How Do Small Cities Lure Tech? Adapt, Invest, Upgrade (and Nudge)," *New York Times*, November 30, 2018, B3.

32. Mark Niesse, "Little-Noticed Agencies Give Big Tax Breaks," *Atlanta Journal-Constitution*, April 2, 2017, A1.

33. Greg LeRoy, "GASB Statement No. 77 Analysis," Good Jobs First, updated April 28, 2017, https://www.goodjobsfirst.org/GASB77Analysis.

34. Gary P. Green and Arnold Fleischmann, "Promoting Economic Development: A Comparison of Central Cities, Suburbs, and Nonmetropolitan Communities." *Urban Affairs Quarterly* 27:1 (September 1991): 145–54.

35. Susan M. Opp, Jeffrey L. Osgood, Jr., and Cynthia R. Rugeley, "City Limits in a Postrecessional World: Explaining the Pursuit of Developmental Policies after the Great Recession," *State and Local Government Review* 46:4 (December 2014): 236–48.

36. Aaron M. Renn, "What Employers Want from Cities," *Governing*, July 2018, 24–25.

37. Ben Casselman, "Nashville Leaves the Pack Behind," *New York Times*, December 17, 2018, B1. Also see Ssu-Hsein Chen, Richard C. Feiock, and Jun Yi Hsieh, "Regional Partnerships and Metropolitan Economic Development," *Journal of Urban Affairs* 38:2 (May 2016): 196–213.

38. Joshua Rothman, "Should We Subsidize Manufacturing?" *The New Yorker*, August 14, 2017, https://www.newyorker.com/news/news-desk/should-we-subsidize-manufacturing.

39. Joe Gose, "Cities Debate Use of Tax Incentives to Raise Skylines," *New York Times*, September 12, 2018, B1.

40. Elaine B. Sharp and Kevin Mullinix, "Holding Their Feet to the Fire: Explaining Variation in City Governments' Use of Controls on Economic Development Subsidies," *Economic Development Quarterly* 26:2 (May 2012): 138–50.

41. Hilary Gelfond and Adam Looney, "Learning from Opportunity Zones: How to Improve Place-Based Policies," Brookings Institution, October 2018, https://www.brookings.edu/wp-content/uploads/2018/10/Looney_Opportunity-Zones_final.pdf; "Boondocks and Boondoggles," *The Economist*, November 17, 2018, 34; Sophie Quinton, "Can Trump's Tax Break Turn Areas into 'Opportunity Zones'?" *Governing* (Finance), November 19, 2019, http://www.governing.com/topics/finance/sl-tax-break-finance-distressed-rural.html.

42. Derek Thompson, "Amazon's HQ2 Spectacle Isn't Just Shameful—It Should Be Illegal," *The Atlantic This Week*, November 16, 2018, https://www.theatlantic.com/ideas/archive/2018/11/amazons-hq2-spectacle-should-be-illegal/575539.

43. Liz Farmer, "The Unexpected Cost of Trying to Land Amazon's HQ2," *Governing* (The Week in Finance), August 17, 2018, http://www.governing.com/week-in-finance/gov-finance-roundup-amazon-giveaways.html.

44. Liz Farmer, "Was Amazon's HQ2 Search a Waste of Time for Cities?" *Governing* (Finance), November 19, 2018, http://www.governing.com/topics/finance/gov-amazon-second-headquarters-waste-cities-time.html; Ben Casselman, "$2 Billion Question: Did Virginia and New York Pay Too Much?" *New York Times*, November 14, 2018, B1; Annie Lowrey, "Amazon Was Never Going to Choose Detroit," *CityLab*, November 9, 2018, https://www.citylab.com/equity/2018/11/amazon-choose-detroit-hq2/575470; Aaron Renn, "Cities That Lost Amazon's HQ2 Contest Can Still End Up Ahead," *CityLab*, November 15, 2018, https://www.citylab.com/perspective/2018/11/cities-lost-amazons-hq2-contest-can-still-end-ahead/575938.

45. Shane Goldmacher, "Amazon Scraps New York Campus," *New York Times*, February 15, 2019, A1.

46. *Village of Euclid v. Ambler Realty Company*, 272 US 365 (1926).

47. For a useful, yet thorough, overview of zoning, see Herbert H. Smith, *The Citizen's Guide to Zoning*, revised edition (New York: Routledge, 2017).

48. Arnold Fleischmann, "Politics, Administration, and Local Land-Use Regulation: Examining Zoning as a Policy Process," *Public Administration Review* 49 (July/August 1989): 337–44.

49. Sonia Hirt, "Home, Sweet Home: American Residential Zoning in Comparative Perspective," *Journal of Planning Education and Research* 33:3 (September 2013): 292–309.

50. Andrew H. Whittemore, "The Experience of Racial and Ethnic Minorities with Zoning in the United States," *Journal of Planning Literature* 32:1 (February 2017): 16–27; Marice Ashe, David Jernigan, Randolph Kline, and Rhonda Galaz, "Land Use Planning and the Control of Alcohol, Tobacco, Firearms, and Fast Food Restaurants," *American Journal of Public Health* 93:9 (September 2003): 1404–8.

51. John R. Nolon, "Mitigating Climate Change by Zoning for Solar Energy Systems: Embracing Clean Energy Technology in Zoning's Centennial Year," *Zoning and Planning Law Report*, December 2015, https://papers.ssrn.com/sol3/papers.cfm?abstract_id=2733319; Daniel Guttentag, "Airbnb: Disruptive Innovation and the Rise of an Informal Tourism Accommodation Sector," *Current Issues in Tourism* 18:12 (2015): 1192–217.

52. Emily Badger and Quoctrung Bui, "Housing Scarce, Cities Erase Single Family Lots, *New York Times*, June 19, 2019, A1.

53. Joel Kotkin, *The Human City: Urbanism for the Rest of Us* (Chicago: Agate B2, 2016), chapter 6.

54. Congressional Budget Office, "Public Spending on Transportation and Water Infrastructure, 1956 to 2017" (Washington, DC: CBO, October 2018), https://www.cbo.gov/system/files?file=2018-10/54539-Infrastructure.pdf.

55. Congressional Budget Office, "Public Spending on Transportation and Water Infrastructure, 1956 to 2017."

56. American Society of Civil Engineers (ASCE), "2017 Infrastructure Report Card," https://www.infrastructurereportcard.org.

57. National League of Cities, "State of the Cities 2018," https://www.nlc.org/sites/default/files/2018-05/NLC%20State%20of%20the%20Cities%202018%20FINAL%20WEB.pdf.

58. Alana Samuels, "How Housing Policy Is Failing America's Poor," *CityLab*, June 24, 2015, https://www.citylab.com/equity/2015/06/how-housing-policy-is-failing-americas-poor/396737. Also see the Urban Institute's summary and links for "A Pilot Study of Landlord Acceptance of Housing Choice Vouchers," https://www.urban.org/research/publication/pilot-study-landlord-acceptance-housing-choice-vouchers; Mattie Quinn, "'Section 8 Need Not Apply': States and Cities Outlawing Housing Discrimination," *Governing* (Health and Human Services), August 29, 2018, http://www.governing.com/topics/health-human-services/gov-section-8-housing-discrimination-income-source.html.

59. Historical income limits by county are available from HUD's interactive website: https://www.huduser.gov/portal/datasets/fmr/fmr_il_history.html.

60. Ayoung Woo, Kenneth Joh, and Shannon Van Zandt, "Impacts of the Low-Income Housing Tax Credit Program on Neighborhood Housing Turnover," *Urban Affairs Review* 52:2 (March 2016): 247–79.

61. Claudine Gay, "A Room for One's Own? The Partisan Allocation of Affordable Housing," *Urban Affairs Review* 53:1 (January 2017): 40–70.

62. Ann Owens, "Assisted Housing and Neighborhood Poverty Dynamics, 1977 to 2008," *Urban Affairs Review* 52:3 (May 2016): 287–322.

63. Center on Budget and Policy Priorities, "Policy Basics: Federal Rental Assistance," November 15, 2017, https://www.cbpp.org/research/housing/policy-basics-federal-rental-assistance; US Congress, Congressional Budget Office, "Federal Housing Assistance for Low-Income Households," September 2015, https://www.cbo.gov/sites/default/files/114th-congress-2015-2016/reports/50782-lowincomehousing.pdf; Maggie McCarty, "Introduction to Public Housing," Congressional Research Service, report R41654, January 3, 2014, https://www.everycrsreport.com/reports/R41654.html.

64. For a detailed history of the Great Recession, including the roles of federal agencies, see Adam Tooze, *Crashed: How a Decade of Financial Crises Changed the World* (New York: Viking, 2018).

65. Dan Immergluck, *Foreclosed: High-Risk Lending, Deregulation, and the Undermining of America's Mortgage Market* (Ithaca: Cornell University Press, 2009), chapter 5.

66. See Dan Immergluck, *Credit to the Community: Community Reinvestment and Fair Lending Policy in the United States* (Armonk, NY: M. E. Sharpe, 2004). For more on the CRA, see reports and other information from the Federal Financial Institutions Examination Council, a federal interagency organization: https://www.ffiec.gov/cra/default.htm.

67. For example, the Colorado Department of Local Affairs worked with various groups to develop a guide for cities and counties: "Planning for Hazards: Land Use Solutions for Colorado," https://www.planningforhazards.com/about-guide.

68. For more information, see the USGBC website, particularly its explanation of LEED (Leadership in Energy and Environmental Design) certification: https://new.usgbc.org/leed.

69. Mike Maciag, "Eviction Epidemic," *Governing*, June 2018, 58–59.

70. Chris Joyner, Jeff Ernsthausen, and Willoughby Mariano, "Eviction Tactics Squeeze Renters," *Atlanta Journal-Constitution*, June 24, 2018, A1. Also see the landmark study of housing issues facing poor renters by Matthew Desmond, *Evicted: Poverty and Profit in the American City* (New York: Crown Publishers, 2016).

71. Fulton County Board of Assessors, "Fulton County Guide to Homestead Exemptions," 2018, http://fultonassessor.org/wp-content/uploads/sites/16/2018/04/2018-Guide-To-Homestead-Exemptions.pdf.

72. Louisiana Tax Commission, "Frequently Asked Questions," http://www.latax.state.la.us/Menu_FAQ/FAQ.aspx#faq7.

73. Isaac William Martin and Kevin Beck, "Gentrification, Property Tax Limitations, and Displacement," *Urban Affairs Review* 54:1 (January 2018): 33–73.

74. Deborah A. Carroll and Christopher A. Goodman, "Assessing the Influence of Property Tax Delinquency on Residential Property Sales," *Urban Affairs Review* 53:5 (September 2017): 898–923.

75. Center for Community Progress, "Frequently Asked Questions on Land Banking," https://www.communityprogress.net/land-banking-faq-pages-449.php#What%20is%20a%20land%20bank?.

76. Center for Community Progress, "Land Banks and Community Land Trusts: A Primer for the Houston Land Bank," May 2018, https://www.communityprogress.net/filebin/180531_Community_Progress__Land_Bank_and_Community_Land_Trust_Primer_Houston_Land_Bank_Final.pdf.

77. National Alliance to End Homelessness, "State of Homelessness," https://endhomelessness.org/homelessness-in-america/homelessness-statistics/state-of-homelessness-report.

78. Tony Robinson, "No Right to Rest: Police Enforcement Patterns and Quality of Life Consequences of the Criminalization of Homelessness," *Urban Affairs Review* 55:1 (January 2019): 41–73.

79. Richard Florida, *CityLab*, December 7, 2012, https://www.citylab.com/life/2012/12/uselessness-economic-development-incentives/4081. Also see Natalie Kitroeff, Patricia Cohen, and Monica Davey, "Trump Heralded a Bog TV Factory in Wisconsin. Now It's in Doubt," *New York Times*, January 31, 2019, A1.

80. Jenney Schuetz and Cecile Murray, "Unpacking the 'Housing Shortage' Puzzle: How Does Housing Enter and Exit Supply?" Report, Brookings Institution Metropolitan Policy Program, April 25, 2018, https://www.brookings.edu/research/unpacking-the-housing-shortage-puzzle.

81. Edward L. Glaeser and Joseph Gyourko, *Rethinking Federal Housing Policy: How to Make Housing Plentiful and Affordable* (Washington, DC: AEI Press, 2008), xv, 4.

82. Glaeser and Gyourko, *Rethinking Federal Housing Policy*, 4–6, 142–71.

13: POLICIES TO PROMOTE QUALITY OF LIFE

1. City of Los Angeles, Office of the Mayor, "Mayor Garcetti Leads 'Climate Mayors' to Oppose US Withdrawal from Paris Agreement," press release, June 1, 2017, https://www.lamayor.org/mayor-garcetti-leads-%E2%80%98climate-mayors%E2%80%99-oppose-us-withdrawal-paris-agreement; Aamer Madhani, "Forget Paris: US Mayors Sign Their Own Pact after Trump Ditches Climate Accord," *USA Today*, December 4, 2017, https://www.usatoday.com/story/news/2017/12/04/u-s-mayors-sign-pact-track-progress-paris-agreement/920305001; Climate Mayors, "Climate Mayors Submit Comments on Proposed Repeal of Clean Power Plan," press release, March 27, 2018, http://climatemayors.org/actions/clean-power-plan; Patrick Sisson, "Climate Mayors: The Impact a Year after the US Left the Paris Agreement," *Curbed*, May 30, 2018, https://www.curbed.com/2018/5/30/17411024/paris-accord-climate-change-climate-mayors.

2. These data and related material are available from the Federal Bureau of Investigation, "Crime Data Explorer," https://crime-data-explorer.fr.cloud.gov/explorer/national/united-states/crime/2000/2017.

3. Alan Ehrenhalt, *The Great Inversion and the Future of the American City* (New York: Knopf, 2010).

4. John Gramlich, "5 Facts About Crime in the US," *Pew Research Center: Fact-Tank*, January 3, 2019, https://www.pewresearch.org/fact-tank/2019/01/03/5-facts-about-crime-in-the-u-s.

5. City of New York, Police Department Bureaus: Counterterrorism, https://www1.nyc.gov/site/nypd/bureaus/investigative/counterterrorism.page.

6. Weiyi Cai and Jugal K. Patel, "A Half Century of School Shootings," *New York Times*, May 14, 2019, A17.

7. CNN, "Trayvon Martin Shooting Fast Facts," updated February 28, 2019, https://www.cnn.com/2013/06/05/us/trayvon-martin-shooting-fast-facts/index.html.

8. Ashley Southall, "Police Officer Who Heard 'I Can't Breathe' Goes to Trial," *New York Times*, May 13, 2019, A16.

9. US Department of Justice, "Investigation of the Ferguson Police Department," March 4, 2015, https://www.justice.gov/sites/default/files/opa/press-releases/attachments/2015/03/04/ferguson_police_department_report.pdf; CNN, "Controversial Police Encounters Fast Facts," updated May 3, 2019, https://edition.cnn.com/2015/04/05/us/controversial-police-encounters-fast-facts/index.html.

10. Jacey Fortin and Jonah Engel Bromwich, "Cleveland Police Officer Who Shot Tamir Rice Is Fired," *New York Times*, May 30, 2017, https://www.nytimes.com/2017/05/30/us/cleveland-police-tamir-rice.html; Minyvonne Burke, "Officer Who Fatally Shot Tamir Rice Quits Ohio Police Department Days after He Was Hired," *NBC News*, October 11, 2018, https://www.nbcnews.com/news/us-news/officer-who-fatally-shot-tamir-rice-quits-ohio-police-department-n919046.

11. CNN, "Controversial Police Encounters Fast Facts," updated May 3, 2019.

12. Vanessa Williamson, Kris-Stella Trump, and Katherine Levine Einstein, "Black Lives Matter: Evidence that Police-Caused Deaths Predict Protest Activity," *Perspectives on Politics* 16:2 (June 2018): 400–415.

13. Manny Fernandez, Richard Pérez-Peña, and Jonah Engel Bromwich, "Five Dallas Officers Were Killed as Payback, Police Chief Says," *New York Times*, July 8, 2016, https://www.nytimes.com/2016/07/09/us/dallas-police-shooting.html; Steve Visser, "Baton Rouge Shooting: 3 Officers Dead; Shooter Was Missouri Man, Sources Say," *CNN*, July 18, 2016, https://www.cnn.com/2016/07/17/us/baton-route-police-shooting/index.html.

14. Federal Bureau of Investigation, "2018 Law Enforcement Officers Killed and Assaulted," https://ucr.fbi.gov/leoka/2018/topic-pages/tables/table-1.xls.

15. David Hemenway, Deborah Azrael, Andrew Conner, and Matthew Miller, "Variation in Rates of Fatal Police Shootings across US States: The Role of Firearm Availability," *Journal of Urban Health* 96:1 (February 2019): 63–73.

16. Hemenway et al., "Variation in Rates of Fatal Police Shootings across US States," 72.

17. *Washington Post*, "Fatal Force," 2018, https://www.washingtonpost.com/graphics/2018/national/police-shootings-2018/?utm_term=.71e47d746a27.

18. Natalie Delgadillo, "Civilian Oversight of Police Appeals to Many. But Is It Effective?" *Governing*, May 25, 2017, https://www.governing.com/topics/public-justice-safety/gov-civilian-oversight-police-charter-amendment.html.

19. Delgadillo, "Civilian Oversight of Police"; Southall, "Police Officer Who Heard 'I Can't Breathe'."

20. Zachary A. Powell, Michele Bisaccia Meitl, and John L. Worrall, "Police Consent Decrees and Section 1983 Civil Rights Litigation," *Criminology & Public Policy* 16:2 (May 2017): 575–605.

21. Mark Berman, "San Francisco's Police Force Will Be under State Oversight after Justice Dept. Rolls Back Federal Program," *Washington Post*, February 6, 2018, https://www.washingtonpost.com/news/post-nation/wp/2018/02/06/san-franciscos-police-force-will-be-under-state-oversight-after-justice-dept-rolls-back-federal-program/?utm_term=.d62355051566.

22. Rahm Emanuel, "Lessons for Police Reform," *New York Times*, May 9, 2019, A23.

23. Innocence Project, "About," https://www.innocenceproject.org/about.

24. "Case Dismissed," *The Economist*, May 4, 2019, 25.

25. Steve Reilly, "Tens of Thousands of Rape Kits Go Untested across USA," *USA Today*, July 30, 2015, https://www.usatoday.com/story/news/2015/07/16/untested-rape-kits-evidence-across-usa/29902199.

26. RAINN, "Addressing the Rape Kit Backlog," https://www.rainn.org/articles/addressing-rape-kit-backlog.

27. End the Backlog, "Why the Backlog Exists," http://www.endthebacklog.org/backlog/why-backlog-exists.

28. End the Backlog, "Test Rape Kits. End Serial Rapists," http://www.endthebacklog.org/backlog-why-rape-kit-testing-important/test-rape-kits-stop-serial-rapists.

29. "Police Department Race and Ethnicity Demographic Data," *Governing* (Data), https://www.governing.com/gov-data/safety-justice/police-department-officer-demographics-minority-representation.html.

30. Federal Bureau of Investigation, "Frequently Asked Questions about the Hate Crime Statistics Program," https://www.fbi.gov/services/cjis/ucr/hate-crime.

31. Federal Bureau of Investigation, "FBI Releases 2017 Hate Crime Statistics" (press release), November 13, 2018, https://ucr.fbi.gov/hate-crime/2017/resource-pages/hate-crime-summary.

32. The US Supreme Court has protected hate speech, perhaps most notably in *R. A. V. v. City of St. Paul*, 505 US 377 (1992). In a unanimous opinion, the court upheld the use of enhanced penalties for hate crimes in *Wisconsin v. Mitchell*, 508 US 476 (1993).

33. Federal Bureau of Investigation, "2017 Hate Crime Statistics," table 6, https://ucr.fbi.gov/hate-crime/2017/tables/table-6.xls.

34. Federal Bureau of Investigation, "2017 Hate Crime Statistics," table 10, https://ucr.fbi.gov/hate-crime/2017/tables/table-10.xls.

35. Federal Bureau of Investigation, "2017 Hate Crime Statistics," table 5, https://ucr.fbi.gov/hate-crime/2017/tables/table-5.xls.

36. On the damage from mussels and carp, see Dan Egan, *The Death and Life of the Great Lakes* (New York: W. W. Norton, 2017).

37. For more detail, see the US Environmental Protection Agency (EPA), "State Oversight Resources and Guidance Documents," https://www.epa.gov/compliance/state-oversight-resources-and-guidance-documents.

38. US Environmental Protection Agency, National Pollution Discharge Elimination System (NPDES), "Combined Sewer Overflows," https://www.epa.gov/npdes/combined-sewer-overflows-csos.

39. Mary Anna Evans, "Flushing the Toilet Has Never Been Riskier," *The Atlantic*, https://www.theatlantic.com/technology/archive/2015/09/americas-sewage-crisis-public-health/405541. Also see the NPEDS's "Combined Sewer Overflows Policy, Reports, and Training," https://www.epa.gov/npdes/combined-sewer-overflows-policy-reports-and-training.

40. Daniel C. Vock, "Toxic Waters," *Governing*, March 2019, 36–39.

41. US National Oceanic and Atmospheric Administration (NOAA), "NOAA Ocean Service Education: Nonpoint Source Pollution," https://oceanservice.noaa.gov/education/kits/pollution/03pointsource.html.

42. Emma G. Fitzsimmons, "Tap Water Ban for Toledo Residents," *New York Times*, August 3, 2014, https://www.nytimes.com/2014/08/04/us/toledo-faces-second-day-of-water-ban.html.

43. Luke Fowler, "Local Governments: The 'Hidden Partners' of Air Quality Management," *State and Local Government Review* 48:3 (September 2016): 183.

44. Fowler, "Local Governments," 183.

45. ICMA, "Sustainable Communities," https://icma.org/topics/sustainable-communities; NLC, "Environment and Sustainability: Air Quality and Emissions," https://www.nlc.org/topics/environment-sustainability/air-quality-and-emissions. There is even a National Association of Environmental Professionals: https://www.naep.org.

46. EPA, "Overview of EPA's Brownfields Program," https://www.epa.gov/brownfields/overview-epas-brownfields-program.

47. EPA, "Superfund Enforcement," https://www.epa.gov/enforcement/superfund-enforcement.

48. Vann R. Newkirk, "Trump's EPA Concludes Environmental Racism Is Real," *The Atlantic*, February 28, 2018, https://www.theatlantic.com/politics/archive/2018/02/the-trump-administration-finds-that-environmental-racism-is-real/554315; Tishman Environment and Design at the New School and the National Resources Defense Council (NRDC), "Local Policies for Environmental Justice: A National Scan," February 2019, https://tishmancenter.org/wp-content/uploads/2019/04/NRDC_FinalReport_04.15.2019.pdf.

49. Thomas L. Daniels, "A Trail across Time: American Environmental Planning from City Beautiful to Sustainability," *Journal of the American Planning Association* 75:2 (Spring 2009): 178–92.

50. For an overview, see Kent E. Portnoy, *Sustainability* (Cambridge, MA: MIT Press, 2015), chapter 1.

51. Portnoy, *Sustainability*, 9.

52. US Environmental Protection Agency, "Advancing Sustainable Materials Management: 2015 Fact Sheet," July 2018, https://www.epa.gov/sites/production/files/2018-07/documents/2015_smm_msw_factsheet_07242018_fnl_508_002.pdf.

53. Michael Corkery, "As Costs Skyrocket, More US Cities Stop Recycling," *New York Times*, March 16, 2019, https://www.nytimes.com/2019/03/16/business/local-recycling-costs.html; Nicole Javorsky, "How American Recycling Is Changing after China's National Sword,"

CityLab, April 1, 2019, https://www.citylab.com/ environment/2019/04/recycling-waste-management-us-china-national-sword-change/584665.

54. Portney, *Sustainabililty*, chapter 6.

55. For example, Edward J. Jepson, Jr., and Anna L. Hines, "Zoning for Sustainability: A Review and Analysis of the Zoning Ordinances of 32 Cities in the United States," *Journal of the American Planning Association* 80:3 (Summer 2014): 239–52; Ajay Garde and Cecilia Kim, "Form-Based Codes for Zoning Reform to Promote Sustainable Development," *Journal of the American Planning Association* 83:4 (Autumn 2017): 346–64.

56. Mike Maciag, "Risky Waters," *Governing*, August 2018, 33–39; Nathanael Johnson, "The US Should Go Dutch to Avoid Building Another Houston," *CityLab*, September 1, 2017, https://www.citylab.com/design/2017/09/ the-us-should-go-dutch-to-avoid-building-another-houston/538734; Billy Fleming, "The Dutch Can't Save Us from Rising Seas," *CityLab*, October 17, 2018, https://www.citylab.com/perspective/2018/10/ the-dutch-cant-save-us-from-rising-seas/573070.

57. US Green Building Council, "LEED," https://new.usgbc. org/leed.

58. US Green Building Council, "LEED Professional Credentials," https://new.usgbc.org/credentials.

59. United State Conference of Mayors, "Mayors Strongly Oppose Withdrawal from Paris Climate Accord," press release, June 1, 2017, https://www.usmayors. org/2017/06/01/mayors-strongly-oppose-withdrawal-from-paris-climate-accord.

60. See National Association for Olmsted Parks, "Frederick Law Olmsted Sr.," http://www.olmsted.org/ the-olmsted-legacy/frederick-law-olmsted-sr.

61. National Trust for Historic Preservation, "Our Work: About the National Trust," https://savingplaces.org/ we-are-saving-places.

62. Jane Jacobs, *The Death and Life of Great American Cities* (New York: Random House, 1961).

63. National Conference of State Historic Preservation Officers, "Federal Rehabilitation Tax Credit (Historic Tax Credit)," http://ncshpo.org/issues/historic-tax-credit. Also see Office of the Comptroller of the Currency, "Community Developments Fact Sheet: Historic Tax Credits," July 2017, https://www.occ.gov/topics/community-affairs/pub-lications/fact-sheets/pub-fact-sheet-historic-tax-credits-jul-2017.pdf.

64. Alan Blinder and Audra D. S. Burch, "Fate of Confederate Monuments Is Stalled by Competing Legal Battles," *New York Times*, January 20, 2019, https://www. nytimes.com/2019/01/20/us/confederate-monuments-legal-battles.html; David A. Graham, "The Stubborn Persistence of Confederate Monuments," *The Atlantic*, April 26, 2016, https://www.theatlantic.com/ politics/archive/2016/04/the-stubborn-persistence-of-confederate-monuments/479751.

65. League of American Orchestras, "Orchestra Facts: 2006–2014," press release, November 15, 2016, https:// americanorchestras.org/images/stories/of/Orchestra_ Facts_2006-2014_press_release.pdf.

66. Elaine B. Sharp, ed., *Culture Wars and Local Politics* (Lawrence: University Press of Kansas, 1999), 3–4.

67. Kenneth J. Maier, *The Politics of Sin: Drugs, Alcohol, and Public Policy* (Armonk: M. E. Sharpe, 1994), 4.

68. Amy Alonzo, "Federal Lawsuit Seeks to Outlaw Brothels in Nevada, the Only State with Legal Prostitution," *Reno Gazette Journal*, February 27, 2019, https://www.rgj. com/story/news/local/mason-valley/2019/02/26/nevada-prostitution-federal-lawsuit-aims-outlaw-brothel-industry-sex-trafficking/2987901002.

69. Data from the Bureau of Justice Statistics, "Arrest Data Analysis Tool," https://www.bjs.gov/index. cfm?ty=datool&surl=/arrests/index.cfm#.

70. *Jacobellis v. Ohio*, 378 US 184 (1964) at 197.

71. See Sara Zeigler, "Book Banning," in *The Encyclopedia of Civil Liberties in America*, eds. David Schultz and John R. Vile (New York: Routledge, 2015), vol. 1, 106–8; American Library Association, "Top 100 Banned/Challenged Books: 2000–2009," http://www.ala.org/advocacy/bbooks/ top-100-bannedchallenged-books-2000-2009.

72. Robert M. Howard, Arnold Fleischmann, and Richard N. Engstrom, *Politics in Georgia*, 3rd edition (Athens: University of Georgia Press, 2017), 69–70, 91; *Goldrush II v. City of Marietta*, 267 Ga. 683, 482 S.E.2d 347 (1997).

73. For an analysis of the Indianapolis ordinance compared to using zoning to regulate pornography, see Lynn Mills Eckert, "The Incoherence of the Zoning Approach to Regulating Pornography: The Exclusion of Gender and a Call for Category Refinement in Free Speech Doctrine," *Georgetown Journal of Gender and Law* 4 (2003): 863–87.

74. For a summary of this period, see Kenneth J. Meier, *The Politics of Sin: Drugs, Alcohol and Public Policy* (Armonk, NY: M. E. Sharpe, 1994), 135–40.

75. Meier, *The Politics of Sin*, 160–62.

76. "Regulating Alcohol Density: An Action Guide," Bloomberg School of Public Health, Johns Hopkins University, http://www.camy.org/_docs/resources/reports/alcohol-availability/strategizer-55-regulating-alcohol-outlet-density.pdf.

77. Jonathan D. Cohen, "The US Has a Lottery Problem. But It's Not the People Buying the Tickets," *Washington Post*, September 13, 2017, https://www.washingtonpost. com/news/made-by-history/wp/2017/09/13/the-u-s-has-a-lottery-problem-but-its-not-the-people-buying-tickets/?utm_term=.edea65232328.

78. Meier, *The Politics of Sin*, 22–58.

79. Meier, *The Politics of Sin*, 251.

80. Tracy L. Johns, "Managing a Policy Experiment: Adopting and Implementing Recreational Marijuana Policies in Colorado," *State and Local Government Review* 47:3 (September 2015): 193–204.

81. Colorado Department of Revenue, "Marijuana Tax Data," https://www.colorado.gov/pacific/revenue/ colorado-marijuana-tax-data.

82. Jon Murray and David Migoya, "Colorado Communities Pocket Big Bucks from Legal Marijuana, but Threats Loom for Some," *Denver Post*, December 30, 2018, https://www.denverpost.com/2018/12/28/ colorado-marijuana-taxes-local-cities-towns.

83. Susan E. Clarke, "Ideas, Interests, and Institutions Shaping Abortion Politics in Denver," in *Culture Wars and Local Politics*, ed. Elaine B. Sharp (Lawrence: University Press of Kansas, 1999), chapter 3.

84. James W. Button, Barbara A. Rienzo, and Kenneth D. Wald, *Private Lives, Public Conflicts: Battles over Gay Rights in American Communities* (Washington, DC: Congressional Quarterly Press, 1997), chapter 3.

85. The Colorado constitutional amendment, which was placed on the ballot through an initiative campaign, was overturned in *Romer v. Evans*, 517 US 620 (1996).

86. Human Rights Campaign, "Cities and Counties with Nondiscrimination Ordinances That Include Gender Identity," https://www.hrc.org/resources/cities-and-counties-with-non-discrimination-ordinances-that-include-gender; Kevin Draper, "Finally, the NBA Comes to Charlotte," *New York Times*, February 15, 2019, https://www.nytimes.com/2019/02/15/sports/nba-charlotte-bathroom-bill.html.

87. For a brief overview, see Tal Kopan, "What Are Sanctuary Cities, and Can They Be Defunded?" *CNN Politics*, March 26, 2018, https://www.cnn.com/2017/01/25/politics/sanctuary-cities-explained/index.html.

88. See, for example, letters from leaders of these organizations to members of Congress: https://www.usmayors.org/2017/06/26/letter-to-house-members-opposing-h-r-3003 and http://www.nlc.org/sites/default/files/nlc-senate-sanctuary-letter.pdf. There is more information on their positions on the websites of these two organizations advocating on behalf of cities.

89. Valeria Hernandez, "Arizona's 'Concentration Camp': Why Was Tent City Kept Open for 24 Years?" *The Guardian*, August 21, 2017, https://www.theguardian.com/cities/2017/aug/21/arizona-phoenix-concentration-camp-tent-city-jail-joe-arpaio-immigration; Jackie Calmes, "Trump Pardons Former Arizona Sheriff Joe Arpaio, Convicted of Contempt of Court for Violating Latinos' Rights," *Los Angeles Times*, August 25, 2017, https://www.latimes.com/politics/la-na-pol-trump-arpaio-pardon-2017-story.html.

Photo Credits

Index